Crossing the Boundaries

Crossing the Boundaries

Geoff Bull & Michèle Anstey

Pearson Education Australia
Unit 4, Level 2
14 Aquatic Drive
Frenchs Forest NSW 2086

www.pearsoned.com.au

Acquisitions editor: Nicole Meehan
Copy editor and indexer: Forsyth Editorial Services
Cover and internal design by Darben Design

Printed in Malaysia

1 2 3 4 5 06 05 04 03 02

ISBN 1 74009 810 2.

National Library of Australia
Cataloguing-in-Publication Data

Crossing the boundaries.

   Bibliography.
   Includes index.
   ISBN 1 74009 810 2.

   1. Children - Books and reading. I. Bull, Geoff. II.
   Anstey, Michele.

808.068

 An imprint of Pearson Education Australia

Table of Contents

Preface

Crossing the Boundaries arose from our participation in a number of Australasian Children's Literature Association for Research (ACLAR) and Children's Book Council (CBC) conferences. We observed that conference participants came from two distinct disciplines, Arts and Education. Each discipline had its own focus and professional literature but seldom shared common ground. As we talked more with colleagues from both areas we began to 'cross the boundaries' of these disciplines, sharing knowledge and interests and valuing each other's endeavours. It was at this stage that we conceived the idea for *Crossing the Boundaries*, as a way of enriching both disciplines for the mutual benefit of each. As we discussed this idea with colleagues from seven countries and the two disciplines it became apparent that others shared our desire to enrich both disciplines, thus *Crossing the Boundaries* was born.

Geoff Bull

Michéle Anstey

About the authors

Professor Perry Nodelman is Professor of English, University of Winnipeg, Manitoba, Canada. He has a doctorate from Yale university in English literature. He has written about a hundred scholarly articles and two books about children's literature, three novels for children, and, in collaboration with Carol Matas, four fantasy novels.

Jane Doonan trained as an art historian, and taught English for many years in secondary schools. She now writes, reviews and lectures on the aesthetics of picture books. Her studies of the works of picture book makers and illustrators, from John Tenniel to Maurice Sendak, and including Quentin Blake, Anthony Browne, Robert Ingpen, Satoshi Kitamura and Lisbeth Zwerger, appear in international journals. She published *Looking at Pictures in Picture Books*, (Thimble Press) in 1992. Her research interests include the art of Japanese picture books.

Evelyn Arizpe is associate researcher on the project 'Reading Pictures' (Homerton College, Cambridge). After her doctoral studies at the Department of Education, University of Cambridge, she was associate researcher on a European Community project on adolescent masculinity. She specialises in the fields of adolescent literacy and children's literature.

Dr Geoff Bull is an Honorary Associate Professor in the Faculty of Education at the University of Southern Queensland. He is a former national president of the Australian Literacy Educators' Association and founding member of the Australian Literacy Federation (ALF). He teaches undergraduate and postgraduate students in literacy and children's literature and has a particular interest in speculative fiction and postmodern trends in children's literature. He has been involved in extensive consultancies with schools throughout Queensland and is particularly interested in community literacies.

Dr Linda Knight is the subject coordinator for Visual Arts Education, University of Technology, Sydney. Her tertiary education and subsequent research centres on children's picture book illustration and her PhD looked specifically at the practice of the illustrator in British picture books. As a reflection of her position as practicing artist, her research is conducted primarily through image making rather than through text.

Dr Michèle Anstey is an Associate Professor in the Faculty of Education at the University of Southern Queensland. She is also Director of the Faculty's Centre for Children's Literature and Literacy Education and Research (CLEAR). One of her major interests is in literacy teaching practices and she has applied this research in a range of long-term consultancies with primary and secondary schools throughout Queensland. She is particularly interested in the literacy practices of isolated rural communities and the implications of these for developing an appropriate literacy curriculum for the schools in these communities. Her major interest in children's literature is in picture books and visual literacy and the use of children's literature in developing literacy. She is a former editor of the *Australian Journal of Language and Literacy*. She has recently been Director of the Literate Futures Project for Education Queensland and continues to work as Principal Adviser to the Project.

Together with Geoff Bull she has published *The Literacy Lexicon* (1996, Prentice Hall), *The Literacy Labyrinth* (1996, Prentice Hall), *Reading the Visual: written and illustrated children's literature* (2000, Harcourt Australia).

Brian Caswell graduated from UNSW with BA DipEd in 1975. After working for twelve years as a high school teacher, he began writing seriously in 1988. Since then, he has published twenty-three books for young people, and numerous short stories. His standing among Australia's writers for young people is shown by his numerous awards and short-listings. He lives in Sydney with his family.

Sue Page has a MA Comm and lectures in the University of Canberra's School of Creative Communication and Culture Studies in the fields of writing for young people, genre writing and literary studies. She is currently conducting PhD research into Australian young adult novels.

Sophie Masson writes for children, young adults and adults. Her novels have been published in Australia, the UK, and the US, and her short stories, articles, essays and reviews also regularly appear in many outlets around the world. Her first play, *The Green Prince*, co-written with Christopher Ross-Smith, and based on her novel, *The Green Prince* (Hodder Headline Australia 2000), was premiered in Australia in 2001. Her latest novel, *The Hand of Glory*, will be published in Australia in 2002.

Linda Christian-Smith is Oshkosh Foundation Professor of Curriculum and Instruction at the University of Wisconsin, Oshkosh. She is the Master's degree program coordinator for her department along with teaching the Master's Seminar. She received her PhD from the University of Wisconsin Madison, concentrating upon critical educational theory and gender studies. She is the author of five books and thirty articles on gender, literacy and women in higher education.

Dr Kerry Mallan is Senior Lecturer in School of Cultural and Language Studies in Education, QUT. She has a DipT; GradDipT-L; BEdSt; MEdSt; and PhD. She currently teaches courses in children's literature, storytelling and teacher-librarianship at QUT. Her research interests include picture books, children's literature, children's storytelling, and gender and sexuality.

John McKenzie is Principal Lecturer, Christchurch College of Education. He is the Head, Centre for Children's Literature, Advanced Education Programmes, Christchurch College of Education. He initiated the development of New Zealand's research journal in children's literature, entitled *Talespinner* (ed. Dr Darnell), and has shown a commitment to closer Australasian relationships through ACLAR (the Australasian Children's Literature Association for Research) and *Reading Time*.

Associate Professor Ray Misson is Head of the Department of Language Literacy and Arts Education, and Associate Dean (International) in the Faculty of Education at the University of Melbourne. He has worked extensively on the implications of literary and cultural theory for the work in English and literacy classrooms.

John Stephens [MA(Hons), DLitt] is Associate Professor in English at Macquarie University, where his main teaching and research is in children's Literature. He is author of

Language and Ideology in Children's Fiction and (with Robyn McCallum) *Retelling Stories, Framing Culture*, along with about sixty articles and two books on discourse analysis. His primary research focus is on the relationships of texts produced for children (especially literature and film) with cultural formations and practices.

Dr Myrna Machet is senior lecturer in the Department of Information Science at the University of South Africa, one of the ten largest distance teaching universities in the world. She has a BA (Hons) English; B.Bibl. Hons, M.Bibl (RAU); D Litt et Phil (RAU). She has been a lecturer at Unisa for the past eighteen years working with both undergraduate and postgraduate students. Her research has focussed primarily on children's reading, particularly in a multicultural context.

Associate Professor Jeri Kroll teaches in the English Department at Flinders University where she convenes the Creative Writing Program. She has a BA (Hons) from Smith College (USA), a Masters from the University of Warwick (UK) and a PhD from Columbia University in New York City. She has published on Samuel Beckett (the subject of her PhD), contemporary poetry and the pedagogy of creative writing as well as on children's literature. In addition, she has published eighteen books for adults and young people; her most recent being a young adult novel, *Riding the Blues*, and a chapter book, *Fit for a Prince* (both in 2001).

Robyn Sheahan-Bright operates justified text, a freelance writing and publishing consultancy service. She is completing a PhD entitled 'To Market To Market: Culture and Commerce in Australian Children's Publishing Since 1945' at Griffith University (Gold Coast) where she teaches a course on writing for young people. She has a BA, Graduate Diploma of Library Science and a Master of Letters (Distinction) in Children's Literature. She has edited and compiled several collections and is currently a member of the Literature Fund of the Australia Council.

Dr Rosemary Ross Johnston is the Director of the Centre for Research and Education in the Arts at the University of Technology, Sydney and the editor of *CREArTA*, an interdisciplinary international journal of the arts. She is Secretary of the International Research Society for Children's Literature, and Associate Secretary of the *Federation Internationale des Langues et Litteratures Modernes*. Her latest publication (with other authors) is *Literacy: Reading, Writing and Children's Literature* (2000, Oxford University Press).

Acknowledgments

We wish to thank the colleagues, teachers and students with whom we have worked over the years, and who have helped shape the ideas which are realised in *Crossing the Boundaries*. We particularly thank our friends and colleagues who have joined with us in writing chapters. Special thanks to Linda Knight who has provided one of her beautiful pieces of art for the cover illustration.

Thanks also to the staff of Pearson Education for your continued support of our work, in particular Nicole Meehan as acquisitions editor. Special thanks to Jon and Alison Forsyth for their work as editors; as always you have been meticulous and remained patient and good humoured through it all.

Part one

Reading illustration
and text and the
development of visual
and new literacies

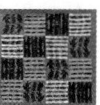

Chapter 1

Something fishy going on:
child readers and narrative literacy

Perry Nodelman

A group of adult students in my course in children's picture books at the University of Winnipeg expresses confusion about David Diaz's illustrations for Eve Bunting's *Smoky Night*. Why, they ask me, do the people have blue and purple faces? The text says nothing about them playing with paint or being sick with some strange disease. It makes no sense. Another group is equally confused by numerous details of the pictures in Anthony Browne's *Willy the Dreamer*. Why is there a pink sofa in the jungle Willy imagines himself exploring? Why does the title page contain a picture of a gorilla labelled 'boat', of a book labelled 'shoe' and of a chair labelled 'flag'? Not only is this inaccurate, but there is also, inconsistently, a picture of a banana labelled 'banana'. It makes no sense.

But it does make sense, I tell them. The faces are blue and purple because the style of the illustration is expressionistic. The colours represent not a visible surface reality, but the emotions of the moments depicted, a complex stew of fear, anger and chaos. Furthermore, I say, the coloured faces represent a shrewd choice on the part of the illustrator, an eminently sensible one. The story is about a riot in an urban neighbourhood — a story that might well have contentious racial overtones. In choosing a style that allows a face to be blue, the illustrator can avoid providing identifiably African or European skin tones. As for Browne's mislabelled gorillas and chairs, they are a reference to a surrealist painting by Rene Magritte, *La clef des songes* ('The Interpretation of Dreams'), which, in one of a number of versions, offers similarly framed images of a horse labelled 'the door', a clock labelled 'the wind', a jug labelled 'the bird' and a valise labelled 'the valise'. This is just one of many references to Magritte's work throughout the book, and other illustrations in the book allude to paintings by Dali and Chirico, to films like *The Wizard of Oz* and *Frankenstein*, to children's picture books by Chris Van Allsburg — to an entire range of art about fantasies and dreams. The jungle Willy's pink sofa sits in is a homage to one found in Rousseau's painting *The Dream*. The sofa itself appears at the point occupied in Rousseau's picture by a similarly curved settee, but the voluptuous nude occupying Rousseau's settee has been replaced by characters from other books by Browne: two children, a woman and a man watching television. Not incidentally, the man looks a lot like Sigmund Freud, whose theories explore the sense hidden in apparently nonsensical fantasies and dream worlds.

Well, my students say, maybe it does make sense — once you explain it to us. But we didn't know all that until you told it to us. It's not fair of the illustrators to make the meanings of the pictures dependent on knowledge of other things that aren't actually in the picture. Furthermore, they add, if we adult university students don't know it, how could children be expected to know it? Surely these overly sophisticated details make these inappropriate as books for children?

What that conclusion ignores is that understanding even the simplest and most readily perceivable features of pictures equally depends on a context of information provided by their viewers. Because a photograph of a cat resembles an actual cat more obviously than does the written word *cat*, it's less obvious that we need special knowledge in order to understand it. But we do. Anthropological literature describing early contact with groups unfamiliar with contemporary Euro-American civilisation frequently contain reports of people without previous knowledge of photographs or representational drawings who could make little sense of the examples they were shown.[1] The pictures in picture books are often much less representational, their meaningfulness much more dependent on viewers knowing how to read small, static, two-dimensional images as depictions of larger, moving, three-dimensional objects — a few sparse lines as depictions of a more complex visual field. The fact that so many children *can* interpret a wide range of different kinds of pictures at an early age doesn't mean that understanding pictures is easy. Instead, I believe, it's a result of their great flexibility and is as great an accomplishment as learning to use spoken language, a skill that children also miraculously more or less teach themselves.

But they aren't likely to teach themselves to read blue faces as expressions of emotion or, without knowledge of Magritte, intuitively understand a reference to his work. The art theorist Arthur Danto says, 'To see something as art requires something the eye cannot descry — an atmosphere of artistic theory, a knowledge of the history of art: an art world' (1992: 431). As my students' experiences suggest, picture books are part of the art world. Rather than dismissing a book as unsuitable for children because it contains blue faces or allusions to Magritte, I tell my students we might better see it as evidence of our adult obligation to introduce child reader/viewers to the art world. We can then find ways of helping them to develop visual literacy — learn what they need to know in order to have a better chance of understanding and enjoying picture books.

Reader response theory tells us that making sense of stories requires knowledge of a repertoire — a storehouse of information about life and other stories and of strategies for engaging that information.[2] But for those of us immersed in the culture of books and reading, it might seem less obvious that equivalents of the blue faces of visual texts lurk in verbal texts — even apparently straightforward ones. Just as there is an art world implied by any visual work of art, there is a literature world implied by any verbal work of art. And just as experienced viewers might take the blue face in an expressionistic picture for granted (I did so myself until my students made me aware of my doing so), there are aspects of verbal texts experienced readers also tend to take for granted.

My example, yet once more, is the response of a group of my university students to a picture book: the American writer and illustrator Chris Raschka's *Arlene Sardine*, a story about a small fish who gets her wish to become a sardine. As the book proceeds, Arlene is netted, boxed, sorted, smoked, oiled, canned and cooked:

At last, Arlene was a little fish, in oil, packed in a can.
A little fish, packed in oil, in a can, is a sardine.
Arlene was a sardine.

My students didn't just dislike this book. They were actively horrified by it, convinced that the author-illustrator must be some kind of child-hating sadist. I was startled by this response. I myself had greatly enjoyed the book. It made me laugh. I simply assumed it would make others laugh too.

Current pedagogical wisdom, in North America at least, would suggest that this difference of opinion was just a question of different individuals responding differently, as we all in our unique individuality inevitably do. Seen in these terms, my reading and response were no more valid than those of the others, and most likely merely represented nothing more than the sadism I shared with the author. That's a conclusion I find myself not wanting to share. Yes, those who don't know Magritte would read an allusion to Magritte differently than those who do. But if the allusion was intended, then those who miss it are missing something important, something the illustrator wanted viewers to be thinking about in order to make what they see more specific, more distinct, more complex. One doesn't *have* to do what an illustrator wants — there's no law enforcing it. But surely it's desirable to try to figure out what it is — to engage in what one hopes will be an actual act of communication with someone else, an act in which one learns of something one did not in fact already know. Once viewers have attempted to be aware of what they think an illustrator might have wanted to communicate, they are free to have different responses to it — even to dislike the picture exactly because it does allude to Magritte. But responses based on lack of awareness of the allusion are, I firmly believe, less valid. They are authentic experiences for a viewer, certainly, but inaccurate nevertheless — a reason for teachers to do some teaching about the art world so that what the viewers experience so authentically shares more with what illustrators intend and knowledgeable viewers are able to see.

I believe that my response to *Arlene Sardine* represents my access to a repertoire of knowledge about stories parallel to my knowledge of Magritte — knowledge that allowed me to place the story in the literature world in a way that my students could not. The students had more to learn about a specific form of literacy we tend often to take for granted and therefore neglect to teach, either to university students or to children. For want of a better term, I'll call it *narrative literacy*.

What narrative literacy consists of becomes clear if we imagine someone without it: a narrative illiterate. Such a person would never have heard a story — would not know what a story was. We are all born that way. Jungian theories of archetypes assert that we don't need to have heard stories to know them — that the basic plots underlying all stories reside in the collective unconscious of the human race. It seems just as likely to me that what appears to be archetypal and universal might be a matter of cultural history — of new stories mirroring what works in the stories the storyteller already knows. One way or the other, however, new human beings only get conscious access to archetypes or widespread patterns by learning to make sense of the stories they actually do hear in their life after birth — by developing narrative literacy.

Furthermore, many of the aspects of these stories that we most take for granted have little to do with the world we actually live in and know. Consider, for instance, the many stories for very young children that are about animals and other creatures. In real life in North America, most contemporary children have little contact with rabbits or pigs. Yet many of the earliest stories they hear are not only about rabbits or pigs, but about rabbits or pigs quite unlike any they might actually have encountered — ones that talk, wear clothing, shop, build houses, make friendships with ducks and spiders and people. For adults in possession of narrative literacy and access to the literature world — particularly, in this case, the children's literature world — all this seems quite natural, perfectly familiar and certainly understandable. But imagine a narrative illiterate, confronted with news about a world quite unlike the one he or she actually experiences outside books. For such a young reader, even the most conventional stories would have to seem just as strange and bewildering as my students found *Arlene Sardine*.

An example is Laura Appleton-Smith's *Frank the Fish Gets His Wish*. Alone in a tank in a pet shop, Frank nevertheless has recognisably human thoughts — including a desire for a 'pal'. How he developed awareness that there was such a thing and could thus be sad without one is left unexplained. So is what Preston Neal's illustrations reveal — that Frank has distinctly human-looking eyes and that the pal he soon finds, a fish named Trish and identified as 'she', has battable human eyelashes and sports what looks like lipstick, presumably the waterproof kind, on her luscious human-looking lips. Anyone even the least familiar with children's literature will not be surprised by these details. Indeed, they are exactly what might lead many adults to classify the book as pedestrian and unimaginative. But for someone without that familiarity, it's hard to imagine that a fish with lips and angst is any less unsettling or strange than one with a wish to be caught and canned. Logically speaking, fish with lips seem to have more to do with the surrealism of a Magritte than with the reality of actual fish. In reality, indeed, being caught and canned is a much more likely fate for a fish than is finding a life partner and signalling camaraderie, as Frank does, by chummily draping his apparently muscle-filled fin over the partner's back. Ironically, then, what distressed my students about *Arlene Sardine* is the way in which it departed from the conventional world of children's stories in the direction of actual extra-literary reality.

It's possible, of course, that what I'm calling reality is not the world as young children usually perceive it. There might be something we identify as childlike thinking that would find a Frank and Trish who have human emotions and occupy conventional human gender roles more believable than an Arlene who lives as real brislings often do.[3] It's assumptions of this sort that lead many adults to view the many books about humanised creatures like Frank as acceptably and incontrovertibly childlike books for children. But there is no evidence that this is true as anything other than a self-fulfilling prophecy.[4] Seeing stories of this sort as appropriately childlike, adults offer children access to many of them, and so children inevitably come to accept their basic characteristics as what stories are. In other words, I want to suggest, children develop an interest in humanised animals, not as something inherent and inevitable in their make-up or development, but as part of their narrative literacy. They learn to accept as conventional the kinds of stories that adults conventionally offer them. The history of Maurice Sendak's groundbreaking picture book *Where the Wild Things Are* is interesting evidence of that.

When it first appeared in 1964, many adults were as horrified by Sendak's book as my students were horrified by *Arlene Sardine*. The wild things — creatures unlike any conventionally found in picture books at that time — would surely give children nightmares. Almost forty years later, *Wild Things* has become a classic and other illustrators have followed its lead and produced picture book after picture book depicting various kinds of monsters, dragons, sandmen, nightmares, and such. One, by the Canadian writer Robert Munsch, depicts a living fart. It's hard for most adults to imagine that such books could upset many children. Our own adult knowledge of what has become conventional causes us to assume that children, too, will find it non-distressingly familiar. We forget that for those new to the experience of books, wild things and Franks are just as strange as Arlenes are.

If children are not inherently drawn to stories about human animals, why are there so many of them? The answer, I think, has to do with the narrative literacy of the adults who produce children's books — their immersion in the children's literature world. Children's literature began as, and has continued to be, a didactic literature, a way in which adults can teach children how to think about themselves and their world. When adults began to write specifically for children some centuries ago, then, they used as models pre-existing stories that did such teaching — stories such as Aesop's fables, which describe the actions of humanised animals as models for readers' behaviour. As a result, and, I believe, more or less by accident, humanised animals came to be identified as characteristic of children's stories — what most people most readily imagine when they think of children's literature. A children's book editor once told me that she received on an average of three times a week, every week of her over-thirty-year career, unsolicited submissions of stories about young humanised animals who were unhappy, went off and had an adventure, and learned a valuable lesson as a result.

Many such stories do get into print. One is *Frank the Fish Gets His Wish*. It's logical then to assume that knowledge of how to read such stories would soon develop in beginning readers — that it would be an early addition to most children's narrative literacy. It's possible to separate some component parts of that literacy:

- The knowledge of a world unlike normal reality and found exclusively in stories, in which animals and other creatures can talk and have human emotions.
- Familiarity with a sequence of events in which a humanised creature wishes for something, gets it, and learns a lesson from having got it; in other words, knowledge of a common basic plot or story pattern.
- Familiarity with the basic concept of a fable — that a story about someone not oneself might contain a message about one's own behaviour, and therefore, associated with this skill:
    - the strategy of identifying with the main character of a story — seeing oneself as somehow like that character so that what happens to the character allows one to derive a message about oneself.
- In more general terms, knowledge of what a plot is — how a sequence of events can fit together to form a satisfying whole, with a sense of a beginning before which nothing particularly notable happened and a satisfying conclusion after which nothing particularly notable will happen.
- Understanding of the peculiar nature of the stories — that they are a form of lie that somehow has the status of a form of truth, that they can be considered convincing or realistic even while never claiming to be true. In other words: knowing how and to what extent to believe in stories.

With further thought, I'm sure I could list many other aspects of narrative literacy embedded in the ability to make sense of a story like *Frank the Fish Gets His Wish* — ones I've thus far so taken for granted that I've not yet become consciously aware that I know them.

I believe my students possessed all these forms of narrative literacy. Yet they still had trouble with *Arlene Sardine*. Why? The answer emerges from my reason for believing that the students possessed these skills. It was their attempt to apply their conventional expectations to *Arlene Sardine* — and their inability to deal with its divergences from the conventions — that caused their annoyance. My students seem to have arrived at a second stage in the development of narrative literacy. They are anything but narrative illiterates, and are well aware of common story patterns and the other basic narrative conventions I just listed. What they don't have is any way of coping with divergences from the conventions they expect — except to reject stories, like *Arlene Sardine*, that diverge too much.

Much of the literature available for both children and adults operates with the assumptions that readers will possess this sort of narrative literacy. Most bestselling fiction, in TV and films as well as in books, offers readers another version of a basic narrative experience — a formula they are assumed to already know and have come to expect. In adult literature, for instance, Harlequin romances always tell of a woman overwhelmed by the lust of a more powerful older man who is eventually overwhelmed by his love for her. A book like *Frank the Fish* is the children's literature equivalent — a story that represents the use of an expectable formulaic pattern, this time one in which a non-human main character with whom children might well identify wishes and gets what is wished for. Readers who enjoy the experience of following patterns they recognise expect the patterns and tend therefore to be upset by serious divergences from them.

In this context, *Arlene Sardine* is likely to be particularly upsetting, simply because it starts out by being so unsurprising. It seems, by and large, an obvious representative of an expectable story pattern — the same one, in fact, as *Frank the Fish*. Arlene, identifiably small and immature, wishes about what she wants to be when she grows up, and gets her wish. But what she gets has required her to die in the process — an upsetting divergence from the pattern.

Arlene is upsetting not merely because it diverges from expectation, but because of the particular nature of the divergence. Once invited to identify with the main character of a story, readers in possession of the appropriate narrative literacy don't expect that character to die. The assumption that child readers will have the narrative literacy to identify with a character singled out for attention, as Arlene is at the beginning of *Arlene Sardine*, underlies my students' conviction that the book is sadistic. It invites children to see themselves as someone who then gets netted and cooked, and thus makes them painfully and necessarily aware of their own fragility.

The death of such a character is not just upsetting in itself. It also prevents readers from obtaining the kind of pleasure they expect to get — what such stories most significantly offer: the experience of a sequence of events that leads to what we call a happy ending. Happy endings occur when central characters who readers can identify with as being somehow like themselves triumph over bad circumstances and powerful enemies, somehow like ones readers have to cope with in reality but cannot in reality move past. The stories people in general know best and like to hear most frequently tend to be ones which offer imaginative versions of what readers might not realistically expect to actually happen in reality. They are wish-fulfilment fantasies. *Arlene Sardine* subverts this process — its ending offers what we might realistically expect to happen in reality rather than what we might have hoped for. Arlene's wish is fulfilled in a way that leaves readers' wishes singularly unfulfilled.

Furthermore, this process of wish-fulfilment becomes complicated for adults, such as my students, who are reading books intended for children. They tend to read them not as books about characters with whom they themselves identify, but in terms of how they imagine children would identify. The wish-fulfilment expected then represents not what real child readers might actually wish for, but what the adults reading the book might wish for children — what they as adults would like children to desire. As many adults view them, then, children's stories turn wish-fulfilment fantasy into fable — teaching children to have the correct wishes for themselves.

Stories can be understood to work this way only in the context of another assumption about the narrative literacy of child readers. We must assume they understand that the process of their expected identification with a main character will lead them to consider what happens to the main character as something that could happen to themselves. In other words, child readers must be imagined as reading all stories as fables — parables about how they themselves ought to behave. If what happens to the character is good — as when Frank gets his wish — then they can read the story as affirming the character's behaviour. If what happens to the character is bad — as when the unnamed fish protagonist of Leo Lionni's *Fish is Fish* (1970) decides to explore the world beyond his pond, described by his frog friend, and nearly dies from lack of oxygen — then they can read the story as discouraging behaviour like that of the character's. Like this fish, young readers should not wish to be what they are not.

In this context, *Arlene Sardine* is decidedly confusing. Is the book suggesting that Arlene's wish was a good thing or a bad thing? When Frank gets what he wishes for, it is a good thing, because what he wishes for — companionship and good times — are clearly good things in the eyes of most adults, things that most adults believe children ought to wish for. The book comfortingly confirms common adult ideas about how children should think about themselves. In terms of its application to child readers, wishing to be a sardine is less clearly wishing for something good. Brislings do often grow up to be sardines and, similarly, children do often grow up to be adults. But becoming adult is not usually a matter of dying and being canned. Or is it?

Perhaps *Arlene Sardine* is an allegory about the stifling conformity of adult values and the danger of children's wishes not being free and childish? But if it is, why does the text not clearly point out that Arlene's wish was bad and is being granted a punishment with a clear negative message for readers? Why does the narrator seem to celebrate Arlene getting her wish, even to the point of ignoring the uglier implications of it? After Arlene dies, the text cheerfully asserts, 'I'll bet she felt well-rested on the conveyer belt'. Or are readers meant to see that as an ironic joke, and understand how ridiculous Arlene's wish was when it led to her being well-rested in this particularly extreme way? Or are we to understand merely that Arlene, being a brisling, would have become a sardine no matter what she did or didn't wish? Is this a happy wish-fulfilment fantasy or a bleak warning about the inevitability of disaster? It's hard to tell — and that's upsetting.

In giving its main character what he wants, furthermore, *Frank the Fish Gets His Wish* confirms that wishing itself is a good thing. Where I live in North America, at least, most adults want children to wish for things — have aspirations and hope for their futures, have dreams so they can make their dreams come through. These are central tenets of our contemporary culture. When Arlene wishes and gets her wish, and both the wish and its result seem so confusing and disastrous, it raises serious questions about the value of wishing in the first place. Wouldn't she have been happier to remain a living brisling, content with her lot? Once more, the book seems either to contradict or to complicate what most adults conventionally expect children's stories to say.

What all this amounts to is two simple facts. First, *Arlene Sardine* diverges from conventional story patterns in ways that render inoperable or misleading the strategies for understanding stories that many children and adults have in their repertoire. Second, however, it does so in ways that seem to invite the use of these conventional strategies. It is no *Finnegan's Wake* or *English Patient*, so beyond the pale of conventional expectations for children's stories that most readers of children's stories wouldn't even know how to begin to read it. The trouble is, exactly, that such readers do think they know how to begin to read it — and then discover that reading it in that way leads to confusion and upset.

So why, then, was I not confused and upset when I read it? I believe it was because my own lengthier experience of reading and studying literature in general and children's literature in particular had immersed me in the children's literature world, and equipped me with a further set of narrative literacies — ones my students, many other adults, and many children have not yet learned. In order to determine what these literacies might consist of, I need to say more about my response to *Arlene Sardine*.

First: the book not only gave me pleasure — but my response to it was focused on that pleasure. I was most aware of my sensuous experience of the bold green and oranges of the pictures, of the sumptuous, confident lines of the apparently handwritten text, of the musical repetitions of the words of the text: 'She was delicately smoked. Delicately smoked was she.' All of this reminded me of the visual and verbal equivalents for music Raschka has so cleverly explored in his pictures and words in other picture books (*Charlie Parker Played Be Bop*, for instance, or *Mysterious Thelonius*), and struck me as being equally jazzy and equally enjoyable. What theme or message it might convey hardly interested me. It was too much fun experiencing it to worry about much beyond that. Paradoxically, then, I was responding in a less intellectual way than my students were, or than my students assumed young children would. We might logically assume that inexperienced readers would be more likely to respond with their senses than with their minds. But since adults invest so much energy in getting children to think about how stories so centrally contain messages about their own behaviour, I suspect the opposite is true. It takes a more sophisticated strategy to move beyond a thematic focus and pay attention to (or at least acknowledge in conversation that one is paying attention to) the more sensuous aspects of texts.

It also takes, I suspect, a certain lack of egocentricity. I wasn't distressed by Arlene's fate in part because I read about her as someone quite unlike myself. I am not, after all, a brisling. I don't even like to swim all that much. And in any case, I tend to find the worlds evoked by stories more interesting for how they differ from my own world than for how they are like it. I tend to read for news of other and different places, other and different people — not so much for news about myself. While I do consider the implications of a story in terms of my own ideas and values, I don't need to agree with its themes before I can derive pleasure or self-understanding from it. I might learn from my perception of a difference. In other words, identification with a protagonist is not a central factor in my reading of fiction. I could enjoy hearing about Arlene's sad fate because it didn't particularly occur to me to think of it as a story about my own existence. Since we tend to assume children are egocentric and offer them stories intended to be read egocentrically, we might well be making them egocentric readers as a self-fulfilling prophecy. That doesn't mean they couldn't with encouragement develop the presumably more sophisticated skill of detachment and have access to a wider range of experiences and pleasures — including the pleasure of *Arlene Sardine*.

Being detached from Arlene may have been at least partly responsible for my willingness to find her story funny — and enjoying its humour was certainly the central feature of my response to it. Why did I find it funny? What was I laughing at?

First, and perhaps sadistically, detached from Arlene, I enjoyed her getting what she wished for in such a spectacularly counter-productive way. Theories of comedy often center on the relationship of laughter to cruelty — our pleasure in the suffering of others, especially those whose behaviour has defined them not only as separate from but also inferior to ourselves and therefore deserving of a comeuppance. Knowing what sardines are — dead and cooked — I know how foolish it is for a young fish to wish to be one, and am happy to see Arlene's folly appropriately rewarded. (And in any case, it's hardly an unusual fate for a brisling. I felt free to laugh because of my knowledge that brislings do often become sardines — including some I have eaten myself.)

Second, I loved the way the narrative played with me: the blatantly (and surely deliberately) incorrect assumption of the opening line, 'So you want to be a sardine', the comment about how well-rested Arlene was on the conveyer belt, the narrator saying, 'I wonder if Arlene was a little nervous for the final inspection'. I loved the sense of sharing a secret with the narrator, the knowledge that what was being reported so positively was in fact not so joyously optimistic a series of events after all. In other words, I was enjoying irony — the perception that what was being said was not quite what was actually meant. Since the perception of irony is usually considered to be a sophisticated strategy for making sense of texts, it's rarely taught to children, who might then not actually possess it. But even infants respond to ironic jokes. I can remember my own children laughing uproariously when I shouted the word 'whisper' and whispered the word 'shout'. More young people might be more responsive to irony if adults were more willing to acknowledge their actual or potential awareness of it.

Third, and I believe most significantly, as I responded to *Arlene Sardine* I found myself thinking of other stories. I particularly enjoyed the ways in which it reminded me of other books only in order to diverge from them and, it seemed to me, comment on them.

For instance, I found myself thinking of Leo Lionni's *Swimmy*. Raschka's images of Arlene as one among 'ten thousand friends' look suspiciously like Lionni's images of schools of fish. Except for the protagonist Swimmy, Lionni's fish all look alike — not surprising, since they all seem to have been produced as impressions of the same block print. Indeed, the basic idea of *Swimmy* is that the fish are so without individuality that they can easily become indistinguishable parts of the one giant fish Swimmy talks them into pretending to be in order to protect themselves from larger fish. Arlene's friends are equally indistinguishable from each other and, except for one red dot on what would be her cheek if she were human, from Arlene. But Swimmy retains his special identity as an exception to the group by masquerading as the black eye of the pretend red fish. Quite differently, finding the little and often faded red dot and identifying Arlene from a myriad of close possibilities is a version of *Where's Waldo* — an almost impossible task. Furthermore, apart from the narrator's identification of Arlene by a human name and claim that she made a wish, nothing happens to her different from the rest of the brislings or from what happens to any brisling on its way to a supermarket. In insisting that Arlene's fate is unique and has special meaning and then offering nothing unique or special, the narrative makes another ironic joke. It also implies a commentary on *Swimmy* and on books like it that ask children to identify with humanised animals and other creatures who have lost important aspects of their natural selves in the process of humanisation. A real fish in Swimmy's situation wouldn't have a name, wouldn't be distinct from others of his kind, wouldn't have a solution to his problem or even be particularly aware of his problem — at least not in human terms. That Arlene *is* just another sardine reveals how far removed from any actual fish experience a story like *Swimmy* is, and how illogical it is to read animal experiences as parables about human ones.

Arlene Sardine reminded me of Lionni's other book about fishes. *Fish is Fish* also invites readers to think about it as a story about themselves. But children, unlike fish, *can* survive out of water. Fish may be fish, but surely only the most protective of adults want children to believe that children are children now and forever, doomed to death if they choose to venture forth from the small pond of their childhood. By insisting that sardines are sardines, *Arlene Sardine* pushes the message about the danger of having aspirations to a comic extreme. As a result, it becomes an ironic commentary on *Fish is Fish* — and on the many other books for children that ask them to identify with creatures quite unlike themselves as a way of manipulating them into accepting a false idea of their own inadequacy.

Clearly, then, much of my pleasure in *Arlene Sardine* emerged from my awareness of ways in which it not only engaged my narrative literacy, but also, in doing so, made me aware of my awareness — thoughtful about the nature and operations of the literacy. By evoking and then diverging from conventional story patterns and other aspects of my narrative repertoire for children's narrative, it led me to think about those patterns and about the strategies that children's books conventionally imply their readers ought to be using in order to understand them. My perception of its relationships to more conventional books made me think of it as a story about specific other stories and what those stories ask of their readers too — and also, a story about conventional attributes of stories for children in general. I conclude that a consciousness of the possibility that literature might be about literature as much as it is about the world outside literature is a further stage in the development of literacy. In this third stage of narrative literacy, readers no longer judge stories on the basis of whether or not they obviously and accurately represent reality or persuasively convey messages the readers agree with or would like children to agree with. Indeed, the point and the pleasure of a story might be exactly the extent to which what it depicts *doesn't* represent reality or imply a truth.

In order to be able to think about the possibility that a story might be misrepresenting the world and take pleasure in it, one needs detachment from what one reads, a willingness to be thoughtful about it, and an awareness of irony. One needs to comprehend the possibility that a text might be in the process of undermining the very things it seems to be confirming. Opening up the door to irony is potentially subversive. It allows detached and non-accepting readings at odds with the intentions of books not intended to be ironic, and thus, makes young readers less susceptible to adult efforts to impose adult perceptions and values on them. In my own reading of *Fish is Fish*, it was my ability to question its apparently wholesome message about accepting yourself as you are that led me to see the dark underside of that message — its apparent denial of the validity of any sort of aspiration at all. Similarly, many readers in possession of a more sophisticated narrative literacy refuse to stop at the positive aspects of the message of Marcus Pfister's *The Rainbow Fish* (1992). In this widely popular book, a fish with sparkling silver scales achieves happiness and is perceived as admirable when he gives the scales to other fish, so that everyone is equally beautiful. While clearly intended to be an allegory about charity, the business of making yourself less beautiful to make others happy also implies that being like others is better than being uniquely individual. If one has any concern over the conformist tendencies of contemporary culture, that seems a strange thing to be trying to persuade children of. Once more, the fact that the characters are fish — creatures we imagine as being more or less identical — makes them a clearly inappropriate metaphor for humanity and opens the door to ironic interpretations.

I believe the opening of the door to be a good thing rather than a bad one. Much of what many adults would like children to agree with is not necessarily healthy or wise. Much of what children's books conventionally support is foolish or even dangerous. Reading with a degree of narrative literacy that makes one aware of stories as stories has the potential to protect young readers from this folly or danger. Knowing how to read *Arlene Sardine* as a commentary on other children's books not only opens up the possibility of taking pleasure in a text that might otherwise seem confusing, it also frees one from being so easily manipulated by all those other books.

Helping young readers to develop this sort of literacy is a matter of some significance. How can we go about doing that? Can children learn more about the literature world — and if so, how?

I have no doubt that narrative literacy can be taught, both to adults like my students and to children. I introduced *Arlene Sardine* in a recent version of my children's literature course in order to evoke the kind of response I've been describing here from a new group of students in order to make the kind of comments about these responses that I've been making here. To my surprise, this group of students had no problem with the book — indeed, they greatly enjoyed it. I speculate that happened because we arrived at the book at a much later point in the course, after the students had spent some months becoming aware of matters like story patterns and the identification strategies that books imply of their readers. In the context of their already established awareness of the literariness of literature and an expanded repertoire of knowledge about children's stories, these students were already in the process of developing a more sophisticated narrative literacy. Furthermore, when some of them decided to share *Arlene Sardine* with various groups of children, their own pleasure and enthusiasm — and, just as important, the conversations they had with the children, based on our class work, about how the book was like other books and such — meant that most of these children were also able to perceive and enjoy the book's humour. They, too, were developing more sophisticated skills for making sense of narrative.

A more formal version of the work I did with my students and my students did with children would be to introduce children to stories using common story patterns in a sequence that moved form the most conventional to the most divergent from conventions, in the context of a discussion about patterns and divergences. In terms of the books I've discussed here, one could begin with *Frank the Fish Gets His Wish*, then move on to *Swimmy*, *Fish is Fish*, and finally, *Arlene Sardine*. As a conclusion to the series, one might then move on to a book that offers an even more intricately diverse version of the same pattern: Arthur Yorinks' *Louis the Fish*. In this book, a young man who likes fish but is unhappily destined to life in his family's butcher shop wakes up one day to find that he has become a giant salmon, and ends up living happily ever after in a tank in a pet shop window — immersed in the fish world. As yet another story about fishes and wishes (are there so many simply because of the rhyme?), self-acceptance and aspiration, this book evokes and comments on all the others — just as knowing all the others allows them to evoke and comment on it.

What I am proposing here — a formal study of texts in which teachers actively work to help children develop the specific literary strategies needed to understand them in something like the way they were intended — defies assumptions about literature and teaching children currently powerful in North America and elsewhere. Those assumptions insist that any and all responses to literary texts are equally valid, and require that children set their own agendas in the learning process — learn what they individually need to learn at their own pace. Consequently, efforts to teach children anything specific about literature are viewed as dangerously elitist — a matter of believing one knows how they ought to be thinking — and repressive of their individuality. I obviously don't share these assumptions. I believe that children's ability to understand themselves can only be enriched through their development of knowledge of the shared means by which human beings communicate their differences to each other. I also believe that not actively teaching children narrative literacy tends to deprive them of that literacy for far too long. The development of this knowledge can and should be a clearly enunciated goal of literary study for children of all ages.

Finally, I believe that those engaged in the study best develop knowledge through active instruction and by means of activities carefully planned by teachers to achieve specific results. Learning takes place in what the developmental psychologist Lev Vygotsky (1996) called the zone of proximal development — the territory between what students already know and what they can learn with the help of others. Good teachers can and should help children move through this zone towards an ever-growing knowledge of the literature world.

Further Reading

Those interested in doing further reading about some of the topics explored in this chapter should take a look at my website, *Reading About Children's Literature: A Bibliography Of Criticism*, specifically under the heading *Writing, Reading, Teaching*. The site is located at:

   http://www.uwinnipeg.ca/~nodelman/criticism.htm

What follows are some excerpts from the website, focusing on just a few of the many materials listed there. The items named here represent foundation work on these matters. Consult the website and recent numbers of journals such as *Children's Literature in Education* for more recent research.

The basic ideas of reader-response criticism are discussed in two books by Wolfgang Iser: *The Implied Reader* (Baltimore: Johns Hopkins UP, 1974) and *The Act of Reading* (Baltimore: Johns Hopkins UP, 1978). Two useful collections of essays about reader response are *The Reader in the Text: Essays on Audience and Participation*, Susan Suleiman and Inge Crosman (eds) (Princeton: Princeton UP, 1980) and *Reader-Response Criticism: From Formalism to Post-Structuralism*, Jane P. Tompkins (ed.) (Baltimore: Johns Hopkins UP, 1980). In *The Reader, The Text, The Poem: The Transactional Theory of the Literary Work* (Cambridge: Harvard UP, 1978), a classic text first produced in 1938, Louise Rosenblatt outlines a persuasive theory of response and its application to teaching literature. The repertoire implied by children's texts is discussed in Peter Hunt's 'What Do We Lose When We Lose Allusion? Experience and Understanding Stories', *Signal* 57 (September 1988), 212–22.

Some stimulating books about the teaching of literary skills to children are Robert Protherough's *Developing Response to Fiction* (Milton Keynes: Open UP, 1983); *Readers, Texts, Teachers*, Bill Corcoran and Emrys Evans (eds) (Upper Montclair: Boynton/Cook, 1987); Ian Reid's *Making of Literature: Texts, Contexts and Classroom Practices* (Australian Association for the Teaching of English, 1984); and Andrew Stibbs' *Reading Narrative as Literature: Signs of Life* (Milton Keynes and Philadelphia: Open UP, 1991). Although Stibbs focuses on work with older children, all his ideas could be used with younger children.

Of the various children's literature journals, *Children's Literature in Education* devotes most attention to questions of teaching. A groundbreaking set of articles, 'Teaching Literary Criticism in the Elementary Grades: A Symposium', Jon C. Stott (ed.), originally appeared in *Children's Literature in Education* 12.4 (1981), 192–206. Articles relating to the specific matters discussed in this chapter include a number by Jon Stott: 'It's Not What You Expect: Teaching Irony to Third Graders', *Children's Literature in Education* 13.4 (1982), 153–61; 'Spiralled Sequence Story Curriculum: A Structuralist Approach to Teaching Fiction in the Elementary Grades', *Children's Literature in Education* 18.3 (1987), 148–63; 'Will the Real Dragon Please Stand Up? Convention and Parody in Children's Stories', *Children's Literature in Education* 21.4 (1990), 219–28.

Among other important articles are Linnea Hendrickson's 'Literary Criticism as a Source of Teaching Ideas', *Children's Literature Association Quarterly* 9.4 (Winter 1984–1985), 202; Sonia Landes's 'Picture Books as Literature', *Children's Literature Association Quarterly* 10.2 (Summer 1985), 51–4 (about teaching meaning-making strategies for picture books); and Roderick McGillis's 'The Delights Of Impossibility: No Children, No Books, Only Theory', *Children's Literature Association Quarterly* 23, 4 (Winter 1998–99), 202–8.

Bibliography

Appleton-Smith, L. (1998) *Frank the Fish Gets His Wish* (illustrated by Preston Neel). Flyleaf, Lyme NH.
Browne, A. (1997) *Willy the Dreamer*. Candlewick, Cambridge MA.
Bunting, E. (1994) *Smoky Night* (illustrated by David Diaz). Harcourt Brace, San Diego, New York, London.

Danto, A. (1992) 'The Artworld', *The Philosophy of the Visual Arts*. P. Alperson (ed.). Oxford University Press, New York and Oxford, pp. 426–33.

Handford, M. (1987) *Where's Waldo*. Walker Books, London.

Iser, W. (1978) *The Act of Reading: A Theory of Aesthetic Response*. Johns Hopkins, Baltimore and London.

Lionni, L. (1963) *Swimmy*. Pantheon, New York.

—— (1970) *Fish is Fish*. Pantheon, New York.

Munsch, R. (1990) *Good Families Don't*. Doubleday, Toronto.

Nodelman, P. (1996) *The Pleasures of Children's Literature* 2nd edn. Longman, New York.

—— (1988) *Words about Pictures: the Narrative Art of Children's Picture Books*. Athens GA, University of Georgia, Pennsylvania.

Pfister, M. (1992) *The Rainbow Fish*. North-South, New York.

Raschka, C. (1992) *Charley Parker Played Be Bop*. Orchard, New York.

—— (1997) *Mysterious Thelonious*. Orchard, New York.

—— (1998) *Arlene Sardine*. Orchard, New York.

Vygotsky, L.S. (1996) *The Vygotsky Reader*. René van der Veer and Jaan Valsiner (eds). Blackwell, Oxford.

Yorinks, A. (1980) *Louis the Fish* (illustrated by Richard Egielski). Farrar, Straus, New York.

Endnotes

1   See, for instance, my discussion of these matters in *Words about Pictures*, 10–16.

2   For a discussion of repertoire, see Iser (1978, p. 69).

3   From a Jungian perspective, indeed, animals that act like humans might be archetypal, and represent the realities of the collective unconscious — realities that children, less hampered by knowledge of surface realities, might access more easily than adults.

4   For a discussion of assumptions about childlike thinking and childhood development as self-fulfilling prophecies see my book, *The Pleasures of Children's Literature* (1996, pp. 77–81).

Chapter 2

Drawing on the text:
Ron Brooks and the art of collaboration

Jane Doonan

Ron Brooks is a picture book maker who practises the art of collaboration; an artist who has said:

> The words are the thing, really, to me … firstly to try and do maximum possible justice to the text, to the writer, and secondly to allow the reader to find their own connections with the story, with the whole work.

(Scobie, 1997: 32)

As a reader, one way in which to apprehend this artist-designer's achievement is to take him at his word, begin as he did, by attending closely to what he was given, follow this through to the presentation of the whole work, and discover some of the forms his 'maximum possible justice' took. The connections will become self-evident.

Ron Brooks has made notable collaborations in particular with Jenny Wagner, Margaret Wild, and Margaret Perversi. His first full scale picture book, *The Bunyip of Berkeley's Creek*, with Wagner's text, won the Children's Book Council Picture Book of the Year Award in 1974. Four years later they were to repeat this success, and collect another of these awards, together with three others, for the enigmatic work, *John Brown, Rose and the Midnight Cat*. In 1994 they collaborated on *Motor Bill and the Lovely Caroline*, a lyrical picture book which explores the concept of difference and celebrates the uniqueness of each individual's personality. The collaborations with his wife, Margaret Perversi, *Henry's Bath* and *Henry's Bed* (1997), were inspired by their third child. They construct a notion of childhood set in a Utopian landscape, and introduce young viewers — although they may not be aware of it — to the concepts of intertextuality and indeterminacy. Brooks has illustrated three texts by Margaret Wild, *Old Pig, Rosie and Tortoise*, and *Fox*. Any of these collaborative partnerships will sustain close study but a choice had to be made; from the viewpoint of the art, *Old Pig* and *Fox* have contrasting writing styles and types of story, but share a linguistically determined anthropomorphism, and encompass some common themes.

As indicated above, my approach to Brooks' collaborative role is primarily an investigation of the picture books themselves, supported by data accessed in Dromkeen Children's Literature Collection (Scobie, 1997), from which Brooks' statements about his work have been taken. The video interview between Ron Brooks and Michèle Anstey (Anstey, 1998), made for the University of Southern Queensland, also has been made available to me. Brooks says, in interview, that in interpreting and visualising the text he does not engage with the writer but with the words, which he reads repeatedly, and considers very carefully over a period of time. The reason for this includes a belief that:

> There is often a great deal more in the text, behind the text, in between the text — it can be greater than even the writer knows.

He says that his role '… is to try and find all those unwritten stories'. My interests in the aesthetics of the picture book as a medium fix the focus and I shall concentrate upon three aspects: the pictorial style which Brooks adopted, as a response to the 'tone of voice', plot and main theme; how he chose to portray characters and the setting; and the layout which he designed to accompany the shape and rhythms of the story.

Old Pig — sacred landscape, light and shade

> … the expandability of the layers of meaning in the whole work is of paramount importance to me. It must become available to different readers, different ages, in different ways at different time, over time …
>
> (Scobie, 1997: 33)

The story Margaret Wild gave Ron Brooks concerns Old Pig and Granddaughter, characters who are anthropomorphised through behaviour and setting, living in a town small enough to walk around, and near open space, trees and a lake. They have lived together happily for a very long time, and their guiding principle is that of sharing. As Old Pig feels the approach of death she puts her practical affairs in order, then she gives Granddaughter a final lesson in how to be fully alive. One of the key concepts in the text is that of nourishment. We are told exactly what the pigs ate and the importance of eating the right food. Old Pig's celebration of life takes the form of a feast, for the senses, in the open air.

The themes of *Old Pig* include the importance of honouring and valuing the mutual responsibilities which two people have who live together, the merits of civilised behaviour, and pleasures to be gained from a wholehearted response to the natural world. A major theme is that of rites of passage, which both characters undergo: death for Old Pig, and the move from a dependent to an independent state of being for Granddaughter. Anthropomorphism is a device which in itself opens a text to a range of readers of different ages. Even the youngest children are familiar with the idea. The device in literary, dramatic and visual arts distances the reader/viewer because the gap between the fantasy world and the real one is made explicit; it is an effective way of entertaining children, socialising them without appearing to teach or preach, and of allowing for the inclusion of potentially painful matters, such as death, in a form which will not alarm them.

The covert narrator's voice is restrained. It gives sufficient information to move the story along, but withholds sufficient information to prompt the young reader to draw inferences. One device which Wild uses to great effect when feelings are running deep is the short sentence, which literally creates breathing space and thinking space. The following example is taken from the episode when Old Pig leaves the house on her own to put her affairs in order.

'I have a lot to do today,' she said. 'I must be prepared'.

'Prepared for what?' asked Granddaughter.

Old Pig didn't reply. She didn't have to. Granddaughter already knew the answer and it made her feel like crying inside.

Wild has created a story which works against the usual narrative thrust to find out what happens next. By the fourth opening, like Granddaughter, the reader knows of Old Pig's impending death. From an artist's perspective this has to be the ideal text to pictorialise because the viewer is encouraged to behold the page rather than turn it.

Brooks first graphic contribution to the text is to make his represented participants so convincing that it is an easy matter to see them as portraying human characteristics. The only clothing is Old Pig's hat, required by the text, and used by Brooks to lend significant point to her personality; he shows her wearing it in town, but she is not a pig to feast with her hat on. However, he gives her a pair of *pince-nez*. In the tradition of the early masters of caricature and the anthropomorphic impulse — Thomas Rowlandson, J. J. Grandville and John Tenniel — Brooks is extraordinarily skilled at investing an animal face with human expression. It's as if these artists work from the human cartoon character type to the animal rather than the other way round; Old Pig's face has the cast of an amiable person with very little chin. The animals are up on two legs, and the ageing process at work in Old Pig is conveyed through the presence of a walking stick, and a progressive loosening of skin and sagging of flesh. They have 'wrists' which flex, allowing their trotters to curve round objects. All the rest is pose. Old Pig and Granddaughter convincingly express a range of human attitudes, they behave and 'move' like humans do. One example will make the point.

In the first frame which accompanies the text, Old Pig is behind Granddaughter, as if gently guiding and urging her forward. Granddaughter looks back over her shoulder. They are attending to each other, with eyes engaged, snouts only inches apart. Their relationship is immediately established through the body language.

Brooks has expanded the layers of meaning in the whole work, which in turn increases the scope for multi-readings, principally in two interlinked ways. Firstly he introduces three activities not mentioned in the text. These take place within the house, the garden and in the wider landscape. They enhance (make more explicit) the theme of rites of passage, and introduce ideas about cultivating the self as well as the immediate surroundings. Secondly, for a greater part of the '*slow walk around the town*' in which Old Pig is going to feast her eyes upon everything, Brooks chooses a cultivated landscape — a small arboretum with a lake — which is imbued with ideas of nature and the religious impulse. Flourishing with trees that are the source of much of its visual vitality, this setting, which has its origins in a real paddock in Tasmania, balances the decline and death of Old Pig.

The three activities are represented through recurring images of a boat, musical instruments and gardening tools. These images are given prominence by featuring in the first pictures which introduce the characters to their audience — on the wrap-around design for the board cover, on the title page and the first frame which accompanies the opening of the text. Here, Brooks is manipulating the physical characteristics of the picture book itself to his own advantage. Beginning on the front cover, the composition shows Granddaughter rowing Old Pig on a lake; with its abundance of water lilies and reflections of a vespertine sky the lake might be at Giverny. The boat recurs, empty, as a small scale detail upon the same lake during a summer storm, and finally it is given large scale prominence on the last double-page frame. On the backboard cover, the picture shows trees at the lake's edge casting violet and dark grey-rose shadows on the surface of the water. Next, to complete the sequence, and appreciate the wrap-around design, one has to open the book and place it face down. Then the presence of sunshine and shadow within the whole composition is apparent, with the lakescape functioning as a metonym for the picture book's themes. Within the meaning of the discourse, the boat first exemplifies one of the pigs' shared pleasures — is there anything half so much worth doing as simply messing about in boats? — then its cessation. The boat also is a symbol for the journey they undergo both physically and psychologically in their respective rites of passage. Brooks adds an associated motif at a pivotal point in the story in which a chord of impending loss is introduced. Two framed pictures hang upon the dining room wall; the one to the left, behind Granddaughter, shows a sailing boat; over to the right, behind Old Pig, is a painting of a lighthouse. As eye and mind connect the two, several interpretations suggest themselves.

An equally important recurring image — that of the means of making music, the food of love — is featured on the title page. Seated at the piano, with her trotters poised above the keyboard, Old Pig looks over her shoulder to exchange a look with Granddaughter who is holding a cello. Old Pig's pose is the one an accompanist adopts — 'Are you ready?' And in the context of this story the implied question reverberates. Music gives way to silence midway through the visual narrative when Granddaughter is depicted sitting on Old Pig's piano stool beside the piano with its lid closed. When she is ready truly, Granddaughter raises her bow again.

The third image, a set of gardening props, is introduced on the first text page where Old Pig carries a flower basket and Granddaughter wheels a barrow. Their garden shares the qualities in miniature of the wider landscape. The barrow and a hoe feature on the last frame where they have special significance.

Brooks' interior setting for Old Pig's home shows comfortable period furniture, sashed curtains, decorated china. His exterior setting is a small townscape in countryside, complete with emblematic weatherboard, nineteenth century houses roofed with corrugated iron. Although this is not an agricultural landscape, the words John Stephens uses (1994: 76) in association with the long tradition of literary pastoral as exemplified in Australian picture books which have such settings most certainly apply to *Old Pig*:

> … the countryside is a world of fulfilled desire, offering peace, general abundance, and innocent pleasures and amusements to lives shaped by seasonal rhythms.

Although I am unable to interpret *Old Pig* in terms of landscape and identity from an Australian perspective, to my European eyes Brooks' abstraction of the paddock belongs equally well within the tradition of the Northern Romantic painters. Romanticism involves attitudes and ideas in the visual arts and shows itself both in the artist's choice of subject and his attitude to that subject.

In *Modern Painting and the Northern Romantic Tradition*, Robert Rosenblum (1975) offers a way of seeing and understanding affinities in the subject, feeling and structure of paintings of a long tradition of artists, working mainly in Northern Europe and the United

States. He suggests that these affinities arose as a response to the religious dilemmas posed in the Romantic movement. Rosenblum's great chain of artists links Caspar David Friedrich and Philip Otto Runge, working in Germany in the early eighteen hundreds, to Mark Rothko and his transcendental abstractions of the mid twentieth century. What all the painters have in common — Blake, Runge, Palmer, Van Gogh, Munch, Hodler, Nolde, Marc, Kandinsky, and others — is that they 'seek the sacred in the modern world of the secular' (1975: 218).

The early Romantic painters, in their search for 'new means to experience God-given mysteries outside the confines of religious orthodoxy' (1975: 36), turned their attention to the landscape in general and to seascapes. Their new sacred icons included trees, flowers, moons, sweeping clouds, water, ships; everywhere the pathetic fallacy was invoked, and luminous skies were used to create the required transcendental effect. Brooks, intuitively or intentionally, employs in *Old Pig* the iconography of the Northern Romantic painters and their successors. What Wild's characters enjoy beyond their own hedge, is a landscape displaying the Romantic attitude.

How is all this pictured? Brooks uses fine pencil line and water paint. The lines on the contours are loose and light and broken open, animating the shapes. The latter are inscribed and re-inscribed in multiple traces which lie very close or cross each other, in search of telling form. Looking at the record of the movement of his hand shows how the image was brought into being, and at the same time invests the image with its own implied movement. It is as if leaves tremble, boughs shake, Old Pig slowly turns her head, Granddaughter perks up her ears. Water paint is floated on, ebbing and flowing and overflowing the contours, details and textures are brushed in, with flurries, twirls, dabbles, and dots. The white of the supporting paper shines through the washes, to luminous effect. Colour is desaturated, until Old Pig takes her Granddaughter feasting upon radiant landscapes.

Throughout the pictorialisation, light and shade are used as a visual metaphor for the Granddaughter's frame of mind and spiritual wellbeing, and to enhance the rites of passage theme, generally. The quiet dignity displayed by Old Pig and Granddaughter in the face of what's happening to them is matched by the scale, tone and weight of the hand-printed text written in pencil; the icons of language are expressive in themselves, functioning as a calligram for how the words might be spoken.

Layout — gathering momentum, grace, and power

The rhythms of the text slowly build towards a first, sustained climactic episode. In the story time this covers a couple of hours or so as the pigs take their walk. This is followed by an early evening interlude, then the tension rises again for the concluding episode which covers their last shared hours from nightfall to morning. Double-page frames carry these major episodes.

The title page and first page opening each show a single large air-frame, the lightest way of marking the edges of a panel or picture. Then the visual rhythms change in the second opening. Occupying a double-page spread are eight air-framed panels which directly illustrate the voice, as it reports all the pigs' practical shared activities in a story time which covers the hours from morning to evening. The air-frame allows the pigs' actions more

One morning. Old Pig did not get up as usual for breakfast.

Illustration 2.1 'One morning old pig did not get up'
(*Old Pig*, Wild, 1995)

psychological 'elbow room' than a bordered panel would, and allows viewers unimpeded movement from one area to the next. Moving through the sequence which shifts scenes, reading captions and looking at what is shown, in itself takes an appreciable period of discourse time. It also builds up the impression that we have been getting to know the pigs and how they go about their chores, over a lengthy period. The third opening introduces a foreboding note and shifts the music into a minor key. Old Pig's chair is empty (see Illustration 2.1).

The next significant change in the story's tempo occurs after Old Pig has put all her domestic affairs in order, and is heralded by her declaration; 'Now … I want to feast'. She moves herself and Granddaughter from the domestic arena into a wider landscape — both literally and spiritually. Brooks now uses four successive double-page frames. For the first time in the layout design, the frames bleed on all sides to the cut edges of the paper — minimising the boundary between the pictured and the real world. Old Pig appears revitalised by the act of marvelling — exhorting Granddaughter to see how light glitters on leaves and clouds gather 'like gossips' in the sky. She points out reflections in the lake, picks up the sounds of parrots in the trees. As a summer storm breaks she asks if Granddaughter can smell the warm earth and suggests they should taste the rain. This intense experience is a recapitulation of the theme of 'doing things together'.

The pictures are accompanied by Old Pig's spoken words, so we have her subjective point of view of the different aspects of the landscape as she directs Granddaughter's regard. In the first two scenes we share her perceptual and conceptual viewpoint, and in the other two we are spectators of the pigs but still hear Old Pig's words. The last scene, sweeping rain, is in effect a portrait of a tree, a glow of orange and gold. Ron Brooks draws on tradition here. 'I see in nature, for example, in trees, expression and, as it were a soul.' wrote Van Gogh, in a letter of 1882 (cited by Rosenblum, 1975: 77). A tree springing from some resemblance to the human form — or spirit — was a prominent Northern Romantic motif in paintings, from Friedrich onwards, and is perpetuated in children's illustrated literature through particular works of contemporary artist-illustrators such as Maurice Sendak, Ian Beck and Angela Barrett. The total effect of the walk around the town is to show that there is no diminishing of Old Pig's zest for life at the approach of death.

Overleaf, the setting then returns within the house and within the relationship between the pigs. Three air-frames show Granddaughter now in charge. After putting Old Pig to bed, and eating her own supper, she suggests she might share Old Pig's bed, and hold her tight, just as Old Pig did, when she, Granddaughter, was little. Effectively, they have exchanged places in their power relationship. This is a moment fraught with sentiment which could so easily slide into sentimentality. But Brooks has prepared for it.

He uses the turn of the page to give his audience a radiant surprise.

Brooks restores the double-page frame and, in an image which perfectly embodies the main themes, shows Granddaughter playing her cello to Old Pig, who is lying peacefully in bed (see Illustration 2.2). She is being 'held' by the Granddaughter's music in a symbolic togetherness rather than a physical one. Such an interpretation is particularly powerful as it acknowledges their separateness. Granddaughter is now a solo performer and her pose shows her playing confidently.

Colour enhances the mood of serenity; dusky violet, muted blue, rose, greyed green and desaturated orange hues play harmoniously together. A framed picture of the cow jumping over the moon, a transcendent nursery image, hangs above the wood-burning stove suggesting that the music is happy — the tune of the rhyme, perhaps, or a piece which Old Pig taught Granddaughter. The character of the composition is harmonious and spacious. Old Pig is placed on the lower left foreground of the picture plane, linked to Granddaughter by a directional glance. Salience and perceptual weight is given to Granddaughter in three ways: she is on the right-hand side of the picture plane; her form is isolated with ample sweep of space in front of it and to either side of the lower part of her body, so that there is

Illustration 2.2 'So Granddaughter switched off the light …'
(*Old Pig*, Wild, 1995)

nothing to distract the viewer's interest in the passage from the front plane to the middle plane where she is positioned; and she is backlit by the moon hovering outside the window like some celestial being, which lends her shape an aura. The vertical and horizontal emphases of window frames, stove door and bed frame give visual stability to the composition, which otherwise is a rhythmic ordering of curving sweeping lines, and elliptical and round shapes. These units repeat themselves in large and small scale in various forms, like variations on a melodic theme.

The next opening is the final double-page frame, and carries the closing segment of text which covers the hours from night until morning. The accompanying illustration, characterised by Romantic extremes of empathy with nature, encompasses the passage of time specified by the words. Brooks' composition shows a bird's eye view of the now familiar territory. On the left of the picture plane is a moonlit landscape, pictured in silvered colour. Old Pig's house is framed by trees, smoke rises from its chimneys; the three poplars which have marked the passing season stand like sentinels in the middle distance. White lilies glimmer in the foreground. On the other side of the picture plane, the sun is rising and dappling the lake with gold. The empty rowing boat and its reflection is given great salience, set in isolation, unrealistically large in scale, painted in saturated white and yellow, and complementary purple. In the wider context, a boat refers to a notion that is very old indeed — the newly deceased have to cross a river or sea to reach the land of the dead, references to which can be found in Egyptian, Greek and Nordic cultures. A dove wings towards the sky — a symbol for Old Pig's departure or of her spirit taking flight or, for younger children, simply an early bird.

The rites of passage for both Old Pig and Granddaughter have been celebrated. But this is not the end of Brooks' contribution to the multi-layered themes, or his exploitation of the construction of the picture book. He extends the story in the final page frame, by creating implied time to function as a continuum, in which the present holds both references to the past and a promise for the future. Granddaughter stands in front of the summerhouse beside the lake, looking at two parrots flying in her direction. She has her arm round a white duck, earlier seen as one of a pair, in what looks like an affectionate or consoling gesture. Beside her are the wheelbarrow and spade.

Fox — elemental landscape and playing with fire

> Each text is different; I endeavour to respond to each according to my perception of its own particular needs … and so, though only superficially I believe, my technique, my 'style' from book to book moves about a bit … It shifts with the words. It hopefully also shifts with the reader.
>
> (Scobie, 1997: 33)

Ron Brooks has a range of pictorial styles at his command. Illustrations for *The Bunyip of Berkeley's Creek* (Wagner, 1973) and *John Brown, Rose and the Midnight Cat* (Wagner, 1977) have an introspective quality stemming from a fine closed line, meshes of texturing and fully realised settings. Their graphic style exhibits a highly wrought 'finishedness'. Nothing is ever quite so settled upon the page in later picture books — *Motor Bill and the Lovely Caroline* (Wagner, 1994) materialise in apparently effortless strokes and flowing brushmarks, in a world perforated with light. Altogether more robust, the artwork for the two *Henry* books (Perversi, 1997) has the spontaneity and immediacy of sketchbooks of family life. Images emerge from swiftly rendered strokes of expressive intensity, in both charcoal pencil and water paints in rich earthy hues. The depths in these pictures comes in part from modelling, and in part from the materials, which include toppings of shellac. *Fox* (Wild, 2000) shows Brooks at his most painterly. Linnet Hunter has written that he has:

> used the archetypal symbols of forest, water, cave and desert in a distinctly Australian way. Past and present associations — which incorporate the influences of other great Australian artists such as Boyd, Olson, Fairweather — are melded and establish this book as part of the Australian artistic tradition.
>
> (Hunter, 2000: 5)

Once again, it seems appropriate to begin with considering the text itself, and the tone of the narrator's voice. Margaret Wild sets her allegory in the Australian outback where, after a bushfire, one-eyed Dog rescues Magpie, who has a burnt wing. In a perfect symbiotic relationship, she becomes his missing eye, and he becomes her wings as he runs carrying her upon his back. They are happy in the passing seasons. Enter Fox. He is dangerous because he cannot love and belongs nowhere. Fox sets out to destroy what he is incapable of expressing through separating the two good friends. The narrative includes the classical elements of tests, separation and a journey of self-discovery. Two major themes are the redemptive power of love, which is directly constructed, and the concept that just as a body may be maimed, so too may a mind, which Wild leaves for her readers to infer. Other themes include the duties of friendship as well as its blessings, the nature of trust, and the potential frailty of humankind in the face of temptation. The story is structured upon conflicts. It sets raw nature, with bushfire and desert, in opposition to the civilising process associated with the cave and water. Magpie is in conflict with Dog initially, then with Fox, who appeals to her senses, against her sense of loyalty; she is in conflict with herself and, finally, with the environment.

The narrator's voice is formal and poetic, delivering the tale in the here-and-now of the present tense. Through the subtleties of the language — the sentence structure, and the narrative gaps and pauses which Wild leaves for her readers to fill — the moral complexity manifests itself.

Magpie is the character about whom we are told most, by the third person narrator who enters her mind. Magpie responds with intensity to everything. In the beginning of the story, as she drags her body into the shadow of Dog's cave, 'she feels herself melting into blackness'. The colour of her black feathers and cultural associations with that colour and death connects with the idea of a loss of will as well as physical consciousness. Later, 'she rejoices' when Dog runs with her on his back. With a convincing mixture of animal instinct and human sensitivity and perception, she fears Fox. When he tempts her once, twice, she is passionate in her refusal to leave Dog. At the end of the story, when she is abandoned in the desert, 'Magpie huddles, a scruff of feathers adrift in heat. She can feel herself burning into nothingness' — 'adrift' suggests powerlessness and her extreme vulnerability, 'burning' reminds the reader of the physical property of the sun, and Magpie's previous suffering through fire.

Dog has a cluster of virtues. In the space of the first few lines, Wild creates his character through action. He rescues Magpie, tries to tend her burnt wing, and console her. His attempts are met with two understandably bitter outbursts, to which he responds with silence. From these telling silences the reader infers his sympathetic nature, tact and honesty. His Achilles' heel is his over-trustfulness. Dog turns a blind eye literally and metaphorically to Fox, and a deaf ear to Magpie's warning about him.

The elements of setting which are associated with Dog are a cave, and a river. The cave is his home and stronghold, and a place of protection and recuperation for Magpie. At the mouth of the cave, Dog and Magpie come to relax in the evenings 'when the air is creamy with blossom'. Scent becomes palpable and visible through the metaphor. Water, which brings nature to life in reality, is the agent Dog chooses to reveal to Magpie that her life is worth living.

Fox, with his haunted eyes and rich red coat, 'flickers through the trees like a tongue of fire', 'scorches through woodlands'. Thus, Wild forges the connections between Fox, fire, the colour red and associations with danger.

Clearly this literary text can stand on its own. It contains vivid figures of speech to promote mental imaging, and specifies settings which, literally and symbolically, may be related to plot and character. Wild has presented her collaborator with a formidable challenge.

Brooks' response is to shift into a painterly style, and exploit the symbolic power of his materials, particularly through texture and colour. He literally fuses words and images through the materiality of the mixed media from which the pictures are constructed. With the exception of the final recto leaf which is left unworked, the total surface, to the cut edges of the paper of every leaf, whether bearing images or not, appears as layered textured paint, and the text is either marked onto or into the painted surfaces, or cited on textured collage cartouches. As in *Old Pig*, the hand-lettering of the text functions as a calligram; in this case, not indicating how the words are to be spoken but rather how they are to be felt.

The icons appear primitive like the emotions, awkward to deal with, coming at the reader from all directions like conflicting thoughts. And coming at the reader from all directions literally as well, for their layout challenges traditional picture book reading. The object itself has to be turned, this way and that, to follow the story trail scraped and scratched in the pictured earth, clay, and rock face surfaces, involving the reader in the action, through action. The challenge extends also to one of the pictures which incorporates two frames of the same episode: Magpie on Dog's back at the river bank (turn the book upside down to appreciate this view) and what she sees mirrored on the surface of the water (hold the book the right way up). Virtual reality becomes Magpie's new reality as she looks at herself from a different perspective (see Illustration 2.3). Brooks finds an equivalent for this mental process through making it necessary to rotate the book to read the text which borders the image.

Rather than anthropomorphise the animals, Dog and Magpie are depicted with naturalism, Fox is a near-natural stylisation. Wild's text makes it clear that Fox eludes conveniently simple judgment. Brooks supports the inherent ambiguity through his portrayal of Fox as a handsome creature, but his 'otherness' is marked. Brooks structures his compositions so that emotional relations between participants are expressed through the position on the picture plane, directional gaze and posture.

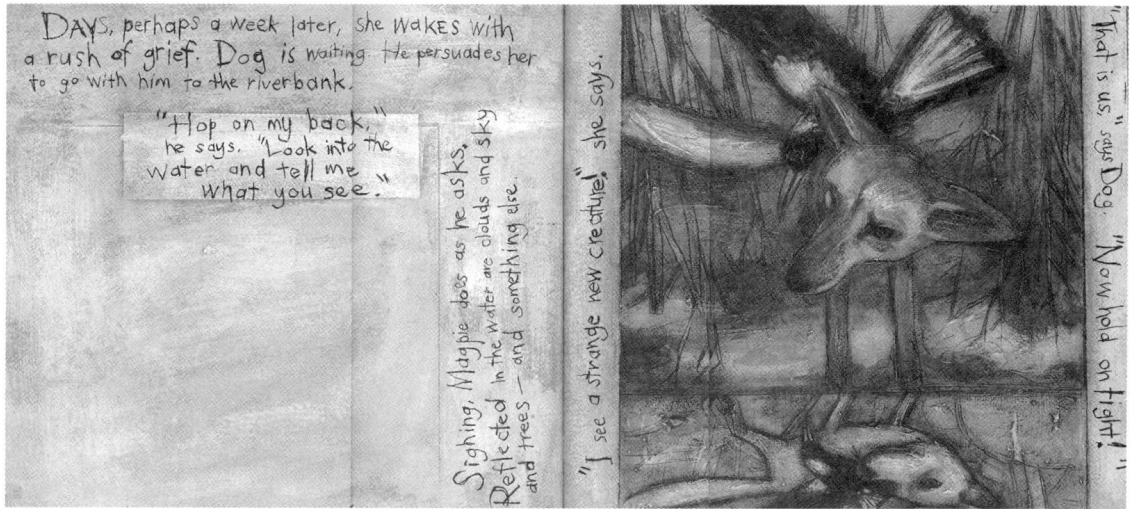

DAYS, perhaps a week later, she wakes with a rush of grief. Dog is waiting. He persuades her to go with him to the riverbank.

"Hop on my back," he says. "Look into the water and tell me what you see."

Sighing, Magpie does as he asks. Reflected in the water are clouds and sky and trees — and something else.

"I see a strange new creature," she says.

"That is us," says Dog. "Now hold on tight!"

Illustration 2.3 'Days, perhaps a week, later ...'
(*Fox*, Wild, 2000)

Good picture books have points of entry across the age and ability range, and I introduced *Fox* to a group of students of only seven years of age because I was curious to learn how much they could make from it. Understandably they had no insights about Fox's deep motive, however they were engrossed from the cover onwards, and recognised the moral dimension in relation to trust, friendship and betrayal. The children interpreted the pictures through the expressive qualities of the images of the animals, 'reading' them through psychological and social experiences at home and in the playground. Following the lead given by the text's focalisation of Magpie, Brooks shows important episodes through her eyes, conceptually and perceptually — a form of visual autobiography which encourages engagement.

Brooks' artwork, in expressionist style, exemplifies graphic and plastic freedom, wrought and wrestled from oil paint, acrylic, water-colour, charcoal and shellac. Marks made by gouging, scratching, scraping, brush trails and flickering black lines agitate the picture surface in patterns as complex as the feelings they express. There is a strong play between the depth and surface of the media itself, with its strata of paint and paper, symbolically mirroring both the underlying and apparent motives in the action.

As an example of a picture which exhibits some of the qualities associated with modern Expressionism I have chosen the double-page frame showing Fox running away with Magpie who has turned her world upside down. The words recount how they '... streak past coolibah trees, rip through long grass, pelt over rocks, Fox runs so fast that his feet scarcely touch the ground' (see Illustration 2.4).

Brooks draws this scene with sharp implements and thick brushes, and a trust in immediacy of statement. The frame cannot contain the limits of Fox's outstretched form, brush up, paws down, on a diagonal plane. He has an incandescent orange-red hue. The fur is composed of predominantly horizontal striations or traces in the thick impasto, the brush strokes inside the shape both modelling his form and mimicking the effect of wind

While Dog sleeps, Magpie and Fox freak past coolibah trees, rip through long grass, pelt over rocks.

Fox runs so fast that his feet scarcely touch the ground, and Magpie exults, "At last I am flying. Really flying!"

Illustration 2.4 'While Dog sleeps ...'
(*Fox*, Wild, 2000)

flattening his coat. The physicality of the paint, whether lying on the surface or gouged — denoting fur, feather, cloud, rocks, earth, trees, and palings — destroys the distance between object and background, drawing freely the object into the background and vice versa. It also minimises distinctions between the surface texture of those objects. This is the 'elemental landscape' — Fox and Magpie and the territory, and the icons of language, all composed of the same kind of·matter, all drawn in a belief in the power of the mark — as it is made — to give form to feeling.

Setting, colour, layout — staging the drama

There are three basic variations for the style in which Brooks represents the setting of Wild's tale. He depicts the location of the cave and river with the greatest degree of naturalism of all three, and this sets the scene for the opening of the text pages which establish Dog's territory. One of the two paintings of the mouth of Dog's cave (the other is described below) is a balanced arrangement of curving shapes and straight sided ones, and variously textured surfaces. A little above the perceptual centre of the composition is the cave entrance, a mysterious darkness, impenetrable to the eye, surrounded by slabs of stone, and huge sun-warmed boulders. Its monumental numinous presence intensifies the sense of place for the story's events, as does the back endpaper, a landscape depicted in golden ochre, cerulean, velvety viridian and gauzy veils of tender new green.

The second variation of setting includes almost monochromatic pictures of the terrain, with the minimum of observed details. The frame which shows Magpie riding on Dog's back for the first time is one example. The restricted colour is playing a significant role; wonderful though Magpie feels this to be, it has nothing like the intensity which she experiences when she flies with Fox. In this second group are pictures which partner pivotal episodes in the story. Brooks minimalises the details, and focuses attention upon the animal participants, as when Dog and Magpie are depicted running through a semi-abstract background which signals the change of seasons through change of hue — and an ominous change in the circumstances of the two friends. On the opposing frame is Fox, who has just come into the bush. In abstract terms, his shape is a strong vertical flame-like curve, an orange red cipher, forming a barrier on the right of the picture plane from top to bottom. In narrative terms, there is no escaping him.

The third variation shows non-figurative or near-non-figurative settings, which draw their meaning from the intrinsic behaviour of shapes, lines and colours. We are able to interpret the abstract pictures in relation to the descriptive; the two are complementary, the same elementary landscape. The near-non-figurative settings are used as expressive mindscapes for Magpie, in episodes of high intensity which record her conceptual viewpoint. Examples of this are when she feels Fox watching her, next when he abandons her, then when the hostile environment sets the fourth test, the final temptation — 'It would be so easy just to die here in the desert' — and, finally, as a setting for the start of 'the long journey home'.

In painting, colour is always interpretation. The colour red is shared by the fire of the bush and the sun, and a fox's coat. This is enough to 'read' fear and danger into anything carrying that colour, for the emotional and symbolic interpretations are factual and from real experience. Brooks uses the symbolic power of colour in a particularly interesting way when he pictures the entrance to Dog's cave after Fox has started sharing it. The text, from Magpie's viewpoint, records that at night Fox's smell 'seems to fill the cave — a smell of rage and envy and loneliness'. The painting is predominantly an arrangement of warm blacks, crimson, and deep green shapes, under-painted and permeated with red and bordered in red. The colour is a visual equivalent of Fox's smell, his control of Dog's territory, and more than that — the inescapable presence of Fox in Magpie's consciousness.

On all but five frames, the characters direct significant looks towards each other, and on the front cover Fox comes bounding into our lives subjecting us to a direct gaze. Generally we can deduce what the gazer is demanding of us, but in this instance there is nothing to go on. That signifies — the gaze is used to menacing effect to accompany the recorded incident when Magpie feels Fox is 'watching, always watching her'. Brooks positions the viewer as Magpie, and shows a close-up of Fox's eyes on a narrow horizontal slit of a panel. Did Brooks depict Fox with eyes which do not reflect the light for aesthetic or symbolic reasons, a visual translation of 'haunted eyes' perhaps? Unlike Magpie's, they lack that white speck of paint which artists use to give lustre to the eye. Without the speck the gaze of the subject seems dead; in the case of Fox, the lack of lustre promotes the impression that moral consciousness is missing.

The rhythm of the story is climactic, with a strong element of suspense. The interrelated episodes accelerate in intensity from the moment when Dog invites Fox to share the cave, until Fox shakes Magpie off his back as he would a flea. The design of the layout builds towards a matching pattern, to this point.

After the title page, the sequence has single page frames to focus attention on the continuous shifts of power in the relationships of the three participants in their psychological drama. The double-page frame is used first to give full conceptual weight to the episode when Dog makes his unwise offer. Then the double-page frame is withheld until a run of four of them, which pictorialises Fox's flight with Magpie, and carries the audience to the moral heart of the text. The run of double-page frames closes on his abandonment of her. Fox tells Magpie: 'Now you and Dog will know what it is like to be truly alone'. The abstract ground is an expression of burnt-out hope, ashen in hue, with an agitated surface. The layout pattern emphasises the great distance travelled, the magnitude of Fox's betrayal, and ultimately raises the question of the likelihood of Magpie being able to get back to Dog.

Brooks then takes the opportunity extended by Fox's sudden disappearance from the text. The narrator concludes in five sentences, reporting the final temptation and Magpie's response. Brooks, as designer, has to balance the energy and duration of the run of four double-page frames, with conceptual weight and significance for the closing stages of Wild's story. He allows three openings for Magpie's trial by burning heat, her vision of Dog's cave, and the last image of her — a metaphorical phoenix — positioned on the picture plane in a rising diagonal and in relatively large scale. He then extends the story on the endpaper which increase the opportunities for multiple meanings. Those with whom I have shared the picture book, from the ages of seven years to the seventh decade, are divided in their opinions about whether this scene may be interpreted as a sign of Magpie and Dog's reunion, or of Dog's forgiveness, or of Magpie's redemption being matched by Nature's regeneration, or simply as a sign of natural regeneration. But everyone agrees that she does the right thing. As such, Fox is an agent for Magpie's transformation; fire tempers steel, and metaphorical fire is able, at best, to temper the human character.

In conclusion, as whole works, the ways in which Brooks has pictorialised and designed *Old Pig* and *Fox* emphasises their text-given difference to each other in form, and the affinity each has with the major genres of narrative art and dramatic art, respectively. They exemplify two types of picture book which Reinbert Tabbert identifies as: '… a narrative one which unfolds a world and a dramatic one which develops a conflict' (1999: 14). *Old Pig* stands in relation to the former, *Fox* to the latter. Each book offers a very different experience. *Old Pig* celebrates and consoles in equal measure, offering a stable world in which virtues can be passed from one generation to the next. Things are as they seem. In *Fox* the arguments about how life should be lived are presented as a conflict of ideas. *Fox* has echoes of a medieval morality play, with good and fallen angels contesting for Magpie's soul. *Fox* is a psychodrama — a psychoanalytic model of human personality, with its elemental landscape symbolising the world of the unconscious — the id colliding with the ego, and the prompting of the super ego, set the stage for the central conflict. *Fox* makes it clear, even to relatively young children, that the moral life is beset with difficulties and complexities. Nothing is quite what it seems.

Brooks' interpretation of *Old Pig* extends the story world, which is essentially a practical one, into a visual expression of creative impulses and practices. *Fox* displays some of those metafictive devices which are intended to contest accepted ways of looking at picture books; however, it may be equally well argued that Brooks subverts this intention. The foregrounding, of material means and conventional viewing practice, functions metaphorically. Although the two works present very different stylistic appearances, and modes of expansion, Ron Brooks supports and thus enhances the values and underlying assumptions of Margaret Wild's texts. Both picture books — through imaginative reach, writing, interpretative illustration and design — exemplify the best that may be achieved through the art of collaboration.

Bibliography

Anstey, M. (1998) *Ron Brooks: Interview and Demonstration of Technique* (video). University of Southern Queensland, I.L.S, Toowoomba.

Hunter, L. '*Fox*: Linnet Hunter looks at a publishing landmark', *Magpies* vol 15 no 2 May 2000, Magpies Magazine Pty Ltd.

Perversi, M. (1997) *Henry's Bath* (illustrated by Ron Brooks). Viking/Penguin Books, Australia.

—— (1997) *Henry's Bed* (illustrated by Ron Brooks). Viking/Penguin Books, Australia.

Rosenblum, R. (1975) *Modern Painting and the Northern Romantic Tradition, Friedrich to Rothko*. Thames and Hudson, London.

Scobie, S. (1997) *The Dromkeen Book of Australian Children's Literature* (comp). Scholastic, Gosford.

Stephens, J. (1994) 'Illustrating the Landscape in Australian Children's Picture Books', *Landscape and Identity: Perspectives from Australia*, Parsons, W. and Goodwin, R. (eds), Auslib Press, Adelaide.

Tabbert, R. (1999) 'Nutshell Theatres: On considering Picture Books as Dramatic Art', Report of Internationale Jugend Bibliothek 1/99, Munich.

Wagner, J. (1973) *The Bunyip of Berkeley's Creek* (illustrated by Ron Brooks). Longman Young Books, Australia.

—— (1977) *John Brown, Rose and the Midnight Cat* (illustrated by Ron Brooks). Kestral Books (Penguin), Melbourne.

—— (1994) *Motor Bill and the Lovely Caroline* (illustrated by Ron Brooks). Viking/ Penguin Books, Australia.

Wild, M. (1995) *Old Pig* (illustrated by Ron Brooks). Little Ark Book, Allen & Unwin, St Leonards.

—— (1998) *Rosie and Tortoise* (illustrated by Ron Brooks). Allen & Unwin, St Leonards.

—— (2000) *Fox* (illustrated by Ron Brooks). Allen & Unwin, St Leonards.

Chapter 3

On a walk with Lily and Satoshi Kitamura:
how children link words and pictures along the way

Evelyn Arizpe with Morag Styles

Lily is a cheery little girl who likes going for walks with her dog, Nicky. She watches the sunset, buys groceries and flowers, looks at the stars, says goodnight to the ducks, arrives back in time for supper with her parents and finally goes happily to bed. This is Lily's story and it is the story told by the words. But to understand why there is always a scared-looking Nicky next to the smiling Lily, we need to 'read' the story told by the pictures. As Lily and Nicky take a walk, the pictures show us that the dog encounters (or he imagines), among other things, a snake, a tree with a wicked grin, a fierce-looking postbox, lamp posts with eyes, a strange man emerging from a poster on the wall and various monsters. When they get home, he tries to tell Lily and her parents what he saw, but they do not seem to be paying attention. Exhausted, he finally lies down, only to be plagued by a group of mice trying to get into his basket with a ladder!

Like the hen in *Rosie's Walk* (Hutchins, 1970) who apparently never notices the fox that is following her, Lily goes out and returns home seemingly unaware of the creatures that frighten her dog. The text tells us that 'even if it is dark, Lily is not afraid because Nicky is with her'. Is she so confident with Nicky that she is oblivious to danger? Or is Nicky so neurotic that he will see monsters wherever he looks? Or perhaps, as one of the young readers we spoke to speculated (and not without reason), Lily is not afraid because she and her family are also ghostly monsters.

Lily Takes a Walk (Kitamura, 1997) is a postmodern picture book in the sense that it leaves the reader to deal with these questions, fill in the gaps and resolve the ambiguities of the pictorial text (Styles, 1996). These aspects belie the apparently simple narrative and lead the reader into a world of alternative meanings where fears can be dealt with through humour and irony. This picture book is also illustrating one of the defining aspects of its genre: the relationship between image and text. David Lewis writes that '… the picture book always has a double aspect, an ability to look in two directions at once and to play off the two perspectives against each other … the picture book is thus not just a form of text, it is also a *process*, a way of making things happen to words and to pictures' (Lewis, 1996: 109–10). In *Lily Takes a Walk* we have two characters, each literally looking in a different direction, and as their perspectives play off against each other, the readers find themselves participating in the process of making a story happen. The reader perceives at least two contrasting versions of the same events at the same time and perhaps understands that reality is never quite simple. If this seems too complicated a concept for young readers, it is worth quoting Karen, a 7 year-old, even if she is obviously struggling to express her reply to why Lily and Nicky are always looking in different directions:

> Because they might have different like … say if Lily heard a joke and Lily laughed but Nicky couldn't laugh because he didn't get it […] so they might have different possibilities.

As he does in many of his other books, Satoshi Kitamura is playing a serious game with the relationship between the illustrations and the texts. In this particular pictorial text he invites his audience to join Lily and Nicky as they walk along, encouraging a reader like Karen to become aware of the complexities in postmodern narrative. As Margaret Meek (1988) tells us, it is the text that teaches what readers need to learn. It may be that some inexperienced readers will require more help in this understanding, and this is where the teacher should come in as a more experienced reader who listens to the children's responses and asks the questions that will lead the young readers to develop their critical awareness of the text and of their role as readers.

But how do the readers learn and become aware of how picture books work? How do they join the artist's game, if in fact they do so? How do they make sense of the discourse of the pictures? How do they relate it to the words? And how do they deal with the incoherent and the incomplete? These are some of the questions that our project, *Reading Pictures*,[1] aims to explore by talking about picture books with children of different ages.

The research: 'interviewing' with children

Reading the multi-image world of this second millennium requires new and sophisticated skills, but how these skills affect reading and looking and how they can be taught and learned are questions that are just beginning to be addressed. Many modern picture books use visual forms from other media and demand some of these complex skills in order to be understood; in this way they aid the reader in becoming 'multiliterate' (Anstey, 2000). By analysing picture books in depth and by asking young readers how they make sense of them it is possible to expand our knowledge about these skills. Many teachers and researchers have convinced us of the value of trying to learn from children's talk about their reading (Heath, 1983; Lewis, 1992; Watson, 1996, to mention a few). Even so, there have been surprisingly few systematic attempts to ask children about their reading/viewing of pictorial text, particularly using the same book and questions with children of different ages and in different schools.

Perhaps one reason for this is that picture books are mainly used with very young readers for teaching reading, but tend to be discarded in the later years of primary school in favour of apparently more 'complex' texts. However, the picture book has proved that it is as complex as any other art form and that it continues to appeal to readers as they develop — including adults. Our project on how children 'read' picture books aims to explore the potential of visual literacy and the skills children need to deal with visual texts. We wanted to look at multi-layered picture books by contemporary artists who we would also interview about their work.

After looking at the work of many talented artists we decided on Anthony Browne and Satoshi Kitamura, and from among their many books, we selected three which we believed would appeal to a wide age range (between 4 and 11) and provide enough material for in-depth discussions: *The Tunnel* and *Zoo* by Browne and *Lily Takes a Walk* by Kitamura.[2]

Lily Takes a Walk was read in two of the seven primary schools that participated in our project, one in Cambridge and one in Essex.[3] Six children were selected by the teacher from each of three groups: Years 3–4, 5–6 and Reception in one school, and Years 2, 3–4 and 5–6 in the other. The selection was based on contrasting 'reading abilities', of which the researchers had no knowledge until after the interviews took place. Twenty-four children were individually interviewed and six group discussions (led by the researchers) took place.[4] During the individual interviews the researchers followed the questions closely, but during the group discussion, although there was guidance from the researcher towards certain key aspects of the text, there was room for the children to expand on their previous answers and to explore other ideas that were brought up at the time.

Some of the questions we asked applied to all three books, while others were particular to each one. We began by asking about the appeal of the cover and how it showed what the picture book might be about (later in the interview we asked if, in retrospect, the covers were 'good' for the book). We asked them to tell us about each illustration through specific questions, to show us their favourite picture and how they 'read' it and to talk about the relationship between words and pictures. We questioned them about the actions, expressions and feelings of the characters; the intratextual and intertextual elements; what the artist needed to know in order to draw and the way in which he used colour, body language and perspective.[5]

Because we felt that constructing meaning from a picture book demands various re-readings, we decided to carry out follow-up interviews six months later with three children from each school. The importance of this was confirmed by the work done by 4 and 5 year-olds in a school where one of our teachers had done further work on *Zoo* after the initial interviews. This resulted in some outstanding artwork and also in a greater appreciation of the more complex issues in the book. In the revisiting, the emphasis of the questions changed from detailed examination of individual pages to the bigger picture, including a consideration of the book as a whole.[6] The transcripts from the initial and the follow-up interviews were analysed according to codes derived from other studies on reader-response (for example, Thomson, 1987) with the added factor of the visual. What follows are some of our findings as we followed Lily and Nicky's footsteps through the book.

Walking with Lily and Nicky

As anyone who has read with young children knows, it is difficult to talk about their response to pictures because their words do not always match the manner in which they look at the pictures. Children's responses include the way they 'look round' moving their eyes from one side to another; enthusiastic gestures; the way they point at things shouting 'Look, look!' when they make a new discovery or solve a puzzle; and even the way in which they go back and forth through the book, crumpling the pages in their excitement. All of the researchers were struck by the intellectual seriousness, as well as the pleasure, with which the children looked at the book. They were absorbed by the task and reacted strongly to the pictorial text, expressing not only likes and dislikes but also ethical and moral preoccupations. They were interested in the smallest details and untroubled by the puzzling nature of the narrative, even when they could not always find an answer to our questions at that time. Sometimes it was as if the children knew that they would eventually solve the puzzles and could leave their understanding 'on hold' for the moment.

Their interest began at the sight of the cover and became keener as they turned the pages. The cover sets the tone for the rest of the book: the seemingly innocuous title which is Lily's story, together with the threatening background of blank, dark windows, empty streets and frightening monsters. It shows a smiling Lily carrying her groceries towards the left side of the page while Nicky stands facing the opposite way with a frightened look on his face, his eyes are wide open, his nose, ears and tail are pointing upwards and his mouth crumpled into a worried grimace (see Illustration 3.1).

From Nicky's expression the children — from the youngest to the oldest — gathered that there would be something menacing to come. This lured them to find out what he was scared of and to read the rest of the book:

> [You think] something like what's the dog scared of, so you like turn the page and then look and then just carry on reading and there's some more monsters and you just want to see the rest of it. (Kevin, 10)

Despite the sinister atmosphere, the children expected a 'scary' but, at the same time, 'funny' book, because they were reassured by the cartoon-like style of the drawing. Colin (8), for example, predicted it might be 'a bit like a comedy'. Readers become involved when they can form analogies between the text and their own experience. For example, Jess (6) was immediately interested because of a building which looks like a church she goes to; others spoke of their own or other people's dogs. Interestingly, for many readers (myself included) it was not until the first reading was over, and the cover was scrutinised again, that they

Illustration 3.1 Cover of *Lily Takes a Walk*

discovered what it was that Nicky was looking at: a scary face made by a tree with fierce looking nostrils, bent lampposts as eyes and a mouth full of tree trunk and iron railing teeth. At this point there was unanimous agreement that the cover was a good one for the book because, as Janet (4) put it: '… it looked like what was going to happen in the story'.

The title page belies the cover in that the dog is actually looking quite happy to be going for a walk. Perhaps this is because they are just starting out or because Lily is actually looking at him for once (it is the only time they actually look at each other with the exception of the back cover where Nicky is again looking worried). Several children noticed the house in the background and wondered whether it was Lily's home. On the next page, back on the pavement, both characters are looking at the reader, Lily is smiling but Nicky is already looking worried and seems to be inviting us to share in his apprehension. Empathy also encourages involvement, and it was not surprising that most readers were more concerned about the feelings of the over-imaginative dog than with the child, while at the same time laughing — not unkindly — at him. This also allows quite young readers to enjoy the experience of feeling a little more grown up or mature than the characters in the book. Some of the children reasoned that the dog was looking worried because he was hungry or tired, but most of them thought he was anxious because of what he might see on the walk. Several children commented on this direct look. Flora (10) said it was as if someone was taking a picture of him from outside the book, while Saul (11) noted that they were looking at 'us, the reader'.

Next we have a double-page spread (like all the remaining pictures in the book) which shows Lily and Nicky once again in the country or a park. Lily has her back to us as she admires the sunset, but Nicky is startled to see a snake as he lifts his leg against a bush. Several children said this was their favourite spread because of the rich colours, especially the blues and greens, and they also commented on the way the grass and the trees were drawn. Karol (10) liked the 'texture' and the way the trees looked 'scribbled' but were actually 'very carefully done'.

As Lily walks along towards the right-hand corner of the page, Nicky's imagination really starts working. He looks behind him to see a tree giving him a wicked grin. Then, when Lily stops at the grocer's stall, his eyes widen in terror when he sees a post box leaning over, with its open top full of pointed teeth and letters dropping from its 'mouth'. Some of the children noticed the empty can and other litter in these two spreads, and, as we will see, they followed this trail and later reached the conclusion that Kitamura was trying to make a point about pollution. The fact that Kitamura was not intentionally making a point about the environment does not invalidate the children's reactions.[7]

As it gets darker, we find ourselves in one of the more frightening places in the walk: while Lily looks up at the stars, Nicky sees a face in the tunnel, a wide-gaping mouth with lampposts for eyes and traffic cones for teeth. The alley is dark and deserted like the rest of the streets, except for a skip full of rubbish. Most of the readers commented on the menacing atmosphere, the older ones being more specific about which details made it frightening:

It's kind of scary, but it's funny because […] street lights with just a tunnel wouldn't scare you at all, but it's just because it's together it makes it look real, like it's actually alive …
All the detail, like even the skip with the rubbish falling out, and another reason why it's

frightening is because not only that the dog's not looking at her, but because the dog's on the other side of the wall looking at something and she's just kind of talking to herself. (Kevin, 10)

A younger child, Jess (6), was probably making an association with her own fears: 'Scary, there might be baddies' houses and as it is dark I thought there might be a baddie in [the skip]'.

The evening has become purple, the moon appears and becomes one of the eyes, together with the clock on the tower, of an owlish looking face with tree trunks for teeth and a lamppost nose. Nicky stares in horror while Lily seems to be waving at us, but the text says that she is waving to a Mrs Hall, whom we cannot see. This gap, the missing Mrs Hall, was only a problem for the younger readers who said that she must be in one of the windows, and pointed at ones behind Lily. The older ones said that she must be off the page, where we (the readers) were:

> It's like you're Mrs Hall because he's looking at you, because you can't actually see the window … so she's waving to you. (Kevin, 10)

As she continues her walk, now almost in the dark, Lily points out to Nicky how clever the bats are, but he is shaking at the sight of a strange-looking man with a top hat who seems to be coming out of a poster, bending a lamppost in the process, and spilling the tomatoes, from the blood-coloured juice he is drinking, onto the pavement (see Illustration 3.2).

Kevin noticed that the dog was not 'round' but 'fuzzy', which meant he's 'even more scared'. When asked what sort of man he was, the children used the picture's clues to define him as a witch, 'because it's got a witchy hat and coat' (Janet, 4) or a vampire, 'because it's got very pale white skin and it's got a blood stain there [on the cuff]' (Hugh, 9). Alice (9) even gave him a part in the narrative:

Bats flitter and swoop in the evening sky.
'Aren't they clever, Nicky?' says Lily. 'Not far, now.'

Illustration 3.2 Spread of Lily looking at the bats

He has that sort of spiky bit there, spiky collar. And maybe he's pretending that's blood, blood juice and also there is a bat swooping around and going 'Oh do not get near this poster or the evil bloodsucking vampire will have you for dinner!'

The next spread shows Lily saying goodnight to the ducks and gulls on one side of the bridge, while on the other a dinosaur or Lochness-like creature stares down at Nicky, who is rooted to the spot despite his fast-moving legs. All the children were able to explain why Nicky seems to have eight legs in this picture and some exemplified it by moving their own legs very quickly. In this spread it is Janet (4) who gives a voice to the monster: 'Aaaggg! He's getting burnt [as he leans over the lamppost]'. There are still a few more monsters to terrify Nicky, popping out at him from rubbish bins just before he and Lily get home. According to Kevin (10) they looked '3D' and one girl described how Kitamura's lines make them look scary:

> … he's made them all like all different angles and all different triangle shapes and all sticking out and stuff and this one's just all straight, then zigzagged. (Karol, 10)

Once at home, over dinner, Lily tells her parents about her walk. We can see the father smiling but we can't see the mother's face. On the opposite page, Nicky has his mouth open, surrounded by little bubbles with the pictures of the monsters he has seen. Many of the children again showed their familiarity with the cartoon-like style by saying these were the dog's 'speech' bubbles (one compared them to those in *Asterix* and *Tin Tin*).

> Well you can see the mother asking Lily and she's just like saying some nice things and he's just thinking 'what are you doing?' And he's just thinking of the things he's seen. (Martin, 7)

As the text says, it's time for bed and Lily sleeps happily underneath the duvet with her name written all over it (only the older ones noticed this). Nicky has also settled into his basket and is just about to relax when, as the flap opens, a group of mice give him a last shock by trying to climb into his basket with a ladder. When asked how they felt about this picture before and after opening the flap some of the readers remarked on the cosiness and messiness of her bedroom (and immediately compared it to theirs) and at the same time noticed details which reminded them of the uncanny atmosphere, such as the fact that three of the stuffed animals look rather worried and sad, that the tiger in what is presumably Lily's drawing looks scared and that dark blank windows are looking into her room. As Alice (9) rightly pointed out, it doesn't seem that Nicky will be happy anywhere because he will always find something to be frightened of:

> It's a place that Lily can be really comfy in and very happy, but Nicky can be like 'Ooh this room!'. There's just something about everything that he can get very scared about.

Reading further into the picture

As readers and researchers walked along with Lily and Nicky, the responses gave us an insight into the more complex discursive aspects of this book in particular and of picture books in general. It also provided insights in relation to the readers' appreciation and awareness of:

- visual features of text and artistic intentions;
- the interaction between words and pictures;
- the implied reader-viewer and children's own reading-viewing process; and
- the significance of the book as whole.

The following sections discuss these insights.

Appreciation of visual features and artistic intention

Questions about visual features were asked throughout the interviews with prompts on colour, pattern, perspective and body language. We also asked if they noticed similarities with other Kitamura picture books. Most of the children noticed colour, and referred especially to the different shades of sky (later, many of them made an attempt to portray these skies in their drawings). They also noticed the cartoon-like patterns of the 'wobbly' lines, the uneven bricks, the flat wheels and the crooked windows. One of the Year 6 boys described this style as 'realistic but not realistic'. Other visual features that were mentioned included perspective (how the trees became smaller in the distance); where the characters were placed (for example, that Lily is always on the side furthest from the monsters and Nicky is nearest); and intertextual references (to Kitamura's *A Boy Wants a Dinosaur*).[8]

The less experienced readers tended to provide less plausible explanations (with no basis in the text) for the way in which Kitamura draws lines. For example, they said the steps were wobbly because:

> They belong to a witch.
> They've been there for thousands of years.
> A heavy man stepped on them.

The more experienced readers tended to give reasons that had more to do with logic (rightly or wrongly) and with the author's intention. Karen (7), for example, said:

> It is hard to draw steps so he might wiggle a little bit cause he is worried about it, that he's going to do it wrong, so he's a bit shaky.

And Martin (7) considered how they added to the atmosphere: 'it's to make it scarier and to stand out more'.

Other children commented on the atmosphere created by the continual appearance of dark colours, the blank windows and empty cars. They described it as 'spooky' and 'upsetting'. Karol (10) spoke of the difference between these dark backgrounds and the way in which Lily and Nicky 'brightened it all up'. Martin also remarked on this contrasting effect:

> It's very good, his use of colour, because he's like used all bright colours on her … I reckon he could have picked different (flowers) like roses or daffodils … but he probably just chose a really bright colour: yellow. And he's chose a really dark colour for the houses.

In general, we felt that the children would have had a lot more to say about the visual features of the text if they had the language to do so; nevertheless, they were able to discuss how these features were used by the artist to make a joke, create an atmosphere or emphasise a message.

Interaction between words and pictures

About the relationship between words and pictures in *Rosie's Walk* (Hutchins, 1970), Nodelman says:

> In showing more than the words tell us, the pictures not only tell their own story; they also imply an ironic comment on the words. They make the words comic by making them outrageously incomplete …
>
> (Nodelman, 1988: 224)

A similar interaction is taking place in *Lily Takes a Walk* and although most of the younger readers struggled to express their understanding of this interaction, some of the older ones managed to explain it quite clearly:

Interviewer: Do you think the pictures are telling the same story as the words?
Saul (11):   Yes plus a bit more … [the pictures] seem to bring out the story.

Almost without exception, the children thought the pictures were more interesting than the words. They felt that *Lily Takes a Walk* would still be good if you only had the pictures, but if there were only words it would be boring, especially, they added, for 'children'. There was definitely a belief that books with pictures (lots of them) were for younger children and the amount of pictures in books decreased in inverse ratio to the words as books were intended for older readers. However, some children did realise that only having the words would change the meaning of this particular book. Hugh's (9) comment about having only words was typical: 'you wouldn't be able to see what was happening'.

In order to appreciate the humour in a 'polysystemic' book like *Lily Takes a Walk*, it is necessary to integrate the meaning from both the words and the pictures — two different signifying systems (Lewis, 1996). When asked if the words and pictures told the same story, most readers found it hard to separate them and answered yes, but some of the more engaged ones recognised they were different:

Interviewer: Do the words and the pictures tell the same story?
Karen (7):   A bit of a yes and a bit of a no because it doesn't say that like Lily is pointing to the leeks or something, but it does say 'today she …'
Interviewer: So if the words are telling that story, who's telling the rest of the story?
Karen: The dog.

The Years 5 and 6 students were more able to articulate the difference between the meanings derived from the text and the pictures. For example, Flora (10) pointed out that 'the pictures tell you about the monsters and the words just tell you what Lily thought'. Kevin (10) described this in more detail, weighing up the contribution of both words and pictures:

(If it were only the words) it wouldn't be good because it would just be a happy book because it doesn't say anything about anything being scary. It's just saying she's not scared and she'll do her shopping, she looks at the stars, she walks past someone's house and waves. You wouldn't see the bats or any of those things that make it scary … Some books are better without the pictures because then you can make up your own thing, but I think this is better with the pictures … the words need the pictures more than the pictures need the words.

Invoking his previous experience as a reader, Kevin recognises the difference between the two signifying systems and how they work upon the reader (the pictures make it scary). His statement also shows us the analytical process by means of which he arrives at a conclusion and makes a judgment on the value of these systems. It is an indication of the processes that are going on in the reader/viewer's head as they attempt to construct a story structure using different kinds of 'building blocks'.

Implied reader-viewer and children's own reading-viewing processes

Perhaps because the 10 and 11 year-olds had little opportunity to look at picture books both at home and at school, *Lily Takes a Walk* was, at first, considered as a book for younger children. This was also true of some of the 8 and 9 year-olds, because, they argued, if it were for older children it would have more writing and 'a bit more detail'. However, by the end of the interview day, this opinion was revised by many of the older readers, such as Peter (9):

> I think this book's interesting because … children enjoy picture books but I think it's also better for older people because if they read it carefully they can like spot things, like what we're doing now, they can sort of have fun with it and spot things.

This and other answers show how their previous experience of books and their knowledge of the type of fiction we were reading comes to bear on their responses. Kitamura's cartoon-like style was an indication that it would be both a fictional and humorous book. Alice (9), for example, when asked if the monsters were real or imaginary, said:

> Well in books really anything can actually happen, it's just your own imaginary world so that could actually be happening.

Asking a reader to describe what happens when he or she reads is always fascinating, especially when they are young children who are searching for a way to describe it. Many answers revealed the importance that detail has for them. The older children described how they spot 'the problem' or the unexpected and then return to the 'normal' and put the two together:

> Peter (9):   I look carefully and I see what may be the problem because you see the dog notices things that the girl isn't noticing so then I split the book into half and I see what Lily's seeing and really what she's saying … seeing and doing, and I will look at the dog and see what he's doing.
>
> Interviewer: So you get sort of one side and then the other side?
>
> Peter: And try and put them together.

Peter's description of what is going on in his head as he reads gives us an indication of what children are noticing as they look at pictures. As they read they are looking at the whole picture and connecting it to the words, as well as seeing through the characters' eyes and trying to pull all this information together. Their processes of deduction involved both imagination and commonsense. For example, Jess (6) speaks of looking for clues to 'get things right'; when Lily smells her supper cooking, she wondered which one of the houses was hers:

> Is that her house? It might be her house. Let's have look in the front. I think it is because on the first page she has got a blue roof, so that might be.

Readers were aware that they were joining in a kind of game which allowed them to go back and forth through the book to look for details they had missed in order to solve the puzzles. They were willing to work hard at making connections and coming up with explanations; evidently they were deriving great satisfaction from participating in the meaning-making process by piecing the picture together.

Significance of the book as a whole

One of the most difficult tasks for any reader is to be able to stand back from a text and view it as a whole; it is perhaps even more difficult when we are dealing with a polysystemic book, where two different discourses must be dealt with at the same time. Yet the children in the study showed that they were beginning to consider overall meaning at various levels. To begin with, we asked children whether they would describe *Lily Takes a Walk* as 'funny' or 'serious'. Many of the younger readers said it was simply 'funny', while some of the older readers said it was both. They pointed out the humorous elements of the picture book and the way in which Kitamura 'makes you laugh'. Hugh (9) summed it up by saying: 'It's funny because the dog keeps getting scared and the little girl smiles'.

As the interviews and discussions progressed, the children raised moral and ethical issues which demonstrated that they were able to perceive more profound implications of this deceptively simple story. This occurred mainly in the group discussions. Often the researcher led up to some of these issues, but in other cases the readers arrived at some surprising conclusions as they discussed possible and alternative meanings. For example, in the following excerpt from a group discussion, the Year 2 children are debating whether the 'monsters' were really there or if they were a product of Nicky's imagination:

Karen (7):	I think he's just looking at it and then he thinks 'Oh no!'
Jess (6):	No, because it is in the dark, because he's staring in the dark and it makes them look different to what they really are.
John (7):	No, I think he's been watching tele about all this stuff … He's thinking of all this stuff and when he looks he sees them there, when they are not really there.
Martin (7):	(Maybe it's a) person holding things up …
Ced (7):	I think that it's that he looks at them and then he imagines that they're scary.

The children put forth their hypothesis, trying to explain it to themselves and the others, based on their own experience of dealing with imaginary terrors. Together they are struggling to reach beyond the literal to a level of understanding that shows psychological insight into the dog's behaviour.

The environmental issue was raised by some children who noticed the litter that appears in many of the pictures. Carl (8) read this as a message Kitamura was trying to put across through his book:

… he might be trying to tell people in just a picture in a little way to clear up your rubbish
… he might be saying to people who read the book to clear up your rubbish.

This idea was also brought up in the Years 3–4 group discussion and for one girl it involved an important consideration about viewpoint and perspective:

Interviewer: So the dog does notice all the rubbish doesn't he?
Lena (11):   Because he's so small he might see it more, because it's a bit bigger than him.

By means of the two stories running alongside, Kitamura leads us to understand that the world can be seen from different perspectives. Saul (11) applied this idea to the fact that the 'vampire' and Lily's dad look quite similar (see Illustration 3.3).

It is interesting to note that he also speaks of the importance of looking carefully at the text in order to notice this sort of detail and understand what he called 'the moral':

Saul: People may look different in a different suit but they could be the same person.
               Some people may not realise that, they just look through it and they don't actually see the dad.

Illustration 3.3 Spread of Lily having dinner with her parents

The interviewer picked up on the idea of 'the moral' and as the children worked collaboratively, they reached a more satisfying explanation of what is going on in the book:

Interviewer: Would you say that there were any other morals in this book?

Lena (11):   People believe in things but not everybody.

Angus (9):   From the dog's point of view when you are little things scare you more than when you are bigger … when you are little sometimes your imagination just wanders and then when you are older you can tell things look like that or not.

The last statement shows a grasp of how characters' perceptions can be different and how these differences may be responsible for their emotions and actions. It also shows an analogical understanding of how the ability to discern between reality and fantasy develops with age. Like Angus, by the end of the group discussions, many other children were showing signs of a much broader comprehension of the picture book.

Preliminary conclusions

Some of the preliminary findings of our research confirmed our expectations, while others proved more surprising. One of the main findings was, as we had expected, an age-related ability to notice and talk about the various features of the text. However, we were amazed to see how quickly even the smaller children moved on in their understanding, given the opportunity to do so. Another expectation that was confirmed was the importance of discussing reader response within a group. Various studies (Fry, 1985; Chambers, 1993; Thomson, 1987, among others) have found evidence not only of how listening to and asking for the opinions of readers can help in their understanding, but how group discussions and teacher-led circles can further extend children's critical skills. We also found this to be especially true of the group discussions where readers worked together to arrive at a more complex interpretation of the pictorial text.

Listening to children respond to a story requires a lot of time and patience and the same applies to making sense of these responses. More research and analysis is needed, but the results so far are already suggesting important implications in relation to the way in which children approach picture books. In the first place, it is worth mentioning again just how positive the response was: all of the children — both girls and boys — had something interesting to say about it and their enthusiasm and engagement with detail increased as they 're-searched' it for themselves and found more and more to see. Their appreciation of the humour and, as Lena (11) put it, 'the jokes in between the pages' grew on further readings. Secondly, we noticed the sophisticated manner in which children deal with many elements of the modern picture book such as gaps, incompleteness and ambiguity that confuse many an adult reader. This has also been observed by researchers such as Bromley (1996), Lewis (1992, 1996), Styles (1996) and Watson (1996).

In English schools, picture books are not often re-read and re-discussed enough because of the constraints of the curriculum requirements. This means that many children remain at a more literal level of comprehension in which they understand the plot sequence, facts and details, but find it difficult to construct meaning at a more critical level. We found that at first the children were trying to make literal sense of the gaps and incoherencies, instead of being able to take a step back and comprehend how they worked within the whole of the story structure. It is necessary to encourage the reading of books like *Lily Takes a Walk* which confound the reader's expectations in a playful and, at the same time, thought-provoking manner. Also, these books should be approached not only as aids for learning to read, but also as texts that have something to teach the reader about reading itself. Frequent and unhurried revisiting of the text will convince the older children that they have much to see and (with help from the teacher) learn from what they might think of as 'babyish' texts. Saul, for example, an 11 year-old who was quite laconic when interviewed on his own, admitted at the end of the group discussion that:

> Now I have read it I thought it was quite good but at the start when Mr Smith brought it up I thought, 'Oh no not another boring story' … (now) every time I look at it I find something new.

The responses also demonstrated the crucial role of the teacher as someone who asks significant questions and leads the readers to notice certain details, to ask their own questions and to answer them individually or collaboratively. There is a need to introduce a language for them to talk about both the visual and narrative elements. They can be encouraged to think of their responses based on their knowledge and experience of 'reading' other media texts which in some cases is actually wider than that of the adults around them.

Finally, one of the most revealing and not altogether unexpected findings of the project so far has been that many times it was the children who were considered by the teachers to be 'struggling readers' who turned out to be some of the more experienced and articulate interpreters of the visual; even those students who had particular learning disabilities were able to make meaning and in some cases actually expanded the possibilities of the pictorial text. Such was the case of Charlie whose slight autism made him speak slowly and not very distinctly. It was Charlie who reasoned that Lily's white face, the fact that the family were drinking the same tomato juice as the vampire and the father's resemblance to this vampire, meant that Nicky was, ironically, living with a family of ghostly monsters. No wonder Lily wasn't afraid of the dark!

Bibliography

Anstey, M. (2000) 'Postmodern Picture books and New Literacies: Implications for teaching', International Symposium Reading Pictures: Art, Narrative & Childhood, Homerton College, Cambridge, September, pp. 1–4.

Bromley, H. (1996) 'Spying on picture books: exploring intertextuality with young children', in V. Watson and M. Styles (eds) *Talking Pictures. Pictorial Texts and Young Readers*. Hodder and Stoughton, London, pp. 101–11.

Browne, A. (1989) *The Tunnel*. Julia MacRae Books, London.

—— (1994) *Zoo*. Red Fox, London.

Chambers, A. (1993) *Tell Me: Children, Reading and Talk*. The Thimble Press, Exeter.

Fry, D. (1985) *Children Talk About Books: Seeing Themselves as Readers*. Open University Press, Milton Keynes.

Heath, S.B. (1983) *Ways with Words*. Cambridge University Press, Cambridge.

Hutchins, P. (1970) *Rosie's Walk*. Bodley Head, London.

Kitamura, S. (1997) *Lily Takes a Walk*. Happy Cat Books, London.

Lewis, D. (1992) 'Looking for Julius: two children and a picture book', in K. Kimberley et al. (eds) *New Readings*. A & C Black, London, pp. 50–63.

—— (1996) 'Going Along with Mr Gumpy: Polysystemy and Play in the Modern Picture Book', *Signal* 80, pp. 105–19.

Meek, M. (1988) *How Texts Teach What Readers Learn*. Thimble Press, Exeter.

Nodelman, P. (1988) *Words about Pictures. The Narrative Art of Children's Picture Books*. The University of Georgia Press, London.

Styles, M. (1996) 'Inside the tunnel: a radical kind of reading — picture books, pupils and postmodernism', in V. Watson and M. Styles (eds) *Talking Pictures. Pictorial Texts and Young Readers*. Hodder and Stoughton, London, pp. 23–47.

Thomson, J. (1987) *Understanding Teenager's Reading*. Methuen, Melbourne.

Watson, V. (1996) 'Imaginationing Granpa — journeying into reading with John Burningham', in V. Watson and M. Styles (eds) *Talking Pictures. Pictorial Texts and Young Readers*. Hodder and Stoughton, London, pp. 80–100.

Endnotes

1   Morag Styles and Evelyn Arizpe are leading the research together with a team of experienced teachers and specialists, including Helen Bromley, Kathy Coulthart, Janet Campbell and Kate Rabey. The fieldwork was carried out in schools beginning in January 2000.

2   Both Browne and Kitamura were interviewed at length and have since shown much interest in the project.

3   Seven primary schools participated in the research: three in Cambridge, another three in London and one in Essex. Approximately 600 children from Reception to Year 6 (ages 4 to 11) answered a short questionnaire on their reading, computing and viewing habits. We carried out 105 individual interviews and 21 group discussions after which the children were invited to draw a picture of what they remembered most about the book.

4   I am indebted to Helen Bromley for the responses from Essex.

5   Questions specific to *Lily Takes a Walk* included, for example: What do you think Lily tells her Mum and Dad? What do you think Nicky would like to tell Mum and Dad? How do you know? Do you think Lily noticed any of the monsters? Did Nicky imagine the monsters?

6   Sample questions included: What does the artist want to make the people who read this picture book think about? What goes on in your head as you look at the pictures? How do you think the artist decides what to write as words and what to draw in the pictures? Tell me about the way Kitamura draws lines. Lily and Nicky are always looking in different directions, what does that tell us about them?

7   When asked about this particular point in the interview, Kitamura admitted that he might have made the reference unconsciously.

8   Kitamura's style is so distinctive that even my 3 year-old daughter, spotting an illustration from *A Boy Wants a Dinosaur* (which she had never seen) as she wandered through an exhibition of contemporary picture book art, exclaimed, 'Look, it's like Lily!'.

Chapter 4

The postmodern picture book:
its place in post-literate pedagogy

Geoff Bull

There has always been a strong link between picture books and the pedagogy of literacy in many classrooms. How we think about literacy has undergone considerable change since the 1970s during which time the picture book has sustained substantial development. With the advent of increasing technological change and globalisation, the literacy demands of everyday life have increased exponentially. As information has become increasingly dependent on visual material and less reliant on the more traditional print forms, so society has entered a period which could be termed post-literate. Literacy is no longer dependent on print material and no longer relies only on the decoding of written symbols on the page into the oral mode. Concomitant with these changes has come the evolution of the postmodern picture book that relies as much on illustrative text for conveying meaning as it does on written text. Since both literacy and picture books have undergone considerable change in recent times, it would seem useful to explore how pedagogy might be adapted to reflect these changes.

In this chapter I will trace the development of the postmodern picture book and focus on how approaches to pedagogy have changed over time. I will then explore how changes in pedagogy and picture books have produced new literacies and new literatures. Finally I will examine how a post-literate pedagogy might be implemented.

What is a postmodern picture book?

Different concepts of what a picture book is, and how it might be created, have emerged over time. Townsend (1987: 304), writing originally in 1965, defined picture books with reference to the illustrations in them, making reference to length and sophistication of the plot as being characteristics of books for older readers. Sutherland and Arbuthnot (1986: 81) also argued that illustrations were the defining characteristic of picture books. They suggested a typology of picture books where either the pictures or the text were predominant, or the pictures and text were extensions of each other. On the other hand Huck, Hepler and Hickman (1987: 197), Cullinan (1989: 29) and Saxby (1997: 184) all suggested that text and illustration must both be part of the narration. There has not always been agreement on the value of the integration of illustration and text with some art historians and even some authors suggesting that picture books were solely the creation of the artist, the text having only a subsidiary or supportive role.

The evolution of the picture book has produced narratives where the interplay of the illustrative and written texts has moved beyond a supportive role to one where new texts are created through the continuous interplay of the visual and graphic messages. The illustrative text has to be read (viewed) in a similar way to the written text, thus potentially producing multiple narratives. This new type of picture book, the postmodern, has far more meanings available to the reader, enabling many more readings to be constructed.

The idea that both the written and illustrative texts work together and that they each assist in the reading of the other is reflected in later definitions of the picture book. Both Kiefer (1995: 6) and Sheahan (1995: 15) alluded to this concept when they spoke of 'combination' and 'harmony'. The greater sophistication of the picture book made it more likely that the reader could take pleasure in the act of reading because more readings were available. At the same time the traditional audiences of picture books were being rethought with many authors (such as Gary Crew in Australia and Anthony Browne in Britain to name but two of many) creating picture books aimed at adult enjoyment as well as students.

Because picture books are now no longer necessarily for young students only, changes have occurred in the categories in the annual Children's Book Council (CBC) of Australia Awards and frequently a degree of controversy surrounds the announcement of the awards. What is becoming more obvious as we learn more about what happens when readers engage with text is that age and experience are not necessarily barriers to young readers. Experience can act as an intervening variable in considerations of age and appropriateness of the subject or content of the book but young readers can sometimes understand very sophisticated narratives or themes. It can be very tempting, as Hollindale (1997) has suggested, to dismiss some books as being too difficult for young readers or, conversely, to expect that some books are too easy for older readers. Readers (and viewers) may make many different readings of a book and it may not be defensible for adults to withdraw books from students on the basis that they believe that a book is at too high, or too low, a level of sophistication.

Where does all this lead us in the quest for a definition of a postmodern picture book? For the purposes of this chapter I suggest a working definition of a postmodern picture book might be *where the written text and the illustrative text are in concordance and work interdependently to produce meaning.* (See Anstey and Bull [2000] for a further discussion of this definition.) I have termed this a 'working definition' because I feel that picture books are dynamic with authors and illustrators continually pushing the boundaries of the genre. As our knowledge of reading changes, so the definition will alter to encompass these modifications. These transformations in reading and how the picture book is viewed produce a literature that is both socially and culturally determined, a factor that highlights the importance of the postmodern picture book.

Changes in how the modern picture book is viewed/read have taken place against a background of adaptations of how such books might be presented to students. Indeed it is very difficult to judge whether the changes in the picture books have come about as a result of changes in pedagogy, or whether developments in pedagogy have set the scene for the creation of the postmodern picture book.

Early views of pedagogy and the picture book

Picture books are increasingly a part of what goes on in everyday literacy classroom pedagogy. Whether it be through teacher use in program development, or student engagement as part of reading instruction, students are increasingly called upon to operate in a semiotic of visual literacy as well as the more traditional linguistic semiotic. How students learn to read picture books is effected, to a large degree, by how teachers structure their instruction.

During the period of time in the 1960s and 1970s when there was a rapid expansion in the production of picture books, there was little thought given to how picture books might be used in the classroom. This rapid expansion of the marketplace was caused by the post-war baby boom producing a concomitant burgeoning of publishing and allowed an increasing number of authors the opportunity to have their work published. In such a flourishing market, ideas of what counted as literature were changing rapidly and the traditional boundaries of literature were being challenged. What counted as children's literature was broadened and redefined by critics in the United Kingdom (Townsend, 1965), the United States (Huck, 1961; Arbuthnot, 1964 and Norton, 1983) and in Australia (Saxby, 1971). This redefining of children's literature had the effect of making more literature available to students and teachers. However, little attention was paid to how this literature might be used or how it might be learnt from.

An unproblematic pedagogy

As a result pedagogical concerns were focussed more on introducing literature of greater quality and scope than that which had been contained in classroom reading materials up to that time. The variety and quality of literature available in the typical classroom was so different from that which had been accessible that the focus was more on incorporating it into everyday teaching. Questions about how it might be selected, who might select it, how it might be read, who might be represented in it, or how it might be taught were rarely considered. Concerns centred more on which books to use rather than possible problems associated with their use and gave rise to an unproblematic pedagogy (see Bull, 1995 and Bull and Anstey, 1996).

The use of children's literature in such an unproblematic way was reflected in the emerging pedagogics of literacy of the time. At the secondary school level through the introduction of the 'growth through literature' approach (Dixon, 1967) and at the primary school level through the advocacy of new approaches to literacy instruction (such as Graves, 1983 and Cambourne, 1984) an 'uncritical immersion in literature' approach was adopted. These approaches to literacy instruction became a feature of the personal growth model in secondary schools and the whole language model at the primary level and represented a tremendous advance in the pedagogy of literature. Where there were problems associated with these new approaches to the use of literature, as opposed to problems with approaches to the teaching of literacy, they were seen as problems of inclusiveness or exclusiveness and were not concerned with questions about the pedagogy itself.

A psychological pedagogy

Once literature became a feature of the literacy curriculum attention changed from the books themselves to the reader, and the focus of research concentrated on the effects that reading had on the reader. Because of prevailing views about reading at the time these new studies were essentially psycholinguistic (Smith, 1971; Goodman, 1976; Harste and Carey, 1979; and Olson, 1977) and centred on an exploration of the motivation and responses of the reader. Earlier work on response by Iser (1974), Rosenblatt (1969) and Holland (1968) had suggested that response was a developmental construct. Work by Blunt (1977), Thomson (1986) and Protherough (1983) proposed a number of stages of response to literature and incorporated psychological constructs such as self-identity, empathy, reflection and projection. These different stages or levels allowed a number of different readings of a text dependent on the sophistication of the reader and led to a more critical pedagogy. Such a pedagogy authorised a complexity in the relationship between reader and text that led teachers to appreciate the potential for learning that the use of literature encouraged. However, this complexity still rested on a somewhat unproblematic pedagogy since it recognised comprehension as the only text-related problem that was present when the reader engaged with text.

Literature as problematic — a critical pedagogy

The challenge to the unproblematic pedagogy came first from the European scene from a number of critics (Derrida, 1975; Foucault, 1970 and Barthes, 1975). They questioned the static, inflexible view of text as unchanging and fixed by suggesting that meaning in text is never entirely fixed, that language is endlessly diverse, and that texts, rather than being unique, are an amalgam of many other texts. To incorporate such ideas into literacy, pedagogy meant that reading could not be seen as merely an interaction between reader and the text. In this new view text contains a number of multiple meanings that can lead to multiple readings by the reader. Alternative scenarios can be set up by the reader depending on how the text is structured and how it is read by the reader. In this view not only are there many possible meanings that can be construed but also many possible contesting constructions of ideas and individuals. Text then becomes an ideological site where individuals can be constructed in particular ways and where certain group views can dominate and so marginalise the views of others. Such a pedagogy is inherently ideological in nature and has led to the development of post-structuralist and postmodern theories of literature. Contiguous with these views of literature, literacy educators (Baker and Freebody, 1989; Luke, 1987,1993; Gilbert, 1989; Fairclough, 1992; Kamler, 1994; and O'Brien, 1994) have developed a pedagogy for examining text that has become known as *social critical literacy*. This pedagogy views the text as problematic and raises a number of issues which are summarised below.

1 Meaning may be constructed for the reader rather than by the reader.
2 Teachers may shape the text (the text may be *authorised* rather than *authored*).
3 The text may shape the reader (sometimes without the reader realising).
4 Every text teaches particular ideologies.

5 The context in which the text is formulated is crucial in the construction of the text.
6 Every text teaches about literacy and literature.
7 There are multiple meanings in text, some of which may be dominant.
8 Texts construct or marginalise ideas/individuals by positioning them in a particular way (from Bull and Anstey, 1996).

Classrooms become sites where differing or contesting ideologies are foregrounded and discussed and where new pedagogies are played out. Pedagogies encourage interrogation, deconstruction and then reconstruction of texts (which include magazines, newspapers, video and advertisement). These critical pedagogies are far removed from that of the 'unproblematic' with its uncontested adoption of literature into the classroom. Response takes place in a more public and explicit ideological forum rather than in a concealed and covert psychological (con) text.

Critical pedagogy and the postmodern picture book

The possibilities of implementing a critical pedagogy using postmodern picture books can be illustrated by reference to texts such as John Burningham's *Come away from the water, Shirley* (1977). Here the written text is accompanied by two parallel modalities (Nikolajeva and Scott, 2001) and conflicting illustrative texts. One of the illustrative texts (see Illustration 4.1), with its accompanying written text, supports the expected discourse between parents and children and the accompanying power relationships that are both explicit and implicit in these situations. It is a typical beach scene where mother and father are filling out their humdrum, rather tedious, day at the beach. The other illustrative text (on the right-hand side of each opening of the book) is a contesting discourse where Shirley has the power and is in control of the situation. Shirley's fantastic adventures could not be more different to the stark reality and conventionality of her parents' non-adventure.

Many readers will be able to identify with the parent/child interaction (or lack of it) that takes place between Shirley and her parents and also the language that is used by the characters. Burningham has selected a particular linguistic discourse that accurately reflects

Illustration 4.1: *Come away from the water, Shirley*

that used by many parents in the context of the beach. The linguistic choices made (for example, vocabulary and syntax) produce a written text of a particular sort. The illustrative texts, through selection of such devices as line and colour, produce an artistic discourse that leaves the reader in no doubt as to who is having the most fun and where all the excitement is happening. The reader has to learn to take note of both the linguistic and artistic discourses in order to uncover the various readings of the narrative. Finally, there is another discourse produced by the interaction and integration of the verbal with the visual that explores family relationships and how different generations fail to communicate with one another.

The implementation of critical pedagogy requires readers to learn to interrogate texts in order to find out how the books work. Picture books are ideally suited to this task because of the presence of both written and illustrative text. The postmodern picture book challenges traditional audiences by presenting plots, characters and format in quite different ways. This new type of picture book contains metafictive elements such as contradictions, multiple or even indeterminate meanings and a mixing or pastiche of illustrative styles and is to be read quite differently.

Metafictive picture books draw the reader's attention to how the text actually works as a narrative by interrupting the expectations or predictions that the reader may be making. The reader becomes self-consciously aware (Waugh, 1984) of particular features of the text. If critical reading is to take place then the mature reader needs to become reflective in order to become aware of how fiction in general, and picture books in particular, work. The 'self-conscious' book assists the reader to stand back while they are reading and watch how the process of engagement with narrative works. The self-aware reader is not a new idea but follows a tradition from Britton (1972) through Harding (1977) and Meek (1988) to Mackey (1990) in investigating the proposition that there is more to reading than meets the eye. The construction of the postmodern picture book, with its metafictive elements, is particularly suitable to highlighting the many processes that the reader has to learn. Many of these processes are learnt from sources other than the words on the page and therefore require new approaches to pedagogy that rely on different literatures and the conceptualisation of new literacies.

New literacies, new literatures and the post-literate society

In considering whether it is necessary to reconceptualise the nature of literature and whether this in turn should direct our attention to new forms of literacy, it is useful to look at the relationship of words and pictures. Critics such as Foucault (1970) have suggested an 'infinite relation' whereas de Certeau (1986) suggested a 'heterology' of difference to indicate the complex interdependence of the two. While this position would seem to be quite useful in terms of the argument that has been presented so far, both Tolkien (1964) and Bettelheim (1976) have suggested that illustrations provide little support for the reader.

There seems little support in modern times for the position that Tolkien and Bettelheim took. In these days of post-technological revolution and globalisation the means of communication are increasingly relying on the visual. The advent of 'visual culture' Mitchell

(1994:16) has meant that we have entered a period of what might be termed a post-literate society where traditional forms of literacy and literature that rely on print only may be threatened. At the least, we have entered a period where visual literacy is as critical as textual literacy if we are to remain communicatively competent both as individuals and as a society. As Stephens (1992) suggested, the new models of literacy and literature require that students not only need to learn how to read the pictures, but also how to interpret them in culturally appropriate ways.

Kress (1995: 5–6) has pointed out that cognitive and intellectual demand made by the syntax of the language has lessened while there had been an 'increasing sophistication' demanded by the visual medium. This increased sophistication has taken the form of more highly abstract visual information and a requirement to make links across different fields of information. Illustrative text has its own set of regularities or a grammar (see Kress and van Leeuwen, 1990; Anstey and Bull, 2000) that is similar to, but different in scope and form, from the grammar of written text. This new type of reading is necessary not only to deal with new technologies, such as the Internet with its increasing use of visual text and iconic language, but also to deal with the new types of texts. These are to be found not only in picture books but also in the media texts of TV, film and video where new information is being increasingly stored.

The traditional roles of written and visual texts may become reversed where the visual carries most of the meaning and the written is used merely to comment on the visual. At a minimum the visual or illustrative texts become central to the gaining of meaning ensuring that students have to become proficient at reading pictures. These texts will take the form of more universal, international and globalised texts on the one hand, and local or community texts on the other. The need to be able to read universal visual images, and yet engage with and valorise local differences, will magnify the necessity for visual literacy and for new literacies.

In this post-literate age readers are beginning to rely at least as much, and perhaps more, on the illustrative text for information and communication. They are more likely to be used to 'reading' a whole range of different visual images quickly for a quick impression and to developing different information gathering, scanning and synthesising skills from the ones we currently associate with reading. New literacies are developing and are likely to foreground illustrative text more than ever before. Given the parallel development of different metafictive techniques and the rise of the postmodern picture book with its multiple discourses, students will need to engage in different readings of fiction.

How might readers construct different readings in picture books?

Early ideas about how readers might construct readings of a picture book focused on the gradual development of response over time (Applebee, 1978; Thomson, 1987) as readers matured in their ability to understand features of the narrative such as character development and motives. In each case the reader was portrayed as a kind of passive consumer of the text where the text had already been constructed (by the author). It was the readers' role to discover the meaning that the author had intended.

Basing their approach on what Barthes (1975) termed 'readerly' and 'writerly' texts, where the reader has to adopt an active rather than a passive role, contemporary critics (Watson and Styles, 1996) have formulated the reader as an active constructor of the text as it is read. In their view the reader pays attention to the written and illustrative discourses in the picture book, becoming an active participant in the construction of the story. This signifies a shift from a view of the reader as a passive recipient *of* the story to an active participant *in* the construction of the story. Readers are therefore more liable to become self-reflexive 'collaborators' rather than 'easily manipulated consumers' (Moss in Trites, 1994: 237). The reader therefore has more choice or agency in how to synthesise information from the different discourses present in the picture book. In postmodern picture books, because of the metafictive elements, the reader has the potential to become more self-conscious and self-reflexive. It is more probable that different readings will be constructed by the reader and less likely that ideological reproduction will occur.

While each reading that a reader makes may be seen as legitimate there are other authorial messages that the reader should hear. Self-reflexive readers should be focusing on issues such as the author's purpose, how characters are being constructed, silenced or marginalised, and why the author/illustrator has left gaps in the narrative. Many of the contemporary illustrators have adopted a postmodern perspective in a very conscious way. Anthony Browne (in Evans, 1998: 194) pointed out that in his picture books it was important to see how much of the narrative was told by the pictures, how much by the words and how much was told 'by the gap between the two'. Browne stated that he used this relationship between words and pictures 'deliberately' to make them open to different interpretations.

The choices that an illustrator makes are part of what can be termed the *grammar* of the artist and would make up part of a new visual literacy. Just as readers need to learn a grammar of written text, a linguistic grammar, so they need to learn an artistic grammar involving such elements as line, colour, form, media, texture, balance, design and layout. In learning a new literacy or literature students may follow a path of self-discovery where personal experience plays a major part. However, not all students will be able to take advantage of this more natural style of learning and even those who can will not be able to access it, or benefit from it, on all occasions. If new literacies are to be learnt then new literacies need to be taught. New literacies depend on new pedagogies for all students to be successful in their learning.

Investigating a post-literate pedagogy

Postmodern picture books form an important part in the learning of the new literacies/literatures that have been discussed so far in this chapter. Nevertheless a new post-literate pedagogy requires more than just the provision of mere resources. Students sometimes need to be exposed to particular content, resources and specific pedagogical structures in order to support learning. It is important to become aware of what pedagogies are operating in an educational setting since learning is always taking place, whether it be planned for or otherwise.

Elsewhere (see Bull in Bull and Anstey, 1996) I have suggested that prior learning can either support or intervene in the desired learning outcomes of a sequence of lessons. In this particular setting in a Year 2 class the students had taken part in a six week unit on science fiction that was designed to supplement their knowledge of fantasy and highlight the differences between the two genres. The culminating activity of this unit of work based around *Professor Noah's Spaceship* by Brian Wildsmith (1980) was for each student to produce their own picture book containing both written and illustrative texts that would reflect the learning that had occurred during the last six weeks. Bull and Anstey (1996) reported that when the texts produced by the students were analysed there was a marked gender difference in the illustrative texts that influenced the construction of the written texts.

The male students had exemplified space in their drawings through the use of dark colours (predominantly black) containing representations of planets, suns, spaceships and all the paraphernalia of space travel. The female students had used bright colours to fashion drawings of kitchens, houses and other domestic scenes. The boys wrote about space travel by spaceship while the girls constructed scenes about cooking and packing in preparation for the adventures that were to take place in space. While the texts produced by the boys reflected the detailed and varied activities that they had engaged in over the last six weeks, the girls produced texts that did not reflect the learning that had taken place. It was not a case of the boys learning and the girls not, nor was it an example of how boys can do science and girls cannot, but rather that the female students chose to represent their experiences in a particular way.

When the students constructed their texts, it became clear that they themselves had been constructed through their exposure to the everyday world of advertising, television, shopping with their parents, and the reading materials that they had read at home and school. (See Gilbert and Rowe, 1989 and O'Brien, 1994 for discussion of this point.) These 6 and 7 year-olds had already 'learnt' that certain subjects (in this case space and perhaps more importantly science) were the province of males and that certain roles (support roles such as packing and preparing food) were appropriate for females. These students had built up quite different views of reality that effected their ability to represent their learning accurately and to deconstruct and to reconstruct text. Or it may be that the girls had not so much learnt that this was the way that they should respond to text, but that in the real world in an adventure in space it was very likely that these would be the roles allotted to them.

Irrespective of the explanation, what mattered was how the students constructed text based on how they saw themselves being constructed. They had reacted to the pedagogies employed in their classroom in an unpredicted way by responding to what Ludwig and Herschell (1998) term the 'explicit and implicit learning' available to them. As Ludwig and Herschell suggest, students may experience lack of success in learning contexts, not because of an inability to learn content, but because they have not learned the required procedures of certain pedagogies. These 6 and 7 year-old students, particularly the girls, may have learnt the content of the unit very well. What they may not have learnt is when and how to demonstrate their learning in the face of certain pedagogies.

What seems to be important, even when successful learning takes place, is that students understand the underlying pedagogies that are in place in a learning context so that the learning is both replicable and transferable. These pedagogies might be termed classroom narratives that need to be assimilated in the same way that students come to appreciate the fictional narratives in literature. Nodelman (in Chapter One) proposes what he calls 'narrative literacy' that refers to knowledge of how stories work and how they come to represent reality. Perhaps this is the true nature of a post-literate pedagogy where classroom narratives operate in contexts where fictional narratives are learnt as students develop more sophistication with narrative literacy. To make some sense of this I would like to return to the same group of Year 2 students that I reported on earlier in this chapter and to reinterpret some work I had completed in their classroom pedagogy (see Bull, 1995 and Bull and Anstey, 1996).

In this earlier research a unit of work on dinosaurs and dragons had been implemented, not only because it capitalised on student interest and continued the science theme from the previous unit, but also because it continued the focus on the real and imaginary begun in the previous unit. It also enabled a number of questions to be proposed at the outset that would give direction to the students' learning. In the original research the investigation was directed towards finding out how much the students drew on the written text and the illustrative text to distinguish between dinosaurs and dragons. The students also considered whether questions about true and imaginary creatures, narrative and expository genres and fiction and non-fiction would assist in these comparisons.

The pedagogy that was being employed in the classroom was based on an attempt to deal with the issues raised by social critical literacy. The classroom narrative was directed towards using the dinosaurs and dragons distinction to address the issue of the construction of meaning for the reader. It also sought to deal with questions of how texts can shape and position readers in particular ways. At the time it was felt that the students would be able to deal successfully with such questions because they had spent some time in the previous unit of work discussing how and why their science fiction texts were so different and what conditions had led to these differences. The dinosaur and dragon texts were thought to be most effective in dealing with these literacy issues because narrative and expository genres and fanciful and factual illustrations were regularly mixed in the one text.

The students were able to make distinctions between dragons and dinosaurs using illustrative style and concentrating on such dragon features as wings, flying, breathing fire and arrow-shaped tails. When discriminations between fantasy and reality were made the focus shifted quickly to setting and what was possible and what could be fairly labelled magic or preposterous (such as dinosaurs in gardens or kitchens). In questions relating to fiction/non-fiction distinctions, students resorted to the written texts contained in the dinosaur/dragon books and focused on the text construction. In each case the students were engaging in what Nodelman has termed 'narrative literacy' (see Chapter One). They had already begun to develop their concept of what stories/fiction/narratives do and this led them to expect that stories were 'forms of lies' that had taken on 'the status of a form of truth'. That is, they were prepared to accept that narratives could reasonably contain untrue, improbable and imaginative content and were ready to reconcile that this was appropriate for a fictive genre. Fiction could therefore be based on a web of untruths yet still be a realistic description of the way things are in the world. The dragon texts where seen by the students to be quite acceptable, even if they contained scenes where dragons were in kitchens, because dragons are imaginary creatures and fantasy is the stuff of narrative.

When the students looked at the dinosaur texts, which they firmly fixed in the real world, they saw these books as non-fiction where truth, not fantasy, could be expected. Dinosaur

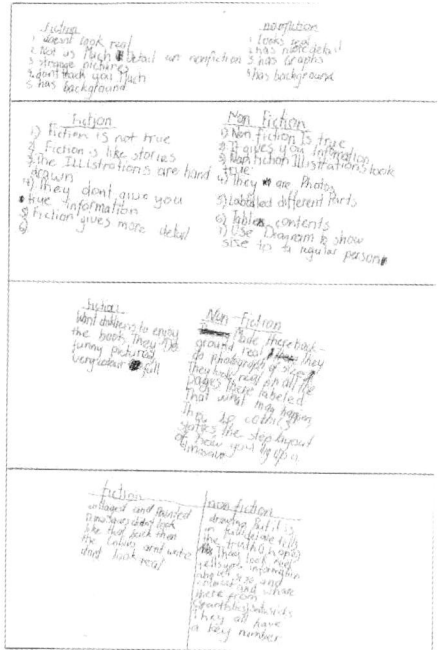

Figure 4.1 Group retrieval charts

books therefore contain factual information that could and should be believed. Problems arose for the students when texts that ought to be factual — dinosaur books — presented the reader with imaginary situations (e.g. smiling dinosaurs). While they were able to accept that there were times when a fantasy story about a dinosaur would be reasonable, the students were only prepared to acknowledge this if the written text was structured in an appropriate way. In other words, non-fiction or expository texts not only had to be factual but they also had to contain written text that was constructed in the form of a report or explanation. In their developing concept of narrative literacy any book that did not conform to these patterns was a poor quality book where the author was in error in terms of style even if some of the content was true.

In Figure 4.1 are examples of the group retrieval charts that the students constructed to illustrate the essential differences between narrative (fiction) and exposition (non-fiction).

The shared understandings that the students recorded sometimes refer to features of generic structure such as graphs, labels, headings, diagrams and statistics and sometimes to the didactic nature of the texts through the relationship of reading for pleasure or information. Just as often the students are grappling with issues of reality, truth, fantasy and imagination that take place within the framework of the pedagogy originally applied to the investigation of written and illustrative text. This is further illustrated in the transcripts that were recorded during the discussions between the students and the teacher about the dinosaur/dragon books.

Transcript One is an excerpt from a discussion about good and poor quality illustration and indicates how the students judged this against the background of questions about truth and reality and how they saw these in relation to fiction and non-fiction.

Transcript One

GB	I think we all agree it's a dinosaur. The question I want to ask you — is it a good illustration of a dinosaur or a poor one?
Patrick	Because dinosaurs don't look happy and they don't sit down at table — they'd be too big.
GB	So that makes it a good or poor quality illustration?
Patrick	Um. Poor.
Bob	They didn't do that and it didn't happen in the olden days when dinosaurs were there.
Jane	Stuffed bears weren't alive then — stuffed bears aren't alive now!
GB	That's true.
Kate	And dinosaurs don't live in houses.
GB	That's true — so what do we know about this book?
Mike	It's fiction.
GB	What makes it a fiction book?
All	It's a story.

Transcript Two occurred during a discussion about written text in fictional material. Here the students concentrated initially on characteristics of the generic structure of narrative to make their judgments but soon turn to the forms of truth and lies that make up Nodelman's notion of narrative literacy.

Transcript Two

GB	What is it about the words which make it fiction?
Jane	Well, with these books they have a beginning 'Once upon a time'.
GB	And what does that tell you that it's going to be?
Jane	Fiction.
Jake	You see — if it's fiction it doesn't have paragraphs — it just keeps on going.
Tricia	Well, I thought it would be fiction because I had a look at a few pages at the words — and he threw cans at his mouth and he ate them — and dinosaurs don't do that.
GB	What's makes Tricia's answer a good one?
Steven	Because if a dinosaur would eat rubbish everyone would know it — but everyone knows it doesn't.
GB	Right! Jake?
Jake	It can't eat rubbish because it can't crunch it up in its mouth.
Jane	Dinosaurs don't eat that junk!
GB	So what are the words telling you?
Chorus	It's not true!
GB	If it's not true it's …?
All	Fiction!

In both the lessons described above (i.e. the former on distinctions between fiction and non-fiction and the latter on the dinosaur/dragon books) the explicit learning that is occurring relates to identifying the generic structures and purposes of both the fiction and non-fiction genres. The teacher has constructed a classroom narrative in order to support explicit learning about different genres. In both the lessons the students have begun to engage with the texts available to them to explore how stories work. They have investigated the forms of truth and the forms of lies present in fiction (and in non-fiction) and are beginning to form a concept of narrative literacy that will assist them to interrogate both types of texts. This is a more implicit type of learning that is nevertheless just as important as the explicit learning that the teacher has allowed for. In terms of post-literate pedagogy the crucial practices that are being employed in this classroom need to be made more visible to both the teacher and the students. The use of postmodern picture books is a way of accomplishing this task because of the inclusion in the texts of metafictive devices that support multiple texts and readings.

To illustrate this point I wish to return to John Burningham's *Come away from the water, Shirley* (1977). As I have previously pointed out in this chapter, the metafictive nature of this postmodern picture book promotes discussion about contesting discourses and about the relationship of illustrative and written text. Implementing a post-literate pedagogy using Burningham's book would facilitate learning about how stories represent reality and explore the relationship between truth and fantasy. The two illustrative texts available in *Shirley* draw attention to the fact that there are at least two narratives in this story that variously represent the truth of what is going on at the beach and what is the nature of the interaction between Shirley and her parents. This is augmented by the written text that accompanies the illustrations because it addresses only one of the illustrative texts, thereby highlighting the differences in the two versions of a day at the beach. Postmodern picture books therefore have the potential to make explicit the development of narrative literacy when post-literate pedagogies are employed.

Conclusion

What I have proposed in this chapter is that, through the use of what has become known as the postmodern picture book, it is possible to focus students' attention on how picture books work. However the mere inclusion, and use of, picture books does not guarantee that student learning will be supported and maximised. A post-literate pedagogy such as I have proposed requires that attention be given to both the explicit and implicit learning that may take place in a classroom. The interplay of such implicit and explicit learning takes place against the background of the classroom narrative that exists in particular lessons or units of work. The pedagogies that are implemented in these classroom narratives impact on the range of literatures and literacies that are available to students.

The pedagogy of the teacher can position the reader such that a particular reading of the text or a highly personalised view of literacy and/or literature is authorised. Particular views of literacy that are resistant to change and highly traditional ideas about what counts as literature can be adopted in classrooms. Conversely, through embracing more dynamic pedagogies, literacies can be constructed that reflect popular culture more accurately, and deal more successfully with the greater range of texts to be found in the fast-changing technological world in which students live.

The research reported in this study concerning 6 and 7 year-olds indicated that students were capable of a great deal of sophisticated learning. It also suggested that literature and learning are inextricably linked and advocated certain action on the part of the teacher as well as the learner. It becomes a question of pedagogy and not just learning. It may be that students of particular ages can engage with narrative literacy only when teaching employs post-literate pedagogies.

Bibliography

Anstey, M. and Bull, G. (1996) *The Literacy Labyrinth*. Prentice Hall, Sydney.

—— (2000) *Reading the visual: written and illustrated children's literature*. Harcourt Australia Pty Limited, Sydney.

Applebee, A.H. (1978) *The Child's Concept of Story*. University of Chicago Press, Chicago.

Arbuthnot, M.H. (1964) *Children and Books*. Scott Foresman, Illinois.

Baker, C.D. and Freebody, P. (1989) *Children's First School Books: Introductions to the culture of Literacy*. Blackwell, London.

Bakhtin, M. (1981) *The Dialogic Imagination: Four essays*. University of Texas Press, Houston.

Barthes, R. (1975) *S/Z*. Jonathan Cape, London.

Barton, D. and Hamilton, M. (1998) *Local Literacies*. Routledge, London.

Barton, D. and Ivanic, R. (1991) *Writing in the Community*. Sage, London.

Bettelheim, B. (1976) *The Uses of Enchantment: The Meaning and Importance of Fairy Tales*. Thames and Hudson, London.

Blumenthal, N. (1989) *Count-a-Saurus*. Little Mammoth, London.

Blunt, J. (1977) 'Response to Reading: How Some Young Readers Describe the Process', *English in Education*, 11, 3, pp. 34–47.

Bradford, C. (1993) 'The Picture Book: Some Postmodern tensions', *Papers* 4:3, pp. 10–14.

Britton, J. (1972) *Language and Learning*. Pelican, London.

Bull, G. (1995) 'Children's Literature: Using text to construct reality', *Australian Journal of Language and Literacy* 18, 4, November, pp. 259–69.

—— (1996) 'Using Children's Literature to Support Children's Learning', in Bull, G. and Anstey, M. *The Literacy Lexicon*. Prentice Hall, Sydney.

Bull, G. and Anstey, M. (1996) *The Literacy Lexicon*. Prentice Hall, Sydney.

Burningham J. (1977) *Come away from the water, Shirley*. Jonathan Cape, London.

Caldwell, H. and Moore, B.H. (1991) 'The art of writing: Drawing as preparation for narrative writing in the primary grades', *Studies in Art Education* 32:4, pp. 207–19.

Cambourne, B. (1984) 'Language, Learning and Literacy', A. Butler and J. Turbill (eds) *Towards a Reading and Writing Classroom*. PETA, Rozelle.

Cullinan, B.E. (1989) *Literature and the Child* (2nd edn.). Harcourt Brace Jovanovich, New York.

de Castell. S., Luke, A. and Egan, K. (1986) *Literacy, society and schooling*. Cambridge University Press, Cambridge.

de Certeau, M. (1986) *Heterologies: Discourses on the Other*. University of Minnesota Press, Minneapolis.

Derrida, J. (1975) 'The Purveyer of Truth', *Yale French Studies* 52, pp. 31–113.

Dixon, J. (1967) *Growth Through English*. Oxford University Press, London.

Dyson, A.H. (1989) *Multiple worlds of child writers: Friends learning to write*. Teachers College Press, New York.

Evans, J. (1998) (ed.) *What's in the Pictures? Responding to the illustrations in picture books*. Paul Chapman, London.

Fairclough, N. (1992) *Discourse and Social Change*. Polity Press, Cambridge.

Foucault, M. (1970) *The Order of Things*. Tavistock, London.

Freebody, P. et al. (1996) *Everyday Literacy Practices in and out of School in Low Socio-Economic Urban Communities*. DEETYA, Canberra.

Genette, G. (1980) *Narrative Discourse: An essay in method*. Basil Blackwell, London.

Gilbert, P. (1989) *Writing, Schooling and Deconstruction: From Voice to Text in the Classroom*. Routledge, London.

Gilbert, P. and Rowe, K. (1989) *Gender, Literacy and the Classroom*. ARA, Melbourne.

Goodman, K. (1976) 'Reading a psycholinguistic guessing game', in H. Singer and R.B. Ruddell (eds), *Theoretical Models and Processes of Reading* (2nd edn). IBA., Newark.

—— (1984) 'Unity in reading', in *Becoming Readers in a Complex Society: 83rd Yearbook of NSSE* (Part 1). University of Chicago Press, Chicago.

Graham, J. (1990) *Pictures on the Page*. England National Association for the Teaching of English, Sheffield.

Graves, D. (1975) 'An examination of the writing processes of seven-year-old children', *Research in the teaching of English* 9, pp. 227–41.

—— (1983) *Writing: Teachers and Children at Work*. Heinemann, New Hampshire.

Harding, D.W. (1977) 'Psychological Processes in the reading of fiction', in Meek, M. *The Cool Web: The Pattern of Children's Reading*. Bodley Head, London.

Harste, J.C. (1985) 'Portrait of a new paradigm: Reading comprehension research', in A. Crismere (ed.) *Landscapes: A State-of-the-Art Assessment of Reading Comprehension Research*, Final report of US Department of Education funded project USDEC-C-300-83-0130.

Harste, J. and Carey, R.F. (eds) (1979) *New Perspectives on Comprehension*. Monograph No.3 in Language and Arts Series, Bloomington, Indiana.

Heath, S.B. (1983) *Ways with Words*. Cambridge University Press, Cambridge.

Heath, S.B. and McLaughlin, M. (1994) 'Learning for anything everyday', *Journal of Curriculum Studies* vol 26 no 5, pp. 471–89.

Hill, K.J. (1984) *The Writing Process: One writing classroom*. Nelson, Melbourne.

Holland, N. (1968) *The Dynamics of Literacy*. Response, Oxford University Press, New York.

—— (1988) 'Ideology and the Children's Book', *Signal*, 55 January, pp. 3–22.

Hollindale, P. (1997) *Signs of Childness in Children's Books*. Thimble Press, Stroud, Gloucestershire.

Hubbard, R. (1989) *Authors of Pictures, Draughtsmen of Words*. Heinemann, Portsmouth, New Hampshire.

Huck, C. (1961) *Children's Literature in the Elementary School*. Holt Rinehart and Winston, New York.

Huck, C.S., Hepler, S. and Hickman, J. (1987) *Children's Literature in the Elementary School* (4th edn). Holt, Rinehart and Winston, New York.

Hunt, P. (1991) *Criticism, Theory and Children's Literature*. Blackwell, London.

Iser, W. (1974) *The Implied Reader*. John Hopkins University Press, Baltimore.

Jungman, A. (1993) *The Little Dragon Nips Out*. Young Corgi, London.

Kamler, B. (1994) 'Lessons about language and gender', *Australian Journal of Language and Literacy*, 17, 2, May, pp. 129–38.

—— (1992) 'The social construction of free topic choice in the process writing classroom', *Australian Journal of Language and Literacy*, 15:2, pp. 105–22.

Kiefer, B.Z. (1995) *The Potential of Picture Books: From visual literacy to aesthetic understanding*. Prentice Hall, Englewood Cliffs, New Jersey.

Kress, G. (1995) 'Literacy or Literacies: Thoughts on an agenda for the day after tomorrow', Unpublished paper.

Kress, G. and van Leeuwen, T. (1990) *Reading Images*. Deakin University, Melbourne.

Lewis, D. (1990) 'The constructedness of texts: Picture books and the metafictive', *Signal*, 62, pp. 131–46.

Ludwig, C. and Herschell, P. (1998) 'The power of pedagogy: Routines, school literacy practices and outcomes', *Australian Journal of Language and Literacy*, 21, 1, February, pp. 67–83.

Luke, A. (1987) 'Open and closed texts: A theoretical model for the critical analysis of curriculum narratives', *Review in the Teaching of English*, IX, pp. 1–41.

—— (1993) *The Social construction of Literacy in the primary school*. Macmillan, Sydney.

Luke, A. in Unsworth, L. (1993) *Literacy Teaching and Learning*. Macmillan, Melbourne.

Mackey, M. (1990) 'Metafiction for Beginners: Allan Ahlberg's *Ten in a Bed*', *Children's Literature in Education*, 21: 3, pp. 179–87.

Matthew, R. (1990) *Triceratops*. Puffin Books, London.

Meek, M. (1988) *How Texts Teach What Readers Learn*. Thimble Press, Stroud.

Mitchell, W.J.T. (1994) *Picture Theory: Essays on Verbal and Visual Representation*. University of Chicago Press, Chicago.

Nikolajeva, M. and Scott, C. (2001) *How Picture Books Work*. Garland, New York.

Nodelman, P. (1988) *Words about Pictures: The Narrative Art of Children's Picture Books*. University of Georgia Press, Athens.

Norton, D.E. (1983) *Through the Eyes of a Child*. Merrill, London.

O'Brien, J. (1994) 'Critical literacy in an early childhood classroom: A progress report', *Australian Journal of Language and Literacy*, 17, 1, February, pp. 36–44.

Olson, D. (1977) 'The language of instruction: The literate bias of schooling', in R.C. Anderson, R.J. Spiro and W. Montague (eds) *Schooling and the Acquisition of Knowledge*. Erlbaum, Hillsdale.

Pride, M. (1988) *Dinosaurs of Australia*. Angus and Robertson, Sydney.

Protherough, R. (1983) *Developing Response to Fiction*. Open University Press, Milton Keynes.

Rosenblatt, L.M. (1969) 'Towards a Transactional Theory of Reading', *Journal of Reading Behaviour*, 1, Winter, pp. 31–49.

Salmon, M. (n.d.) *There's a DINOSAUR in the garden!* Lamont, Melbourne.

Samuels, S.J. (1970) 'Effects of pictures on learning to read, comprehension & attitudes', *Review of Educational Research*, 40, pp. 397–408.

Saxby, M. (1971) *A history of Australian Children's Literature 1941–1970*. Wentworth, Sydney.

—— (1997) *Books in the Life of the Child: Bridges to literature and learning*. Macmillan, Melbourne.

Schallert, D.J. (1980) 'The role of illustrations in reading comprehension', in R. Spiro, B.C. Bruce and W.F. Brewer (ed.) *Theoretical issues in reading comprehension: Perspectives from cognitive psychology, linguistics, artificial intelligence, and education*. Erlbaum, New York, pp. 503–25.

Sheahan, R. (1995) 'Invisible Words, Visible Pictures', *The Literature Base*, 6: 2, June, pp. 15–20.

Smith, F. 1971, *Understanding Reading*. Holt, Rinehart and Winston, New York.

Stephens, C. (1990) 'Peepo Ergo Sum? Anxiety and Pastiche in the Albergs' Picture Books', *Children's Literature in Education*, 21: 3, pp. 165–77.

Stephens, J. (1989) 'Language, Discourse and Picture Books', *Children's Literature Association Quarterly*, 14: 3, pp. 106–10.

—— (1990) 'Intertextuality and *The Wedding Ghost*', *Children's Literature in Education*, 21: 1, pp. 23–36.

—— (1992) *Language and Ideology in Children's Fiction*. Longman, London.

—— (1994) 'Illustrating the Landscape in Australian Children's Picture Books', in *Landscape and Identity: Perspectives from Australia* Proceedings of the 1994 Conference, Auslib Press, Adelaide, Australia.

Story, D. (1985) 'Reading comprehension, visual literacy and picture book illustrations', *Reading Horizons*, 25, pp. 54–9.

Sutherland, Z. and Arbuthnot, M.H. (1986) *Children and Books* (7th edn). Scott Foresman, Illinois.

Thomson, J. (1987) *Understanding Teenagers' Reading: Reading processes and the teaching of literature*. Methuen, Melbourne.

—— (1986) 'Developmental Stages of Literacy Response', *English in Australia*, 78, December, pp. 16–25.

Tolkien, J.R.R. (1964) *Tree and Leaf*. Allen & Unwin, London.

Townsend, J.R. (1987) *Written for Children* (1965). Penguin, London.

Trites, R.S. (1994) 'Manifold Narratives: Metafiction and ideology in picture books', *Children's Literature in Education*, 25:4. pp. 225–42.

Turbill, J. (1983) *Now We Want to Write*. PETA, Rozelle.

Walker, K. (1989) *The Dragon of Mith*. Allen & Unwin, Sydney.

Watson, V. and Styles, M. (1996) *Talking Pictures*. Hodder and Stoughton, London.

Waugh, P. (1984) *Metafiction: The theory and practice of self-conscious fiction*. Methuen, London.

Wildsmith, B. (1980) *Professor Noah's Spaceship*. Oxford University Press, London.

The 'art' of research

Dr Linda Knight

Deconstruction of the image

This chapter discusses research into illustration practice via a project that concentrates specifically on Australian picture books. I am a research artist, conducting academic study through artworks that may resemble, but which are not, commercially produced illustrations. My work, some of which is described in this chapter, aims to develop new thoughts and perspectives on how to look at/understand the art of children's picture books.

This chapter contains both written and visual analysis, reflecting the structures I usually adopt when making investigations. Arts-based research is necessary and particularly appropriate for studying picture books, because it promotes development of the visual, without the overbearing influence of the written. This type of bi-faceted research also has further advantages, in that it facilitates understanding for writers and artists — that is, those who read and those who look. Importantly, this includes the illustrator (who unbelievably has been pretty much left out in the cold in terms of having critical work to reference), as well as the critic, publisher, writer, educator, etc.

Visual research into children's book illustration is quite new[1] but necessary, especially because unlike many other studies which may interpret significance or meaning, it is purely concerned with the process by which illustrators 'practice' — that is, create their wonderful work. To obtain specific information I assess illustrations via a methodology, which I define as Post-Modern Deconstructivist (PMD) Method. PMD Method is an important facilitator in the study of children's book illustration. It not only has very definite aims and benefits, but a distinct objective to remove, as much as possible, any 'outside' agenda — an issue which has sometimes dogged previous studies. This methodology also provides a necessary addition to extant theories that have in the main critiqued illustration via other disciplines, including history, English literature, psychology, cultural studies, librarianship, and so forth.

Specifically then, PMD Method gathers information on the practice of the illustrator. It is important that this should not be confused with the art of the illustrator, as that aspect requires a different technique of assessment.[2] Instead, PMD Method focuses on the ways in which the artist physically constructs an illustration.

Roland Barthes (1977), in his essay on the press photograph, proposed that there were three separate stages to its production. The stages of producing an illustration can likewise be identified as:

1 stage 1 — the concept, or idea, of the image;
2 stage 2 — the physical production of that image;
3 stage 3 — how the finished image is received (by any form of audience).

PMD Method concentrates on the second stage of this tripartite process. Most significantly it does not look at illustration via significance, semiotics, or connotation. This is very important as all these aspects are covered through studies on the art of illustration. Instead this methodology works by *deconstructing* illustrations to identify marks, colours, composites, functions and so forth in order to record commonalities of practice and technique.

These aspects may be interpreted to discuss notions of conventionality, stereotyping, or standardised representation — in respect of how the illustrator has created the image. Postmodern philosophy produces research that challenges patterns of practice evident in published picture books and allows for examination of the subject via its own medium, in much the same way that other artists are doing so in film, video, painting, sculpture and so forth.

Although this methodology is not concerned with interpreting meanings in illustration, it does involve a process of 'reading' the image, although essentially it is about dissecting and recognising set responses by which illustrators work. Its major benefit to the wider subject of children's literature is that it aids understanding of the impulses that drive the illustrator. This is not to force assumptions upon why illustrators create the images they do, but to explore what is evident. Additionally, PMD Method specifically benefits other illustrators because it presents alternatives to previous external[3] writings on aesthetics or taste, via a more internal, tacit understanding of process and professional practice. This tacit model is vital to illustrators, because it's often the method by which they learn their art. One example of this is that when illustrators talk about their art, it is often via introspective reflection (aspects of this are highlighted in interview excerpts later in the chapter). This form of discussion is the most natural way for many illustrators to conceptualise their work. However, while this presents no problem to other illustrators (due to a shared understanding of concept and terminology), it may not readily translate to other readers, who more commonly think in the literal.

This chapter then presents research via both text and image, to try and 'bridge the gap' between those who are interested in illustration, and those who create it. Consequently, the bi-faceted nature of my research, plus the methodology that supports it, presents a new visual literacy in understanding illustration.

The research discussed in this chapter concentrates on the practice of illustrators in Australia — a country that interests me for a number of reasons. The quality of illustration in Australia is extremely high, and the children's picture book on the whole is well supported — both in terms of patronage and academic regard/support. What really interests me however is the particular nature of the visual culture. Australia is essentially made up of indigenous and non-indigenous people, which in itself is not wholly unusual, but the artistic differences that emerge from these two groups is.

Unlike many other countries, indigenous art in Australia is held in equal (and sometimes higher) regard to non-indigenous art. Not only is this the case, but much indigenous art uses an entirely different representational visual vocabulary to the non-indigenous, including concepts of narrative, perspective, representation, sequence and so on. And I mean it is entirely different (see also the work of Morphy, 1998). Incredibly and delightfully, this beautiful form of painting has filtered through into the more commercialised world of children's book illustration. This mix of Australian indigenous and non-indigenous illustration, which explores two traditions — the oral (Aboriginal) and the literal (Western) — provides a basis for the research discussed in this chapter.

I have previously conducted research into anthropomorphic animal characters in British picture books, and in it I proposed that there are ten ways, or 'functions', for making these animal characters humanistic.[4] I would extend on this and suggest that these same functions have been used globally without change since animal characters have appeared in books (which is a very long time!). This implicit statement supports the idea that as cultures we continue to uphold national heritages and conform to representational stereotypes, perpetuating what semioticians identify as the arbitrary nature of signs. It could further be assumed that many cultures too produce representational stereotypes, even if they are realised in various ways, or with different symbols.

To investigate representational stereotyping in this wider context I applied PMD Method to look at basic commonalities of practice and then explored it in my own painting. By concentrating on the dual nature of Australian illustration I was able to explore the distinctly different set of creative functions within indigenous and non-indigenous work. Anthropomorphic animals form the core resource of the Australian project, not only because animals play such a large role in the country's stories, but it was useful to combine familiar functions with new, unfamiliar ideas of practice and to present possible comparisons/oppositions in my images.

I have found that 16 functions describe Aboriginal illustration practice in terms of creativity and image construction.[5] This suggests there is an identifiable, or signatory, visual language being used that is particular to the culture (i.e. it helps us to recognise it as 'Aboriginal'). Various of these functions are discussed at length later in the chapter, via critiques of published work, and samples of my visual research.

The exposure to Aboriginal illustration has expanded my existing visual vocabulary, challenging those conceptions which are founded on my own well-established Eurocentric visual heritage, built as it is on a long history of aesthetic convention. Exposure to Australian illustration has helped me learn how to conceptualise and create work that is ephemeral and abstract, allowing me to gain understanding of how to apply the same creative approaches as the indigenous illustrator. This way of painting was extremely difficult initially, as it works in virtual opposition to what I had been previously taught at art school. However this was a welcome creative challenge, particularly because more critically it reflects differences between Aboriginal culture, and the fundamentally literal nature of my society — in which books are very highly regarded. However the presence of Australian indigenous-produced illustration in the market is a testament to its appropriateness and sophistication.

Indigenous Tradition vs Eurocentricity

To highlight the particular differences between Aboriginal and Eurocentric Australian illustration practice, I have focused on four published titles (two examples of each style) to indicate technique, resource leads and quality. Using specific examples also helps to understand how PMD Method works and how it can be applied to other illustrations. All four books contain images of anthropomorphic animals, as a reflection of my research project. However, due to costs and copyright laws, I would suggest obtaining copies of the books for reference[6], where you will also be able to view them in colour.

The books I have chosen are:

- *Tjarany/Roughtail* (Greene and Tramacchi, 1987), illustrated by Lucille Gill;
- *Kun-Man-Gur* (Cowan, 1994), illustrated by Bronwyn Bancroft;
- *Possum Magic* (Fox, 1983), illustrated by Julie Vivas; and
- *Minton goes Trucking* (Feinberg, 1999), illustrated by Kim Gamble.

Tjarany/Roughtail is chosen because of its high quality. It won the Eve Pownall Award for non-fiction and is excellently designed, incorporating colour and explanatory illustrations, plus two texts — English, and Kuktatja, which is the language of the people to whom these stories belong.

Bronwyn Bancroft is a highly respected and prolific indigenous illustrator, who is a descendant of the New South Wales Bundjalung tribe. She has produced a number of contemporary children's books, of which I believe *Kun-Man-Gur* is one of her best.

I have chosen *Possum Magic* for two reasons — one because Julie Vivas is a highly respected and accomplished illustrator and, two, because *Possum Magic* is possibly one of the best-known contemporary picture books in Australia. It was highly commended in the Children's Book Council Picture Book Awards in 1984, and received an IBBY honour diploma in 1986.

Finally, I have chosen *Minton goes Trucking* because I am such a fan of Kim Gamble's work. He is very popular in Australian picture book circles, producing work for older readers also. I feel he is one of a select group of artists who consistently maintain the high standard seen in Australian illustration.

While the purpose of this chapter is to look at illustrative difference, it is worth contextualising my chosen titles through a brief description of their stories, to help indicate the breadth by which animals are used as characters.

Tjarany/Roughtail centres on a number of Dreamtime songs (stories) that the Roughtail Lizard Man gave to the local men. The particular story I shall discuss is called 'The Crow and the Eagle', recounting how the crow's feathers became black. *Kun-Man-Gur* imparts a moral message to treat everyone with equal respect regardless of difference, and tells how the two flying fox children of the Rainbow Serpent come to fly at night. These indigenous-produced books both contain stories that are creational and mostly involve animal 'identities'. This is possibly too vague a term, but I am reluctant to categorise animal beings that are intricately woven into Aboriginal histories, which seem to transcend between being actual animals, people, and spirits/Gods.

By contrast, the two non-indigenous books contain stories that are quite different to the Aboriginal ones, but show similarities to each other. They each treat the animal in a singular, personal sense, by giving them individual personalities and unique problems. Additionally there is no mistaking that the animals in these books are essentially common animals that have been awarded human attributes to varying degrees, and so theirs is a much more constructed presentation. *Possum Magic* is about an invisible young possum and his efforts to become visible. *Minton goes Trucking* is one of a series of books that concentrate on various methods of transport, through a narrative about two friends (a lizard and a turtle) who live and work in a circus, but who are trying to return 'home'.

Influences are important to any illustrator, as they guide concepts of populism, which help to maintain consistency and continue the audience's cultural arbitrary understandings of their visual language. This is fundamental to the success of a children's book; because understanding the visual is just as important as understanding the language it is written in. Books in Australia then have twice this responsibility, as they need to appeal and communicate to both indigenous and non-indigenous children (and the adults) who read them. This may seem a very obvious statement, but it is worth remembering how different the visual language of these two communities is, and how that must transcend into something as 'innocent' as the picture book.

For example, while Bancroft's work emerges via the Eurocentric book format, her strategy for visualising pays conscious homage to her cultural and artistic heritage. Her use of repeated symbols to suggest land, sea, and the Rainbow Serpent utilise a reduced system of codes/icons that emerge from a strong history/knowledge of pre-existent art techniques.[7] This too is seen in Gill's work, in that her illustrations also rely upon established methods of painting for the representation of animals and environments, using Aboriginal techniques of presenting narrative. The patterned 'grounds' that the two illustrators have used bring a true sense of animation to their work and with it a strong sense of Aboriginal identity, consciously learning from and building on an already powerful fine art tradition. Bancroft also brings in elements of Western influence, seen particularly in illustrations where she combines suggestions of perspective, linear narrative, and side-on viewed environments.

Gamble and Vivas's works show different influences. Gamble's environments, props and styling show a more Eurocentric method of resourcing that relies upon cinematic strategies of creating narratives[8] and eclectic cultural referencing,[9] while Vivas is more selective about what art she prefers, seeming instead to be influenced by personal creative strengths.[10] Effectively both Gamble and Vivas make choices about what should influence them, picking randomly (and globally) from any number of cultures and histories. Despite this eclecticism their work shows cultural consistency, because it eventually utilises methods of representation which are based upon established Westernised schema.

Although there have been many previous writings on looking at children's books, use of the PMD Method brings out interesting additions to these readings. What follows are a number of discussion points that highlight some differences of practice — for instance how each illustrator approaches and formulates creative solutions such as 'perspectival viewing' (by the audience).

Both the non-indigenous illustrators manipulate side-on perspective to varying degrees. Vivas uses both bird's-eye and worm's-eye views, whereas Gamble's work is more uniform with changes occurring in terms of distance or nearness. This nearness is a common feature of children's books as there is often a desire to keep the detail up close, to maintain the reader's involvement and interest. Gill uses plan perspective in her second illustration, called 'Tjukurrpa Kaarnka Kamu Kurnkangulku' (Dreaming of the Crow and The Raw Meat Eater [Eagle]). This is prevalent in the portrayal of the creek, camp, animals, and emu tracks. Because it shows plan perspective it is possible to approach the illustration from a number of sides, unlike Gill's first illustration which, because of its side-on perspective, has much more of a conceived 'top' and 'bottom'.

Interesting differences occur in terms of depth of perception also. Although Gill's work is composed of many dots, these dots collectively represent solid elements, and depth. Although the perspective is 'flat' there is still a *sense* of depth through the careful use of colour that suggests fire crackling over grass, the creek meandering through clusters of rocks, and the rounded bodies of the animals. The image dances when you look at it. Bancroft too uses similar ways to achieve density, in that she portrays light and shadow via pattern — as variations in colour washes, or repeated objects which diminish in size (such as the flying fox shapes on page 14). Both Vivas and Gamble use established Western fine art methods for representing depth. Vivas's work is the most classical in this sense as she achieves depth of field and solidity by building up layers of darker tones over light, whereas Gamble, being much more the graphic artist, relies upon more cinematic techniques of placing props, characters and environments as if on a stage — so the illustration approaches us in staggered layers of detail.

A number of the indigenous practice functions I identified are interlinked, as they focus on the use of single icons within the image. Gill's illustrations are seen to be almost entirely constructed out of dots, the only variation being their size, such as the smaller dots that create 'lines', which edge areas containing larger dots. These shaped areas of dots represent environments such as land, water, rocks, sky etc. This not only shows how the reduced visual vocabulary — the same dot icon — can be repeated to construct an entire image, but it makes direct reference to an extensive art history which also uses such marks. These collective dots give the image busyness, as they jostle like the atoms seen in science textbooks. Bancroft's work, although it uses a wider range of shapes and marks, also shows a very reduced schema that is used in repetition. It's almost as if Aboriginal art recognises that everything in the world is made of millions of tiny particles, all working together to form the earth and its creatures. Furthermore, each of these symbols also commands its own space within the illustrations, sitting in isolation to other marks, and for this to work successfully in an image requires strong understanding of formal spacing — again a skill which directly relates to historic cultural painting traditions.

By contrast non-indigenous illustration relies upon an entirely different symbolic technique, often referencing a long history of allegory and metaphor in Eurocentric fine art. This is an equally powerful message, seen especially in terms of Vivas's *Possum Magic* illustration on page 19, and the image of the downcast young possum. The shape of the poor creature droops, representing his sadness, seen through downward lines and brushstroke marks, the use of blue/purple colours, and the close perspective — bringing the viewer in to a more personal level. Gamble uses a slightly different technique — again because his work is inspired by the more iconic graphic arts seen through his use of the archetype, including caravans, buildings, trees, bread, etc. There is no association to a particular item, but rather a visualisation of his imagination, cleaned up and rounded off and presenting a very accessible, appealing world to children.

Differences of practice also emerge when using PMD Method to focus on the actual drawing and painting of the image. Again it is very important to stress that I'm discussing the *construction process* here rather than a symbolic interpretation of the finished product.

What's apparent is that the two non-indigenous illustrators have drawn their final illustrations out first and then painted them, whereas the two indigenous illustrators have used paint only, and built up their images systematically in layers. This means that Vivas and Gamble have 'mapped out' their work prior to colouring it — that is, drawn it out in pencil first, including the details, features, composites and so forth before the image is painted. This is in contrast to the process of Gill and Bancroft who have laid a ground of opaque, blocked in shapes and then layered on smaller opaque marks to build up detail. The opacity of the paint would make it impossible to plan or draw out the image first, as all marks would be obliterated with the first layer of paint. Gamble retains the expressive aspect of his drawing marks, and Vivas's drawing is also quite noticeable, with a controlled expressiveness that shows through her watercolour. This seems quite intentional, as Vivas prefers the drawing part to the painting.[11] Bancroft has a wonderful technique of representing the earth and the underwater by firstly filling in large areas with base colour, then painting clusters of dots and concentric circles on top, to suggest the texture of each element. This process of piling opaque paints on top of each other is one of the fundamental differences between non-indigenous illustration (which is based upon a distinct formal history of structure and aesthetics), and indigenous illustration (which is based upon historic techniques that are systematic, but less restrictive).

One aspect of Australian illustration I noticed immediately was the amount of white space left on a page and many have informed me that it aims to reflect the wide spaces and bright light of Australia — and it is a highly effective decision. However, this sense of bright light and vast space is not generally dealt with in the same way in Aboriginal illustration, as it is portrayed more via careful approaches to design which leave large areas of the page saturated with colour (representing the intense Australian heat). In respect of the four books discussed, Vivas and Gamble both leave large areas of their illustrations white, whereas Bancroft bleeds all her illustrations off the page, and Gill's, although framed by a white page, are essentially full colour paintings that have been photographed for the book.

This sense of the Australian light (which seems to have a quality and intensity of its own) can be further assessed by deconstructing the techniques illustrators use to portray 'light' and 'dark'. Gamble shows a particular grasp of how light bounces off objects, by painting strong shadows contrasted with equally strong highlights in a realistic manner. Bancroft projects how the intensity of the heat affects colours at different times of the day by combining many ochre tones with turquoise, magenta and yellow details. Gill also achieves a notion of dark and light, through natural pigment colours that are layered in contrasting tonal qualities which reference Aboriginal tradition. The subtle difference in techniques used by each illustrator is actually highly significant because it reflects the major role colour theory plays in the art training of any culture, because whatever the artist learns affects their subsequent work.

This can be seen more specifically when PMD Method is used to observe how colour is layered and combined. I have discussed how Bancroft particularly applies colour and tone using ochres against chemical dyes, which she layers from dark colours to light. This layering technique is distinctly reminiscent of Aboriginal fine art and can be seen particularly in work that starts with a black base (which is also evident in some children's books; see Laurel et al, 1997). This contrasts considerably with the Eurocentric practice of working from light tones to dark. Indeed, because many illustrators work in watercolour, the paper or base colour should be white and the translucency of the paint limits other colour layering sequences. Vivas and Gamble apply this painting theory to their watercolour painting, by going from light tones to dark and layering transparent washes of paint.

These aspects so far show how sophisticated both Western and Aboriginal tactics are for illustrating. Gill's *Tjarany/Roughtail* shows particularly high quality illustrations, seen through her formal approaches to pattern and composition, plus the complexities of representational devices she uses such as multi-directionality.[12] This establishes her work as distinctly different to the two non-indigenous illustrators and notably also to Bancroft's work. Collectively however, all four illustrators' work links to, and supports an ideal of, quality that is at least on a par with fine art traditions.

I have mentioned previously the ten basic functions for anthropomorphising animals (Knight, 1999: 63, 78). However, do such functions appear in Australian illustration?

Gamble utilises many functions for humanising his animals[13] — in fact his animal characters in *Minton goes Trucking* adopt all ten functions in various combinations, with his main characters wearing clothes in one illustration and not in others (compare pages 5 and 11). Vivas's *Possum Magic* characters also portray levels of anthropomorphism, although the illustrator is more reticent about their manipulation:

> … you don't cross that line … so that you destroy the integrity of the animal — as an animal. So I've done one picture book with animals that are anthropomorphic and it's because I'm actually uncomfortable with it.
>
> (Interview, November 2000)

Bancroft by contrast explores anthropomorphism in various ways although the characters in *Kun-Man-Gur* do emerge via a number of the ten functions already established. There is the toadfish that stands on hind fins, using side fins as arms that also have the human ability to grab a spear. There is also a bat that displays human facial expressions, sits around a campfire and it too stands on hind legs. More iconic are the flying foxes as they are largely portrayed in group form, and it is here that Bancroft relies upon the process of repeating one identical symbol to represent them. Their anthropomorphism emerges through their human adult/child's relationship with the snake. The snake, while playing a humanesque father/God figure is the most 'traditionally' treated visually, as he is simultaneously viewed from side-on and above, and his importance is established through high decoration, in the form of a repeated pattern comprising dots, concentric circles, u-shapes, lines and so forth.

Gill more consciously references both art traditions, as done in the first illustration for 'The Crow and the Eagle'. Animal characterisation is clearly Eurocentric, with an interplay of traditional symbolism seen through treatment of the rock-hole, sky, hill and camp. The animals too show evidence of traditional reference, as they appear as silhouette shapes — a common aspect of Aboriginal art. However this in itself does not present the animals as anthropomorphic in a Eurocentric sense, as they do not seem to overtly possess human attributes. James Cowan, the author of *Kun-Man-Gur* holds the view:

> … while the myth speaks of animals, we are in fact dealing with anthropomorphic figures … not only animals, but also the antecedents of the Aborigines, since the Aborigines, through their totemic affiliations, believe themselves to be derived from individual animals at the time of the Dreaming.
>
> (Cowan, 1994)

I regard Gill's animals as anthropomorphic because the 'text' (which is representative of something much older, already established and familiar to Kukatja people) suggests they interact and behave as humans would — the crow particularly taking on the role of the human hunter.[14] Incidentally, the animals do use the function 'same size' which is common in Western illustration, although usually it is combined with other functions. So while it seems that humanesque aspects do not appear in the image, they would be apparent to a reader who knows the story. This understanding facilitates a continuing tradition of storytelling for those who 'read' imagery rather than written text.

Gill's animals are anthropomorphic through their roles in a culture's history, intertwined with stories of creation both of the land and its people. If Gill's practice can be seen as representative of Aboriginal illustration — and there are a number of artists who have worked in similar ways — then it would be fair to propose that many of their methods for anthropomorphising are different, because their stories are so different. It seems Aboriginal illustrators use as reference their knowledge and familiarity of surroundings that include animals and stories indigenous to each region of Australia, thus bringing totally disparate processes of practice into children's picture books. Essentially, indigenous anthropomorphic representation is established by confirmation of what the animal is *not* — a creature which behaves completely naturally.

Non-indigenous practice reflects Eurocentric styles of illustration, and Gamble's work in *Minton goes Trucking* is a good example of this. His animals are more representative of humans, which means they act as vessels for singly human emotions and characteristics. Particularly the supporting cast of characters, such as the building site worker (a bulldog), use animals as vehicles to portray human stereotypes. This suggests that the character of 'building site worker' came first (via the text), with the bulldog being chosen as a suitable repository. The main characters are also presented this way, evident in certain situations where their reactions are more human than animal.[15] This is most notably seen in the illustrations on pages 16–17, where the turtle is in a dangerous situation and is showing great fear. The turtle, with his legs splayed, head stretched out and underside up, shows comic book characteristics which are almost slapstick but not natural — normally, in such a situation, a turtle's more likely response would be to retreat into its shell and feign death. Because this pose may not have been as visually stimulating to Gamble, he relied instead upon filmic traditions of dissipating fear via comedy or humour.

If Vivas's *Possum Magic* was interpreted via other methodologies for reading images (such as those that concentrate on connotation, semiology, codes, etc.), then the animals are seen as faithfully drawn, true to nature, dignified, real possums. Vivas has consciously tried to uphold this in her drawings.[16] Alternatively, comparing illustrations on pages 15 and 21 via PMD Method allows for additional observations. Page 15 shows Grandma Poss hanging by her tail, poised above her reflection in a pool and about to clean her teeth. There is no direct evidence of anthropomorphic behaviour in her ability to hang by her tail, or to be able to hold an object (in this case a toothbrush), but she is wearing glasses, and her pose represents a moment of contemplation rather than a pause in natural activity. Page 21 shows the same character riding a bicycle which is the correct size for her. Here she is clothed in shoes and socks, apron and glasses and the illustration is a freeze-frame moment of her cycling. These two illustrations show that, despite Vivas's intentions of remaining faithful, the possum wears clothes, has the human ability to ride a bicycle, possesses human emotion and is human adult-sized.

The four illustrators use quite different and distinctive ways of approaching and representing the animal character, and while certainly there are many levels of characterisation and manipulation, by applying PMD Method it seems that whatever the illustrators' intentions, there is very little chance of animals being used as characters in books without their being anthropomorphic in some way.

The ten Eurocentric functions for anthropomorphising animals are consistently and identically visually upheld in non-indigenous practice, being instantly recognisable to Eurocentric audiences who have learned to decode such representations. Interestingly, these ten functions *also* exist in indigenous practice, but Aboriginal illustrators seem to delve into the visual schema of both cultures when portraying them. Consequently it could be tentatively suggested then that there is a third visual language being created here.

Identical to Eurocentric illustration, Aboriginal practice utilises visual schema in addition to its own — in fact some examples seem to make a point of doing this, such as Ray Meeks's images for *Pheasant and Kingfisher* (Berndt, 1987), which reference various cultural styles.[17] Meeks's example and others like it is so rich in symbolism, it is perfectly feasible for indigenous and non-indigenous children alike to interpret the illustrations without prior knowledge of the stories.

This multi-faceted containment of narratives makes these books wonderfully postmodern, as they operate on interdependent text/image relationships, challenging notions of how children's books can be regarded and read/understood while successfully building new extensions for Aboriginal art. It is worth discussing at this point the resistance by some critics to labelling this work 'illustration', calling it instead 'Aboriginal painting'. While this could be positively interpreted as an acknowledgment of artistic strength and quality, I fear it has more to do with the reputation of illustration being a 'low' or easy art form, and the consequent associations for the artists. This is sadly because children's picture book illustration is still regarded by some as glorified commercial art, seen only by children who would possess 'low' critical judgment. Therefore, classifying the work of Bancroft, Gill et al. as paintings 'frees' them from such confines. This generally does not happen within

European illustration, due to its larger audience being able to 'read' and 'decipher' Eurocentric artworks. Aboriginal illustration can indeed seem quite abstract to this Eurocentric readership, but this does *not* change the art form. It is extremely beautiful illustration, and should be regarded as just that — representing the quality of children's books.

I have discussed how indigenous illustrators are seen to paint with very opaque pigments, allowing them to systematically work from dark colours to light. This process of layering opaque grounds seems to stem from the traditions of hiding sensitive or secret parts of a Dreaming story, or as Howard Morphy's investigations show, to achieve the essence of light (1998: 185–9). This technique is a major difference between indigenous and Eurocentric practice. My training has taught me to construct art via a pyramid-like structure that starts with large areas of light tones and ends with small details of the darkest colours — the object being to leave areas of each tonal layer exposed. Furthermore, if illustrators in the UK are representative, the most popular medium used is watercolour, and the transparent qualities of this paint makes it almost impossible to work from dark to light.

Several studies, including those conducted by Morphy, acknowledge that traditional Aboriginal art is constructed of complex coded systems, where composites are painted and layered in a systematic fashion. This is also true of Aboriginal illustration, particularly in the works of Bancroft, but also Meeks, who consistently uses one ground colour of red ochre. Systematic schema is also used in Aboriginal contemporary fine art, such as Lin Onus's *Fish 1994–5* (Onus Estate) that contains repetitions of a fish icon, which also appears in his other works.

While it seems Aboriginal art houses many varied styles just as Western art does, process techniques still differ between the two cultures. These it seems are inherently/inevitably linked to their respective cultures, art traditions and histories and while there are conscious crossovers by both sets of artists, basic visual/creative languages pervade.

Practice as research

This section contains some of my visual research. The structure of this entire chapter (being in written and visual form) reflects how my research benefits both *readers* and *viewers*. The two previous sections detail specific aspects about the understanding, assessing and critiquing of Australian illustration, and this section too has those objectives — it's just that they emerge via visual works. For those who comprehend in the literal, sections one and two help to provide a canon of conceptual understanding, while for artists, this section may suggest new ways of approaching personal practice to break down common response. What this section must promote overall, however, is that visual research is as much a host for theory as written research.

Each piece included in this section consciously explores the functions I have identified — both for anthropomorphising animals, and Australian illustration practice. These functions are not rigidly applied or restricted to certain paintings however, but for the purposes of providing exemplars, I have linked each piece with an individual function. Also, rather than explaining the images with text, there are a number of 'prompts' that accompany each image, which if needed can relate artworks to issues discussed earlier.

Illustration 5.1 Red Panda XVII
Acrylic, pastel on white cartridge, 120 x 150 cm, 2000

Reduced visual vocabulary

- A reduced system of marks and icons are used to mean various things.
- This is reliant upon the placing of such marks/icons in a number of contexts or constructions.
- Enlarging and reducing creates image or abstraction.
- New experience of using a much-reduced reference 'bank' to create an image.
- A repetitive working method of creating and then completing images.
- Using the same brush-strokes, or drawing strategies.
- Using a single cognitive pattern to draw out the animals.

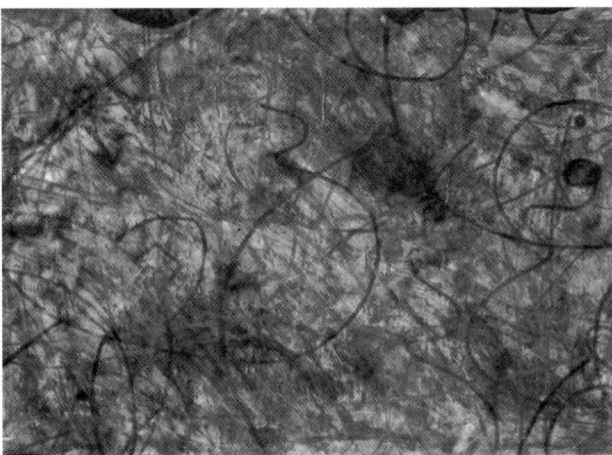

Illustration 5.2 *Red Panda XIV*
Acrylic, pastel on white cartridge, 105 x 150 cm, 2000

Colours used

- Colours reflect Australian light.
- The colour of the sky, and the trees in shadow against it.
- Tones and colours which make direct reference to immediate surroundings.
- Mimics the colours found in published Aboriginal illustration.

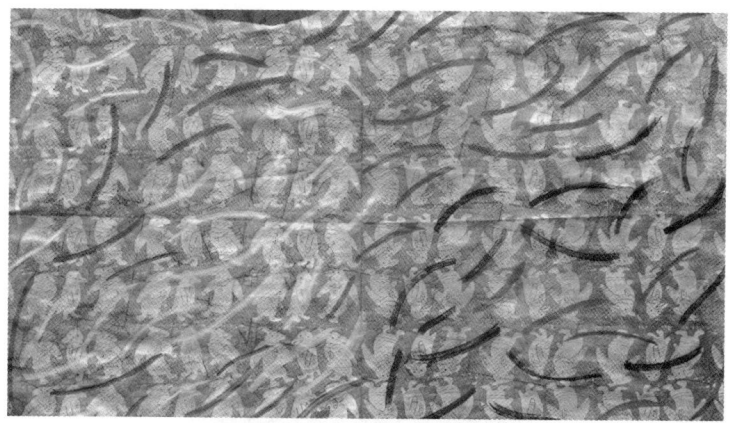

Illustration 5.3 Penguin XXXIX
Acrylic, linocut, pastel on map, 100 x 68 cm, 2000

Opacity

- Use of opaque paints, as opposed to transparent washes.
- The challenge to previous working practices with colour.

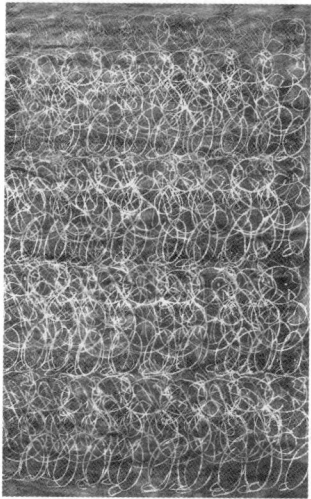

Illustration 5.4 Red Panda V
Acrylic, pastel on white cartridge, 90 x 150 cm, 2000

- New ways of creating illustrations.
- Each medium is used over each other, rather than in combinations.
- No inter-relationship between each medium.
- Allows for developing the image via stages of separated events.

Repetition

- Repetitive use of an icon or mark within the image.
- Creates levels of importance, or represents textures.
- One symbol of the red panda repeated.
- Creates an abstraction of the original symbol.
- Emerges as an abstract image.
- Repeating one icon, to give it new identity.

Illustration 5.5 Red Panda IV
Acrylic, pastel on white cartridge, 73 x 105 cm, 2000

Dark to light

- Works in opposition to my conventional Western practice.
- Challenges my art school training of working from light to dark.
- Links closely with use of opaque paints/grounds.
- Requires different aesthetic working practices.
- Reflects the practice of constructing images systematically.
- Makes the process of sketching out obsolete.
- Presents new visual/creative challenges.

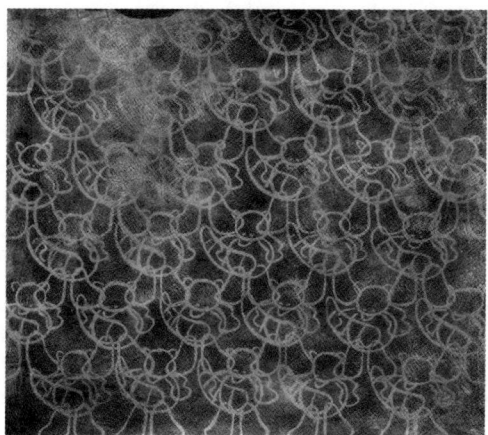

Illustration 5.6 Red Panda XXI
Acrylic, pastel on white cartridge, 75 x 75 cm, 2000

Same symbol

- Links closely with repetition and reduced visual vocabulary.
- Forms part of creative basis for many Aboriginal illustrations.
- This explores one aspect of the repetition 'trio'.
- Abstraction is achieved via patterning.
- One symbol is used to create more complex structures.
- The eye acknowledges the symbol in other contexts.

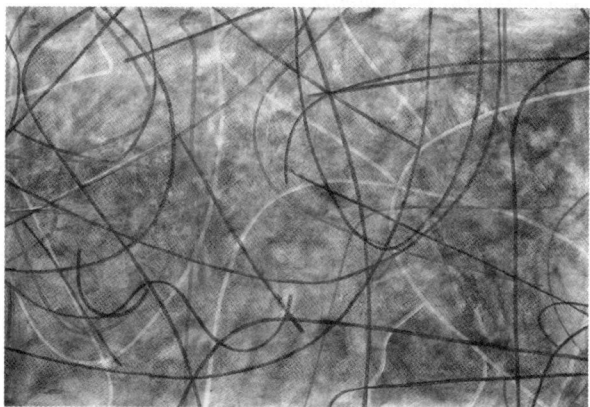

Illustration 5.7 Red Panda XIII
Acrylic, pastel on white cartridge, 150 x 105 cm, 2000

Symbolic

- Symbolic of Australian grassland, and native plants.
- The panda symbol, when used in an abstract construct, suggests new representations.
- The panda symbol resembles tracks, or marks in the ground.

- Symbolism emerges through colour and through contextual placement.
- Static shapes/objects become the emotive possessors of strong symbolic meanings/messages.

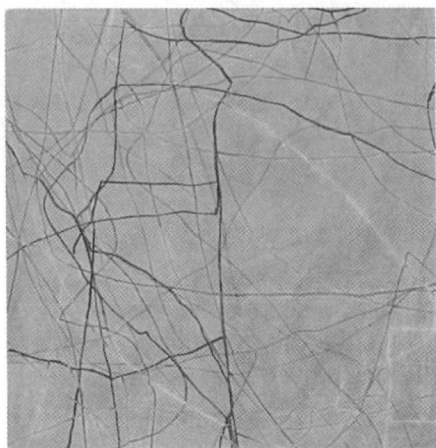

Illustration 5.8 Red Panda XII
Acrylic, pastel on white cartridge, 75 x 75 cm, 2000

Silhouette

- A common mechanism in illustrations.
- Usually consists of a black filled-in shape.
- Abstracted by many transparent silhouette shapes over-layered.

Illustration 5.9 Penguin XXXVIII
Acrylic, linocut, pastel on maps, 100 x 120 cm, 2000

- Concepts of the archetype, or the anonymous presence.
- Work is also suggestive of the fissure lines in rocks.

Layering

- An illustration process which directly references indigenous fine art tradition.
- Hides/protects information which may be regarded as sensitive and not for public view.
- Utilises the process of hiding, or semi-covering.
- Layers are systematically built up.
- No previous planning or sketching out.
- Conscious adopting of indigenous practice.
- The image changes each time a layer is added.
- Past elements/details become changed, or concealed.
- Distinctive qualities alter with each layer.
- Virtually all the visual research uses this process in some form.

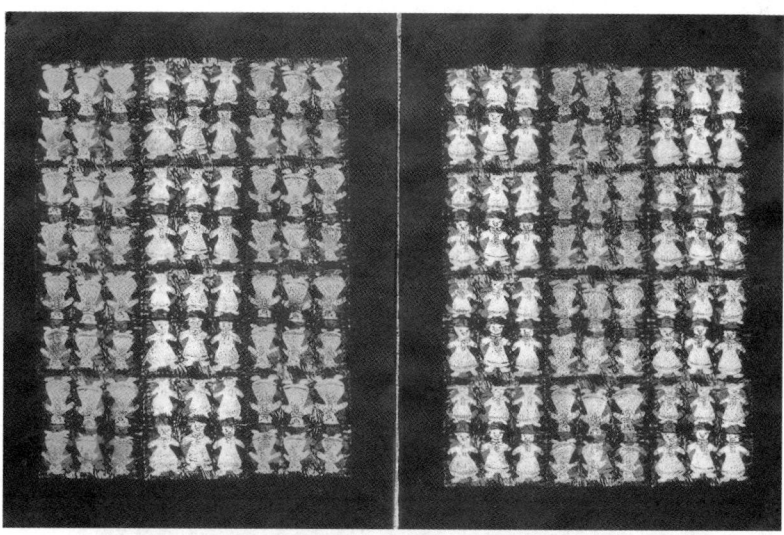

Illustration 5.10 Penguin XXX
Linocut on black Saunders, 56 x 75 cm, 2000

Black base

- More commonly found in fine art than illustration.
- Some illustrators prefer to start with a black base.
- Refers to concepts of achieving illuminosity.
- There is a distinct glowing quality to colours.
- Works closely with processes of constructing via dark to light colours.

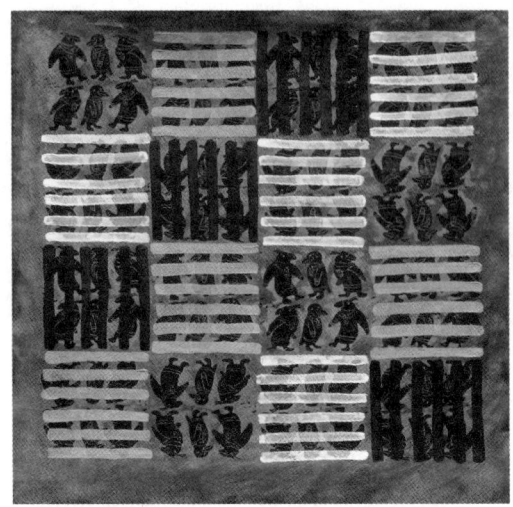

Illustration 5.11 Penguin XXXVI
Acrylic, linocut on white cartridge, 75 x 75 cm, 2000

Multi-directional

- Constructive nature facilitates readings form a number of directions.
- Images do not always have a top and bottom.
- Reflective of traditional art practice.
- References fine art paintings that are created by one, or more, artists sitting around a canvas on the floor.
- Canvases are worked on at various random points.
- Generally the artists work toward themselves.

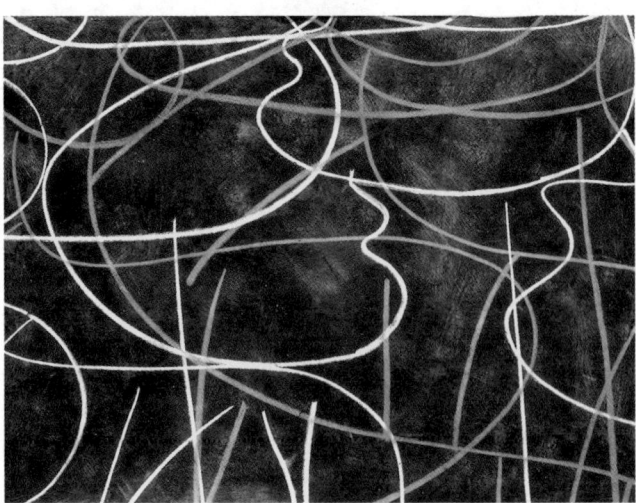

Illustration 5.12 Red Panda IX
Acrylic, pastel on white cartridge, 74 x 58 cm, 2000

- Prints face many directions.
- Striped colours form a diminishing spiral.

Flat perspective

- Opaque quality of paints used causes a flatter perspective.
- Does not preclude possession of any perspective.
- Perspective instead is suggested, rather than represented.
- The dark colour naturally recedes, but is presented as a flat ground.
- The line colours, because they are much lighter, sit forward.
- The lines individually have no depth, but represent a solid panda object.

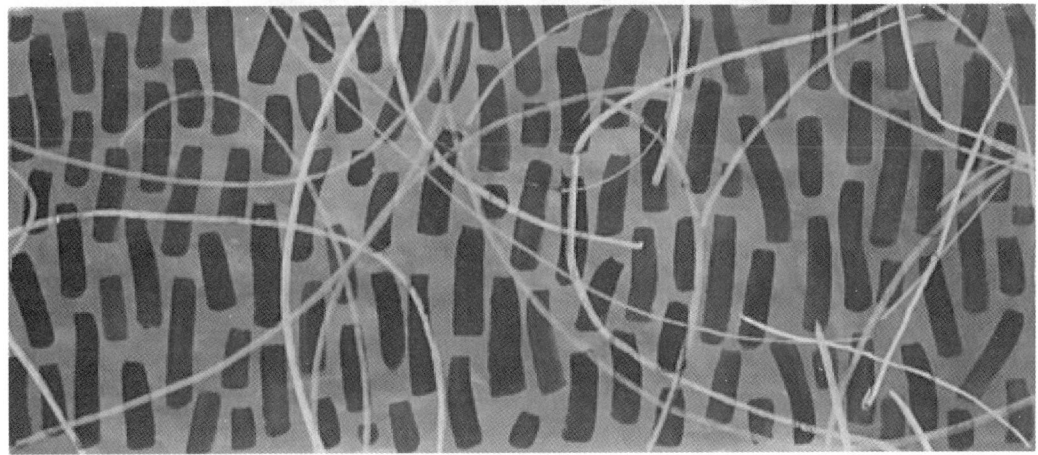

Illustration 5.13 Red Panda XL
Acrylic, pastel on white cartridge, 150 x 50 cm, 2000

Formal spacing

- Concentrates on design aspects.
- Stems from observations of the formal spacing of individual components.
- Based on the premise that each mark contributes something to the image.
- Has equal importance to the design as a whole.
- Each component (mark, icon, etc.) has its own place in the image.
- Creates complex systems of arrangement.
- Gives a sensation of flowing, or movement.
- Each mark is placed in respect to all others.
- No-one part is more important or prominent than any other.

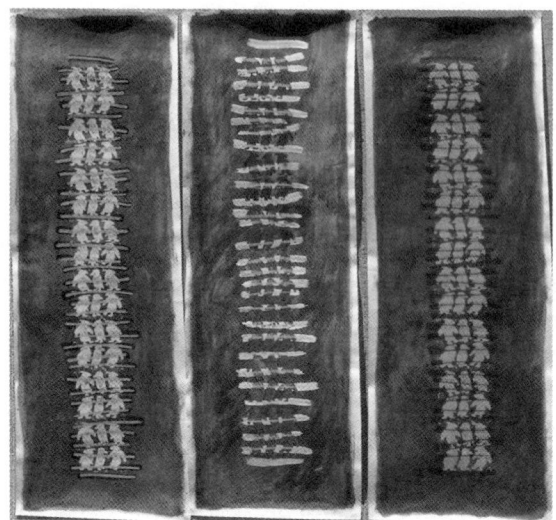

Illustration 5.14 Penguin XXXIII, XXXIV, XXXV
Acrylic, linocut, pastel on white cartridge, 40 x 150 cm (each), 2000

Strong design

- Indigenous illustration shows strong aspects of design.
- Systems for creating and building differ considerably to Western practice.
- Stems from a patternesque composition.
- Relies upon a strong knowledge of cultural history.
- Provides a number of design solutions, which have been perfected over time.
- Combines a number of learnt processes, with my own visual design heritage.

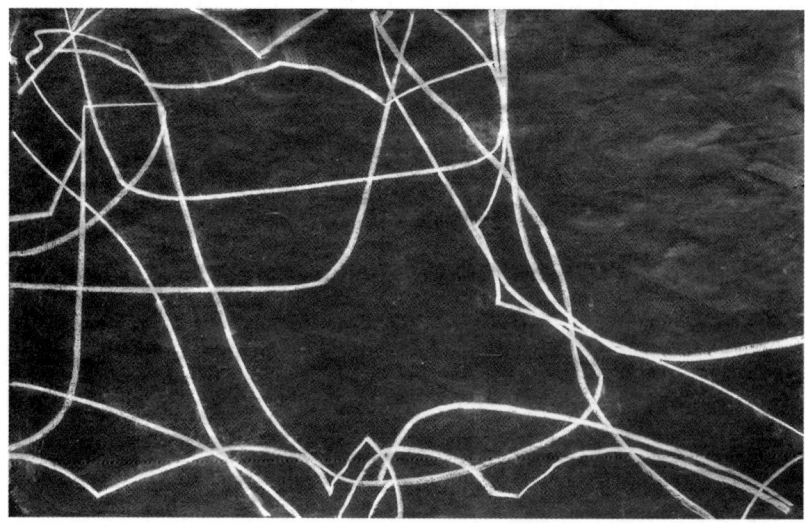

Illustration 5.15 Red Panda X
Acrylic, pastel on black paper, 103 x 50 cm, 2000

Sophisticated composition

- Links with other design aspects.
- Informed again by a strong visual, cultural heritage.
- Helps to maintain the particular visual identity of the culture.
- Distinct from other types of illustrative practice.
- Emerges particularly when many small elements are contained in one illustration.
- Sustains a sense of order, equality and balance despite business.
- A number of similar marks can maintain separate identities.
- At the same time have equal importance within it.
- Combines Eurocentric values of composition with those found in Australian illustration.

I hope that by presenting research art as a major part of this chapter, I can help to break down, or indeed 'cross the boundaries', between understanding/comprehending text and illustration in children's picture books. However a fundamental aid to this is that this research art is not seen as 'illustrating' my research — these images are an equal, if not primary, process of investigation for my work, and therefore my images and text must share the same output platform. This is the reason why my work is not overly explained, or minutely dissected via textual explanation, as to do this would subjugate it.

Some readers may find it hard to look at the images and gain full understanding of the concepts I explore, or may feel the techniques and skills needed to interpret art are beyond them, but this creates the need for my research. Because I am both an academic and an artist, the language I speak merges the terminology of the literal and the visual, to present an insight into how illustrators react to text and create visual responses. By looking at this visual research, and reading the text, elements or aspects of the artwork will become more apparent, even to those who do not draw. Essentially this allows for the subliminal and somewhat closed world of illustration practice to be accessed, and understood, by those who do not create this art.

Bibliography

Barthes, R. (1977) *Image Music Text*. Fontana Press, London, pp. 15–31.

Berndt, C. (1987) *Pheasant and Kingfisher* (illustrated by Raymond Meeks). Bookshelf Publishing Australia, Gosford.

Caruana, W. (1993) *Aboriginal Art*. Thames and Hudson, London.

Cowan, J. (1994) *Kun-Man-Gur* (illustrated by Bronwyn Bancroft). Peribo, Mount Kuring-Gai.

Feinberg, A (1999) *Minton goes Trucking* (illustrated by Kim Gamble). Allen & Unwin, Melbourne.

Fox, M. (1983) *Possum Magic* (illustrated by Julie Vivas). Omnibus Books, Adelaide.

Greene, G. & Tramacchi, J. (1987) *Tjarany/Roughtail* (illustrated by Lucille Gill). Magabala Books, Broome.

Knight, L. (1999) *An Investigation From the View of the Illustrator into the Representational Stereotypes Contained Within UK-Published Children's Picture Books, 1960–1994*. University of Wolverhampton, pp. 63, 78.

Laurel, Y. et al. (1997) *Wulungarra Stories* (illustrated by Yangkana Laurel et al.). Kadjina Community School, Kadjina.

Morphy, H. (1998) *Aboriginal Art*. Phaidon Press Ltd, London.

Onus Estate (1994–1995) *Fish*. Lin Onus's idea for commission — gouache on illustration board.

Schwarcz, J. (1982) *Ways of the Illustrator: Visual Communication in Children's Literature*. American Library Association, Chicago.

Endnotes

1   At the time of going to press, to my knowledge I was the first person in the UK to have completed a practice-based PhD in children's picture books.

2   See for instance works by: Moebius, W. (1986) 'Introduction to picturebook codes', *Word and Image*, 2(2), pp. 141–58; Alderson, B. (1986) *Sing a Song for Sixpence: The English Picturebook Tradition and Randolph Caldecott.* Cambridge University Press, Cambridge. Nodelman, P. (1988) *Words about Pictures: The Narrative Art of Children's Picture Books.* The University of Georgia Press, London.

3   Defined as an assessment or discourse provided by a non-artist.

4   These functions are: human body, correct representation, clothed, human emotion, human characteristics, human habitat, human ability, human adult/child roles, hind legs, same size. See Knight, L. (1999) *An Investigation From the View of the Illustrator, into the Representational Stereotypes Contained Within UK-Published Children's Picture Books, 1960–1994.* University of Wolverhampton, pp. 63, 78.

5   These are: reduced visual vocabulary, colour, opacity, repetition, dark-to-light, same symbol, symbolic, plan viewing, silhouette, layering, black base, multi-directional, flat perspective, formal spacing, design, composition.

6   Better still, you could try to find the originals — look out for exhibitions, or see if some are stored in special collections.

7   For instance, see Clifford Possum Tjapaltjarri, *Honey Ant Dreaming Story* (1983), National Gallery of Australia, for an example of this painting technique.

8   Gamble has stated: 'I'm inspired by all kinds of art forms — masks, dance, most music, film, sculpture, poetry — I'm fairly indiscriminate'. (Interview with Dr Linda Knight, Sydney, August 2000.)

9   Gamble has also said: 'Given that I've grown up with the history of other people's work, from Egyptians, to Disney and Jim Henson, I'm bound to be influenced by all of it, and I freely take and adapt whatever I need, within the overall needs of the story'. (ibid.)

10 Vivas has stated:

> People like Albrecht Durer — I like people's drawings, I'm not so keen on paintings … To me a painting is too complicated, but drawing I like, before the solidness has gone into it. And see, that's the thing with me too — the drawing and the inventing …
>
> (interview with Dr Linda Knight, Sydney, November 2000)

11 ibid.

12 Howard Morphy (1998: 103–5) in his treatise on Aboriginal art states: 'Paintings are frequently produced on the ground, with the artist adding features from different sides …'.

13 Gamble states: '… there are many ways to humanise animals … From simply placing them in human predicaments … to putting our clothes on them, to giving them our voices.' (Interview with Dr Linda Knight, Sydney, August 2000.)

14 The story recounts how the crow, 'had a hairstring tied around his waist and he used a long, hollow reed to breathe underwater' (Greene and Tramacchi, 1987: 5).

15 When asked about creating animal characters, Gamble has said, 'Beyond that, it's basically the same as with people, regarding facial expressions and body language'. Interview, November 2000.

16 On drawing Grandma Poss, Vivas has said, 'Where she's cleaning her teeth I think if I had put the brush in her mouth, I would have thought, "ooh Yuk". I didn't want to … see the possum's teeth, and I wouldn't go that far'. (Interview, November 2000.)

17 There seems to be a number of references in his work, including Natural History illustration, Egyptian iconism, traditional Aboriginal.

More than cracking the code:
postmodern picture books and new literacies

Michèle Anstey

In keeping with the theme of this book, *Crossing the Boundaries*, this chapter crosses boundaries between the study of children's literature as literature and its utility as a site for literacy instruction. In terms of recent trends in literacy, particularly the redefining of literacy as multiliteracies involving multiple modes and technologies, children's literature could be seen as an 'old literacy', comprising traditional print and visual literacies. Following this argument the use of children's literature as a context in which to teach new literacies could be seen as limited, as it would not provide opportunity for students to practice new literacies. However an examination of what reading is in terms of new literacies, and the ways in which a literate person needs to be able to read in new times, indicates that if literature exhibits particular characteristics it can be most useful for teaching new literacies. One area of children's literature has these characteristics — the postmodern picture book.

The postmodern picture book is in itself a product of new times and incorporates many of the characteristics of new literacies, requiring the reader to read and engage with the text in new ways. It is the purpose of this chapter to show how the new literacies of the postmodern picture book can be used as a context in which to teach multiliteracies. The chapter will begin by defining the new literacies and what it means to be multiliterate by describing the reading practices associated with multiliteracies. This will be followed by a description of the postmodern picture book and how it can challenge the reader to use the reading practices associated with multiliteracies. The role of the teacher as mediator of text and literacy teacher will also be explored.

Defining 'new times' and their effects on literacy

Change is the overarching characteristic of the later twentieth and early twenty-first century and will continue to be so. Change affects all aspects of our lives, from the global to the local — it is realised in our leisure and our workplace. It is so influential on all aspects of our lives that life in the twenty-first century is often referred to as 'new times'. It is appropriate to look briefly at the different sectors of our lives and how change has influenced the practice of literacy in these sectors.

Globalisation has had great effect on working lives (The New London Group, 1996). A post-Fordist economy (Piore and Sable, 1984), sometimes also termed fast capitalism (Gee, 1994), is characterised by business and markets focussed on flexibility and niche (as well as mass) marketing in order to cope with economic change. Workplaces in a fast capitalist culture often move to a less hierarchical organisation where teamwork and multiskilling are valued (Cope and Kalantzis, 1995). In these new workplaces different literacy, communication and social skills are necessary to those of the previous hierarchical organisation structures in which each employee had a specific task which required a specific set of skills.

Other global changes effect our public (state and civic) lives. Recently we have seen the breakdown of 'amalgamated states', such as the USSR in Europe, into individual nations characterised by religious, ethnic and/or cultural affiliations. Similar trends are manifested in Asia and the Pacific — the unrest of the Philippines, Indonesia, Fiji and the Solomon Islands. Change is also a feature of state and civic lives within countries that were largely settled by immigrants; for example, Australia, the United States and Canada. In these countries change is characterised by acknowledgment and acceptance of difference in terms of ethnicity, culture and religion as views about the culture, identity and rights of indigenous people in such countries change.

The effects of these changes on literacy are many. Although these global and state level changes are marked by fragmentation and difference the technological and economic changes of the times mean that in both our public and private lives we must interact with these different groups on a daily basis. This occurs not only face to face, but also through digital electronics: the internet, email and other technologies (e.g. film and media) which are now an everyday part of our workplace, home and leisure-sites. Indeed print is only one of many available technologies for communication these days (Durrant and Green, 2000). The literacy, communication and social skills necessary for firstly mastering the technology and secondly interacting with these very different groups are both new and different.

Technology has also changed our private lives. The concept of one largely shared set of community values and conventions promulgated by the print and electronic media has been challenged by the availability of multi-channel media systems (The New London Group, 1996) and growth in the print media. Concomitant with the trends to niche marketing, such systems cater for *different* audiences, rather than one large homogenous audience. Subcultures and specialist groups have therefore become a viable and important part of the market share to be courted and serviced. Issues and topics that previously were largely kept private have suddenly emerged in these various media, accessible to all. However it is not only the details of subgroups and subcultures that are now available to all. The print and electronic media, through magazines and current affair shows, now present details of the private lives of people from celebrities and royalty to the general public. The availability of this information, the associated viewpoints, values and attitudes presented with it and the way in which it is presented (bias, sensationalism etc.) once again place new literacy and social demands on the viewers and readers of such material (Kalantzis, 1995).

The influence of change in business, marketing and technology on private lives of people is not all targeted at subgroups nor is it confined to the local level. Parents are all too aware of global marketing aimed at their children that moves across a range of media and commodities; for example, the Pokémon phenomenon which transcends computers, games, TV programs, T-shirts and other accessories such as caps and pencil cases (Luke, 1995).

Once again the literacy and social skills necessary to examine and accept or resist such marketing influences are more sophisticated than those previously required.

Defining multiliteracies

The changes in work, public and private lives detailed in the preceding section indicate that one set of literacy skills and one set of social skills will no longer be sufficient to participate fully in the economic, social and leisure life of the future. In our working lives we will be required to change tasks, multiskill and/or change occupations and each of these changes will require us to acquire new literacy skills and interact in different ways. Furthermore, the changing technologies of our work, public and private lives mean the acquisition of new literacy skills which will continue to change. Technology in all aspects of our lives will bring us into contact with a range of cultures and subgroups each of which may require us to use different literacy skills or ways of interacting. Finally, the availability of vast amounts of information, and the ideologies represented in it will also require new and sophisticated literacy and social skills in order to examine, accept or resist the variety of ideas presented.

Recently literacy educators have coined the term *multiliteracies* to focus on the ways in which literacy education will need to change in order to address the social diversity, technology and globalisation which are features of our new and changing world (The New London Group, 1996). The term literacy is no longer appropriate as it focuses on language alone. Multiliteracies focus on the many modes of representation and forms of text that have been made available through multimedia and technological change. Therefore being multiliterate requires not only the mastery of communication, but an ability to critically analyse a range of texts and other representational forms. It also requires the ability to engage in the social responsibilities and interactions associated with these texts.

New times and new literacies mean new goals for literacy education. The acknowledgment of change as the one constant of life in new times indicates that literacy education must focus not only on the mastery of certain knowledge and skills, but in addition, on the use of these skills in various social contexts. Furthermore literacy education will need to foster the attitudes and abilities needed to continue to master and use the evolving languages and technologies of the future. Literacy education must also focus on critical engagement and understanding of text and its inherent ideologies, in all its forms, as well as competency in creating such texts. Such competency will empower the citizens of the twenty-first century, enabling them to take more informed and critical control of their workplace, public and private lives. Literacy education in the twenty-first century might aim to inculcate the following understandings in its students:

- all texts are consciously constructed and have particular social, cultural, political and economic purposes;
- text comes in a variety of representational forms incorporating a range of grammars and semiotic systems;
- the reader/viewer may need to draw upon several grammars and semiotic systems in order to process some texts;
- changes in society and technology will continue to challenge and change texts and their representational forms;

- there may be more than one way of reading or viewing a text depending on a range of contextual (social, cultural, economic or political) factors; and
- there is a need to consider the possible meanings of a text and how it is constructing the reader and the world of the reader.

The characteristics of reading new literacies in new times

Reading is one of the literacies of new times and, as the preceding paragraphs indicate, it will require critical engagement with a range of text types, representational forms and technologies for a range of social purposes. Clearly this means that there are different ways in which a reader will practice reading and therefore different skills and knowledge needed to engage in these practices. In order to focus literacy education, and in particular the teaching of reading, on the requirements of reading in new times Freebody and Luke (1990), investigated and grouped reading practices. They concluded that at various times a reader will engage in four reading practices, mostly simultaneously, and suggest that a reader must be competent in all four practices. A model, the Four Resource Model, was developed, defining and describing each practice. It incorporates coding practice (code-breaker), semantic practice (meaning-maker), pragmatic practice (text-user) and critical practice (text-analyst). Table 6.1 presents the model and defines each area in terms of the practices a reader should be able to engage in.

Table 6.1 The Four Resource Model of reading

Coding Practices	Semantic Practices
Developing your resources as code-breaker: - How do I crack this text? - How does it work? - What are its patterns and conventions? - How do the sound and marks relate singly and in combinations?	Developing your resources as text participant: - How do the ideas represented in the text string together? - What cultural resources can be brought to bear on the text? - What are the cultural meanings and possible readings that can be constructed from this text?
Pragmatic Practices	**Critical Practices**
Developing your resources as text-user: - How do the uses of this text shape its composition? - What do I do with this text, here and now? - What will others do with it? - What are my options and alternatives?	Developing your resources as text-analyst and critic: - What kind of person, with what kind of interests and values, could both write and read this naively and unproblematically? - What is this text trying to do to me? - In whose interests? - Which positions, voices and interests are at play? - Which are silent and absent?

Based on Freebody and Luke 1990, in Luke and Freebody 1999.

Mastery of the first of these practices, coding practice (code-breaker), is particularly challenging in terms of the range of texts available in the twenty-first century. A knowledge of phonics, spelling, grammar and the left to right, top to bottom organisation of the page is inadequate given the range of textual forms the reader now encounters. Representational forms now require us to process visual images, the written word, design, and the interface of visual and linguistic meaning (oral and written) in electronic media. The reader/viewer often has to draw on a variety of resources including the grammars of various semiotic systems such as languages, film, photography and body language. Furthermore the reader/viewer may be required to bring together a range of the elements of these semiotic systems in a particular setting; for example, visual and aural in film; or visual, design, aural, symbolic, language and illustration all in one internet site. 'Cracking *the code*' (singular) is an inadequate description; the reader today must crack many different codes simultaneously.

Competence in semantic practice requires the reader to bring previous experiences with texts and life to the reading situation in order to make sense of the text at hand. Thus all prior readings of text and media and all one's social, cultural and everyday community experiences provide a knowledge resource which aid in the interpretation of the text's possible meaning.

Pragmatic practice (text-user) is essential to the reader's ability to function competently in society. The reader may be able to crack the code and even make sense of the text, but be unfamiliar with how, where and when this text might be used. For example, a reader may be able to read a menu in a restaurant but be unable to engage in the appropriate oral interaction of ordering food, which is part of reading and using a menu. Pragmatic practice also refers to the use of text for learning and then applying that learning in life.

One could suggest that a reader is competent if he or she is a successful code-breaker, text-participant and text-user. However, while these skills may enable the reader to make meaning of and use text successfully, it also means the reader is accepting the text without question. Texts are not neutral — they represent cultural, economic, social and political ideologies, attitudes and values. As such, they position the reader in particular ways and present particular readings of the world. Unquestioning acceptance of text leaves the reader powerless and vulnerable. It is essential that a competent reader learns how to interrogate text. That is, the reader should consider how he/she is being constructed in relation to the text, and think about the implications of the origins of the text, and the reason it has been written. The reader must be able to identify gaps and silences in the text as well as analyse what is present.

New literacies, new times and reading

The Four Resource Model has been discussed as a way of ensuring the teaching of reading meets the requirements of literacy education in new times with new literacies. This is further clarified in Table 6.2 which summarises how the understandings required of literacy education in the twenty-first century are realised in the four practices of reading and their associated skills, knowledge and strategies. In the column on the left are the previously presented understandings about text that a multiliterate person will need in the twenty-first century. In the column on the right are *the essential* (not *all*) reading practices required to process such understandings. For example, if a reader is to be able to read the underlying social, cultural and political purposes of a text, understand what the text's purpose is and how it is used, then the reader will need to be able to engage in pragmatic (text-user) and critical (text-analyst) practices. Clearly engaging in these practices will also require the reader's skills as code-breaker and text-meaning maker, but the most essential practices to these understandings about text are pragmatic (text-user) and critical (text-analyst) practices.

Table 6.2 Relationships among understandings about text in the twenty-first century and the Four Reading Practices

Understandings about text required in order to be multiliterate in the twenty-first century	Related reading practices*
All texts are consciously constructed and have particular social, cultural, political and economic purposes.	**Pragmatic** **Critical**
Text comes in a variety of representational forms incorporating a range of grammars and semiotic systems. The reader/viewer may need to draw upon several grammars and semiotic systems in order to process some texts.	**Coding** **Semantic**
Changes in society and technology will continue to challenge and change texts and their representational forms.	**Coding** **Semantic** **Pragmatic** **Critical**
There may be more than one way of reading or viewing a text depending on a range of contextual and other factors.	**Critical**
There is a need to consider the possible meanings of a text, how they are constructing the person themselves and the world around them in particular ways, and why this construction is being made.	**Semantic** **Critical**

*Definitions:
Coding: Texts may use various semiotic systems. Need to know how these systems work, their patterns and conventions.
Semantic: Text presents ideas. Need to be able to bring together previous experiences to make sense of the text.
Pragmatic: Text has been constructed for use and for a particular purpose. Need to know its use/purpose, how it has been specially constructed to fulfil this purpose/use, how to use it.
Critical: Texts are not neutral and have been constructed with particular ideologies. Need to be able to interrogate the text, its purpose, how it is constructing and positioning the reader and the world, its gaps and silences.

Clearly one aspect of literacy education in the twenty-first century will be the development of all four of these reading practices to enable engagement with multiliteracies (or new literacies). Interaction with texts that provide opportunity to use and develop these reading practices will be essential. While reading will often involve the use of new technologies and engagement with a variety of social contexts, it will not be possible or appropriate to base all literacy education experiences around technology. However it is important that the texts used exhibit some of the characteristics of the new literacies. For example, finding texts which encompass a variety of semiotic codes, layouts, design, and format in order to provide experience with 'cracking various codes' is essential.

Crossing the boundary: literature for literacy education

Literature has always been a site that reflects social, cultural, economic and political features of the times. It is because of these features that most children's literature is also an important site for students to engage in three of the four practices of the Four Resource Model; semantic (text-meaning), pragmatic (text-user) and critical reading (text-analyst) practice. A recent trend in picture books is the move to unusual layouts and formats and the mixture of different semiotic systems within the illustrative and written text. This trend reflects the general changes in the representational forms of text which are a feature of the twenty-first century and as a result picture books are also a suitable site for development of the fourth practice, coding practice (code-breaker). It is this practice which helps crack the code of these new and different representational forms. The recent changes in picture books have been termed postmodern and are a reflection of similar postmodern trends in other aspects of society. It follows then that postmodern picture books are a logical and important site for teaching literacies of the future, particularly, the four reading practices.

The postmodern picture book

The postmodern picture book challenges the reader with change at a number of levels. Author and illustrator have consciously employed a range of devices which are designed to interrupt reader expectation and produce multiple meanings and readings of the book. These books also challenge the traditional audience of picture books. Previously the picture book has been seen as the province of the young, inexperienced reader. However the postmodern picture book has features and readings which appeal to a much wider age group, level of sophistication and range of reading abilities.

The devices consciously employed by author and illustrator have been termed *metafictive* (Waugh, 1984; Bradford, 1993; and Grieve, 1993). They are found in the development and representation of both written and illustrative text and even in the overall design and physical construction of the book. The development of different relationships between the written and illustrative text is also an important feature of the postmodern picture book. The following devices are those most commonly found in postmodern picture books (Anstey and Bull, 2000):

- non-traditional ways of using plot, character and setting which challenge reader/viewer expectations and require different ways of reading and viewing;
- unusual uses of the narrator's voice to position the reader/viewer to read the book in particular ways and through particular character's eyes (this can be achieved by the written or visual text);

- indeterminacy in written or illustrative text, plot, character or setting which requires the reader to construct some of the text and meanings;
- a pastiche of illustrative styles which require the reader/viewer to employ a range of knowledge and grammars to read;
- change to traditional book formats with new and unusual design and layout which challenge the reader/viewer's perception of how to read a book;
- contesting discourses (between illustrative and written text) requiring the reader to consider alternate readings and meaning;
- intertextuality which requires the reader/viewer to access and use background knowledge in order to access the available meanings; and
- the availability of multiple readings and meanings for a variety of audiences.

In summary, the postmodern picture book, like many of the texts available today, looks different and is meant to be read differently. It has the potential to engage the reader in all four reading practices and therefore make an excellent site for teaching the knowledge, strategies, and skills necessary for engaging in these practices. In Table 6.3 the four reading practices have been juxtaposed with the features of postmodern picture books in order to demonstrate how postmodern picture books provide an opportunity to engage with each of the four reading practices.

Table 6.3 How postmodern picture books provide experiences with new understandings about literacy and the Four Reading Practices

Understandings about text required in order to be multiliterate in the twenty-first century	Related reading practices	Features of postmodern picture books which provide experience with these understandings*
1. All texts are consciously constructed and have particular social, cultural, political and economic purposes.	Pragmatic Critical	Conscious Construction Positioning the Reader
2. Text comes in a variety of representational forms incorporating a range of grammars and semiotic systems.	Coding Semantic	Pastiche of Illustrative Styles Unusual Formats
3. Changes in society and technology will continue to challenge and change texts and their representational forms.	Coding Semantic Pragmatic Critical	Pastiche of Illustrative Styles Unusual Formats Conscious Construction
4. There may be more than one way of reading or viewing a text depending on a range of contextual and other factors.	Critical	Positioning the Reader Indeterminacy Contesting Discourses Intertextuality Multiple Readings

Table 6.3 How postmodern picture books provide experiences with new understandings about literacy and the Four Reading Practices (continued)

5. There is a need to consider the possible meanings of a text, how they are constructing the person themselves and the world around them in particular ways, and why this construction is being made.	Semantic Critical	Positioning the Reader Indeterminacy Contesting Discourses Multiple Readings

*Definitions:
Conscious Construction: The postmodern picture book is consciously constructed to challenge and engage the reader in new and different ways.
Positioning the Reader: Unusual uses of the narrator's voice position the reader/viewer to read the book in particular ways and through a particular character's eyes (this can be achieved by the written or visual text).
Pastiche of Illustrative Styles: A pastiche of illustrative styles require the reader/viewer to employ a range of knowledge and grammars to read.
Unusual Formats: Changes to traditional book formats with new and unusual design and layout challenge the reader/viewers perception of how to read the book.
Indeterminacy: Indeterminacy in written or illustrative text, plot character or setting requires the reader to construct some of the text and meanings.
Contesting Discourses: Contesting discourses (between illustrative and written text) require the reader to consider alternate readings and meaning.
Intertextuality: Intertextuality requires the reader/viewer to access and use background knowledge in order to access the available meanings.
Multiple Readings: The availability of multiple readings and meanings for a variety of audiences.

In order to demonstrate further the utility of the postmodern picture book for developing multiliteracies and engaging in and learning about the Four Reading Practices several Australian postmodern picture books will be examined. The five understandings about the text in the twenty-first century, the relevant reading practices and the associated postmodern features identified in Table 6.3 will be used as an organising structure for discussion of how postmodern picture books facilitate learning about reading, and learning how to read. Clearly not every feature of each book can be discussed. The aim is to discuss only those features that best demonstrate the understandings about new literacies and their relevant reading practices.

Understanding one

Understandings about text required in order to be multiliterate in the twenty-first century	Related reading practices	Associated postmodern features
All texts are consciously constructed and have particular social, cultural, political and economic purposes.	Pragmatic Critical	Conscious Construction Positioning the Reader

Two books have been chosen to illustrate this understanding, the related reading practices and associated postmodern features — *Memorial* by Gary Crew and Shaun Tan (1999) and *The Rabbits* by John Marsden and Shaun Tan (1998).

There are multiple readings of both these books, but in both cases one reading may be interpreted as historical, social and political. For example, one reading of *The Rabbits* might be allegorical where it is read as a retelling of the invasion of Australia in 1788. One reading of *Memorial* is that we should fight for our beliefs and that people will remember and respect your stand even if you lose; that fighting for your beliefs is what counts. Both books therefore have been consciously constructed and have historical, social and political purposes.

In using these books as part of classroom pedagogy about literacy, *pragmatic practices (text-user)* may be encountered. Pragmatic practices are about a text's use. If the teacher asks students to engage in an allegorical reading of *The Rabbits* then it will be read as a white invasion of Australia in 1788 and is being used as a reinterpretation of Australian history. Similarly, because *Memorial* contains narrative and illustrative material about the wars in which Australia has been engaged, a teacher may encourage students to read it as a source of information on these wars and their times. Thus, these postmodern books can become sites in which pragmatic reading practices are engaged in, but only when the teacher mediates the reading. However such post-literate pedagogy (see Bull in Chapter Four) should not only *engage* students in the use of these texts as perspectives on history but demonstrate and actively teach *how* such readings can be made, what contributes to these readings, and how the reader can explore these readings' accuracy or bias.

The exploration of the accuracy or bias of the readings will engage the reader in *critical practice (text-analyst)*. Again it is essential that students explore how the different readings of these books were constructed through illustrative and written text, how they as readers came to be positioned to read these books in particular ways and whether there are alternative readings of these events. Such investigations will require the explicit teaching of

Illustration 6.1 *The Rabbits*

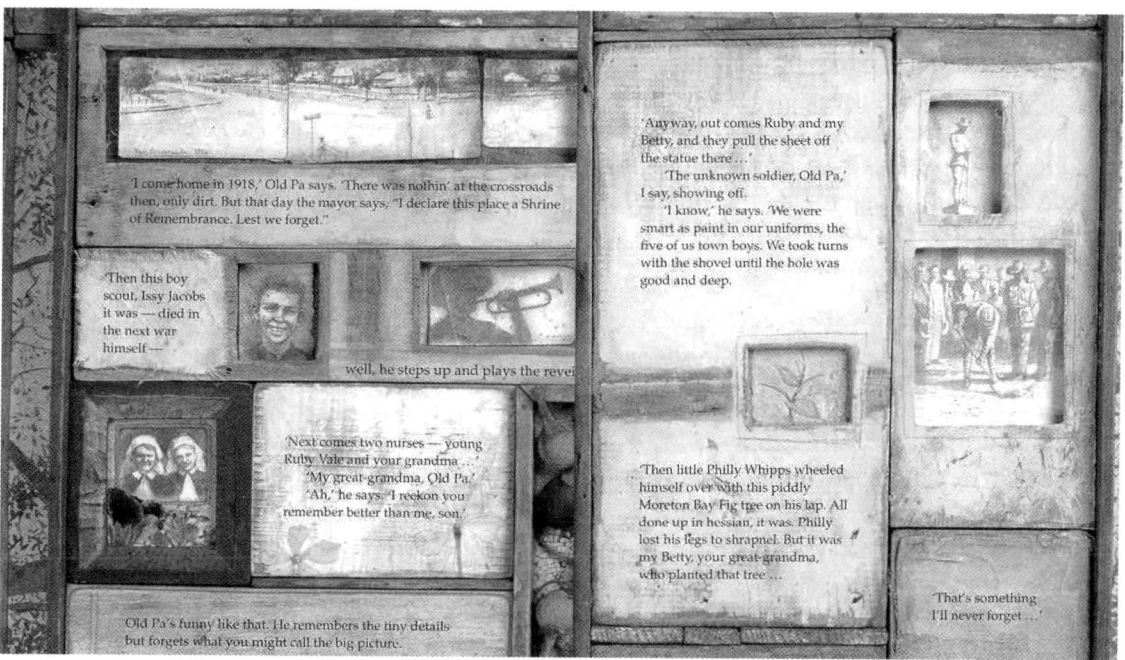

Illustration 6.2 *Memorial*

how to read illustrative text (see Anstey and Bull, 2000: Chapter 7) and the different discourses in the written text.

Both books challenge and engage the reader in new and different ways. The illustrations in *The Rabbits* provide much of the information that encourages reading it as a white invasion of Australia, for example the landscape, the animals depicted and the uniforms and mode of transport (ships) used by the rabbits (see Illustration 6.1). The reader is therefore challenged to use the illustrative text as well as the written text to access other readings of the book.

Memorial uses unusual layouts, unconventional forms of illustration, such as historical artefacts and unusual media, to engage the reader (see Illustration 6.2). Again reading both the written and illustrative text provides additional readings and meanings. For example, facsimiles of old photographs, wall paper and building materials of the times provide additional information for the reader.

The Rabbits and *Memorial* are narrated in the first person, a retelling. They position the reader on the narrator's shoulder, seeing the event through the narrator's eyes and encouraging the reader to take on the attitudes and values of the reader when viewing events in the stories. In *Memorial* the illustrative and written text seem to be told by different narrators. The written text is told by a boy talking to his Grandpa about a memorial and how his Grandpa recalls the events. The illustrative text would seem to be a visual representation of the actual fragmented memories of the Grandpa, particularly as the illustrative text consists of artefacts from those times (for example, wallpaper, fabric, tiles, window frames, photos and pressed flowers). Thus the reader can be positioned in two different ways when reading this book and view the content through two different sets of eyes. Each position will have a different focus and emphases, revealing other possible readings and meanings.

It can be seen from the above analyses that the postmodern characteristics of these two books — that is, their conscious construction, their challenges to the reader to read in different ways, and the positioning of the reader through the narrator's voice — all facilitate the development and use of pragmatic (text-user) and critical reading (text-analyst) practices.

Understanding two

Understandings about text required in order to be multiliterate in the twenty-first century	Related reading practices	Associated postmodern features
Text comes in a variety of representational forms incorporating a range of grammars and semiotic systems.	Coding Semantic	Pastiche of Illustrative Styles Unusual Formats

The book selected to illustrate this understanding, the related reading practices and associated postmodern features is *Tagged* by Gary Crew and Steven Woolman (1997). It has been chosen particularly because it demonstrates the use of a variety of representational forms within one book and therefore provides engagement with a range of grammars and semiotic systems.

Tagged is often referred to as a graphic book rather than a picture book because of its unusual style and format, mixing the genres of comic book and picture book, and in places, film and television. The integration of written and illustrative text is so complex that it is necessary to read both almost simultaneously to make meaning. There are also multiple plots in the book, real and imaginary, told in different representational forms. It is the identification of these different representational forms and the ability to read their grammar and semiotic system that enables the reader to make meaning from the illustrative and written text. The reader needs to know how these different representational forms work, how to crack their particular codes.

In the opening pages of *Tagged* a boy, Jimmy, is dreaming about fighter pilots and his dream is presented in black and white cartoons, complete with written and illustrative text (see Illustration 6.3). At the bottom of the page a colour illustration of Jimmy and his dog, Max, waking from the dream is accompanied by written text beginning the main plot. In subsequent pages the main plot shows Jimmy searching for his dog, Max, and finding a Vietnam veteran living in an abandoned building. The main plot continues to be told in colour. The layout however is not traditional, the text and illustrations are segmented across the page, outlined in black lines. The effect is of cinematic images reminiscent of the 'movietone news' reports of other wars, complete with different camera angles and close-ups. As Jimmy searches for Max he is still playing out imaginary scenes from his fighter pilot dream and these continue to be represented in black and white cartoons, interspersed among the colour images.

Illustration 6.3 *Tagged*

A third plot is introduced when Jimmy meets a Vietnam veteran and the veteran tells of his experiences in Vietnam, particularly losing his mate, Thommo. At this point the black-framed, coloured illustrations move between scenes in the building and scenes from the veteran's experiences. Their size and shape vary. Occasionally a sequence of grey and white illustrations depicting Vietnam war scenes appear. These are framed in television screens, reminding the reader that much of the Vietnam war was seen 'at home' on television. It can be seen from this brief description and perusal of Illustration 6.3 that a number of semiotic systems must be utilised when reading *Tagged*.

Having cracked the code of these various semiotic systems the reader also needs to access previous experiences and general knowledge in order to gain further meaning from the text; that is, engage in *semantic* (text-meaning) practices. For example, an adult who lived in Australia during the Vietnam War will make different meanings from the text to a teenager who has only experienced Australia's participation in Vietnam through history lessons, movies or television documentaries. Each of these readers will draw on different knowledge and experience to make meaning.

The pastiche of illustrative styles (and semiotic systems) combined with the unusual layout and format of the text in *Tagged* makes it an excellent site in which to engage in post-literate pedagogy, exploring how these systems work, what they contribute to the meanings available and identifying the knowledge and experiences which cause different readers to make different meanings.

Understanding three

Understandings about text required in order to be multiliterate in the twenty-first century	Related reading practices	Associated postmodern features
Changes in society and technology will continue to challenge and change texts and their representational forms.	Coding Semantic Pragmatic Critical	Pastiche of Illustrative Styles Unusual Formats Conscious Construction

In order to discuss this understanding, the related reading practices and associated postmodern features, we will return to *Memorial* by Gary Crew and Shaun Tan (1999). *Memorial* as a book is an example of the effects of change which have created new literacies and new times. Change in the technology of producing picture books enabled a book with illustrations incorporating such a range of materials in its illustrations (eg tiles, fabric and wood) to be printed. Similarly, change in society — that is, changes in people's perceptions of what a picture book is and its potential audience — enable such a book to be accepted and nominated for the Children's Book Council Picture Book of the Year Awards in 2000.

Memorial has previously been discussed in terms of *semantic* (text-meaning) *practices* and the possibilities for its use as *pragmatic (text-user) practice* teaching Australian history. The book also challenges the reader in terms of *coding practices* (code-breaker). Because of its unconventional layout and the use of realia or artefacts together with more conventional paint, collage and pencil, the reader needs to consider how these different media and layouts are to be read. Where should the reader first direct his or her attention, are some aspects of the text (illustrative and written) to be read first, or in a particular order? A conventional semiotic of left to right, top to bottom reading of the page does not work.

Cracking the code in this case means bringing previous experiences with other unconventional texts and media to the task in order to engage in *meaning-making practices*. Furthermore, consideration of the author's and illustrator's intent in writing *Memorial (critical practice)* may help with making meaning, and cracking the code. Because the reading of *Memorial* forces the reader to engage in at least three of the reading practices more or less simultaneously, it is an ideal site for post-literate pedagogy. Teacher and students can actually analyse how they make meaning from the text and what it was that aided the development of that meaning. This process engages students in metacognition, understanding and monitoring how they learn what they learn, or in this case how they read and made meaning of this text. Through a careful discussion and analysis of how the readings were derived and what it was in the text or in the readers' experiences which led to those meanings, students will become more self-conscious readers who can transfer and access appropriate skills and strategies with different texts and for different purposes.

Understanding four

Understandings about text required in order to be multiliterate in the twenty-first century	Related reading practices	Associated postmodern features
There may be more than one way of reading or viewing a text depending on a range of contextual and other factors.	Critical	Positioning the Reader Indeterminacy Contesting Discourses Intertextuality Multiple Readings

The book chosen to illustrate this understanding, the related reading practices and associated postmodern features is *The Watertower* by Gary Crew and Steve Woolman (1994). It is an excellent example of a text that can be read in multiple ways. These different readings are provided through various postmodern features of the text, particularly the indeterminacy of the plot, intertextuality, the contesting discourses of illustrative and written text and the unusual formatting and layout of the book. All these features invite the use of critical practice (text-analyst) in order to unlock the various meanings and consider the author's and illustrator's purposes.

The Watertower has challenged the parameters of the picture book genre, introducing science fiction to the genre, although there is no suggestion of science fiction in the written text. It is the features of the illustrative text which may cause the reader to access previous experiences with science fiction texts (books, magazines and movies) and make meanings in this way. Steven Woolman has used shape, line and colour to turn a harmless looking water

Illustration 6.4 *The Watertower*

tower into a sinister and alien spacecraft. By repeating the spiral shape of the tower steps throughout the book, Woolman has created the feel of the windows of an alien spaceship above the earth, through which the characters are being watched (see Illustration 6.4).

This atmosphere is reinforced by a strange symbol on the tower which reappears all over the town and on clothing. This symbol appears to have power over the characters in later scenes in the book, particularly the double spread featuring the people in the main street of the town (see Illustration 6.5). The people are facing the reader but their eyes are focussing on the tower with an eerie expression reminiscent of other science fiction (eg. *The Kraken Wakes* and *The Midwich Cuckoos* by John Wyndham).

In terms of literary pedagogy this book provides opportunity to explore exactly how symbolism and intertextuality work to provide other readings and meanings. It provides opportunity to examine how gaps in written text (no mention of science fiction) can be filled by illustrative text. It is important to remember however that simply reading and finding the multiple meanings in the text is not going to teach students *critical practice (text-analyst)*. It is through the examination of reading, and understanding how meaning is constructed, that aids the student in becoming a critical reader. This can only be achieved with focused discussion and analysis of reading and meaning-making processes; that is, explicit teaching practices.

The design and layout of *The Watertower* also position the reader to read in particular ways and question the usual coding practices (code-breakers) used to crack the code (left to right, top to bottom and so on). The green-black cover and background throughout the book emphasise a science fiction theme. Binding and page layout challenge the 'normal' reading of a book; that is, from top to bottom, left to right, front to back. Instead the reader must manipulate the book, turning it to read it. It is so unusual in its design that some readers actually do not know where to begin and have been known to read it backwards! Again, discussion of why the author and illustrator want the reader to read that way invites critical practice (text-analyst).

Illustration 6.5 *The Watertower*

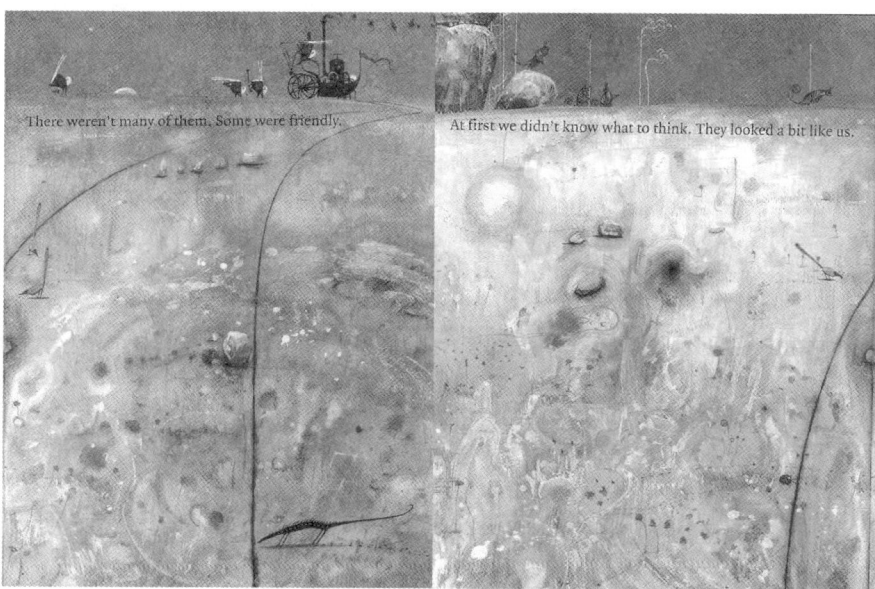

Illustration 6.6 *The Rabbits*

Understanding five

Understandings about text required in order to be multiliterate in the twenty-first century	Related reading practices	Associated postmodern features
There is a need to consider the possible meanings of a text, how they are constructing the person themselves and the world around them in particular ways, and why this construction is being made.	Semantic Critical	Positioning the Reader Indeterminacy Contesting Discourses Multiple Readings

We will return to *The Rabbits* by John Marsden and Shaun Tan in order to explore understanding five, its related practices and associated postmodern features. In order to consider the possible meanings of *The Rabbits*, how they construct particular people and events and why these constructions might be made, it is necessary to engage in all reading practices, but in particular *semantic (text-meaning)* and *critical (text-analyst) practices*. The particular postmodern features which aid the use of these practices are the narrator's position, the indeterminacy of the text, and the possibility that the illustrative and written text contest one another.

To explore semantic (text-meaning) and critical (text-analyst) reading practices it is necessary to engage in post-literate pedagogy. One way this can be accomplished is by identifying the possible meanings of *The Rabbits* and their underlying ideologies and then exploring the features of the illustrative and written text which encourage such readings. It is also necessary to consider the reader's past experiences and knowledge which combine with these features to provide particular meanings. For example, we have previously ascertained that one possible reading of *The Rabbits* is the white invasion of Australia. This reading is encouraged by the setting of the illustrative text, and portrayal of the animal characters. The setting and animals are reminiscent of Australian landscapes and native animals (see Illustration 6.6).

If the reader is also familiar with the different telling of the white settlement of Australia, told from various points of view, then interpretations of the illustrative text together with the written text and the reader's knowledge might favour this reading. Other possible readings are the actual invasion of a country by the animal, the rabbit, or the invasion of a country or planet by aliens. The first of these other possibilities might be favoured by readers who combine a reading of the landscape and animals as native Australian with a knowledge of rabbits as agricultural pests. The second possible reading might be favoured by readers who construct the landscape and characters as alien, and have a familiarity with the science fiction genre.

Regardless of the readings and meanings made, exploration of how they were achieved enables the reader to understand how indeterminacy, narrator's voice and contesting discourse of written and illustrative text contribute to meaning. Having discussed the possible meanings, the issues of intent and underlying ideology of such readings can then be explored.

Conclusion

The purpose of this chapter was to cross the boundaries between exploring literature as literature and literature as a context for teaching literacy. In doing so it was necessary to examine the world in which literacy exists and reconstruct definitions of literacy in new times. Similarly it was necessary to re-examine the postmodern picture book as a product of new times and a representation of new literacies. It was demonstrated that Freebody and Luke's Four Resource Model provides a useful framework for examining picture books and identifying opportunities to examine, learn or practice new literacies.

Above all, however, this chapter indicates that in times of change literacy must to be self-conscious. That is, the truly literate person must have the resources to consciously and constantly monitor texts and how they work to construct or represent the world.

Bibliography

Anstey, M. (2000) 'Postmodern Picture Books and New Literacies: Implications for teaching', paper presented at *Reading Pictures: Art Narrative and Childhood*, Homerton College Cambridge, United Kingdom, September 1–4.

—— (in press) 'It's not all Black and White: Postmodern Picture books and Teaching New Literacies', *Journal of Adolescent and Adult Literacy*, International Reading Association.

Anstey, M. and Bull, G. (2000) *Reading the Visual: written and illustrated children's literature*. Harcourt Australia Pty Limited, Sydney.

Bradford, C. (1993) *The Picture Book: Some postmodern tensions. Papers*, 4:4, 10–14.

Cope, B and Kalantzis, M. (1995) *Productive Diversity: Organisational life in the age of civic pluralism and total globalisation*. Harper Collins, Sydney.

Crew, G. (1994) *The Watertower* (illustrated by Steve Woolman). Era Publications, Adelaide.

—— (1997) *Tagged* (illustrated by Steven Woolman). Era Publications, Adelaide.

—— (1999) *Memorial* (illustrated by Shaun Tan). Lothian, Melbourne.

Durrant, C. and Green. B. (2000) 'Literacy and the new technologies in school education: Meeting the l(IT)eracy challenge?', *Australian Journal of Language and Literacy* vol 17 no 2, 89–108.

Freebody, P. and Luke, A.(1990) 'Literacies' programmes: Debates and demands in cultural context', *Prospect: A Journal of Australian TESOL*, 11, 7–16.

Gee, J.P. (1994) 'New alignments and old literacies: From fast capitalism to the Canon' in B. Shortland-Jones, B. Bosich and J. Rivalland (eds) *Conference papers 1994, Australian Reading Association Twentieth National Conference*, Australian Reading Association, Carlton South, 1–35.

Grieve, A. (1993) *Postmodernism in picture books. Papers*, 4:3, 15–25.

Kalantzis, M. (1995) 'The New Citizen and the New State' in W. Hudson (ed.) *Rethinking Australian Citizenship*. University of New South Wales, Sydney.

Lewis, D. (1990) 'The Constructedness of Texts: Picture books and the metafictive', *Signal*, 62, 130–46.

Lewis, D. (1992) in Dombey, H. (ed.) *Literacy for the Twenty-First Century*. University of Brighton Press, Brighton.

Luke, A. and Freebody, P. (1999) Further Notes on the Four Resource Model, http:www.readingonline.org/researchlukefrebody/html

Luke, C. (1995) 'Media and Cultural Studies', in P. Freebody, S. Muspratt and A. Luke (eds) *Constructing Critical Literacies*. Hampton Press, Crosskill, NJ.

Macaulay, D. (1990) *Black and White*. Houghton Mifflin Company, Boston.

Marsden, J. (1998) *The Rabbits* (illustrated by Shaun Tan). Lothian, Melbourne.

Piore, M. and Sable, C. (1984) *The Second Industrial Divide*. Basic Books, New York.

The New London Group (1996) 'A Pedagogy of Multiliteracies: Designing Social Futures', *Harvard Educational Review*, 66:1.

Watson, V. and Styles, M (1996) *Talking Pictures: Pictorial texts and young readers*. Hodder and Stoughton, London.

Waugh, P. (1984) *Metafiction: The theory and practice of self-conscious fiction*. Methuen, London.

Part two

Fantasy, speculative
fiction and other worlds

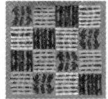

Chapter 7

Bilbo Baggins, or Lara Croft?
Writing for teens in the ruins of the post-Pentium apocalypse

Brian Caswell

All that non-fiction can do is answer questions. It's fiction's business to ask them.

Richard Hughes

Shaking the tree

Reluctant readers. The (predominantly male) victims of the post-literate video/cyberspace society … Or are they? Victims, I mean.

Much has been spoken and written in recent years on the subject of the modern child's (and especially the modern boy's) inability to 'connect' with the written word in a meaningful way. Theories abound, purporting to find reasons for this gradual degradation of our literary way of life.

In fact, there are far more theories than there are practical, meaningful solutions to the problem.

Of course, we could ask the unthinkable: Is there really such a serious crisis, or are we simply experiencing the inevitable reaction of the outdated to any rapid evolutionary process? Perhaps the reason for the growing sense of alarm and hopelessness lies, not in the failures of our children (or even our education system), but rather in the fact that those who are most worried about the problem are, in some ways, too close to it to make a balanced assessment of its real nature.

There can be no 'magic-bullet' solutions to this generation's precarious relationship to the written word, because we are not dealing with a single definable problem.

Perhaps a more effective starting point might be to shake the tree a little — to question a couple of the cherished assumptions accepted as articles of faith by the missionaries of The Universal Church of Reading.

Cherished Assumption #1

There was indeed a 'golden age' when virtually all children read widely — and devoured the classics of literature from *The Secret Garden* to *Treasure Island*, from Enid Blyton to Charlotte Bronte. When we were kids, reading held some sort of mystical position in the world of the under-eighteens. I mean, it *should* have, shouldn't it? After all, I was ten years old before my family got its first TV. What else was there to do but read, if you weren't at school?

Did such a 'golden age' ever really exist? Maybe for some, but there is certain revisionist rose-coloured hindsight at work here.

What kind of person even worries, in any more than a passing way, about *literature* as opposed to basic *literacy*? Obviously, the person to whom books are important, the person who, by choice, will curl up with the warm comfort of a novel, and escape into the world of the imagination. But what about the legions of adults whose sum total literary intake in a good week is the *Daily Telegraph* or *Who Weekly*?

The debate over child and youth literacy is carried on by interested parties, and their published perceptions of the past literary realities must be viewed with suspicion.

How many of these commentators went through school in the top English classes? I did. And if I were to base my recollections of teenage literacy in the late sixties on that experience, I would probably be horrified at the current state of play. But I don't.

I don't, because although I was always top in English, and although I devoured four or five books a week, I also played in the soccer and basketball teams — at school and on the weekend. More than half my friends at South Sydney Boys' High were not from the rarefied heights of the 'A' stream — or even the 'C' stream — and none of *them* ever read anything. Not even the set texts.

To compare today's 'average' reading levels — so beloved of statisticians, politicians and newspaper commentators — with such a flawed vision of past glories is to invite depression.

I will believe that there is a real and demonstrable decline in across-the-board literacy standards, when those who believe in the 'objectiveness' of 'objective' tests administer those same tests to the parents of their victims. I wonder how *they* would fare.

Cherished Assumption #2

There is some intrinsic value in the very act of reading that somehow magically transforms the reader.

I'm sorry, but there is nothing magical about the act of reading. At heart it is a decoding skill, which some people pick up more readily than others.

Which is not to say that it cannot be more — much more — that it cannot open up new worlds of understanding and insight into the human condition, that a book cannot change forever the way an individual sees him or herself. It is just not inevitably the case.

And we need to be open to it. Literature has only ever spoken to the reader who comes to it hungry.

Please remember, I write as one who lives for language, who has built a life on trying to encourage the young to choose books over other pursuits, because I know the thrill of discovery, the total immersion that only happens when you connect on a visceral level with the world created between the pages. Even so, a deep and abiding passion for reading should not blind us to the fact that it is not the same (has never been, and will never be) for a large percentage of the population. That true, devoted readership has always been — and probably always will be — a minority obsession.

So, are the doomsayers' predictions true? Are our children turning into illiterate and monosyllabic post-literate techno-junkies, incapable of appreciating the wonders of the written word? Is the book already an archaic artefact, ridiculously out of place in these days of microchips and macro-networks? Has the revolution rolled on and left it floating forlornly in some small literary backwater that is already doomed to slow stagnation?

I think not. In fact, I believe that there is still a role — and a vital one at that — for written literature in the lives of our youth.

In the process of examining this belief, I may provide some incidental insight into how this writer for young people approaches the somewhat daunting task of writing serious teenage literature, in a post-Pentium world ruled by Bill Gates, Rupert Murdoch, the movers and shakers at Dreamworks — and, of course, that digitally enhanced paragon of assertive femininity, Ms Lara Croft.

The literary continuum — fiction and context

Perhaps it was the historian in me, perhaps it was a legacy of my youthful obsession with mythology and legends, science fiction and fantasy, but since I began writing for young adults (around 1986) I have tried to create stories that contextualise current social structures and problems, by drawing on historical or legendary examples, or by projecting contemporary trends forward to their logical conclusions.

Often, I will attempt both in the same story. A novel that looks to the past and the future is more likely to be able to create a sense of continuity, an environment in which the reader can make some sense of the frustration he or she might be feeling.

Science fiction, fantasy, speculative fiction — call it what you will — allows us to move outside ourselves and outside our society, with its prejudices, its habits of thought and behaviour, and its straitjacketed, politically correct (or incorrect) definitions of truth, to look back at ourselves and all that we accept as inevitable.

More effectively than all the graphic-realist, tell-it-as-it-is-warts-and-all-and-don't-spare-the-feeble-hearted novels you can name, a well-structured piece of speculative fiction can force us to think about issues and about history, precisely because it *is* outside of accepted truth and reality.

Intuitively, we 'know' that what we are reading is a fictional construct. We know, but in order to experience the world that the writer's imagination has created, we make a contract to suspend our disbelief, as the writer takes sometimes huge creative leaps in areas such as social structures, mores, basic physics, biology or history — or even magic and the paranormal.

But (and herein lies the power of speculative fiction with a socio/political bent), in accepting this newly coined reality, we discard our preconceptions, even our socialisation, so we are able to look at contemporary issues with new unblinkered eyes, to ask the unaskable question, to reach the 'unreasonable' conclusion. To see beyond our personal conditioning to the kernel of truth — about ourselves and our world — that social realism often keeps us too close to focus upon.

Removing issues from their contemporary context often enables the reader to consider the wider implications — and to do so in an environment freed from the particular prejudices and 'politically correct' considerations of a story set exclusively in the 'here and now'.

Humankind is the only animal that finds itself equally at home in the present, the past or the future, and I believe that this is because we already spend so much of our time locked inside that part of us which might best be described as 'imaginary'.

Even our present is, to a substantial extent, 'imaginary' — events and stimuli, interpreted through the filter of our own peculiar consciousness.

Am I a predominantly visual learner, or is my preference for the auditory, the kinaesthetic or the audio-digital? The answer to this question may well determine what I notice and what I discard from the two million bits of sensory information which I absorb every second.

No two individuals see exactly the same things when sharing an experience. Nor do we feel the same things, gain the same understandings, react in the same ways.

Which suggests that the 'reality' of my personal present is, to a greater or lesser extent, a fiction to anyone not living inside my head. And if that is the case, then how much more of a fiction is the past — my own, or that belonging to the memories of my ancestors?

It is said that history is written by the victors. To Henry Ford, history was 'bunk'. Herodotus, the father of history as we know it, shares the title (with Satan, I believe) as the 'Father of Lies'. Which is to suggest that somewhere there is an intrinsic 'truth' about any event. One single uncorrupted version of the way the world was/is that the historian consciously or unconsciously distorts. Perhaps there is, but if no-one but God can ever access it, and God isn't letting on, then its existence is at best academic.

Of course, for me, history was never really about unearthing the absolute truth. It was always about understanding — people, morality, the world … Just understanding.

Which is why, when I began teaching history, the first thing I realised was that you don't just teach dead 'facts'. A date is meaningless, a list of monarchs and dynasties says nothing. History is simply a way of understanding — yourself, your place in the world, your fellow humans. It involves imagination, empathy and creativity — and the realisation that in a very real way it is — must be — a fiction, a story created around a skeleton of commonly agreed (or contested) 'facts'.

Which is not in any way a criticism. In the end, fiction, imagination, the ability to look beyond ourselves, is what makes us human.

I am a fiction writer, and for me, there is no distinction in the context of a story, between the present, past or future, the 'real' or the 'created'.

Fiction is fiction, and for me, it serves the same purpose as history. It feeds my passion to understand, and to examine what it is that I believe about the world and being human, and if that means delving into the past, or creating a future history — or creating a future history from events of the present and past, then so be it.

For the epigraph to my 1995 novel, *Deucalion*, I borrowed the wisdom of George Santayana, who said, 'Those who cannot remember the past, are doomed to repeat it'.

Deucalion is set three hundred years in the future, but it is about a post-colonial society coming of age, and learning to deal with its past, its future, its prejudices and the particular rights of the vital culture it dispossessed and almost destroyed.

It is not about Australia at the turn of the twenty-first century, but in a sense, it seeks to contextualise some of the broader issues of our current society, by using the future as a mirror to reflect both the past and the present.

It might be termed 'allegorical future history', because it places the events of the novel's futuristic 'present' against the background of an imaginary historical context — which in turn suggests an actual historical context, with which we are intimately familiar.

On reading the novel you will see, in the legend of the Elokoi heroine Gaita and in the story of Saebi, strong parallels to the Old Testament stories of Joseph and Moses (the former bringing his people from famine to the relative safety of Egypt, the latter challenging the doomed Pharaoh, then leading his people into the wilderness and onward to the Promised Land). You might also have noticed that the map of the Inland Sea, which borders the Elokoi's 'Promised Land' of Vaana, bears a striking resemblance to a map of Israel, or that the east coast of the continent is made up of segments of coastline from most of the colonised continents on Earth — including Australia.

Or maybe you didn't …

The map is a small, self-indulgent visual allusion, but I think it symbolises quite well the allegorical processes at work in the construction of both the plot and the imaginary history of Deucalion the planet.

The View From Ararat — the sequel to *Deucalion* — examines the same society in a time of grave crisis a century later, and is in part a study of the nature of civilisation, asking the question: 'How deeply ingrained is civilised behaviour, and how much is our adherence to "the rules" dictated by the power of society to sanction and enforce its standards of "civilised" behaviour?'

Of course, the answer is very different for different individuals, but a quick glance at recent history — Hitler's Germany, Pinochet's Chile, Pol Pot's Cambodia, the genocide in Bosnia, Kosovo and the countries of West Africa — is less than encouraging.

On Deucalion, the range of human responses to the novel's crisis is huge, from the most selfish to the most self-sacrificing. Which makes this planet — far away in space and time — very Earth-like.

One of the main narrators of *Ararat* is Natassia — who is, in fact, an historian, in a family positively saturated with them. Very early in the novel, as she awaits her first experience of an Elokoi Telling — which is that race's communally (telepathically) shared history — she discusses the value of her role as chronicler of the world-changing events through which she has lived, when she writes:

> And so I await tonight's Telling with mixed emotions.
> Will words ever be quite enough again?
> It's not such an idle question, when you consider exactly what tonight promises.
> Or what it commemorates.
> The Crystal Death.
> The Creeping Apocalypse.
> The End — and the Beginning.

For ten years, I have lived with it, turned it over and around, tried to come to terms with the enormity of it. I have even used my precious words to write a book about it. To try and make some sense of it.

But I know, in my heart, that there are depths I do not have the words to show. For if ever a story needed more than words, this is that story.

It is in the nature of words to make connections. It is in the nature of a story to find its own voice.

But when we die — we who lived it, we who ultimately survived — who will really remember? For all the volumes written, all the minutely researched accounts of events. Deep down at the core of their understanding, who will know?

The terror of the riots. The staring eyes of a dying child. The smell of death. The racing of the pulse.

The overwhelming fear.

Who will even remember how it all began?

(*The View from Ararat*, pp. 5–6)

With those words, Natassia touches on the dilemma of the historian. Knowing is not understanding. 'Facts' are not truth. Perhaps one key role of fiction today is to create a resonance that provides an emotional context in which to interpret historical events.

This understanding forms part of the subtext of both *Deucalion* and *The View from Ararat* and for the final book in the trilogy, *The Dreams of the Chosen* (still, at the time of writing, a 'work in progress').

In a very real sense, all fiction — even so-called 'realism' — is, at its deepest level, allegorical in nature. For what is fiction if not an author's re-interpretation of reality through the lens of imagination? No story — even in the areas of science fiction or fantasy — can hope to move the reader, unless it draws on recognisable archetypes or shared experiences.

The universal 'what if … ?', the source of all story, is a question based firmly in the context of the present. It is the author's act of will (or Act of God, if you prefer), drawing on a shared understanding of what is — and what has been — and moving wilfully beyond it into a created reality. But no fiction can exist without a consciousness — on the part of both the writer and the reader — of the reality that it seeks to alter.

Stendhal alluded to this, when he described the novel as 'a mirror carried along a main road'.

For me, history and the future are all the stuff of fiction. And fiction serves, in part at least, to remind us that we are not alone. That our present is merely a step along the journey from the past to the future, that the problems besetting us are universal problems, and that there have always been solutions, which human beings have always shared.

In a world obsessed with the all-consuming here-and-now, where yesterday's news is tomorrow's landfill, and history doesn't earn enough university-entrance 'brownie points', we are in danger of losing our connection with the human continuum that earlier cultures celebrated in song and story. Our notion of history resembles, at best, picture postcards of the good bits, and at worst, *Bill and Ted's Excellent Adventure*.

But Santayana reminds us that to forget the hard-won lessons is to be condemned to repeat the mistakes of the past.

Adrift on an ocean of unbelonging

The tragedy for many in the 'global village' created by the ongoing communications revolution is that, for all the access we have to the different world cultures, and to the billions of human beings on this planet, too many of us — and far too many of our youth — feel alienated and disenfranchised.

The global scale is simply too vast. Problems seem unsolvable, barriers unscaleable, disempowerment all but complete.

And this is not limited to the cynical street kid or the social outcast. For a real wake-up call, take a look at the demographic statistics on youth suicide.

Alienation, disempowerment, cynicism.

Punks, Goths, Sk8 Fanatics.

Ecstasy, rave parties, graffiti and street-crime.

It all sounds like an editorial from the *Daily Tabloid* — except that some of the words have too many syllables.

Partly, it is a consequence of the breakdown of social institutions like the extended family, or even the church.

Partly, it is a malaise brought on by the overwhelming negativity of the mass media, an environment in which bad news for individuals translates into excellent news for ratings. A society where violence sells more movie tickets and videos than mere adventure, and 1930s style racism and preference swaps win enough electoral votes to manufacture a 'mandate' to tax the poor. Where the politicians and big business worship the bottom-line and 'rationalise' the social consequences, by finding ways to blame the victims.

Partly, it is due to the competitive ethic, which divides us as we strive for success, and stresses the results of failure in terms of our relative inability to possess what 'every successful person' must have.

But most importantly, it is due to a widespread feeling of isolation. Of being alone and insignificant in the unimaginably vast ocean of global humanity.

For some adolescents, adrift on such an ocean, the questions circle like sharks. How can one single, insignificant person possibly make a difference? How can I even find a meaningful way to belong? How can I fit the image, if I can't fit into a size six?

Literature can help reduce that sense of unbelonging. The intensity of identification experienced in reading is far higher than that achieved in 'viewing'. We can empathise. We can relate. As readers, we can — we *must* — place ourselves within the flow of story, instead of allowing it merely to wash over us, because the act of reading demands the conscious involvement of the reader's imagination.

In film and on TV, the illusion of reality is created for us on the set, or in the SPFX departments of Dreamworks or Industrial Light and Magic, but no written story can come to life for us until we become co-creators of the narrative, and it is this cooperation, this 'intensity of identification', which defines the reading experience.

The problem with many of the recent 'graphic realist' offerings — too often masquerading as teenage fiction — is that they use the inherent power of this experience to present — and reinforce — the inexorably isolated individual, the dysfunctional as the norm.

The characters in these stories are cut off from the flow of history; 'decontextualised', if you will. Many are stories without hope, disempowering the reader through a reinforcement of the negative stereotypes promulgated in the media. There are no solutions, because the protagonists are trapped — like the teen who suicides — in a negative context, without access to alternative realities.

Excised from the collective unconscious, these characters are soulless. And so are their stories.

Want to be a hit in the genre? It isn't all that difficult.

First, take a character (preferably teenaged), place him/her into a dysfunctional (preferably single-parent) family and surround him/her with an equally dysfunctional peer group (also with totally ineffectual adult role models). Now you have successfully removed all of the traditional support mechanisms (which, amazing as it may seem, do actually still exist in society).

Once you have totally isolated your character, start piling on the problems. With no coping strategies, and no-one to model them, your character will tragically (inevitably) fail to cope, and you can have your teen audience — and some of their slightly older gatekeepers — reaching for the tissues.

Your publisher's publicity department, smelling sales (and hopefully a Children's Book Council Award short-listing), cranks up its 'this-is-gritty-realism-that-all-teenagers-need-to-know-about' publicity spiel, developed for the five or six 'wrist-slashers' they published last year.

The publicist's pitch might work as a spin-doctor's apology for this particular form of 'negativity-profiteering', but it begs the question: If you claim to write for young adults, does that not pre-suppose a difference between the *young* adult and the *adult* adult? In which case, what is that difference?

In most cases, it is not the ability to deal with complex prose. In spite of the flood of propaganda to the contrary, I have yet to be convinced that today's youth are significantly worse readers than their counterparts in previous generations.

For me, the difference is that the young adult is a person who is still developing a world-view, still asking the questions, and looking for answers to the complex riddle of belonging to the human race. If you choose to write for this readership then, ethically, this factor must be taken into consideration.

Today's teens exist in an environment that is already steeped in negativity. Surely the role of teenage fiction should be not to ignore the problems and present an unrealistically positive view of the world, but rather to present a balanced response to human experience.

To try, today, to avoid the seamier aspects of existence is naive. Negativity is the 'ether' through which the mass media transmit themselves, and no writer of fiction can simply ignore such a pervasive element of the prevailing society. In my own writing, my characters have faced death, betrayal, political and economic immorality, sexual identity crises, drug problems and some ethical dilemmas that would challenge Solomon.

However, what I have always tried to do in my novels is to place individuals into situations that demand decisions — choices which test their ethical, moral, intellectual, emotional and physical limits. And I have attempted to show that human beings are capable of an incredible *range* of responses — from the most selfish and destructive, to the most altruistic and self-sacrificing.

The actions of the characters and the results of those actions are not black and white, good and bad; they are human — fallible, cowardly, heroic, vindictive, warm, cynical, loving, destructive and magnificent — just as they are in real life.

When writing for today's youth, it is not simply a matter of avoiding the hard issues, but rather of showing that, as human beings, we have a range of responses available to us — both positive and negative. A novel or short story can reveal — more efficiently than a 30 second news-grab, and more completely than a Hollywood movie — that while we may not have the power to alter the momentum of events on a global scale, we can develop strategies which work on the local scale — for ourselves, for our family and friends, for our community.

In spite of the pressures alluded to above, and in spite of the growing influence of the media's negative bias, the vast majority of teenagers still cope, still lead full and fulfilling lives. In general, most are no more depressed or dysfunctional than they were in my day — or in my mother's, for that matter. But increasing the negative pressure incrementally, especially in a medium as intensely interactive as the novel, is doing a major disservice to the readership.

In this context, I would add that this misguided notion of 'bibliotherapy' totally fails those individuals with the problems depicted in the stories, because generally they are not the ones reading the books. Bad news sells newspapers, vicarious tragedy sells novels — and the bottom line looks good to the bean counters.

I realise that, at this moment, I am in danger of sounding like an out-of-touch wowser, and an advocate of reactionary censorship, but those who know me know that I am neither.

I was thinking about how to rebut that particular accusation a couple of nights ago, while I was watching *Fight Club* (1999) with my 17 year-old twins, and I realised that it isn't the subject-matter that is the issue. Rather, it is how it is treated — and discussed.

In two hours of screen time, *Fight Club* contains more violence and social dysfunction than a whole shelf full of teen-realism tomes. The difference is, I can sit down with my boys, and watch it — and discuss what we saw.

Besides, the violence depicted borders on caricature, and in spite of the valiant attempts of the director and the actors, it is all happening 'over there' on the screen — not inside their heads.

The very power and intensity of the identification I alluded to earlier, makes the same actions and thought processes far more affecting when written into a novel. And, of course, reading is a more private pursuit. It is not nearly as easy to discuss with a teenager the book he or she has just finished reading, as it is to deal with the techniques and superficialities of even an MA or R-rated film.

So, for me, the superficial allure of 'graphic realism' is not the ideal answer to creating readers in the age of the world wide web. However, the real danger with this approach to youth literature is that it has a surface appeal — and not only for teenagers.

For those among us who believe that, in the face of competition from the electronic media and the ubiquitous PC, we must get the kids reading 'at any cost', the temptation is to say (as the Children's Book Council did in the slogan for their first National Conference) 'at least they're reading'. I didn't agree with the statement in 1991, and I believe it even less now.

Soldiers in the literary rearguard

So, how *do* we prepare to do battle with the Gigabyte monster? How do we keep our young people reading in the face of insurmountable odds?

In a sense, even though the Net was only embryonic at the time, it was that exact question which led me to begin writing for teenagers in the first place.

I came to writing from teaching, and like many teachers, I spent most of my teaching career, from 1976 to 1991 (and particularly the second half of that time) fighting the attempts of the New Right rationalists and industry to hijack the education system and convert our schools from educational institutions into vocational training centres.

I argued long and hard that my role was to try to produce rounded human beings, not channelled automatons, pre-programmed for jobs, which might or might not be in existence in 10 or 20 years time.

That battle has become (to a great extent) a rearguard action, and in spite of the 'positive-spin' political rhetoric being trumpeted about 'key learning areas', the reality is that the Arts and the Humanities have been consigned to the backwaters of the curriculum, in favour of more 'practical' subjects and a higher TER (or whatever is the current acrostic).

Of course, training is not learning, and there is a huge, hidden danger in this promotion of 'channelling' among our youth. Without a 'rounded' world-view, it is too easy to lose context. Without an historical sense of connection to the past — to things outside their own immediate experience — their problems and frustration become almost meaningless.

As a high school English teacher, I faced the constant challenge of finding books to which my charges would respond without the usual litany of, 'This is boooring', or 'This sucks. Majorly'. Or, as was more often the case, the challenge of turning those responses into, 'It didn't suck too badly, considering …'.

Considering what? That it was a book? That there was no video to cheat from?

I loved teaching. It was all I had ever wanted to do, but by the mid 1980s, after a decade of 60 hour weeks, I was reaching my use-by date as a teacher — a process accelerated by the constant attrition of politics and New Right interference in my chosen profession.

I awoke one morning at about 1 a.m. (which is the time I always do my best work) with the decision already made. What I really wanted to do was find a way of creating the books that I, as a teacher, was always looking for. Books that were challenging, relevant, non-patronising and 'didn't suck too badly, considering …'.

So I began.

I had chosen as my audience, a young adult readership. I wanted to write for that large group of readers who were technically capable of reading adult fiction, but whose emotional development was perhaps not ready for the themes presented in such books. I wanted to extend them. I wanted to write books that were demanding, both technically and philosophically, but not remote.

I never did accept the myth that today's teenagers are substantially less literate than we were at their age. There are more demands on their time, certainly, they do show a disturbing tendency to do 47 things at the same time and their reading habits are different. However, on average, their technical ability to read is, I believe, nowhere near as bad as the newspapers would have us believe.

Of course this does not mean that they are as likely to read — by choice — at the same rate as most people reading these words did at their age. The competition for their time is intense, and there is, of course, the omnipresent lure of the electronic; the TV, the PC, the Playstation, the Nintendo 64.

Games like *Tomb Raider*, *Carmageddon*, *Tekkan 3*, *Street Fighter*, *Mortal Kombat* and *Perfect Dark* or any of the myriad driving games, provide action, competition and an overload of sensory stimulation. They are physically, if not mentally, interactive and, as one of my sons' game-playing friends informed me recently, they relieve stress better than … well, almost anything else.

They also consume a significant amount of time.

Characters like Sagat, Vega, Screwy Louie, Sub-Zero, Max Damage, Kuma the Bear and Joanna Dark may not be three-dimensional in the traditional literary sense, but their 3-D graphics are 'awesome'. With gaming, action replaces narrative and instant gratification substitutes for the deeper insight gleaned from the interaction of carefully rounded characters.

The Hobbit, *A Wizard of Earthsea*, *Obernewtyn*, *The Dark is Rising* … so many of our favourite works of juvenile fiction offer worlds far more complete and intricately realised than the shallow electronic environments of the games, and characters like Bilbo Baggins, Ged the Sparrowhawk, Elspeth or Merriman have the potential to leap vividly to life in the reader's imagination, but it is a challenge to make them accessible. To break through the barrier of 'the immediate' — to defer the gratification for a fuller and more satisfying result.

Breaching that barrier was a challenge I undertook when I chose my readership. By surveying teens — what they were reading, watching, experiencing; where their interests lay; what 'turned them on or off' in relation to reading — I began to realise that the problem was not one of content, but rather, of narrative style.

Given the influences at work, I developed a theory of narrative aimed specifically at the 'post-Spielberg readership' — whose primary source of story was not the traditional book.

I had chosen to write for teenagers, which meant that my entire readership was born after *Jaws*, *Star Wars* and *E.T.* were made — after the wizards at Industrial Light and Magic and Dolby had transformed forever the visual and audio 'reality' of the film (and later, the TV) universe.

The slogan for the first of the Christopher Reeve *Superman* movies (1978) proclaimed, 'You will believe that a man can fly'. How tame that seemed only a few years later, after we were blown away by the computer-generated mega-storms in *Twister* (1996), after *Jurassic Park* (1993) had brought dinosaurs to life before our eyes, using digital effects to achieve what cloning has not yet managed, after we cringed beneath the city-sized invading spaceships of *Independence Day* (1996).

The predominant sources of story available to the modern adolescent are electronic and visual. Different studies will give different results for the exact amount of time that a modern child spends in front of the TV or the PC, but all agree that it is substantial. It is inevitable, therefore, that the perception of narrative of the 'post-Spielberg generation' is moulded by their experience.

A film is concerned with action — not introspection. It relies on economy of dialogue and makes the most of what might be called the 'lamination' technique — achieving revelation through the sequential 'laying-down' of scenes or images.

More even than in a novel, there is a focus on plot structure.

Beginning with *Merryll of the Stones* (1989) and the short stories in *A Dream of Stars* (1991), then the novel *A Cage of Butterflies* (1992), I started developing a kind of 'cinematic narrative'. I had always been interested in film, and the way movies constructed story, and I believed that I could adapt some of the narrative techniques from film to novel, while still maintaining the essential literary elements, which make reading an infinitely more demanding and interactive experience than mere viewing.

It was never my aim to write screenplays in novel form. I firmly believe that the gravest crime we can commit against our youth is to underestimate their abilities — to write down to them. My novels for the young adult readership are technically demanding, and work (hopefully) on a number of levels — including the allegorical. They demand a recognition of the moral and ethical dilemmas of living at the turn of the twenty-first century, and attempt to provide a cultural continuum within which to place the decisions of the protagonists.

By choosing a narrative technique that closely mirrors the techniques to which they are accustomed, I am beginning at a point which is, I believe, relevant to my readership. From there, I can lead them to consider issues and ideas which the modern media often skirt as 'too difficult' — or 'too uncommercial'.

Dreamslip (1994), as well as presenting a futuristic post-economic-rationalist apocalypse, places its protagonists — physically — into the continuum of human existence, from the earliest pre-history to the future.

In *Asturias* (1996), the parallel stories examine the relationship that exists in society between art and power. In the modern-day music industry, the power is money, the driving philosophy materialism. During the Spanish Civil War, military and political power holds sway, and the young resistance fighters battle a totalitarian regime which almost destroys them. In both stories, the creative side of human nature is represented by music, and the guitars of Ardillo and Alex are the weapons which eventually win a victory for the artistic regions of the soul.

The dream which drives the Vo family in *Only the Heart* (Caswell and Chiem, 1997) is the dream of freedom. It is a novel about choice and the sacrifices that people will make in pursuit of a future for their children. It is the story of the migrant and the refugee, and looks at how the dream can change even as it is achieved.

The story of 'think tank' kids and the Babies in *A Cage of Butterflies* examines the twin questions: How do people treat you if you are different? and How different do you have to be before people stop treating you as human?

Being different, the politics of prejudice, the power of money, our place in our world and in history — these are some of the themes I have tried to examine in my work so far. They raise questions that are, I believe, important and relevant for today's youth — and they are not easy questions.

Literature, if it can be kept relevant, if its voice is one that speaks to today's and tomorrow's generations, can raise all kinds of essential questions. And as Richard Hughes points out, that has always been fiction's role.

Of course, all this is just one writer's journey. There are as many ways of catering for today's emerging readers as there are authors, and Australia has a dazzling variety of writers for young people.

From the visionary writing of Isobelle Carmody and Victor Kelleher, to the irreverent comedy of Paul Jennings, Morris Gleitzman, Andy Griffiths and John Larkin, from the pure insight of Libby Gleeson and David Metzenthen, to the compulsive excitement of John Marsden's *Tomorrow* series, and the lyrical embodiment of the teen culture as depicted by Glyn Parry, the list goes on.

Every author finds his or her unique way of making the written world relevant to a generation weaned on the flickering of video images. Never has the feast been more varied or sumptuous. And in the end, it is this variety that provides the best weapon in the battle against the electronic enemy.

Remember, it is a battle for the most precious commodity in a young person's life — time. With so many demands, with so many alternative activities, there has to be a reason to invest valuable hours in a book, but match the book to the reader, and you create an experience that becomes a habit.

Every addict starts with a first fix. Every reader starts with a first book.

In the process however, it is essential not to underestimate young readers — and not to confuse issues of 'literacy' with developing a love of reading. Any education system that can refer to novel or poetry as a 'text-type' has some severe soul-searching to do.

I always believed that if I could teach a child to love reading and writing — to become immersed in the magic of words on paper — then the rest would fall into place. You can teach students to 'do' comprehension tests, or you can teach them to comprehend.

Achieve the former, and you create a robot, a clone, factory-fodder. Achieve the latter, and you open up the universe of the imagination — and the student will still be able to do a comprehension test.

Find the right book, and you can achieve miracles.

Perhaps *The Hobbit* (1998) is just the book to win your able, but reluctant, reader away from the simplistic interactivity of *Tomb Raider* or the cartoon mayhem of *Carmageddon*. Perhaps your secret weapon is a John Marsden or a Paul Jennings or the cyber-world of Michael Pryor's *Mask of Caliban* (1996). Only time, and perseverance, will tell.

Just keep telling yourself that all is not lost. Lara Croft may well have digitally enhanced attributes, which your teenage boy will pretend not to notice all that much, except in private conversations with his friends. She may represent every girl's assertive alter-ego, battling the ghouls and the slavering wolves with cool and ruthless precision, but her conversation is somewhat restricted, and her range of responses is severely constrained by the limitations of the technology.

You can only swim so many rivers, climb so many obstacles and kill so many creatures, before the lack of coherent narrative begins to take its toll.

Bilbo on the other hand is a whole lot less attractive — what with all that hair between his toes, and his vertically challenged physique — but what he lacks in digital enhancement, he more than makes up for in charm and narrative drive. And the dragon Smaug has more personality in one of his scales, than all the mindless creatures that sexy Lara ever blasted to a bloody pulp.

Reading might never assume the importance in the lives of many of our children that it did for us — long, long ago, in a universe far, far away, in the time before *Star Wars* and the world wide web — but we can still create readers. When we have, we can definitely provide them with stories that will keep them reading. Along with the 47 or so other things they just have to do simultaneously.

Further reading

Australia boasts an amazing array of writing talent for the young adult. Below is a list of some of the more prominent names of recent years. I have chosen writers specifically for their ability to connect with teen readers today and inform, amuse or challenge them. Their approaches are varied and they provide reading for every mood and purpose. They are the new priests and priestesses of the Universal Church of Reading (Reformed):

Allan Baillie; Ian Bone; Isobelle Carmody; Judith Clarke; Gary Crew; Simon French; Libby Gleeson; Morris Gleitzman; Andy Griffith; Sonya Hartnett; Libby Hathorn; Paul Jennings; Catherine Jinks; Victor Kelleher; Robin Klein; Melina Marchetta; John Marsden; David Metzenthen; Garth Nix; Glyn Parry; Michael Pryor; Gillian Rubinstein; Marcus Zuzak.

Of course, this list is neither complete, nor particularly scientific. It contains the names of Australian authors whose voices and styles, I believe, speak to today's teenaged readers. For thorough and far more detailed analyses of modern books for teens, and for a variety of views on teen and young adult fiction, you would be well served to consult the following books:

Matthews, S. (1998) *The Eye of the Soul*. Magpies, Brisbane.

Moloney, J (2000) *Boys and Books*. ABC Books, Sydney.

Nieuwenhuizen, A. (1992) *Good Books for Teenagers*. Mandarin, Melbourne.

—— (1995) *More Good Books for Teenagers*. Mandarin, Melbourne.

—— (1994) (ed.) *The Written World (Youth and Literature)*. D.W. Thorpe, Melbourne.

White, K. (1994) *Australian Children's Fiction (The Subject Guide)*. Jacaranda Wiley (updated 1996), Brisbane.

Bibliography

Carmody, I. (1987) *Obernewtyn*. Penguin Books, Melbourne..

Caswell, B. (1989) *Merryll of the Stones*. University of Queensland Press (UQP), Queensland.

—— (1991) *A Dream of Stars*. UQP.

—— (1992) *A Cage of Butterflies*. UQP.

—— (1994) *Dreamslip*. UQP.

—— (1995) *Deucalion*. UQP.

—— (1996) *Asturias*. UQP.

—— (1999) *The View from Ararat*. UQP.

Caswell, B. and Chiem, D. (1997) *Only the Heart*. UQP.

Cooper, S. (1976) *The Dark is Rising*. Puffin Books, London.

Fight Club (motion picture) (1999) Twentieth Century Fox.
Independence Day (motion picture) (1996) Twentieth Century Fox.
Jurassic Park (motion picture) (1993) Universal Pictures.
Le Guin, U. (1973) *A Wizard of Earthsea*. Victor Gollantz, London.
Pryor, M. (1996) *The Mask of Caliban*. Hodder Headline, Sydney.
Superman (motion picture) (1978) Warner Bros.
Tolkien, J.R.R. (1998) *The Hobbit*. Harper Collins, London.
Twister (motion picture) (1996) Universal Pictures.

Chapter 8

Looking for action — women in young adult fantasy

Sue Page

Introduction

'Seek and ye shall find' is one of the implicit promises of high fantasy — but not one that is necessarily true when it comes to finding multi-faceted female protagonists. The hero's journey too often sees female protagonists as passengers, not drivers. This chapter examines some of the possible reasons, and highlights psychological theories of adolescent self-concept that demonstrate why it is important to address the issue. The use of archetypes in fleshing out fantasy characters to make them more credible, less predictable and more interesting is one recommended approach.

Fortunately, increasing numbers of authors are reconstructing female heroes, and providing central, multi-dimensional female characters who act as catalysts for the novel's action. Among the fantasy writers who, I believe, are leading the way are Garth Nix with *Sabriel* (1995); Isobelle Carmody with *Darkfall* (1997) and the *Obernewtyn* series (1987, 1990, 1995, 1999); Sophie Masson's *The Gifting* (1996) and *Red City* (1998); Sally Odgers' *Translations in Celadon* (1998); and David McRobbie's *Mandragora* (1991).

The use of different interpretations of this literature can help reveal the strengths and possibilities offered by a multi-dimensional protagonist. To demonstrate the benefits of the multiple readings approach, I undertake two interpretations of one novel, with suggestions for others.

But first, given the range and variety of novels published under the term 'fantasy', it was necessary to limit this chapter. The books I am looking at are:

* those marketed primarily for readers twelve to sixteen years of age;
* written by Australian authors;
* published within the last ten to fifteen years and, most importantly,
* those novels which contain the characteristics of 'high fantasy': a quest motif, a mythological structure, and a secondary world setting (either open, where there is contact with our world and time, or closed, where the world exists in its own reality, with no reference to our world).

In describing the elements of modern high fantasy, Barbara Safford (1997) drew on the oral and literary traditions from which fantasy has developed (pp. 23–4):

The structure of these modern children's stories with secondary worlds whose unique characteristics are determined by magic rather than science, by the holy rather than the material, by the sacred rather than the profane shares with myth and fairy tale the notion of gods and magic as the underlying fundament of being. They share with folklore the humor of the human situation. They share with legend and with romance and epic the predestined nature of the hero and the loyalty of his companions. From all they derive their goals of the defeat of evil through the emergence of the good.

Although she was describing children's fiction, these elements can be applied to high fantasy novels in general.

The proliferation of young protagonists in fantasy, particularly for young adults, is no coincidence. Not only is the 'coming of age' motif a useful mirror for the external journey of the protagonist, and the use of a naif a practical technique to highlight the sense of wonder inherent in fantasy, but it is also an aid in identification of reader with character. (Likewise, readers may find it easier to identify with open worlds, where there is the overt connection to contemporary experiences, than with closed worlds.)

However, the high fantasy genre has a preponderance of male protagonists, providing limited opportunities for female readers to directly identify.

The female hero

To find strong female characters in fantasy is difficult; to find multi-dimensional female protagonists, who drive the action and develop into integrated personalities (as their male counterparts do) is extremely rare. Roberta Noel's statistical analysis of fantasy novels for young adults demonstrated the lack of suitable female role models within the fantasy genre, and particularly the high fantasy sub-genre (Noel, 1997). Her work and my own impressions led me to increasingly question the validity for females of the traditional 'hero's journey' portrayed in fantasy.

Joseph Campbell (1993) analysed the protagonist's journey developed from the separation–initiation–return monomyth.

The Adventure of the Hero:

DEPARTURE (separation)
The Call to Adventure
Refusal of the Call
Supernatural Aid
The Crossing of the First Threshold
The Belly of the Whale
INITIATION
The Road of Trials
The Meeting with the Goddess
Woman as Temptress
Atonement with the Father
Apotheosis
The Ultimate Boon

RETURN
Refusal of the Return
The Magic Flight
Rescue from Without
The Crossing of the Return Threshold
Master of the Two Worlds
Freedom to Live

With some amendment of the 'initiation' stage, I consider Campbell's outline of the heroic journey could be applied as easily to a female hero as to a male. The difficulty I have is with his interpretation. Where he perceives the male hero as 'the king's son' and 'God's son' (p. 39), he perceives a female hero as 'the one who, by her qualities, her beauty, or her yearning, is fit to become the consort of an immortal' (p. 119).

In other words, according to Campbell's view, what is accepted as the male hero's birthright can only be achieved by a female hero through marriage or association; her achievements are only second-hand.

As Rita Haunert points out:

Although he claims that the rite of passage is a universal ritual for both males and females, Campbell gives very few examples of myths where females are heroes … They [women] either function symbolically in the male hero's adventure or are seen in such roles as goddesses, temptresses, or prize. Campbell's schema does not deal with the female and her rite of passage but with the male and his rite of passage, how, uniting with the sexual opposite (anima), he becomes a complete adult individual. The monomyth deals with the development of the male psyche.

(Haunert, 1997: 4–5)

Likewise, high fantasy itself — presumably because the prevailing convention in fantasy is to mirror that 'hero's journey' drawn from mythology — has largely failed to develop female characters of depth, and in fact has tended to go to the opposite extreme, showing female characters as simplistic stereotypes. Examples are, sadly, easy to find in fantasy, including more recent Australian novels:

- women are rewards or prizes to be won
    - e.g. Adious, the young widow Argus settles with in *The Journey* (Marsden, 1988)
- women need to be rescued by the hero
    - e.g. Julia, who becomes a tool for the Ragwitch's return to her world, then is absorbed into the witch's mind in *The Ragwitch* (Nix, 1990)
- they are wise women or witches
    - e.g. Circe Cruel-Claw in *Mandragon* (Aaron, 1998)
- they are innocent, or the 'good' characters to contrast with the male hero's flaws, such as pride
    - e.g. the Princess in *The House of Many Rooms* (Pryor, 1998) who controls her powers and uses them for the benefit of her followers, including the susceptible protagonist, Saul

- they are 'woman as temptress'
  - e.g. Sari/Princess Fame-Bright in *Translations in Celadon* (Odgers, 1998).

I would like to emphasise that my comments do not necessarily mean that I believe those books are 'bad' novels — in fact, the majority I find entertaining stories, well-delivered. However, the limited facets of sometimes central characters, who happen to be female, is disappointing.

The common characteristic in the 'good' or 'neutral' depictions of females is their relative passivity. In fantasy, until very recently, only 'bad' women can be active. An example of this is Sari/Princess Fame-Bright in *Translations in Celadon* (Odgers, 1998); another is the *Ragwitch* (Nix, 1990). Even when a female is the main character, she is often surprisingly passive, and seldom acts as catalyst for the story's action. It would be fairer to call many of them the main object, rather than a protagonist.

Campbell developed his theory by studying the same myths psychologist Carl Jung (1964) drew on in developing his theory of the 'collective unconscious'. Both have definite strengths but, from a feminist perspective, they suffer from the same problem. They drew their theories from limited data — the implicit assumption that myths were unchanging over time; that what Ovid, for example, had written was the way the stories had always been told. The words and symbols Jung and Campbell based their analysis on came from a patriarchal rather than matriarchal world view.[1]

Despite that serious reservation, I agree with Gordon-Wise (1991) that there is much from Jung's theories, as Campbell's, that can be useful in developing female heroes in fantasy. This is particularly true in terms of providing psychologically-credible character development. I contend that a more balanced use of archetypes — incorporating both positive and negative attributes — would improve the depiction of female characters in fantasy, and move beyond the simplistic and sometimes androcentric renderings that have dominated the genre as a whole. (This will be addressed in the archetypal analysis later this chapter.)

However, in works for the young adult, a number of other psychological theories are relevant. Particularly, the issue of psychological (and social) development — most importantly, in terms of this chapter, how this influences self-concept and self-esteem. It is the nature of this development that demonstrates why the presentation of female characters as active, multi-faceted protagonists is so important.

Adolescent self-concept[2]

Whether you follow Havighurst's (1953) developmental tasks model, Piaget's (Gruber and Voneche, 1977) and Elkind's (1984) cognitive development theories, Rosenberg's (1965, 1979) social psychology approach to personality development, or any of the many other theorists examining the nature of the changes undergone during adolescence, there are some common assumptions we can make.

Firstly, that adolescence is a time of great change, both internally and externally. Secondly, that these changes are part of a life-long continuum of development; and thirdly, that the ability or failure to successfully negotiate these changes will in large part determine adolescents' future fulfilment as adult members of society.

There is no single definition of self-concept, or one recognised way of assessing it. However, for the purposes of this chapter, we'll use the broadest definition of self-concept — how someone sees him/herself.

The way we see ourselves, especially during adolescence, is closely bound up with how we wish to be seen, the expectations (our own and others') we are judging by, and how we think other people see us. The development of self-concept during adolescence is a particularly intense process, and has caught the attention of many researchers. Of particular interest to educators is the work of Marsh (1988, 1989, 1990; Marsh and Smith 1987; Marsh et al. 1983, 1984). He developed a self-description questionnaire for adolescents and pre-adolescents, looking at self-concept through a range of lenses. This model has been used with both genders, and tested internationally. Cultural differences were also examined in Smith's (1999) comparison of results from Thailand and Australia.

Research results from a gender perspective, including Alpert-Gillis and Connell (1989) and Knox et al. (2000) reinforce others' findings that on entering adolescence, girls' self-concept is considerably disrupted. While boys' sense of self may also be affected at this age, the research findings consistently show boys' view of themselves is significantly more positive than girls' at the same age. Given the physiological, psychological and social changes that all adolescents go through, the fact that girls' idea of self (which is significantly affected by their perception of their appearance) is so much more negative than their male peers' should give us concern.

One aspect that may be constructive, from a literary viewpoint, is providing a range of femininities in fictional characters. If, as Maslow (1954: 44) contends, there is a hierarchy of needs that must be met before adolescents can become fulfilled and productive adults, one of the most important is 'social affection', or love. The next on his hierarchy is self-esteem '(strength, achievement, adequacy, mastery and competence, confidence, independence and freedom, and reputation or prestige)' (quoted in Reed, 1985: 11). The factor of perceived attractiveness is one aspect that can affect both of these needs. Examples of female fantasy characters who demonstrate their secure self-concept are Nico, in the Doorways trilogy (Pryor, 1998, 1999) and Sabriel (Nix, 1995). Their acceptance of themselves enables them to act decisively and confidently in the situations they confront. An example of a female character who lacks that positive view of self is Rosanna in *Translations in Celadon* (Odgers, 1998). She feels powerless, is easily led, and has extremely negative views about her appearance. Changing her perceptions and improving her self-concept is an underlying but crucial aspect of the story.

Morris Rosenberg (1979, 1965) is a social psychologist, who puts down the growth and changes of adolescence to social influences as well as a developmental process. He argues that it is society's lack of clear expectations of adolescents that causes many of the confusions in teenagers. His work on personality development examines relationships between self-esteem and social influences, including family, peers, school, politics, religion, culture/ethnicity, propaganda and work. Because of the society we are born into, there are specific tasks and roles we are expected to perform as part of that society.[3]

Rosenberg contends the 15–18 year-old age group is the one that is most caught up in self-image. The three reasons he provides are:

1   that major decisions are required of that age group (such as career choice, study options, relationships);

2   they go through huge changes psychologically and physically (including developing sex drives) that shake up the individual's view of themselves; and

3   their in-between status (ie, between childhood and adulthood) involves an inconsistent mixture of external expectations and rules, which is complicated further by both the past and the future influencing their self-image.

He breaks self-concept down to three elements — how someone sees themselves, how they want others to see them, and how they present to the world. He further adds that while these elements are cognitive, people also have strong wishes and feelings about them.

Clearly, there are many differences in approach by psychologists. However, I contend that anyone working with adolescents, young adults and literature can benefit dramatically through an understanding of some of these issues, and therefore how they apply to the novels we recommend to students. It is accepted that adolescent readers want to recognise themselves in what they read. However, arguably, the self they want to see could be either (or both) the one they see or the self they wish to be seen by others. Providing a range of multi-dimensional characters, particularly female characters (given the issue of negative self-concept in adolescent females), ensures that recognition is more likely to occur.

Seeking and finding

A multiple-readings approach is a useful way of drawing out the strengths and weaknesses in how the key characters are portrayed, as well as providing a richer appreciation of other aspects of the novel (such as themes). To illustrate how this approach can be used, I have provided several interpretations of one text — *Translations in Celadon* (Odgers, 1998) — as well as briefer examples from other novels. No single interpretation will provide all the 'right' answers — it is the possibilities opened up by a number of interpretations that is important. In line with that philosophy, I have ignored any stated intentions by the author, and looked only at the text itself.

Translations in Celadon

Self-concept is the key to the characters in Sally Odgers' quest fantasy *Translations in Celadon* (1998). The story is told through two characters. Rosanna Hopestill, whose powers of imagination create the land of Celadon, is a self-conscious and unconfident observer who sees herself on the periphery of the action. The other narrator is the beautiful and manipulative Sari Roberts, confident she is the hero of her own story — and everyone else's.

Although Rosanna resolves in the opening paragraph to 'see it all for real', she is talking specifically about a scene that is not 'real', but one she has imagined — or s'imagined (seen and imagined). Only as the story progresses is the powerful reality of her imagination reinforced. At Sari's instigation, Rosanna begins to imagine a land called Celadon; at Sari's suggestion she envisages characters to fit the names Sari provides. After Sari pretends to have been there, the land becomes more believable to Rosanna. She, Sari, Suzanne Wise, Asher

Phillips and Rafe Winter are 'translated' to Celadon, becoming Horse Still-Hoping, Princess Fame-Bright, White Lily Wisdom, The Happy One and Wolf Shield respectively.

From the start, Rosanna's vision is presented as the 'true' one. Not only does her interpretation begin the book, but also her narration dominates the story. However, her vision is swiftly shown to be flawed — she sees herself only in negative terms, only in relation to what she sees in others, and those perceptions are built on appearances rather than the evidence provided by actions. Her translations subconsciously reveal underlying truths of the characters' personalities, truths she has seen but not acknowledged in the 'real' world. Sari, in contrast, is aware of her 'poor visual imagination' (p. 24) — she demands the reflections and translations of others to reinforce her strong sense of self. In Elkind's (1967) terms, Sari demonstrates both the 'personal fable' and 'imaginary audience' traits.

Names have power in this story, the power to shape and reveal the named. Unlike Le Guin's (1968; 1992 edition) *A Wizard of Earthsea*, where a true name is concealed because it gives power to any who know it, in *Translations* the names are obvious indicators of the characters and/or their roles. All names are known in the world of St Boniface College, but when translated into alternative meanings (just as their five bearers are translated into the imaginary Celadon) the names determine the role of each character. Placenames, too, are deliberately descriptive. (Snowstorm Ridge, for example, in 'our' world.) The old Royal City, Cerulean, where the travellers are heading, carries the expectation of a heavenly or mythical destination (Cerulean, sky blue, heaven/Parnassus, home of the gods). Only the name of the imaginary land Celadon is open to interpretation and invention.

While apparently bringing the story full circle by the end (snowstorms and snowball waltzes), the symmetry is incomplete. Five began; two return — and those two have returned changed. It is Rosanna's journey we follow.

This fantasy stands up well to a variety of readings. There are a number of texts providing a range of approaches to literary criticism, one of the most accessible being Terry Eagleton's *Literary Theory: An Introduction* (1996). To illustrate how different facets can be brought out through multiple readings I will look at two possible approaches to *Translations in Celadon* — feminist and archetypal.

Feminist

There is not one feminist reading; the range of femininities and 'feminist' interpretations is as broad as the possibilities of any other form of literary criticism. For example, Bell Hooks' approach as a black feminist (see, for example, Hooks, 1999, 1989) highlights a different perspective from that shown by Tillie Olsen (1980) or Carla Kaplan (1996). A psychoanalytic feminist approach (such as Chodorow, 1999) is very different from one that looks from the materialist perspective (such as Kuhn and Wolpe, 1978). However, the main assumptions when referring to a 'feminist' reading include:

- that the focus will be on representations of gender;
- that *central* to literary and other discourses are issues of gender and sexuality — they cannot be ignored or denied in valid critical assessment;
- that literature reflects — implicitly or explicitly — power relationships in society;
- that those power relationships are intertwined with identity, lived experience and the politics, or discourse, of the body.

Although five characters are involved in the story, the two key players are the young women who narrate the story — Rosanna and Sari. The binary opposition of these characters is a twist on the more usual male–female dichotomy.

However, the characteristics traditionally assigned to males and females can be seen in Sari and Rosanna respectively. For example, 'Roberts' clearly has masculine connotations, and Sari Roberts takes on the 'masculine' role of driving the action. Where Rosanna's responses are emotional, imaginative and passive, Sari's are calculating and active. Sari is the musician, Rosanna the instrument.

'Hopestill' has connotations of the redeeming nature of hope, the last — and saving — item released from Pandora's box. Like Pandora ('all gifts' [Cotterell 2000]), whose act of opening the forbidden jar released all the world's evils, Rosanna's unwitting actions lead to conflict, division and despair. However, her name shows that there is 'still hope'. Readers can presume that the resolution of this story will not be entirely negative.

In many ways, Sari is more clearsighted than Rosanna. She recognises her own weapons — her sexuality, her popularity, her strength of will, and through them her ability to manipulate others — and is prepared to use them to determine her own future rather than waiting to be rescued as the traditional 'Princess' would do. She sees herself as a warrior, and like a warrior, thinks in terms of tactics (p. 6):

> Knowing when to take a chance and act is most of the battle. Catching people when they're feeling weak or just plain unsettled. Strike then and you've got them in your palm.

Although she describes Translations as a game (e.g. pp. 6, 247), she plans her moves as a general would a war. She is prepared to intimidate, flatter, hurt, woo, injure, cajole, kill and dissemble to win.

Where Rosanna watches the popular students in envy (see the section on self-concept), Sari recognises how insubstantial that power is: 'In five more years they'll be nothing' (pp. 6–7). She also sees Rosanna's weakness — 'that mouse … I bet she doesn't know … who she really is' (p. 7). However, like the other characters, Sari has flaws in her perception. By seeing herself so clearly as a 'winner' (p. 5) she underestimates others; for example, seeing Rafe as 'stupid' (p. 7).

Sari's aggressive pursuit of her goals (a trait generally attributed to male rather than female behaviour) and her willingness to sacrifice others to get there are directly opposed to the traditional rendering of woman-as-nurturer and woman-as-pacifist (both roles allocated to Rosanna). Continuing the male-female analogy, Sari implants the idea of Celadon in Rosanna; Rosanna is the one who brings it to fruition. By naming the characters and land, Sari claims ownership of Rosanna's children/creations as well as defining their roles. Rosanna is the vessel, the tool, the object, the subjected.

Sex, sexuality and identity

As space is limited, it is impossible to provide a full interpretation of the text. Therefore, I will focus on one of the aspects seldom included in fantasy novels for young adults — the interrelated issues of sex, sexuality and identity.

How Sari appears is essential to her. Rosanna is more concerned with disappearing — hiding against the wall at the school dance, escaping into her imagination rather than dealing with the 'real' world, and imprisoning herself in the silence and limited awareness of Horse Still-Hoping.[4] Her self-concept is drawn largely from her negative view of her physical appearance; because she fails to recognise herself within the prevailing (masculine) construct of 'beauty' and 'desirability', she denies her physical and sexual identity. By devaluing other aspects of her sense of self, because she views appearance as the main definer (i.e. she accepts patriarchal values of women-as-object, in which sexual appeal to males is deemed the key element of female worth), she sees herself as powerless — a follower, not a leader.

Sari's outfit for the school dance is described as bright, revealing, clinging and attention-getting. Where Rosanna chooses to hide in asexual baggy jeans (despite having bought an 'awesome velvet skirt' for the social), Sari deliberately highlights her sexual awareness and availability. Although Asher/Happy One falls ready prey to Sari's sexuality, Rafe/Wolf Shield recognises her ploy and resists it (e.g. p. 8). Rosanna denies her sexuality or the possibility of being sexually attractive until the very end of the novel, when she finally accepts that Rafe 'isn't kissing [her] to be kind' (p. 263). Her acceptance of her sexuality is a symbol of accepting herself as an integrated, mature person.

Sari's exotic beauty ('an island angel' [p. 107]; 'looks very sexy' [p. 84]) is made much of — her skin's 'satiny sort of sheen, as if it has just been rubbed up with silver polish' (pp. 8–9); her 'silvery eyes' (p. 11); her 'beautiful brown body' (p. 154); her long, 'sooty-black' hair (p. 9). Sari's skin is described as a very pale brown, 'like weak coffee made with milk' (p. 8). Interestingly, in the world of Celadon, where her power is made manifest, Fame-Bright's skin is described as darker than Sari's (p. 55). The coffee is stronger, the milk diluted. (What a wealth of interpretations could be made of this!)

Although Sari/Princess Fame-Bright derives much of her self-concept from her physical appearance, she also recognises beauty as a form of power. She both identifies via the masculinist value system, and observes from outside it. Like a building, the construct looks different depending on where you stand. Sari epitomises Mary Wollstonecroft's view in *A Vindication of the Rights of Women* (1792):

> Women are told from their infancy, and taught by their mothers, that a little knowledge of human weakness … will obtain for them the protection of man; and should they be beautiful, everything else is needless, for, at least, twenty years of their lives.
>
> (Schneir, 1994: 6)

Sari has taken her great-grandmother's example to heart: 'Great-granny knew her power … good old S.E.X.' (p. 6). It certainly gives Sari power over Asher/The Happy One, who seeks to 'protect and serve her' (p. 84); her knowledge of Rosanna's poor self-image gives her power of a different kind. Sari's connection with her great-grandmother is not simply through adoption of her example. She presents herself to her school peers as 'an island princess', strengthening the status she already has through popularity and beauty by reinforcing people's perceptions of her as above her peers through her royal bloodline. In Celadon, she *is* a princess. In other words, she also seeks status through class.

These female characters' preoccupation with appearance shows two different reactions to the unquestioning acceptance of a masculine construct of femininity. By adopting its inherent value system, Sari seeks power within the traditional and prevailing social construct. Only as the story progresses does Rosanna begin to see that appearances are a false or irrelevant system of valuation, and she begins her tentative construction of an alternative framework.

Sari is happy to play upon the convention of seeking assistance from the men; however, when she is actually in danger of drowning and is saved by Wolf Shield she claims a wolf attacked her. (Although there is not space in this chapter to offer a full archetypal analysis, let alone a psychoanalysis, this illustrates an aspect of Sari's personality that stands more attention.) Her view is — like many of her other attitudes — the hegemonic masculine view that winners refuse to show weakness/vulnerability. As she has positioned herself as a winner, and her self-concept denies the possibility of an alternative, she therefore cannot admit to being vulnerable, weak or a loser (hence she refuses to admit any blame or responsibility for what happens in Celadon).

Rosanna, however, repeatedly needs and accepts help and protection from the male characters — for example, Wolf Shield/Rafe saves her life in both this world and Celadon. Just as she has allowed herself to be comforted, she also comforts; helps as she has been helped (e.g. p. 237). One interpretation of this could be that needing help indicates Rosanna's powerlessness and providing comfort demonstrates the 'maternal' or nurturing aspect of traditional femininity. An alternative interpretation is that this balance of giving and receiving, which only develops as the story progresses, is an implicit acceptance of the equality of her relationship with Rafe/Wolf Shield, where each has the power and resources to share with the other. Again, in this interpretation, she is constructing a new framework for the gendered relationships in her life.

Sari claims absolute rights over her own body — how it is displayed, whether and who she shares it with. Her choice to sleep with Asher/Happy One is not glossed with courtly romance. She sees no need to justify her actions, even to herself. In contrast, Rosanna/Horse Still-Hoping reads it as a sign that Fame-Bright may be falling in love with Happy One. Like the Happy One, Rosanna sees Fame-Bright's decision as the bestowal of a gift (probably, in their innocence, believing it to be Sari's virginity), and project their emotional interpretation of the act. The reader knows how misplaced their interpretation is, with Sari's experience obvious in her discussion of what she would prefer sexually and the lie she tells about those '*new* delights' (p. 138; my emphasis).

Sari/Fame-Bright chooses to sleep with Asher/Happy One to strengthen her hold over him; Rosanna/Horse Still-Hoping, despite her shape-shifting between horse and naked woman in Celadon, only acts sexually once she has been returned to our world. Even then, when she and Rafe/Wolf Shield are alone in a hut in the middle of a snowstorm, we are only told that they kissed, then talked. Whether they took it further is not explicit. We are shown intimacy, not sex.

This overt/covert pattern is repeated in other ways; for example, Rosanna's internal journey is more important than the physical journey that Sari engineers; Sari flaunts her appearance, Rosanna hides or disguises it.

The granting and withholding of sexual favours to Happy One when she knows she would rather sleep with Wolf Shield (p. 138) shows how removed Sari is from the moral judgments Rosanna makes (and, through her, the intended reader). Sari has removed herself from those limits. She wants to possess and control the male characters, whether with their consent or against their wishes. Where she uses intimidation, anger, violence and contempt to control the women, she treats the men differently. Sex is the weapon that she calculates will be most successful; the one she believes the men will be most vulnerable to. Significantly, it fails (foreshadowing her later failure).

Rafe is angered at her attempts to manipulate by using sex as currency in her quest for power (see, for example, pp. 20–1). The 'sensible and sane' (p. 158) Rafe (cf 'mad' Sari, p. 246) refuses to acknowledge any attraction to someone he knows is trouble (pp. 220–1); his attraction to Rosanna involves her mind, her generosity and company (p. 201) as well as her body. He sees her as a whole person, as Rosanna learns to see him; even when he has no memory of the world they came from, he trusts what Rosanna tells him, as Rosanna trusts the man-wolf. This trust is not misplaced. Even when the power to possess is handed to her by Wolf Shield, in the form of his pelt, she instantly rejects it (p. 220).

It is illogical to look at the femininities presented in a text, without also considering the various masculinities. If we accept Foucault's view (1980) that there will always be resistant discourses as well as the dominant discourse, it is obvious that feminists are not alone in developing ways of reassessing culture and how it is represented in novels (as well as in other ways).

In recent years, following the success of feminism in providing alternatives to the masculine and patriarchal ideology of the dominant discourse (or society's implicit and explicit assumptions), much attention has been given to how masculinity is represented. The need for this re-examination appears increasingly accepted in a range of fields, including education. Kenway et al. (1997) emphasise the need for a broad range of possible masculinities and femininities to be available to adolescents. Warner (1994) looks at the way males are socially constructed, and how the idea of 'manliness' has changed over the years.

While in Australia the 'dominant model of masculinity' (Buchbinder, 1998) or 'hegemonic masculinity' is still white, heterosexual, Christian, 'macho' and 'sporty' rather than 'arty', it is only one of several masculinities available. People such as Paulsen (1999) are working in schools to deconstruct the hegemonic masculinity, which he sees as 'inhibiting school life for both girls and boys' (p. 12). Research is also underway into providing models of masculinity that challenge the 'macho' discourse. The ramifications for identification, self-concept and psychological and social development are clear.

Wolf Shield and the Happy One are secondary characters in this story. However, in keeping with the analysis of gender, sex and sexuality above, a brief examination of one aspect concerning the male characters is appropriate as an example of the approach that can be taken.

Wolf Shield's sexual orientation is a matter of interest to both Sari/Fame-Bright and Rosanna — primarily because he refused Sari's sexual overtures. The traditional and embedded (masculine and Judeo-Christian) view is that women are either innocents or temptresses; if temptresses, men are the innocent victims, and therefore men are not responsible for their sexual acts. We may have moved from the Garden to the mall, but at some underlying level, all women are seen as Eves or Marys. Both women expect he will take what is offered — their assumption being all men will sleep with a beautiful woman, given the chance; and that testosterone will overpower any mental, emotional or moral considerations. Rosanna makes the assumption explicit: 'Why did you send her packing?

God, you're a guy and she's a girl and she was throwing herself at you …' (p. 220). This is despite her knowing that Rafe 'doesn't hold any brief' for Sari (p. 114).

When he rejects Sari/Princess Fame-Bright, first at the school dance, then at the mall, then in Celadon, it is clear Rafe fails to fit the dominant model. Another model of masculinity is required. At first Rafe's sexual orientation is questioned. After all, the women think, how could he turn Sari down unless he's gay (see pp. 165–6)?

However, Rafe puts forward another model — a less simplistic interpretation of masculinity being an either–or option. He takes responsibility for his decisions, making conscious choices about who he wishes to sleep with and why. 'Liking girls' (p. 167) is not enough; he does not feel he has to prove his sexuality that way. He knows that Sari 'means trouble' (p. 220); he is angered by Sari's attempts to manipulate and cause division between Asher and himself (p. 221). He knows that Rosanna would never act like Sari (p. 218). It comes as no surprise to the reader that his values lead him to want Rosanna as his partner.

Archetypal interpretation

Archetypal theory provides a range of possible masculinities and femininities. Carl Jung's groundbreaking work on the collective unconscious (refined over his career and made accessible to a wider public in the 1960s, e.g., in *Man and his Symbols* [1964]) drew on myths, stories, situations and roles that represented universal human concerns — concerns that crossed time and geography.

Characteristics are seen as the important factors; the repeated patterns from myths of different cultures and different times. In this chapter, I am looking not at the patterns of themes, images or plots in archetypal mythology, but only the characteristics of the actors. A fuller archetypal analysis would be able to draw out, for example, the significance of the half-human, half-beast nature of Rafe and Rosanna; the repeated image of blood; the image and role of the wolf in mythology, or the implications of Rafe's shedding his pelt, sharing it with Rosanna, and receiving it again. However, the charter here is to look at the characters in terms of archetypes and stereotypes.

Labels for and the number of these characters can change over time, and between researchers. For example, Carol Pearson (1998) in *The Hero Within* named six archetypes[5] (orphan, innocent, magician, wanderer, warrior, altruist); her more detailed work *Awakening the Heroes Within* (1991) identified twelve archetypes (orphan, innocent, seeker, warrior, care-giver, destroyer, lover, creator, ruler, magician, sage, fool). As she acknowledges, 'Archetypes are not bounded entities that are easy to pin down and label' (1998: 321). This helps explain the multiplicity of labels.

The idea of archetypes has struck a popular chord in recent years, with references to archetypes in a wide range of contexts. For example, Caro LaFever (1999) identified eight male 'hero archetypes' in romances and other genre fiction (chief, bad boy, best friend, charmer, lost soul, professor, swashbuckler, warrior). (I will leave open the question of whether these are really all archetypes. Her approach certainly does not follow the Jungian theory of integration.) The new age emphasis on personal growth has also seen archetypes held up as mythical frameworks through which we can examine and change our lives (e.g. Pearson, 1998, 1991; Pinkola Estes, 1992; Thunder Strikes, 2000).

POSITIVE	NEGATIVE
MOTHER: nurturing (birth) fertile protective	MOTHER: devouring (death) fateful suffocating
MAIDEN: innocent awakening sexuality relates to others as an individual	MAIDEN: unquestioning, naive, easily used seductress, flirt; plays with men's feelings 'puella aerterna' (the foolish maiden) whose identity is submerged in the primary father/daughter relationship
WISE WOMAN: healer advances culture magical authority	WISE WOMAN: poisoner (as witch) promotes evil secretiveness
WARRIOR: courageous fierce defender exemplifies independence lover of animals	WARRIOR: ruthless bloodlust emotional withdrawal hunter

Figure 8.1 Some aspects of the female quaternity

Given that this chapter is examining female heroes, I have developed a model of the female quaternity using terms adapted by Gordon-Wise (1991: 33–5). This is a very cursory example of female archetypes, but enables us to demonstrate the interpretation.

One of the problems with the selective use of archetypes has been the development of stereotypes. For example, the great mother can destroy as well as nurture, but she is frequently seen as just the giver of life, the nurturer — few would see 'mother nature' as a negative image — which makes it far removed from the original archetype, which included both negative and positive aspects.

The facets of female characters shown by fantasy writers tend to rely on just one attribute of one archetype — for example, the innocence of the maiden, the nurturing aspect of the mother, the courage of the warrior, or the herbal skill of the wise woman. While contemporary novels may use females as their main characters, they rarely have the depth or strength of purpose of their male counterparts in other books — perhaps because of authors' reluctance to incorporate any negative archetypal characteristics.

Restricting the archetypal characteristics to the pretty, passive and positive has resulted in too many flat, limited female characters in fantasy.

When an author incorporates more aspects — positive and negative — of an archetype, we cannot help but be intrigued by the possibilities it opens up. The more aspects and possible contradictions, the less predictable a character becomes.

For example, in Victor Kelleher's *Master of the Grove* (1982) (a particularly good book for an archetypal reading), Marla has a very ambiguous role. Kelleher has taken the traditional 'wise woman' archetype, and blended both positive and negative attributes, making her complex and rewarding as a character. She is secretive, and has authority. She has magical powers, and uses (abuses?) them over others. Although not the protagonist, it is the relationship Marla develops with Derin that enriches our understanding of him. It is that combination of trust and suspicion; the dependence and independence; the apparent conflict in values and goals; the learning both characters go through as part of the journey that make us believe in them both. Like Derin, we as readers are unsure whether to like or dislike her, trust or distrust her; will she bring redemption or betrayal?

An archetypal analysis of the protagonists of *Translations in Celadon* brings out new possibilities of interpretation.

For example, using the model above, Rosanna typifies the maiden. She is unquestioning, naive, easily used — all seen as negative attributes. However, she also has the innocence of the maiden. She is discovering her own sexuality (see feminist interpretation), yet shies away from the associated negative attribute of flirting or playing with the males' feelings. When she ignores her shyness and self-consciousness, she relates to Rafe/Wolf Shield as an individual. Even at the end of the novel, she seeks to break through to the increasingly 'robotic' (p. 232) White Lily Wisdom on a human and personal level by using a specific reference from Suzanne's past — the blouse that Suzanne made and wore to the school social (p. 231).

Rosanna also shows positive attributes of the mother, with her fertile imagination giving birth to Celadon — a Celadon she defends and refuses to harm on Sari's command (p. 231). Her vision of Celadon springs from the earth itself; mankind's efforts are visible only in the form of Cerulean — a city reduced to ruin, overtaken again by nature. In human relationships, she protects Happy One from the truth (e.g. p. 175). Rosanna also comforts and nurtures Rafe/Wolf Shield (e.g. pp. 237, 266), and in her horse form attempts to comfort Happy One (p. 104).

Sari, on the other hand, has the ruthlessness of the warrior (see feminist interpretation). She also demonstrates the bloodlust of the warrior archetype (pp. 235, 250) — an aspect echoed by White Lily Wisdom (e.g. p. 234) but repeatedly rejected by Rosanna (e.g. p. 236), whose fear and dislike of blood are made clear (e.g. p. 168).

From the first, Rosanna's connection to the natural world is repeatedly reinforced. In her opening vision she sees two figures struggling through the snow — but only after the power of the landscape itself has been recognised (p. 3). She thinks of flowers to distract her from Sari and Asher (p. 3); she looks for Asher 'as a sunflower looks for the sun' (p. 17). She consistently s'imagines (sees and imagines) landscapes before characters.

Rosanna's concentration on the surface rather than the visceral at the start of the book is a twist on the familiar feminist accusation against men seeing women as objects rather than people. Her judgments are based on appearance rather than substance; not only does she see Asher as golden and desirable, she sees Rafe as his binary opposite, the 'dark on the other side' (p. 3). Unsurprisingly, neither she nor the other characters can see what is hidden in the dark. In Jungian terms, recognising our shadow is a crucial step; losing ourselves in it is a danger.

The sexual manipulation Sari delights in, as outlined in the feminist interpretation, fits neatly into the negative aspect of the maiden as seductress and flirt. Like most 'bad' (p. 3) women in fiction she will be punished for it. The temptress is to be feared as well as desired.

Another negative characteristic is from the mother archetype. Sari seeks to devour, or kill, Rosanna's true identity (e.g. '... with the horse now nothing but a horse' p. 225; addressing Rosanna when she is in human form as 'Horse Still-Hoping' p. 231). By translating the names, she is both giving birth to new manifestations of the students and devouring their old identities — in the case of Rafe and Rosanna, only partially successfully. However, Suzanne and Asher disappear into their new personae; they are dead to their past selves.

The nature of archetypal characteristics is not static, and age and experience do not dictate which characteristics will manifest themselves. Although there may be a dominant archetype, Jungian psychologists argue that it is learning how to integrate other characteristics that balance and complete a person. It is the integration of various attributes — positive and negative — of the different archetypes that show us how a character can change; their contradictions, complexity, possibilities, self-awareness, maturation. Different facets enable characters to act in certain ways at certain times. There may be times when a person — or a character — exhibits independence, and other times when their sense of self is intertwined with another.

In other words, the broader possibilities available through the development of an integrated, multi-faceted character can alleviate the predicability of a genre with strong conventions. The hero's journey is a wonderfully dramatic vehicle. We know it works, as it has worked so well for centuries. It satisfies us on some fundamental human level. But the journey does not have to be taken always on the same road. Nor should it be always the same hero. Strengthening secondary and tertiary characters by fleshing them out with new characteristics — faults as well as strengths — will strengthen the whole.

For example, Michael Pryor's Doorways trilogy (1998, 1999) failed to engender any complexity in one of his key characters, the Princess. She is consistently presented as stunningly beautiful and attractive (to all males, not just the protagonist Saul); of royal lineage; she heals and nurtures her followers; she understands and forgives; she can fight — and does — to defend herself, but her followers are the active protectors. She is, in other words, the ideal traditional female ('She has that effect on most people . . she's pretty extraordinary' [*House of Many Rooms*, p. 40]). The only time we see even a slight crack in the facade is when she confesses to Saul that she finds it difficult to always be the leader — a serious flaw indeed, and one that Saul is more than willing to alleviate by letting her talk with him.

By the end of the trilogy, the Princess is still beautiful, understanding, nurturing and so on. She has not changed a jot in the course of three novels, she is still unbelievably ideal; pretty and positive and utterly predictable. Saul reluctantly accepts that he and the Princess will never be a couple, so he accepts the offer of Nico to be his partner instead. (Never mind, Saul. Weren't you lucky that Nico was still prepared to offer herself to you, when you'd made it clear for three books that she was second-best?) With such a good concept for the house of many rooms, and the pacy telling of the stories, I found it disappointing that such an important secondary character was so limited in facets. Some negative attributes, some internal conflict or confusion over different archetypal characteristics, would have 'fleshed out' this character considerably.

Just as we change and develop, so must a fictional character be seen to change — if we are to believe in them. An example of such a change is Rosanna's development of the warrior characteristic, courage (p. 232) — a characteristic we recognise as necessary if she is to move beyond the limitations she lived with at the start of the book. She needs to become independent (another warrior characteristic) of Sari's will before she can oppose it and make the choices that are right for her. It is the learning of these warrior characteristics that is a necessary part of her development as a credible personality. We believe her change because it is a gradual integration, part of a learning process and not an abrupt about-face. Sari has not changed, essentially, from the character who began. The characteristics became more embedded, no new attributes were adopted, and her failure to adapt sealed her fictional fate. Hubris, the traditional downfall of the warrior archetype, proves the downfall of Sari.

The fifth character among the travellers, Suzanne/White Lily Wisdom, who has not been discussed previously, is a pertinent reminder of what happens when the selected characteristics of an archetype become obvious and hackneyed. Suzanne, who reads tarot cards at the school social, becomes the wise woman/witch in Celadon. By making her an 'old' character, uninterested in the males, the author has effectively removed her from the sexual issues of the other two women.

White Lily Wisdom is constantly weaving futures and brewing potions, both curatives and poisons, in the 'witch' traditions. She guards her knowledge closely, she wishes harm on — and causes harm to — other characters, and connected with that she shows the bloodlust of the warrior. But as Rosanna says (p. 198), 'it's as if [she is] acting to a script or plan — according to someone's idea of the way [she] ought to be … She acts like someone's *idea* of a wise woman, mixed up from films and stories' (p. 199).

Likewise, Asher's appeal lies purely in his surface attractions; similarly, his personality is revealed to lack depth. There is apparently no shadow to discover. He never learns to see below the surface, and his lack of perception makes him blind to others' true natures as well as his own ('I [Wolf Shield] know him well but he often reads me poorly.' [p. 199]). Asher is unwilling to see the dark side — either of Fair-Bright's actions and motivations, or the nature of Rafe's double existence ('I am what I am. Sometimes I've tried to tell you, brother. You didn't want to know.' [p. 233]). As Rosanna says, 'He's almost too good to be real' (p. 199).

Odgers reinforces the stock nature of these characters by the increasingly robotic responses of White Lily and Happy One (p. 232), highlighting their lifelessness and lack of other dimensions.

Rosanna explains to Wolf Shield why he seems more real than Happy One and White Lily Wisdom, despite the fact that he is a werewolf — 'a stock type in fantasy but you don't fit your prototype any more than I fit mine' (p. 200). In other words, Wolf Shield and Horse Still-Hoping are not as predictable as the stock characters, because they have more to them than the conventional 'types'. Their personalities offer more for the reader to explore, because the use of archetypal characteristics gives them more dimensions, and therefore less predictable actions and reactions. Rafe/Wolf Shield seems 'more himself — more of a proper person' (p. 198).

Conclusion

The high fantasy genre has a strong tradition of males in the primary (protagonist) role, and females in simplistically depicted, passive, secondary roles. This is despite the fact that there appears to be nothing inherent in the nature of the hero or in the hero's journey that would preclude female protagonists. The genre has been slow to recognise that tradition (or habit) may be masking unexamined assumptions.

That no longer need be the case. Over at least the last two decades, there have been a number of successful feminist challenges to the widely accepted/traditional masculine interpretation of mythology (on which rest both the fantasy genre, and assumptions about the mythical journey of a hero). Jessica Salmonson (1979: 13–14) argued that this highlights the need to present strong, heroic female characters in fantasy literature:

> Fantasy as a literature, more than any other form of storytelling, is mythological in scope — and if we are the product of our myths, the ways we change our myths today will change the kinds of people we become tomorrow.

We need to reappraise our views of female fantasy characters — what we expect them to be, and why. The fantasy genre has endless possibilities, even within its strong conventions, provided we can also use the 'journey' motif to explore the many potential femininities and masculinities available for both heroes and secondary characters.

Only in relatively recent novels does the reader see female heroes who — like their male counterparts — are able to grow and change through the novel, actively drive the story and achieve success in the heroic tradition. As we've seen, this development is still sadly inconsistent. However the number of novels now being published which include multi-faceted female protagonists is certainly an encouraging trend.

The use of archetypes, specifically the incorporation of both positive and negative characteristics of the different archetypes, provides character depth, fresh element(s) of internal conflict, and enables the credible emotional and psychological development of the character. The increasing use by contemporary authors of these different archetypal characteristics is a key element in 'fleshing out' all fantasy characters — particularly female protagonists — and providing credible, active female role models for readers.

Given the evidence of conflicted and negative self-concept of female adolescents, the more effort is made in novels for this age group to provide positive, varied and — crucially — believable female protagonists, the better.

That action is there to be found — and I suspect both readers and the female protagonists to come are more than keen to seek it out.

Bibliography

Aaron, M. (1998) *Mandragon*. Random House, Milsons Point NSW.
Alpert-Gillis, L. and Connell, J.P. (1989) 'Gender and sex role influences on children's self-esteem', *Journal of Personality*, vol 57, pp. 97–114.
Bleich, L. (1980) 'The developmental role of adolescent literature', *Texas Technical Journal of Education*, vol 7, No 1 (Winter), p. 44.
Buchbinder, D. (1998) *Performance Anxieties: Reproducing Masculinity*. Allen & Unwin, Sydney.

Campbell, J. (1993) *The Hero with a Thousand Faces*. Fontana Press, London, HarperCollins Publishers (copyright 1949).

Carmody, I. (1993) *Obernewtyn*. Penguin, Ringwood, Vic.

—— (1993) *The Farseekers*. Penguin, Ringwood, Vic.

—— (1995) *Ashling*. Penguin, Ringwood, Vic.

—— (1997) *Darkfall*. Penguin, Ringwood, Vic.

—— (1999) *The Keeping Place*. Penguin, Ringwood, Vic.

Chodorow, N. (1999) *The Reproduction of Mothering: Psychoanalysis and the Sociology of Gender* (2nd edn). University of California Press, Berkley, California.

Connell, R.W. (1995) *Masculinities*. Allen & Unwin, Sydney.

Cotterell, A. (2000) *The Pimlico Dictionary of Classical Mythologies*. Random House, London.

Donalson, K. and Nilson, A.P. (1980) *Literature for Today's Young Adults*. Scott, Foresman and Company. Glenview, Ill.

Eagleton, T. (1996) *Literary Theory: An Introduction* (2nd edn). Blackwell, Oxford.

Elkind, D. (1967) 'Egocentrism in adolescence', *Child Development*, vol 38, 1967, p. 1029.

—— (1984) *All Grown Up and No Place To Go: Teenagers in Crisis*. Addison-Wesley Publishing Company, Reading, MA.

Erikson, E. (1968) *Identity: Youth and Crisis*. W.W. Norton & Company, New York.

Foucault, M. (1980) *Power/Knowledge: Selected interviews and other writings 1972–1977*. C. Gordon (ed.). (Translated by L Marshall, J. Mepham, K. and Soper). Harvester Wheatsheaf, New York.

Frye, N. (1963) 'The Archetypes of Literature', In *Fables of Identity: Studies in Poetic Mythology*. Harcourt Brace, New York, pp. 7–20.

—— (1982) *The Great Code: The Bible and Literature*. Harcourt Brace Jovanovich, San Diego.

Gordon-Wise, B.A. (1991) *The Reclamation of a Queen: Guinevere in Modern Fantasy*. Greenwood Press, Westport, Connecticut.

Gruber, H.E. and Voneche, J.J. (eds) (1977) *The Essential Piaget*. Routledge & Kegan Paul, London.

Harper, J.F. and Marshall, E. (1991) 'Adolescents' problems and their relationship to self-esteem', *Adolescence*, vol 26, pp. 799–808.

Haunert, R.M. (1997) *Mythic Female Heroes in the High Fantasy Novels of Patricia McKillip*. UMI Dissertation Services (degree date 1983). Ann Arbor, Michigan.

Havighurst, R. (1953) *Human Development and Education*. Longman, Green and Company, New York.

Hooks, B. (1989) *Talking back: thinking feminist, thinking black*. South End Press, Boston, MA.

—— (1999) *Remembered Rapture: The Writer at Work*. The Women's Press, London.

Jung, C. (ed.) (1964) *Man and his Symbols*. Aldus Books, London.

Kaplan, C. (1996) *The Erotics of Talk: Women's Writing and Feminist Paradigms*. Oxford University Press, Oxford.

Kelleher, V. (1982) *Master of the Grove*. Penguin Books, Harmondsworth, England.

Kenway, J., Willis, S., Blackmore, J. and Rennie, L. (1997) *Challenging Macho Values: Practical ways of working with adolescent boys*. Falmer Press, London.

Knox, M., Funk, J., Elliott, R., GreeneBush, E. (2000) 'Gender Differences in Adolescents' Possible Selves', *Youth & Society*, vol 31, no 3 (March), pp. 287–309.

Kuhn, A. and Wolpe, A. (eds) (1978) *Feminism and materialism: women and modes of production*. Routledge and K. Paul, London; Boston.

LaFever, C. (1999) 'Beyond Alpha: The eight male archetypes'. http://www.romance-central.com/Workshops/heroes.htm

Larrington, C. (ed.) (1992) *The Feminist Companion to Mythology*. Pandora Press, London.

Le Guin, U. (1968) *The Wizard of Earthsea*. Published in the volume *The Earthsea Quartet* (1992). Penguin, London.

McRobbie, D. (1991) *Mandragora*. Mammoth, Port Melbourne.

Marsden, J. (1988) *The Journey*. Pan Books, Sydney.

Marsh, H.W. (1988) *The Self Description Questionnaire (SDQ): Manual and Research Monograph*. Psychological Corporation, San Antonio, Texas.

—— (1989) 'Age and sex effects in multiple dimensions of self-concept: Preadolescence to early adulthood', *Journal of Educational Psychology*, vol 81, pp. 417–30.

—— (1990) *Self description questionnaire (SDQ) II: A theoretical and empirical basis for the measurement of multiple dimensions of adolescent self-concept: An interim test manual and a research monograph*. Psychological Corporation, San Antonio, Texas.

Marsh, H.W., Parker, J.W. and Smith, I.D. (1983) 'Preadolescent Self-Concept: Its relation to self-concept as inferred by teachers and to academic ability', *British Journal of Educational Psychology*, vol 53, pp. 60–78.

Marsh, H.W. and Smith, I.D. (1987) 'A cross national study of the structure and level of multidimensional self-concepts: An application of confirmatory factor analysis', *Australian Journal of Psychology*, vol 39, pp. 61–77.

Marsh, H.W., Smith, I.D. and Barnes, J. (1984) 'Multidimensional self-concepts: Relationships with sex and academic achievement', *Journal of Educational Psychology*, vol 77, pp. 581–96.

Maslow, A. (1954) *Motivation and personality* (2nd edn). Harper & Row, New York.

Masson, S. (1996) *The Gifting*. HarperCollins, Pymble, NSW.

—— (1998) *Red City*. HarperCollins, Pymble, NSW.

Mills, M. (1997) 'Boys and masculinities', *Education Links*, No 54 (Autumn), pp. 22–4.

Moore, J.N. (1997) *Interpreting Young Adult Literature: Literary Theory in the Secondary Classroom*. Boynton/Cook Publishers, Heinemann, Portsmouth, NH.

Muus, R.E. (1982) *Theories of Adolescence* (4th edn). Random House, New York.

Nix, Garth (1990) *The Ragwitch*. Tor Books, New York.

—— (1995) *Sabriel*. HarperCollins Publishers, Sydney.

Noel, R.C. (1997) *The Borrowed Cup of Courage: A Descriptive Comparison of Archetypes Presented by Male and Female Authors in Fantasy for Adolescents*. UMI Dissertation Services (degree date 1987). Ann Arbor, Michigan.

Odgers, S. (1998) *Translations in Celadon*. HarperCollins Publishers, Sydney.

Olsen, T. (1980) *Silences*. Virago, London.

Paulsen, M. (1999) 'Deconstructing hegemonic masculinity: An approach for high school students', *Youth Studies Australia*, vol 18, No 3 (September) pp. 12–17.

Pearson, C. (1998) *The Hero Within: Six Archetypes We Live By* (3rd edn). HarperSanFrancisco, San Francisco.

—— (1991) *Awakening the Heroes Within: Twelve Archetypes to Help Us Find Ourselves and Transform Our World*. HarperSanFrancisco, San Francisco.

Pinkola Estes, C. (1992) *Women Who Run with the Wolves: Contacting the power of the wild woman*. Random House, London.

Pryor, M. (1998) *The Book of Plans*. Hodder Headline, Rydalmere, NSW.

—— (1998) *The House of Many Rooms*. Hodder Headline, Rydalmere, NSW.

—— (1999) *The Unmaker*. Hodder Headline, Rydalmere, NSW.

Reed, A.J.S. (1985) *Reaching Adolescents: The Young Adult Book and the School*. Holt, Rinehart and Winston, New York.

Rosenberg, M. (1965) *Society and the Adolescent Self-Image*. Princeton University Press, Princeton, NJ.

—— (1979) *Conceiving the Self*. Basic Books, New York.

Safford, B. R. (1997) *High Fantasy: An Archetypal Analysis of Children's Literature*. UMI Dissertation Services (degree date 1983), Ann Arbor, Michigan.

Salmonson, J.A. (ed) (1979) *Amazons!*. Daw Books, New York.

Schneir, M. (ed) (1994) *Feminism: The Essential Historical Writings*. Random House, New York.

Shavelson, R.J., Hubner, J.J. and Stanton, G.C. (1976) 'Self-concept: Validation of construct interpretations', *Review of Educational Research*, vol 46, pp. 407–41.

Simmons, R.G. and Blyth, D.A. (1987) *Moving into Adolescence: The impact of pubertal change and school context*. Hawthorn, New York.

Smith, I. D. (1999) 'Cross-cultural research into children's self-concept in Thailand and Australia', *Asia Pacific Journal of Education*, vol 19, No 1, pp. 7–20.

Thomson, J. (1987) *Understanding Teenagers' Reading: Reading processes and the teaching of literature*. Methuen Australia, North Ryde, NSW.

Thunder Strikes (2000) 'Elder Wisdom: Re-inventing the male archetypes', http://www.dtmms.org/readingroom/male-archetypes/elder-wisdom.htm

Walmsley, D. (1997) *Adolescent self-concept: An analysis and comparison of selected young adult fiction and current theories on adolescent psychology*. UMI Dissertation Services (degree date 1988). Ann Arbor, Michigan.

Warner, M. (1994) *Managing Monsters: Six myths of our time. The Reith Lectures 1994*. Vintage, London.

Watkins, D. and Gutierrez, M. (1989) 'The structure of self-concept: Some Filipino evidence', *Australian Psychologist*, 24, pp. 401–10.

Wollstonecraft, M. (1792) *A Vindication of the Rights of Women.*

Wylie, R.C. (1979) *The Self-Concept (Vol. 2).* University of Nebraska Press, Lincoln.

Yates, L. (1993) *The Education of Girls: Policy research and the question of gender.* Australian Centre for Educational Research (ACER), Hawthorn.

Endnotes

1   More recently, psychologists and mythologists have tried to avoid that androcentric bias by delving further back in time, to the millenia where the Great Mother was the chief or only god — to discover interpretations which apply more closely to the female consciousness. See, for example, Larrington 1992.

2   A number of publications outline some of the key theories of psychological and social development in adolescence. Among the clearest are Walmsley's (1988) doctoral thesis *Adolescent self-concept: An analysis and comparison of selected young adult fiction and current theories on adolescent psychology*; or Donalson and Nilson's standard text *Literature for Today's Young Adults* (1980).

3   This fits in with Havighurst's (1953) model of developmental tasks. These tasks were predicated on the assumption of teenagers' maturation into citizens who are able and willing to participate in a democratic and capitalist society.

4   For further discussion of female voices, silence and taboos, see Olsen (1980) *Silences.* London, Virago.

5   Carol Pearson's archetypes are not identified as 'belonging to' one gender or the other; she sees them as characteristics that — at least in the modern world — are necessarily found in both genders. The closest she comes to identifying an archetype with a gender is her acknowledgment that certain behavioural characteristics (such as warrior attributes) are more likely to be found in one gender than another.

Chapter 9

The once and future kingdom of the soul

by Sophie Masson

In this chapter, I am not concerned with setting down answers, but hope rather to set off sparks, little ideas to shoot off in all directions; a magpie's treasure-trove of little notions and ideas which may illuminate or provoke or perplex the reader, or cause them to laugh out loud. Whatever. What I certainly hope it will not do is close off options or discussion! It is as concerned with the personal as the cultural, the historical as much as the here-and-now. For this is about the realm of *once upon a time*.

Fantasy, tradition and modern literature

There has always been a bit of an apartheid, in literature, between what is loosely called 'fantasy' and 'realism'. Even in the Middle Ages, which we tend to see, rather simplistically, as a marvel-prone time, writers were routinely criticised for writing 'things that aren't true'. The great twelfth century French narrative poet and romancer (as a novelist is still known in French), Marie de France, whose works of romance and magic and adventure based on Celtic and Arthurian motifs and legends, along with those of her near-contemporary, Chretien de Troyes, proved both very popular in their time and enormously influential in the history of Western literature, was told off in just this fashion. One Denis Piramus took her to task for writing 'works that everyone reads, which are about untrue things!'. How dare readers prefer such escapism to his own inestimable, thumpingly worthy 'non-fiction' tomes? The aggrieved, contemptuous tone Piramus uses is a wryly familiar one to many modern writers.

More than 800 years down the track, it also helps to explain why two very popular and impressive areas of modern literature — children's books and fantasy — have also been amongst the most ignored literary forms, at least as far as the mainstream media is concerned, in the twentieth century. When *The Australian Magazine* commissioned, in late 1999, an issue on 'The Greatest Writers of the Century/Millenium', children's authors were notable by their absence. I would argue that in fact children's books have been the great success story — both artistically and commercially — of the century that has just passed, and of course most of the great children's literature of the century was in the fantasy mode.

Adult fantasy is also routinely ignored, though it happens to be one of the most popular genres around, with a huge, intensely loyal readership. In my view, adult fantasy is in general much less accomplished and exciting than fantasy written for children, but it has some marvellous writers working within the field, and a great potential before it. As more and more good writers are liberated from the tyranny of photographic-style 'realism', or dusty modernism, it may well become *the* great genre of the twenty-first century, with as great an influence, as extraordinary an effect, as the works of the Romance writers in the twelfth century had on the development of European literature. We are seeing the beginnings of that at the moment: in the extraordinary cross-generational success of the Harry Potter books, for example, and those of extraordinary writers such as Philip Pullman, but also in the growth of genres such as magic realism. For fantasy liberates the spirit!

Traditional and modern culture — differences and benefits

Our times are often described by commentators, both negatively and positively, as being unlike any other. Old ways of thinking, it is claimed, have been destroyed; children living in a so-called visual culture no longer respond to the same stories as their ancestors did. Nonsense! For a start, our times share many features in common with other times. And next, I think the idea that we are living in a visual culture is a mistake; this is not a visual culture so much as an *abstract* culture, the product of universal literacy. A true visual culture, combined with orality, is to be found in the Middle Ages, in fact. People derived much of their view of the world from visual things, and most especially from churches. If you look at a medieval church or cathedral, in a country which did not experience the Reformation, such as France, for instance, you will see that it is full of visual images — of paintings, carvings, statues, gargoyles, frescoes, etc. These were all intended to perform several functions: to tell stories, to embody the sacred truths, to humanise abstract concepts such as God and the Devil. In the churches are all kinds of visual stories, many of which do not at all fit in with the false image we have of medieval religion, for there are many frankly pagan, irreverent, erotic or even obscene elements to them. Combined with the powerful oral storytelling of the priest, it helped to ground people's sense of themselves and their culture. And it wasn't only in Europe that these things occurred — you've only got to look, to take an example I am familiar with, at the Javanese Buddhist temple of Borobudur to know that there, too, the visual and the oral combine powerfully to give an extraordinary sense of a robust, richly developed, multi-layered agrarian culture with a keen sense both of human life and of the dimensions of the sacred and the magical — the 'Otherworld', if you like.

In agrarian-based societies, folk and 'high' culture are not as separate as they are in industrial and post-industrial societies: the stories of Marie de France and Chretien de Troyes had both aristocratic and folk culture elements to them; Shakespeare's plays appealed both to the 'groundling' and to the courtier. It was assumed then that people got what they needed out of stories, at whatever level they chose to, or were capable of. Our modern post-industrial world, supposedly so much less class-conscious, by contrast entrenches false distinctions between fantasy and realism, 'highbrow' and 'lowbrow', male and female, black and white, past and present. That is because in fact it is an abstract culture, which values concepts and ideas — the domain of the so-called 'rational' — very much more than it values the fluidity of storytelling, in whatever medium. Rigid, often banal and tendentious categorisation, a lumbering obscurantism of expression and a muddling of clear thought seem to be the results of an over-reliance on the abstract. In the age of the mass market, strangely, we seem to have less of a sophisticated understanding of real human beings than the folk culture of the Middle Ages did, myth and fancy and all! And strangely enough, the real 'fantasy', as in destructive fantasy, lies there. The bigger corporations get, the less contact they seem to have with reality; the more distanced writers get from folk culture, from storytelling, the more analytical they become, the less readers are interested. This is the case even in films; Hollywood has learnt (at its expense) that movies made to some kind of cookie-cutter template just don't wash with the public; the real success stories in films, as with books, is where directors and producers have remained true to the storytelling instinct. Clever-clever camera shots and clumsy analytical devices are simply boring — just as tricks in books, clever-clever nudges and winks at critics are a big turn-off.

And here's the other side of modern culture that may surprise you, for it's very seldom mentioned. Far from being uninterested in the past, far from being removed from it, this is actually one of the greatest ages of recovery and rediscovery of the past, to be compared perhaps to the Renaissance in importance. Before the twentieth century, for instance, we did not know what medieval music sounded like, for no-one had bothered deciphering the many musical manuscripts from the time deposited in libraries all over the world. The great Elizabethan 'metaphysical' poets like John Donne and George Herbert were virtually forgotten; the Middle Ages seen as one long thousand-year period of darkness; pre-Roman societies hardly known at all. Compare that to now, when countless people are beavering away at all kinds of wonderfully esoteric and exciting projects that continually add to more of an understanding of the world. And surprise, surprise — tradition, history, human life and thought and story over the ages and all over the world turn out to be vastly more complex, vastly richer, vastly stranger and more troubling and exciting than any anxious categoriser could imagine.

The importance of children's books in forming modern culture

In an agrarian world, children were not seen as a separate part of society, and certainly their world view was not seen as separate from that of their parents. Therefore, fairytales and folktales, myth and legend, the lives of saints and stories of the Devil, were told to all and for all, not just children. With the disappearance of agrarian society in England after the Industrial Revolution and the emergence of an industrial world came, first, the exploitation of children, then their protection. And also a yearning for that vanished rural Otherworld which now only children were imagined to inhabit — an earthy world yet also one of effortless, natural fantasy and grace: the world of the agrarian society, which produced not only fairytales but also Shakespeare. And out of that yearning was born children's literature; which embodied the view of childhood as the last place of enchantment.

The first children's books were often turgid homilies, but as the nineteenth century advanced and dissolved into the twentieth, and the sense of distance from that rural Otherworld grew, so, paradoxically, did the beauty, freedom, grace and sheer fun of children's literature in English-speaking cultures, culminating in an explosion of talent in the twentieth century. (In other cultures, less distant perhaps from agrarian society, things were different. For instance, in my country of origin, France, there are only a few great children's writers — St Exupery, De Brunhoff, Herge, Goscinny/Uderzo being four who spring to mind, but they are not novelists.) In fact, the twentieth century produced so many good children's writers, so many beautiful works of art that one can profitably compare it to the heyday of the adult novel in the nineteenth century.

Following on from the glorious seeding of the nineteenth century — with its Andersens, Grimms, Nesbits, Lears, Collodis, Carrolls and MacDonalds — we have seen a flowering of literary talent and beauty unmatched since Elizabethan times, in any form of fiction. That's not an idle comparison — the lightness of touch, melancholy, humanity, deft fantasy, sheer storytelling magic and lyricism which characterise Shakespeare's equally tormented and hopeful and energetic time have all found a home in children's literature in the twentieth century, and look set to continue into the twenty-first. The rollcall of the last 100 years is extraordinary, and could fill several pages: A.A. Milne, Kenneth Grahame, C.S. Lewis, J.R.R. Tolkien, Alan Garner, Leon Garfield, Patricia Wrightson, L. Frank Baum, Tove Jannsson, Rudyard Kipling, Dianne Wynne Jones, Philip Pullman, to name but a tiny percentage of brilliant writers, right up to the first years of the twenty-first century. And although the modernist king tide in the early and middle part of the twentieth century, and then post-modern trickery, all but swamped storytelling and passion and fantasy in adult literature until very recently, they have been alive and well in books for children throughout the modern period. There have been hits and misses; there have been times when it seemed issues and agenda might swamp story; but that never completely happened, and we have had a number of 'golden ages' in children's literature, over the last 100 years or so.

Children's writers have never forgotten about story: the central plank of any writer's art throughout the ages. In part, it is a necessity: you simply cannot afford to forget about such things if you want your readers to stay with you! Shakespeare knew that he had to keep large play-going crowds entertained, that they would not put up with dullness; Dickens knew that the readers of his serials must be kept breathlessly hanging till next time. Children's writers today know they must keep their readers entertained; an audience that does not put up with dullness either! The extraordinary success of the Harry Potter books, which in my opinion are helping to usher in a new golden age in children's literature, is a case in point. The success was not created by a marketing machine, but by the readers themselves. For the first time since the days of Charles Dickens, adult readers queued up all night to get their own hands on a copy of a book! And that book had been written for children.

What is more, children's books have influenced, and been read by, far more people than perhaps any of the great modern writers' books for adults. In times to come, which may see these things more clearly, children's literature may well be recognised as *the* greatest and most important literary movement of our times. The best children's books transcend their time; being archetypal, and built on story, they survive much better than fashionable or socially or politically driven adult novels. Winnie-the-Pooh or the BFG or Bilbo Baggins or the Muddle-Headed Wombat are much more a part of people's mental furniture than Leopold Bloom or Lady Chatterley or Humbert Humbert or Lucky Jim. On the other hand, books such as Herge's adventures of Tintin, going from Stalin's Russia to the moon landings, have formed clearer pictures of modern history for many readers than any number of history books or personal witness. This is also because childhood is the great time for reading. Many people, in fact, go from being voracious readers in their childhood (as is still very much the case, despite periodic panics about children not reading any more) to scarcely reading at all as adults, and certainly very little fiction.

Modernism sought to break with the past, and was energised in part by its commitment to newness; but without a vital source, a stream soon dries up, and peters out in the wilderness. And only a dedicated explorer bothers then with trying to find out why such an experiment was tried in the first place. And this is what leads many modern critics to bewail the state of the (literary) adult novel, and to periodically predict its demise. The literary novel is criticised (often justly, but sometimes unjustly) for its anaemic and enervating atmosphere, its introverted characters, and its lack of narrative drive. Genre novels, such as crime or fantasy/science fiction, in the adult field have kept to traditional storytelling, but they often cannot take risks with character, for instance, and tend unfortunately to repeat modern formulae — in fantasy's case, usually Tolkien's groundbreaking model, without Tolkien's vast understanding and depth of knowledge of traditional culture. However, modern children's books, because they have by and large kept the continuity with fable, with medieval romance, with legend, mythology and fairytale, with *story*, in short, whilst taking risks with new subjects, exploration of character, and playing around with reality, have been able to present something which is both new, and timeless.

Both a popular form of entertainment and a potential outlet for extraordinary literary gifts, children's literature bridges both 'popular' and 'high' culture in a way which I think is unique in modern literature in general, and which, as time goes on, has more and more implications for culture as a whole. The return of narrative, of passion and playfulness and moral seriousness as well, in film as well as books, has come about in part because of children's books, and children's stories, within the fantasy genre. It has been an underground thing for the last 20 years or so, perhaps since the time of Tolkien and Lewis and the first of the *Star Wars* movies — but now it is bursting out into the open air, and yeasting the culture as a whole. And it makes me feel greatly excited and optimistic. For the first time in years, the cinemas are full of wonderful things, fantastic stories such as *The Sixth Sense* and *Shakespeare in Love* and *Gladiator* and *Galaxy Quest*: stories with heart, depth, wit, intelligence, subtlety, yet also thrilling and exciting. Wonderful writers, those who have beavered away for years unnoticed, have suddenly come into their own: people like Kevin Crossley-Holland and Dianne Wynne Jones, for instance. Great classics are being rediscovered, as well as new writers with great power and originality in using traditional motifs, such as J.K. Rowling and Lemony Snicket and Philip Pullman. Strangely enough, in my opinion, the rediscovery of the childlike sense of wonder in story does not make a society or a culture less adult — but more so. People had been gulled for too long into thinking that agenda-setting and issue-raising was the right way to go; but now, writers everywhere are bursting the boring bonds of such conventions.

Tradition is not dead, but is continually refreshed

Listen up! Once upon a time, there was a boy who grew up in a foster home, unknowing of his true parentage, taunted for it by his foster-brother. He was a boy who nevertheless had a great destiny put on him, a child set apart from all other children. One day, this child would be put to the test, would learn who he really was, and begin to understand what his burden and destiny, his blessing and curse, was to be, and begin to take up the tasks that were expected of him. He would learn, too, the sacrifices that would have to be made along the way. One day this child would be the centre of a new beginning, a new just kingdom. And knowing this, the forces opposing him would stop at nothing to compromise and destroy him.

Remind you of anyone? Did you say Harry Potter? Well, that's perhaps his most recent name. But go a bit deeper — try Arthur — King Arthur, the legendary King of the West who strode out of Celtic legend and Breton folktale to bequeath to Western culture, through the Romance writers of the twelfth century, probably the most enduring, rich and complex archetypes and motifs ever in the history of literature. Arthur, the once and future king, in the stories bridges the gulf between the world of action and the world of meaning, the mundane world and the Otherworld, who embodies within himself and his legend so many of the contradictory streams of Western culture, streams that seem never to run dry. He is perhaps the most extraordinary example of the fantasy, or legendary, archetype; the clearest picture we have of the paradoxical reality of fantasy, and of just how much relevance it has to our lives as human beings.

Just as the freshness of rediscovered Celtic fantasy reinvigorated the narrow culture of the early Middle Ages, so too the freshness of children's books has touched off a reaction within writers, and readers, the world over. People are realising that we don't have to say goodbye to the past in order to live in the present; that the once and future kingdom of the soul is right there, at hand; that the magical Otherworld is not in some place beyond the world, but within it, exciting, inspirational, lively and fresh as ever. Story is back, in a big way. Myth, that most clearly shows us what it is like to be human — not through preaching or analysis, but through story — is intensely, freshly relevant, once again.

And so, what a wonderful time to be writing in! What wonderful riches we can access! What fantastic stories we can tell! But what is it actually like, using traditional stories, myth and legend, to tell stories that modern readers want to read? I'd like to tell you my own story.

Writing from tradition: a view from the coalface

I've always been interested in traditional stories, from a very young age. Perhaps because of the way in which I was brought up, these stories seemed to me to describe the world and life much more truly than any so-called 'fact' I knew. Born in Java of French parents who are themselves of very mixed ancestry — Basque, Portuguese, Spanish, French and French Canadian — I was taken back to France to live with my grandmother before I was one year old, as I was rather sick and my parents were afraid I might die in Indonesia.

My parents spent another four years in Java, and so my earliest memories are of being with my grandmother and aunts in the ancient south-western city of Toulouse. There I was brought up in an atmosphere of story and legend, for my grandmother told lots of fairytales to me, mostly traditional French ones like *Puss in Boots* and *Beauty and the Beast* and *Cinderella* and *Toads and Diamonds*, but also lesser-known ones and stories of her childhood, and of people she knew. When I came to Australia in 1963, reunited with my parents at last, we were still brought up between and within two worlds, as we were often going back to France.

Even in Australia, though, we spoke only French at home, yet English at school. My schooling was in Sydney and the tiny South Western French village of Empeaux, which nestles near one of the oldest woods in the region, Goujon, part of which has remained standing since Neolithic times. And always I was in an atmosphere of story, of legend, of myth; my parents, especially my father, used to tell us many stories, particularly European ones, but also from Indonesia, from Africa, from India. He was also interested in Australian folk culture, and in Aboriginal myth, and so we had lots of books to read on subjects that were not all that popular in Australia at the time, but that coloured all my way of thinking.

My family has a very long and colourful, not to say melodramatic, past history, and we were full of the exploits and strangeness of our ancestors as well. We also had shelves and shelves of books on history, religion and mysticism, and I devoured these to the sound of lots of music from many different regions.

When we went back to France, Dad would take us on long walks in the forests and up mountainsides where strange old ruined castles teetered on the edges of cliffs. For me, the stories and people of the past were not long ago and far away; they lived in every breath we took, their voices so close to me, their passions and horrors under my skin. We were encouraged to discuss and challenge and explore; to follow our noses and our hearts wherever they took us; an extraordinary background for a writer of fantasy. And always, too, I was aware of the world beyond the world, the things I could glimpse not only of the past but also of some eternal, mysterious presence — the thing I think of as 'the silent singing of the universe', the thing within everyday existence that is at the heart of all myths and legends.

I became particularly interested in Celtic mythology when I was about 11 years-old, whilst still delving very much into other stories and other ways. Later, as a teenager, I discovered Shakespeare, with whose bright and dark spirit I fell immediately in love, and whose work has never ceased to nourish and intrigue and tease me in every way. And all these influences, all these experiences fed into my understanding of ourselves as myth-making creatures, of our lives in this extraordinary world as being rich with meaning, of following ancient patterns that were constantly renewed, and constantly reinvented. And it was exciting to write within those frameworks, in short story, poetry and novel, and to retell and reinvent and renew the old stories, to constantly discover the deep, subtle, not always comfortable meanings within the light-hearted magic, the gory battles, the archetypal love stories.

But when I started professionally as a writer for children and young people, in the very late 1980s (my first short story for young people was published in the New South Wales *School Magazine* in 1987, my first novel in 1990), it seemed to me then that the literary climate in Australia was not conducive to straight-out explorations of myth and legend and fairytale. The ultra-realistic, or rather hyper-realistic, or exaggerated-realism novel was in vogue, and its popularity would go up and up in the years that followed.

After the 'golden age' of the 1960s and 1970s, it seemed as if traditional literature had been put to one side, in favour of the supposedly 'relevant'. Fantasy was not as visible as it is now: though there was quite a lot for younger readers, there was certainly not so much for older readers, and little for adults at all (many Australian writers of adult fantasy had to go offshore at this stage to get published). There also seemed to be a trend for post-holocaust, science fantasy novels rather than those based on traditional stories: the end of the Cold War seems to have reduced the incidence of those kinds of nuclear-Dark Age novels, however. Their place has been taken to some extent by the environmental-disaster futuristic novel. But fantasy novels based on fairytale and myth and legend were not common in the Australian scene (incidentally, they still aren't, unlike, say, in the UK!), and it was not easy to interest publishers in such a concept, especially if the novels were for older readers. The idea that myth told what it was like to be human without boring lectures, that the stories were all about human beings and our journey in life, was not, it seemed, of general mainstream interest at the time.

And so I decided at the time to tell the stories I wanted to tell mostly through the medium of realism, but still with the underlying patterns of those stories I loved. Since traditional stories tell the story of us, because they're the realism of the human soul, as it were, it is actually quite easy to reinterpret them in modern, even non-magical, terms in a way that is not possible if you're departing from an ideology or a fixed idea, or even social observation as such. So, some of my early novels had strong elements of myth, legend and fantasy in them; for example, the time-slip *Fire in the Sky*, or the Celtic-influenced *A Blaze of Summer*. In others, traditional stories featured as underlying motifs and patterns. Therefore, for many years I did not write fantasy novels as such, though I had plenty of ideas for them in my notebook! Meanwhile, as well as jotting down those ideas, I read and read and read and thought and thought and thought; and eventually, when the climate in Australia changed and publishers in Australia were actively seeking out fantasy, all that long reflection bore fruit.

My first two fantasy novels were published in the same year, 1996, and they expressed very different aspects of my interest in traditional stories. *Carabas* derives very much from that inner core of my identity, that very French tradition of the tough, worldly, yet romantic and mysterious story of enchantment; *le conte de fees*, or fairytale, in this case *Le Chat Botte*, or *Puss in Boots*. This story had been around for centuries in French folk culture before it was written down with a characteristic lightness of touch by the great Charles Perrault in the late seventeenth century. The story expressed a great deal about France as a culture, as well as about the nature of power, the possibility of change, the meaning of metamorphosis. I connected it too with a mysterious passage in Genesis, about the sons of God mating with the daughters of men; unexpected, even surprising connections are a bit of a speciality of my magpie mind. (I might add that I'm often as surprised as the next person at the results!)

The writing of *Carabas* was a sheer unalloyed delight. I revelled in the freedom the vehicle of fairytale gave my voice to fully express itself, and I re-experienced that wonderful state of deep, instinctive, toe-wriggling pleasure that we get from stories in our childhoods. But it also explored the deep realism of aspects of human nature and human life that never go away: for instance, the ostracism of people who are different, the nature of evil, the power of love. Here is what the simple, gentle and guileless Frederic, miller's son turned to Marquis of Carabas, says to the being known as Monsieur Balze, who has been attempting to make him turn against his strange companion, the shape-shifting Catou, or Serafin (p. 170):

> It is possible she has a divided nature, as you say. I have seen her powers with my own eyes.
> I have been disquieted by them, for she is not exactly like the rest of us. Yet I cannot believe

the rest. And my heart tells me she is not as you say, not because I am clever or know much at all, but because my blood and my flesh tell me so. We may be dust, Monsieur Balze, but I would rather be dust than a prince of the air without a soul. I would rather be dust than an empty darkness, a hungry abyss. At least dust mixed with water becomes dirt, and dirt grows crops and sustains life.

Now, when I wrote that I had in mind, as well as Frederic and his dilemma, the long rollcall of hatred and inhumanity to strangers and neighbours who are different, that has occurred throughout human history. I thought of the hysteria of witch-burnings, of the Holocaust, of innumerable stories of horror and pain, when human beings acted in ways that makes one despair and bitter with sorrow. However, even in the worst times, there were individual acts of heroism, of selflessness, of compassion, of sheer *love*, even from strangers. And those acts matter, they matter a great deal. But I did not want to expound on it, or even to present it in a historical or political framework; I wanted it to emerge naturally, in a story.

Stories, especially those kinds of stories, do that much better than any kind of analysis. Long before Freud and Jung, people in traditional cultures knew that stories carry within them the essence of what it is to be human, in all our terror and beauty and horror and humour and tragedy and joy. As complex as human nature itself, yet as simply told as a life story, fairytales can be told to a little child every bit as well as to the oldest and wisest person of all, and to everyone in between — each will get what he or she needs or wants out of it. That's because there are no boundaries to them; no closed-off meanings. 'Fairy' or 'faery' is another name not for little things with butterfly wings, but for the mysterious, yet simple essence of human life, a meaning beyond, no, *within* the everyday. It is about everyday magic, everyday heroism, everyday prowess, yet transmuted into a timeless and wonderfully coloured thing.

The Gifting explored another greatly loved area for me: that of Celtic myth, and the historical affront of Roman versus Celt. This dualistic affront has been an underlying pattern in Western culture ever since: urban versus rural, power versus mystery, technological versus magical, figurative versus abstract. The two streams are within Western culture, of course, and it's not only cultures which experience the age-old conflict, but individual people too. I've always been much more interested in exploring those things through people, through character rather than analysis, and so it is within those characters that the very complex story is brought out. The title, and the climax of the novel, refer to an ancient Celtic custom, known as 'gifting', where two rival chiefs competed by giving each other more and more costly or valuable gifts — the loser was the one who had no more gifts to give. It was a way of solving disputes without resorting to war; a typically Celtic custom, I think: down to earth yet extraordinary, a mad idea in one way yet deeply imbued with commonsense. It seemed like a fitting symbol for the novel!

The enchanted world is the green kingdom of the soul

Since those two novels (*Carabas* and *The Gifting*), most of my books have been fantasy novels; always set in the real world, yet in a parallel dimension, where magic and the mundane literally exist side by side. Because writing is always a process of discovery, I have learnt that I am more comfortable (happier) in a world like that of *Carabas* than *The Gifting*, though *Carabas* is the world of the fairytale, a world not really similar to, say, *The Lord of the Rings*, but closer to *The Hobbit* (Tolkien, 1998). For I am exploring what Tolkien called 'the perilous realm', the realm of folklore and fairytale, the world that lies within and beside our 'everyday' world; that *is*, in fact, our everyday world, in its essence.

And so *Cold Iron, Clementine, The Green Prince, The Firebird,* and the recent novels for adults too (based on the stories of Marie de France), *The Knight by the Pool* and *Lady of the Flowers* (which will, with a third, be soon published as *The Forest of Dreams*) all explore that realm, which is the nexus between folk and aristocratic culture, enriched by both, both light and deep, sprightly and serious. And I have found that such travel to the perilous realm most clearly calls forth not only my own gift, but the enthusiasm and response of readers.

The Green Prince, for instance, which specifically travels to the wondrous and traditionally Celtic Otherworlds under the water, has been riding on a great tide of reader response. I know that it is in this kind of story that I most clearly, yet subtly, say what I want to say, through story and character and the sheer fun and delight of fantasy. Whilst I continue, and will continue, to write all sorts of books, I have learnt that these are my true love, my once and future kingdom of the soul, if you like. And I feel very strongly that I want to help reconnect modern readers to the beauties and fun of traditional culture. Too many people seem to think that the way to the enchanted world is closed to us now, that indeed we no longer need it because we have science and technology and are so much more clever than people in the past! As Oberon, King of the Fairies, says sadly in *Cold Iron* (p. 165):

> … Cold iron drives us away because it shows you have no more need of us. Iron is cold like the hearts that no longer want us. Iron is mortal yet immortal. It banishes us from field and forest, from sky and earth. You think you rule it all, with iron. You can explain it all. You can master the Earth and all within it. We who are creatures of air and dream and shadow and hidden meanings, we who are the opposite of cold iron, we fade away then, we are no longer seen …

But Oberon is not telling the whole truth. As the heroine Malkin comes to understand, later, cold iron does *not* have to do that. Transmuted into the living gold of love and wonder, it can remind us of our earthly realities, so we don't, too, become creatures of dream and shadow and hidden meanings. We need to live robustly in our flesh and blood, and iron (the symbol of human ingenuity) is necessary to us. But so are the fairies, so is the green kingdom that is the realism of the soul. Without iron, we might well have difficult, even terrible, material lives; without the green kingdom, we have difficult, even terrible inner lives. We might be satiated to the eyebrows with material things; but if we are not satisfied in our souls too, it's every bit as deadly as being hungry or uncomfortable. Or as a great 'understander' of story and inner meaning once said, 'What does it profit to gain the world if you lose your soul?' (paraphrased from Jesus' saying, as recorded in the Gospel of Mark, 8:36–7). We need both myth and flesh; both the past and the present; we need to feel at home in both — neither to demonise nor to glamorise, but to recognise that tradition still has a great deal to offer us. And to remember that today's latest thing is tomorrow's old hat!

The letters and comments I have had from readers show that this is not just an individual perception of mine. It is the fairytale novels, the novels that most clearly evoke the supposedly vanished world of pre-industrial folk culture, that most deeply seem to speak to readers from all over the world. Recently, I was discussing my fantasy novels with a Javanese friend, and he observed that the atmosphere and underlying patterns in them would be thoroughly familiar and understandable to anyone from Java, for the perilous realm is known to everyone there too; stories of people who go in and out of it are known to all. Indeed, he said, in each village there are such stories; and he proceeded to tell me one about someone from his own village who had disappeared in the forest for three days and three nights, and had only been found on the third night. When he was found, he told of how he had been in a hidden village, a 'fairy' or Otherworldly village, deep in the forest, where he had been invited to a feast, but had not eaten anything, for he knew if he did he could never come home again.

He had seen everyone searching for him, but they had not seen him, and until three days and three nights had passed, the man could not return to his village from this strange place. Just as the Otherworlders had experienced some mysterious longing to see him the day he was lost, so there was some secret law which prevented him returning to human ken before a certain, pre-ordained time. Now, said my friend, this same man who in the past had been thought of as somewhat simple, had a clear and even respected place in the village as something of a *dukun*, or second-sighted healer. And the fact was, he went on, we didn't find the man before the three days and nights were up, though we looked and looked; and the place where we found him was one where we'd looked before; he was found right in the middle of the path, leaning up against a tree. And he had talents after this event that he'd never had before.

Oh, it gave me goose bumps, that story! Not only because it, amongst other Javanese stories, is of course going to form the basis for the Javanese fantasy novel, *The Dukun's Daughter*, which I am planning, but also because of what it says about the relevance of traditional meanings, traditional stories. The once and future kingdom of the soul is there, open to all of us, for it belongs to the whole human race. Ever since the first storyteller told the first story we have known this, deep within ourselves: myth and legend and fairytale is the story of us, in the world. And fantasy is not for deserters who want lies, but for those who want to 'escape' the dull and the habitual for the purpose of really knowing, and rediscovering the truth of the world itself, and of our short, sweet, tragic, glorious, terrifying and mysterious human lives. We are not fairies, not inhabitants of the perilous realm ourselves, for we are mortal, subject to time and sadness and grief. But to us has been given, in compensation, a gift greater even than that of fairy immortality: and that is the gift of story. And is that not the greatest gift of them all?

Epilogue

There too is old Father Gaston, the priest who once christened Candide himself. He is an old friend of the fairy sisters; he is not afraid or wary of them, for he is a woodsman's son, and spent his wild, lonely childhood in the forest. He met Alice (one of the fairies) long ago, when, taken by his childish beauty, she had rolled a little golden ball before him, and he had followed it, laughing and singing. He has told Alice that he does not think God would have created such a beautiful world and so many mysteries if He meant humans to ignore or be afraid of them. He has also shown her a little book he has written and illustrated, in which he propounds the theory that fairies and other immortal beings are really the sons and daughters of lost angels, wandering the earth, forgetful of their heavenly lineage, bound tightly to the earth and its children. He has sought to question Alice about her people. But Alice does not know any of their history; no fairy has ever kept a genealogy book, that is for humans, who need, poor things, to cling to time with as many words and as much understanding as they can muster. When you are immortal — or almost immortal, for fairies do not die, but fade away — you do not need such reassurances, or such reminders. Tradition is not the way of the ancestors, for fairies; it is simply the way things have always been done. They do not tell legends or stories, for they live in an eternal present.

(*Clementine*, 1999: 24–5)

Further Reading

Celtic legends: The Mabinogion, the great Welsh cycle of legends, has been beautifully retold for young people by Haydn Middleton in *The Island of the Mighty* (Oxford, 1986). Irish sagas, such as that of Cuchulain, Finn and others, can be found in many collections and retellings, including Rosemary Sutcliff's *The Hound of Ulster*, *Chronicles of the Celts* by Iain Zaczek (Hodder and Stoughton, 1996) and many others.

Arthurian legends: There are many collections of these, and many good retellings, including a recent volume by British author Michael Morpurgo, which retells Malory's version. Good novels based on the Arthurian legend, suitable for children and young people, include Kevin Crossley-Holland's *The Seeing Stone*, T. H. White's *The Once and Future King*, and Rosemary Sutcliff's trilogy on Arthur.

Good source or discussion works about the stories, their characters and settings include Ronan Coghlan's *The Encyclopedia of Arthurian Legends* (Element Books, 1993) and *The New Arthurian Encyclopedia*, edited by Norris J. Lacy (Garland Reference Library, 1996).

Marie de France: *The Lais of Marie de France*, Penguin Classics 1986,

Proud Knight, Fair Lady, The Lais of Marie de France, translated by Naomi Lewis and illustrated by Angela Barrett (Viking Kestrel, 1989).

Collections of fairytales: Look for those by Charles Perrault (many translations available), the Brothers Grimm, Joseph Jacobs. Also many modern versions, especially those by writers such as Berlie Doherty, Geraldine McCaughrean, Angela Carter.

Folktales and fairytale source books and discussion: Katherine Briggs' collections especially are excellent, as well as her source books such as *A Dictionary of Fairies* (Penguin, 1977) which, for instance, include many creatures to be found not only in traditional literature but also in Harry Potter! Other books by Briggs include *The Anatomy of Puck* (Routledge, 1959), about Elizabethan and Jacobean ideas of fairies and other spirits; *The Personnel of Fairyland* (Alden Press, 1953); *Folktales of England* (Routledge & Kegan Paul, 1965); *The Fairies in English Tradition and Literature* (University of Chicago Press, 1967); and *The Vanishing People* (Batsford, 1978), also about fairies. She is the great expert in the field.

A recent, and excellent, book on the whole fairy phenomenon is British academic Dianne Purkiss' *Troublesome Things* (Penguin, 2001). Tolkien's famous exploration of why fairytales are important, *Tree and Leaf* (Allen & Unwin, 1964), is also well worth seeking out.

General: A good book to read for the history of the novel is Margaret Anne Doody's *The True History of the Novel* (Fontana, 1998), which takes the form's sources back thousands of years, and covers the medieval romance period very well. An interesting, if at times rather opinionated, view of children's fantasy literature is provided in John Goldthwaite's *The Natural History of Make-Believe* (Oxford, 1996).

An excellent biography of William Shakespeare is Park Honan's book, *Shakespeare: A Life* (Oxford, 1999) which has some very good sections on his childhood and influences, and indeed is the best biography of the playwright that has appeared so far; the most readable and the most comprehensive.

Philip Pullman's novels are well worth reading, including his Dark Materials Trilogy: *Northern Lights, The Subtle Knife, The Amber Spyglass* (Scholastic Books, and David Fickling Books, through Scholastic); and his younger readers novels such as *I Was a Rat*, or *The Satin Slippers* (Corgi Yearling through Transworld, 2000); *The Firework-Maker's Daughter*, and *Clockwork* (Corgi Yearling, 1997). As well, there is his series of Victorian thrillers with supernatural elements, the Sally Lockhart Quartet: *The Ruby in the Smoke, The Shadow in the North, The Tiger in the Well*, and *The Tin Princess* (all Scholastic, various editions).

Bibliography

Baum, L.F. (1939) *The Wizard of Oz*. Bobbs-Merrill, Idianapolis.
Crossley-Holland, K. (2001) *The Seeing Stone*. Orion, London.
Garfield, L. (1980s) *Black Jack*. Hear-a-book, North Hobart, Tas.
—— (1980s) *Smith*. Hear-a-book, North Hobart, Tas.
Garner, A. (1967) *The Owl Service*. Collins, London.
—— (1967) *Elidor*. HZ Walck, New York.
—— (1975) *The Weirdstone of Brisingamen*. Collins, London.
—— (nd) *Red Shift*. Harper Collins.
—— (nd) *The Moon of Gomrath*. Harper Collins.
Jannsson, T. (nd) The *Moomintroll* series. Puffin, London.
Jones, D.W. (2000–2001) *The Chrestomanci* series (and others), Harper Collins.
Kipling, Rudyard (1901) *Kim*. Macmillan, London.
—— (1908) *The Jungle Book*. Macmillan, London.
—— (1987) *The Just So Stories*. Children's Classics, New York.
Lewis, C.S. (1988) *The Chronicles of Narnia*. Macmillan, New York.
Milne, A.A. (nd) The Winnie the Pooh Books, published in various editions, Methuen, London.
Masson, S. (1990) *Fire in the Sky*. Angus and Robertson/Collins.
—— (1992) *A Blaze of Summer*. UQP Young adult Fiction.
—— (1996) *Carabas*. Hodder Headline Australia. Also published in 2000 as *Serafin*, St Mary's Press, USA; and to be republished in 2002 as *Carabas*, Hodder UK.
—— (1996) *The Gifting*. Harper Collins Moonstone.
—— (1998) *Red City* (sequel). Harper Collins Moonstone.
—— (1998) *Cold Iron*. Hodder Headline Australia. Also to appear in 2001 as *Malkin*, St Mary's Press, USA.
—— (1999) *Clementine*. Hodder Headline Australia. Also to appear in 2001 under same name in the USA and in 2002 n the UK.
—— (2000) *The Green Prince*. Hodder Headline Australia.
—— (2001) *The Firebird*. Hodder Headline Australia.
—— (2001) *The Forest of Dreams*. Bantam Books.

—— (in production) *The Hand of Glory.* Hodder Headline Australia (due for publication in June 2002.)

—— author website: *http://www.northnet.com.au/~ s masson*

Rowling, J.K. (nd) The Harry Potter books. Bloomsbury, London.

Tolkien, J.R.R. (1954–1955) *The Lord of the Rings.* Various new editions from Allen & Unwin, Harper Collins.

—— (1964) *Tree and Leaf.* Allen & Unwin, London.

—— (1998) *The Hobbit.* Harper Collins, London.

Wrightson, P. (1987) *The Song of Wirrun.* Century, London and Melbourne.

—— (1988) *The Nargun and the Stars.* Hutchinson Australia, Hawthorn, Vic.

—— (1993) *A Little Fear.* Puffin, Ringwood, Vic.

Part three

New constructions of femininities and masculinities

Part three

New constructions of femininities and masculinities

Chapter 10

Chills and thrills:
childhood, boys and
popular horror fiction

Linda Christian-Smith

Introduction

Swamp monsters, werewolves, nightmarish summer camps, sinister theme parks and the things in the basement … These are the dark entities and places of many childhoods. They take on life through the media and horror fiction written especially for children. Horror, once the province of adult fiction, is rapidly becoming an established genre in children's and adolescent literature through Christopher Pike's novels and R.L. Stine's *Goosebumps* series written for second to fourth graders. (Stine also writes *Fear Street*, the horror series for adolescent readers.) Hardly noticeable a few years ago, horror fiction for young readers represented three of the top four best-sellers on *Publishers Weekly's* list of children's trade books in 1992 (Gray, 1993).

In this chapter I examine the *Goosebumps* horror series. I first explore the larger socioeconomic and political context of childhood and children's publishing. Then I present a reading of selected books in the *Goosebumps* series. In this regard, I examine how readers make meanings from *Goosebumps* and reveal how their interpretations construct and are constructed by their understandings of what it means to be a male child.

According to Anderson (1989) researchers need to account for the background and biases they bring to their inquiry and delineate the social and political forces shaping the social universe studied. Who is the 'I' mentioned in the previous paragraph? I am a European American woman who is a university teacher and researcher of curriculum and instruction, working from the perspectives of feminisms, critical theory, postmodernisms and anti-racism. I incorporate insights from poststructuralisms in my teaching and research. The following assumptions and positions inform my study of the '*Goosebumps*' children's horror series.

My story

Reading several of the *Goosebumps* books for this study transported me back to my childhood as a working-class girl of Eastern European background residing in northern Minnesota in the 1950s. I found much in these books I could identify with and yet much that was different than my childhood. I have always been fascinated by the strange, macabre and unexplained. Stine's *Say cheese and die* (1992) reminded me of my visits to the remains of a reputedly haunted burned-out house near the school where I attended kindergarten.

Leading to the old house was a boardwalk, under which trolls were thought to live. This was the quintessential dare of my experiences of childhood. My early home-alone fears were fed by and made sense of through horror fiction. Yet there were family members available to comfort and care for me which is seldom the case in *Goosebumps*. Alongside my reading of Nancy Drew and Jane Austen were H.P. Lovecraft and Edgar Allan Poe stories and the Saturday monster movies such as *I was a teenage werewolf*. In high school I graduated to Mary Shelley's *Frankenstein*, Robert Louis Stevenson's *The strange case of Dr Jekyll and Mr Hyde* and Bram Stoker's *Dracula*. I was hooked on the older versions of films loosely based on these novels.

Today I read little contemporary horror fiction except for the latest instalment of Anne Rice's Vampire chronicles. I remain a fan of vintage horror films such as *Night of the living dead* and modern classic thrillers like *Alien*. However, as a feminist critical educator, I am horrified by the general violence and women's mutilation in the 'slice and dice' scenes prevalent in contemporary horror fiction and films. As one who subscribes to critical literacy frameworks, I am well aware of the utopian and socially incorporated aspects of popular fiction. Reconciling my intellectual frameworks with my feelings of revulsion and my interest in horror is an ongoing process.

The social construction of childhood and masculinities

Childhood often assumes a natural status in psychological discourse, although it is a social construct varying across different historical and cultural sites (Steedman, Urwin & Walkerdine, 1985). The form that childhood takes in a society is closely related to the ways work and leisure are organised as well as school, family and peer relationships. According to Luke (1990), social, political and economic relations shape concepts of childhood. In Western societies, children are often regarded as low-status, economically dependent, incompetent individuals who achieve competency and normality through their interactions with adults who initiate children into larger cultural values. Adult society is constructed as the norm and desirable state, whereas children's society seems to be different and often aberrant. These notions of childhood are of recent origin.

According to Aries (1962), children in Western societies participated freely in everyday events with adults and acquired the knowledge of living from these interactions. During the late Middle Ages childhood as an historical construct and discourse developed as children were increasingly regarded as separate and different from adults. Luke (1989) identifies the large social, economic and political changes brought on by the printing press, the Reformation, the social rebellion of peasants and the rise of the mercantile class as key moments in this shift in thinking. By the sixteenth century, a discourse on childhood was systematised through the printing and disseminating of information on family life, child-rearing and education by pastors and itinerant evangelists. Gradually the school and family were constituted as 'disciplinary sites' where children were defined as needing moral guidance and protection. Valerie Walkerdine (1984) suggests that the 'normalization' of the child continues to underlie today's schools and families, which endeavour to produce self-regulated individuals who fit into the dominant social structure.

Luke (1991) suggests that the above dominant notions of childhood actually mask assumptions that the 'normal' child is a white, middle-class, heterosexual boy. How do boys acquire a sense of themselves from which masculinities are constructed? What 'normalizing' processes do boys experience? How does literacy position boys within 'gender hierarchies' of masculinity? Askew and Ross (1988: 2) suggest that there exists a dominant construction of masculinity in the press and media, representing men as tough, strong, aggressive, independent, brave, sexually active, intelligent and so forth. Connell (1987) notes that configurations of masculinities are hierarchically ordered on the basis of physical size and strength. Individual men also occupy positions along the continuum of action–emotion, sexual experience–sexual inexperience, sport–art and manual/sporting orientations.

These locations are mediated by race, ethnicity, class, sexuality and age. For example, white middle-class men are expected to use their minds, be independent and competitive as well as physically strong. The masculinities of white working-class men and those of colour are constructed around toughness, roughness, physical strength, and action.

Connell (1987: 184) refers to these configurations as 'hegemonic masculinity', defined as 'a social ascendancy achieved in a play of forces that extends beyond contests of brute power into the organization of private life and cultural processes'. Hegemonic masculinities are constructed in the public sphere in relation to women and to subordinated masculinities. However, 'hegemony' does not imply a totalising process without alternatives and resistances to dominant masculinities. For many men personal and social difficulties often arise from the pressures to prove their masculinity and hide their vulnerability.

Hegemonic masculinity especially creates conflicts for the youngest men, because children in general are not expected to manifest such characteristics. Yet boys' gendered subjectivities are the object of intense regulation through subtle and overt pressures on them to start taking up miniature versions of hegemonic masculinities from early on. Literacy, particularly popular children's horror fiction, is a part of this regulation process. However, through the reading of this genre boys may make sense of their life worries and accept, resist and accommodate themselves to this regulation of their gendered subjectivities as will be shown in the subsequent readings of *Goosebumps*.

Chills and thrills: the horror genre

We are living amid a large scale revival of horror in everyday life; in films, television, videos and video games, especially in fiction. A recent segment of the TV news magazine 'Dateline' examined the proliferation of a subculture of vampirism represented by video games and clubs called 'Gothics' where patrons are attired in clothing reminiscent of the many 'Dracula' films. Moreover, a Louisiana vampire enthusiast actually killed family members and drank their blood. Popular media is saturated with images of the occult. Recall the tremendous success of Michael Jackson's 1984 'Thriller' cassette heralded by a video linking sex with zombies, vampires and wolf men. Fox Network's 'X Files' has gone beyond cult status as more and more viewers grit their teeth at the weekly horrors confronting Agents Scully and Mulder. Stephen King now boasts an adolescent readership in addition to his strong following among adults. And then there is Stine's aptly named *Goosebumps* series for children.

Although horror has social, economic, political and psychological aspects, it is first physiological. The word itself stems from the Latin 'horrere' meaning to bristle as when the hair stands on end during excitement. The flesh also becomes bumpy in an attempt to increase body temperature during a chilling experience (Twitchell, 1985: 10). These 'Goosebumps' represent the frightful encounter with the strange and horrible.

Twitchell (1985) notes that horror has always been present in English literary tradition from Grendel in *Beowulf*. Then monsters were the vehicle for promoting the protagonist's heroism. Once the monster was destroyed, readers would value the protagonist all the more. The notion of the monster changed during the eighteenth century when William Hogarth produced social commentaries in the form of engravings of humans becoming monsters through alcoholism, drug addiction, cruelty and murder as responses to the social transformation brought on by urbanisation and capitalism. At the end of the nineteenth century horror classics, such as *Dracula* (Stoker, 1965), *Frankenstein* (Shelley, 1965) and *The Strange Case of Dr. Jekyll and Mr. Hyde* (Stevenson, 1967), became the sites for extended commentaries on social changes wrought by the rise of technology and the scientific mentality. In the United States Poe and Lovecraft mingled themes of forbidden desires with horror. In today's horror genres fictional monsters more frequently take center stage, with the victims and protagonists in the back rows.

What accounts for the enduring attraction of horror? Twitchell (1985) suggests three scenarios:

1. satisfaction with overcoming fears;
2. imaginative consideration of objects of sublimated desire; and
3. rites of passage to reproductive sexuality.

Horror depends on not knowing enough and being kept from complete knowledge. The revelation constitutes the moment of supreme horror. During horror scenes one is cut off from ordinary comforts. Only individual efforts allow one to deal with the threat. Horror monsters frighten by acting out desires, usually sexual, that are feared or taboo and are in turn punished for doing so. Horror is a mode of incorporation into the existing economic structure through buying and collecting books and memorabilia. Horror's socially regulative aspects may be glimpsed in the current stalk-and-slash horror films where women are routinely mutilated and/or murdered when they move beyond traditional notions of femininity and men such as Michael Meyers and Freddie Kruger do the mutilating and murdering. Horror regulates men's actions, but in ways that are different (which will be explored later in this chapter).

Tales from the dark side: popular children's horror fiction

Rose (1984) indicates that children's literature is a contradictory term because children figure mainly as objects of an essentially adult enterprise. Adults control all aspects of book preparation and economically benefit from the increasingly lucrative children's publishing industry. Children are positioned as consumers of versions of childhood provided by adults.

Profiting from childhood is a more recent development in the larger children's culture. In publishing this most likely originated in children's series books like bestsellers *Tom Swift*, *Nancy Drew* and the *Hardy Boys* published by the Stratemeyer Syndicate earlier in the century (Christian-Smith, 1991). The era of quick multi-million dollar sales from children's series books was ushered in 1979 when Scholastic Books developed the first teen romance series, *Wildfire* (Christian-Smith, 1990). With *Wildfire* sales of 2.25 million in the first year, other publishers raced to develop their own romance series.

Scholastic has remained a strong contender in the series books field through its popular *Baby-sitters Club*, *Goosebumps* and other series books. In just over ten years Scholastic corporation has grown from a small educational publisher on the verge of bankruptcy to an international employer of 3300 with annual revenue of $552.28 million in 1995 from subsidiaries in the United States, Canada, England, Australia and New Zealand (Standard & Poor's, 1995: 2292; Director of Corporate Affiliations, 1993: 962). Responsible for this growth are Scholastic's numerous school and home book clubs, trade book series, educational magazines, textbooks and software divisions. Scholastic is making inroads into television, video and film productions through its popular teen program 'Charles in Charge', 'Baby-sitters Club' home videos and the current film versions of *The Indian in the Cupboard* and *Baby-sitters-Club* (Nathan, 1995).

Stine's *Goosebumps* books represent Scholastic's latest foray into the series market and another first in publishing — a horror fiction series just for children. Robert Lawrence Stine's professional relation with scholastic books began in 1966 as assistant editor of *Junior Scholastic Magazine* and the humour magazines *Bananas* and *Maniac*, all aimed at middle school readers (Verney, 1994). He was also the head writer for 'Eureeka's Castle', the highly esteemed children's television program on Nickelodeon. Stine is a prolific writer of more than one hundred adolescent and children's fiction and information books, including some horror titles for Scholastic and Archway's best-selling young adult *Fear Street* horror series. Parachute Press, a book packaging company owned and managed by Jane Waldhorn, Stine's spouse and former editor of Scholastic's *Dynamite* magazine, holds the copyright on *Goosebumps* and *Fear Street*. Part of *Goosebumps*' success is the savvy packaging and marketing aimed at child consumers and their parents. Collecting the books is actively promoted through advertisements at the end of each book. Christian-Smith and Erdman (1999) found that boys legitimate the reading of *Goosebumps* through absorbing these books into the pre-existing practices of collecting sports cards and so forth.

On hooking readers: critics speak out

With millions of copies in print, *Goosebumps* and *Fear Street* have become a force to be reckoned with, which is well-recognised by their critics. Critical opinion of Stine's books is mixed, ranging from lamentations over contrived plots, slim characterisation and predictable events to a begrudging admiration for Stine's ability to keep readers on the edge of their seats (Verney, 1994). Eaglen (1989) comments that Stine, like Pike, is giving readers practise in reading the horror genre that may enable them to graduate to adult horror writers. Others like Gray (1993) are concerned with the level of violence and the fostering of a siege mentality in young readers: because life is dangerous, defence is the best strategy.

Stine maintains that 'kids as well as adults are entitled to books of no socially redeeming value' (Verney, 1994: 216) and the books are 'safe scares. You're home in your room reading. The books are not half as scary as the real world' (Gray, 1993: 54). According to Stine, events in the books are once-removed from children's everyday lives. However, Stine retains enough elements of children's culture to make the books appealing to young readers. There are the rivalries, insecurities, mysterious adults, little league games and family outings. Are *Goosebumps* books as innocuous as Stine claims? Are they only entertainment? What about the versions of masculinity the books offer boys who read them? These and other issues will be discussed in the following sections.

Reader beware, you're in for a scare! — *Goosebumps*

To address the above questions, I read 44 *Goosebumps* books written from 1992 to 1996, being the first to the most current books in the series. I attempted to read the entire series. However, because of the books' immense popularity, it is difficult to purchase the books or secure them from a library. As 44 books would be unwieldy in an article, I chose a sample of ten representative books to discuss in depth. This selection of ten books contains many of the elements found in the larger sample. Details of supporting books from the larger sample, as well as those from the sample of ten, are indicated in the parenthetical references and complete citations are provided in the references at the end of this chapter.

Sample of ten books

#4	*Say cheese and die* (1992)
#8	*The girl who cried monster* (1993)
#9	*Welcome to Camp Nightmare* (1993)
#14	*The werewolf of Fever Swamp* (1993)
#16	*One day at Horrorland* (1994)
#17	*Why I'm afraid of bees* (1994)
#19	*Deep trouble* (1994)
#23	*Return of the mummy* (1994)
#29	*Monster blood III* (1995)
#33	*The horror at Camp Jellyjam* (1995)

Written to the marketing formula described earlier, each book has a common structure. The settings are usually small towns (Pitts Landing, Timber Falls), summer camps (Jellyjam, Nightmoon) and international locales such as the pyramids of Egypt or a Caribbean island. Families are mostly of European-American background and economically comfortable. Children, usually twelve for the main characters, nine and eleven for friends and siblings, are faced with monstrous situations that only they can solve. As in many series books, child characters are somewhat older than readers so that they can participate in events beyond what is available to readers. Adults in families rarely render assistance to children during the ordeal, because they are usually absent (#9, #22, #29,#37, #50), lost (#11, #16, #33, #36, #43) or incapacitated (#6, #13,#21, #23, #48), and children often cannot share their fears with parents. Moreover, adults do not believe the stories of monsters and strange happenings their children tell (#4, #8, #14,#19, #26, #40). The lack of familial support profoundly upsets the children, who must use their ingenuity or band together to save themselves. The horrendous events usually occur outside of children's immediate homes, often in a summer camp or amusement park. However, they often strike close to home. The amusement parks have their Main Streets USA with picket fences and neat houses. The camps are structured like a home with their bunkhouses and names for employees like Uncle Al and Buddy. Children's family relationships and friendships are strained by the horrible events and uncaring attitudes of others.

Goosebumps features breakneck action and excitement reminiscent of the early Stratemeyer Syndicate series for boys such as *The Rover Boys* and *Tom Swift*. That series prompted the Boy Scouts head master Matthews to launch a vituperative attack on the books earlier in the century (Christian-Smith, 1991). However, there are no such outcries today.

Just when one peril disappears, another appears to keep readers in *Goosebumps*. In *One day at Horrorland*, Lizzy, Luke, Clay and parents are trapped in a theme park that lives up to its name. They only recover from the terror of the 'Doomslide' when they find themselves in an equally frightening Hall of Mirrors with walls that threaten to flatten them. Escaping this horror, they encounter bats in a barn and then are pursued by creatures called 'Horrors'. Similarly, Gary Lutz of *Why I'm afraid of bees* exchanges bodies with Dirk Davis. As in the film *The fly* (1986), the presence of an insect during the procedure causes Gary to become a bee. Gary's dreams of better times than the torments of his former life come crashing down when he is nearly run over, attacked by the family cat Claus, caught by the next door neighbour who keeps bees and pursued by his hive mates. *Welcome to Camp Nightmare* features disappearing campers, chilling howls at night and children left untreated. In *The werewolf of Fever Swamp* Grady becomes lost in Fever Swamp, encounters a mysterious 'Swamp Hermit' reputed to be a werewolf, is bitten by a snake, terrorised by nightly howling and is finally attacked and bitten by the werewolf.

In many of the novels, the monsters are adults or peers. In *Say cheese and die* (#4), *Welcome to Camp Nightmare* (#9), *The werewolf of Fever Swamp* (#14), *Why I'm afraid of bees* (#17), *Return of the mummy* (#23) and *Deep trouble* (#19) adults act in monstrous ways towards children. The adults routinely scare children by playing on their fears of insects (#17), wearing monster masks and a mummy disguise (#9, #11, #23, #36) and terrorising and physically harming them (#4, #8, #9, #16, #19, #23,#33). Children become profoundly upset when adults are not caring and echo these sentiments.

> 'It wasn't a nightmare!' Jay yelled shrilly. Larry turned his back on us and continued eating his breakfast. 'Don't you care?' Jay screamed at him. Don't you care what happens to us?'
>
> (#9, 1993: 77)

In *The girl who cried monster* (#8) and *One day at Horrorland* (#16) the adults are themselves monsters. Adults who act in monstrous fashion are usually punished (#4, #8, #16, #19, #23) or revealed not to be monsters after all (#9, #17) or are under the control of sinister forces (#33). In *The werewolf of Fever Swamp* (#14) young Grady's friend, Will Blake, is not only the werewolf, but preys upon his friend at the end of the novel. While Lucy (*The girl who cried monster*) is trying to convince others that public librarian Mr Mortman is a frog-like monster, Lucy and her family are revealed to be the resident monsters of Timber Falls.

Lucy and her brother calmly watch as her parents devour Mr Mortman who is invading their territory. Lucy also terrorises her younger brother Randy with stories of monsters. *One day at Horrorland, Return of the mummy, The werewolf of fever swamp* and *The girl who cried monster* are the only novels with actual monsters: the horrors, the mummy, the teenage werewolf, the frog-like librarian and the monster family. These monsters are probably familiar enough to readers from film and television that they may not constitute a real threat.

The *Goosebumps* series seems to walk a line between things that 'gross out' children in Stine's estimation (Verney, 1994), such as the smelly blob represented by King Jellyjam (#33), the monster blood (#29) that turns a child into a giant and the rubbery Horrors (#16), and the fears children have when being in bizarre situations outside of their control. Just when readers may believe that the mayhem causes the death of friends and family, Stine uses some conventional narrative mechanisms. In *One day at Horrorland* Lizzy believes her parents may not have survived the ordeal.

> *Three out of five. Three out of five.*
>   'Noooooo!' I finally found my voice and let out a horrified wail that echoed off the walls.
>   'Excuse me. A slight mistake', the deep voice boomed. 'Make that five out of five survivors.'
>
> (#16, 1994: 109)

In *Welcome to Camp Nightmare* the missing campers seem to magically reappear when it is revealed to Billy that his ordeal constituted a series of tests regarding his fitness for accompanying his scientist parents on a expedition to a dangerous planet — Earth. When all seems to return to normal at the end of the novels by reuniting children with their families, the unexpected happens. Arriving at home, Lizzy and Luke find a Horror clinging to the back of the bus the family has commandeered (*One day at horrorland*). In *The werewolf of Fever Swamp* Grady himself becomes a werewolf after being bitten by his friend Will. While Gary Lutz is no longer a bee, he continues to extract pollen from flowers for a meal in the manner of a bee (*Why I'm afraid of bees*). The monster blood remains the green 'slime that never dies!' (*Monster blood III*). Although Greg returns the cursed camera, Joey and Mickey steal it, thus beginning another cycle of mishaps each time a photo is taken (*Say cheese and die*). The tenuous endings reinforce for readers that horror is never ending and the world is a dangerous place.

The characters in *Goosebumps* are not well developed as the books' focus is the horrendous situations in which characters find themselves. There is a sameness between characters despite superficial differences. In nine out of the ten books, the story is told from the point of view of the 12 year-old primary character, which is equally divided between girls and boys. Both groups are continually under siege by monsters and are resourceful in extricating themselves from terrible situations. The girls are decisive, resourceful and problem-solvers and at times stronger than their male relatives and friends. Lucy is more courageous than her friend Aaron in seeking the truth about Mr Mortman (*The girl who cried monster*). In *Why I'm afraid of bees* Gary's younger sister Krissy easily opens the jar that will not budge for Gary. Gabe's cousin Sari (*Return of the mummy*) constantly wins arguments and possesses more general knowledge. There are also tensions between male and female blood relatives as to cleverness and strength (#14, #16, #17, #19, #23, #29, #33). Another character trait is a strong physicality. Stine presents this as normal or typical behaviour for the age group. Although both genders continually run, jump, punch and are punched in return (#14, #16, #17, #19, #34) this is more common with boys. Some of these activities are generated from the monster genre itself as individuals are compelled to escape their predicaments. Others pertain to the ways masculinities are constructed in the ten novels.

These masculinities are hegemonic in opposition, organised hierarchically in terms of toughness, strength, sporting abilities, wildness and intellect as Connell (1987) suggests. Masculinities in *Goosebumps* have social class and racial dimensions as well. All the male characters are European-American upper middle-class, other than Gabe, who is of Middle Eastern middle-class background (*Return of the mummy*). Gabe visits his archaeologist uncle, Ben Hassad, and his cousin Sari on a dig in Egypt. This background is all that distinguishes Gabe from other male characters. *Goosebumps* constructs social subjectivities stemming from European-American and middle-class notions of masculinities. For the purposes of analysis, the masculine subjectivities of *Goosebumps* may be grouped as follows: 'regular guys', 'macho men' and 'brains'. However, these subjectivities are not fixed. *Goosebumps* provides glimpses of the struggles surrounding masculinities in the 1990s that carry over into the twenty-first century.

Many of the main characters have doubts about themselves and are somewhat fearful. Although quite intelligent, these 'regular guys' dream of being physically strong and popular. The best example of this is found in Gary Lutz 'the klutz' of *Why I'm afraid of Bees*:

I'm scared of a few other things too such as:
   dogs, big mean kids, the dark, loud noises, and swimming in the ocean. I'm even scared of Claus. That's Krissy's dumb cat.

(#17, 1994: 3)

Being good in math and computers does not win Gary friends. Chosen last for baseball and continually beaten up by neighbourhood bullies, Barry, Marv and Karl, Gary opts for a body switch with Dirk. Dirk is everything Gary is not and wants to be: 'a tall, athletic-looking blond boy in black Lycra bike shorts and a blue muscle shirt' (p. 36) and an expert skateboarder. Dirk needs a 'brain' to earn good grades in a summer school math course. In the aftermath of the transformation accident, Gary's fortunes are not reversed. As a bee he experiences the same harassment and difficulties. Only at the end of the novel does Gary's resourcefulness return to force Dirk to vacate Gary's body. The Dirk–Gary persona becomes popular with girls and puts the neighbourhood bullies in their places. It is only through this magical solution that Gary finally acquires a new confidence. Gary's new masculinities are a blend of strength, sensitivity and intelligence, a kind of 'new man' of the end of century. However, Gary's inhuman side in the form of his bee legacy is responsible for Gary's new sensitivities towards people and nature. Just when readers may believe that all is once again normal at the end of the novel, Stine unsettles them with the vision of Gary extracting pollen from flowers like a bee. Readers are left with the impression that magic can solve their life dilemmas and to be a boy like Gary is to be not quite human.

Most of the novels contain various child versions of the 'macho man'. Dirk Davis (#17), Elliot (#33) and Will (#14) are powerfully built boys, good at sports, and popular. Luke Morris (#16) and Elliot (#33) exude a bravado in the face of danger that disguises their fears. The boys at Camp Nightmare (#9) are constantly repressing their fears because, according to counsellor Larry, 'Uncle Al doesn't believe in coddling' (1993: 34). Another facet of this masculinity is represented by bullies such as Joey and Mickey (#4), Jay (#9), Barry, Marvin and Karl (#17) and Conan (#29). Mean-spirited and constantly quarrelling for a fight, they are the monsters of many readers' everyday lives. These boys verbally abuse, terrorise and beat up the regular guys who live in fear of them.

Which way do you want your nose to slant?' Conan asked Evan.
To the right or to the left?

(#29, 1995: 10)

'You want that stupid smile to be permanent?' He raised a big fist.

(#4, 1992: 96)

'The Klutz is up and walking around. That must mean we didn't do a very good job of pounding him yesterday.'

(#17, 1994: 30–1)

There is a wildness about these boys that coalesces in Will Blake, the preteen werewolf of Fever Swamp (#14). Will's attack on his friend Grady surpasses in savagery other physical attacks in the novels.

He raised his fur-covered face to the moon and uttered an animal howl. Then, snarling out his rage, he lowered his beastly head and dug his fangs into my shoulder.

(#14, 1993: 118)

Through Will's bite lycanthropy is transmitted to Grady.

But I don't mind. I'm not upset. I mean, with Will out of the way, the swamp is now mine! All mine!
I'm climbing out of the window now. There's Wolf 'companion dog' waiting for me, eager to do some night exploring.
I drop easily to the ground on all fours. I raise my fur-covered face to the moon and utter a long, joyful howl.

(#14, 1993: 123)

The wild and rapacious masculinities represented by lycanthropy are romanticised; presented as a joyous romp in the woods. This glosses over not only the brutality of the werewolf, but also a highly disturbing characteristic: he preys on those he loves. Under the werewolf spell, Will savaged his friend Grady. Will Grady's family and friends be next?

In the ten book sample there are few 'brainy' boys. Presented as 'geeky' and weak, they receive little respect and are not admired (#20, #23, #25, #38, #49). It would be difficult for readers to be sympathetic towards Kermit, the child genius of *Monster blood III* because of the ways Stine presents him. Kermit's scientific brilliance is presented as quirky and not normal.

He didn't want to play video games. He didn't want to watch TV. He refused to go outside and play ball or toss a Frisbee around. He didn't even want to sneak down to the little grocery on the corner and load up on candy bars and potato chips.

All he wanted to do was stay downstairs in his dark, damp basement lab and mix beakers of chemicals together. 'My experiments,' he called them. 'I have to do my experiments.'

(#29, 1995: 7)

Kermit does not use his expertise to benefit people, but to make them miserable, especially his sitter, Cousin Evan. When Evan laughs uncontrollably at Conan upon unwittingly inhaling Kermit's laughing gas, Evan is severely beaten by this neighbourhood bully. Furthermore, Kermit's lies get Evan in trouble with Kermit's mother. Kermit's constant pranks cause Evan to dab some monster blood (blobby mayhem-creating substance) on one of Kermit's favourite candy bars. Evan's attempt at revenge backfires when the monster blood is spattered on Evan, who grows to a monstrous height. While Clay (*One day at Horrorland*) is not Kermit's intellectual equal, this thoughtful boy is constantly the object of the rough play of his friend Luke and his innuendoes questioning Clay's sense of courage (manliness) because of his fearful responses to the horrors of the theme park. However, Clay's attitudes are sensible while Luke's bravado is revealed as pretence. Through these representations, readers are offered various subject positions within intellectuality, some of which they may be reluctant to assume.

Goosebumps certainly engages with many of the fears children have today regarding lack of control, violence and isolation. It subverts children's expectations of support from friends and family. *Goosebumps* presents the world as a dangerous place where there are few safe havens for children. However, these children are not passive victims of the fearful aspects of life. With little support and understanding from adults, especially parents, these children are forced to solve their own problems individually or with a few friends. While achieving self-reliance is a traditional theme in books for children, *Goosebumps* does not incorporate the power of the social collective in this process.

Goosebumps may also be thought of as a series of cultural narratives representing the regulation of masculinities. In the novels, boys are pressured to take up miniature versions of hegemonic masculinities: they desire physical strength and control but not to be bullies. Yet, in *Goosebumps* boys' fears and their sensitive sides are repressed as important parts of their masculinities. These competing masculinities represent the multiple gender subjectivities offered to male readers of *Goosebumps*.

Conclusions

The horror genre, with its monsters, is traditionally a site for commentaries on social changes as exemplified by classics like Mary Shelley's *Frankenstein*. Today's children's horror novels also chronicle the psychic struggles involved in growing up at the end of the twentieth century, as children seek, and also fear independence and separation from their parents. As Moretti (1992: 81) notes, the monster 'makes bearable to the conscious mind those desires and fears which the latter has judged to be unacceptable and has thus been forced to repress'. A series like *Goosebumps* imaginatively re-codes the struggles around those desires and the social changes surrounding childhood today. Although *Goosebumps* constructs these transformations as primarily relational and psychic, they are economic and political as well. Moretti (1992: 68) also suggests that the monster expresses anxiety of a monstrous future. *Goosebumps* describes a fictional world in which adults are not there for children. Children must solve their problems and in so doing become powerful. In becoming more adult-like, these children do not, however, acquire social power and recognition. They are still regraded as dependent by their parents and other adults.

Cherland (1994) notes that children often chafe at the restrictions adults place on them and use fiction reading to fulfil in fantasy their desires to occupy more powerful discursive positions than those they perceive to be available to them in everyday life. In her study of popular children's fiction reading, Cherland found that readers experienced satisfaction with overcoming their fears.

Series novels like *Nancy Drew*, teen romance fiction and *The Baby-sitters Club* facilitate children's incorporation into existing capitalistic social and economic relations (Cherland, 1994; Christian-Smith, 1991, 1993). *Goosebumps* presents a striking example of the ways children's literature connects the socioeconomic with psychic structures. Through collecting books and purchasing *Goosebumps*' spin-off products, children are being positioned as male 'possessive individuals', so central to the continuation of capitalism. *Goosebumps* taps into boys' existing pastimes of collecting sports cards and so forth. *Goosebumps* may also work 'intertextually' with other fiction and social texts in children's everyday lives (video games, name brand clothing etc.) to situate them within a children's culture increasingly organised and orchestrated by the corporate sector. Through the 'collection' discourse, book reading may become a more acceptable leisure activity for boys, even though fiction reading is still regarded by many men as a feminine activity (Cherland, 1994).

Goosebumps is primarily read by boys and presents a striking example of how popular children's fiction constructs subject positions around masculinity. The book analysis suggests how contentious and contradictory this is. In taking up gendered social subjectivities as an increasingly separate person, children are engaged in constant social negotiation as they struggle to develop a sense of self out of a diversity of possible, actual and contradictory selves. In *Goosebumps*, macho hegemonic masculinities are promoted at the expense of other masculinities involving caring and empathy. However, these masculinities do surface in the texts. Perhaps boys who are caring and sensitive may find there is a voice for their perspectives.

Is *Goosebumps* as safe a scare as Robert Lawrence Stine contends? As entertainment and a window on childhood today, *Goosebumps*' tales from the dark side present dark visions of what it means to be a child at the end of the twentieth century. In combating the dark forces, the child characters become self-reliant and resourceful. As the child readers of *Goosebumps* chart the stormy waters of the twenty-first century, they will need these characteristics in great abundance. So will all of us.

Bibliography

Anderson, G.L.(1989) 'Critical ethnography in education: Origins, current status and new directions', *Review of Educational Research* 59 (3), 249–70.
Aries P. (1962) *Centuries of childhood. A social history of family life.* Alfred Knopf, New York.

Askew, S. and Ross, C. (1988) *Boys don't cry: Boys and sexism in education*. Open University Press, Milton Keynes, England.

Cherland, M. (1994) *Private practices*. The Farmer Press, London.

Christian-Smith, L.K.(1990) *Becoming a woman through romance*. Routledge, New York.

—— (1991) 'The perils of Nancy Drew: Social identities in popular children's fiction', paper presented at the Mid-Western Educational Research Association's Annual Meeting in Chicago, 18 October.

—— ed. (1993) *Texts of desire: Essays on fiction, femininity and schooling*. The Falmer Press, London.

Christian-Smith, L.K. and Erdman, J.I.(1999) ' "Mom, it's not real": Constructing childhood through reading horror fiction', in S. Steinberg and J. Kincheloe (eds), *Kinderculture: The corporate construction of childhood*. Westview Press, Boulder, CO. pp. 129–52.

Connell, R.W.(1987) *Gender & Power*. Polity Press, Oxford, England.

Cooper, D. (1993) 'Retailing gender: Adolescent book clubs in Australian schools', in L.K. Christian-Smith (ed.), *Texts of desire: Essays on fiction, femininity and schooling*. The Falmer Press, London, pp. 9–27.

Director of Corporate Affiliations (1993) *US Private Companies* (vol 3). National Register Publishing, New Providence, NJ.

Eaglen, A. (1989) 'New blood for young readers', *School Library Journal*, 35, December, p. 49.

Gray, P. (1993) 'Carnage: An open book', *Time, 142* (5) 2 August, p. 54.

Luke, C. (1989) *Pedagogy, Printing and Protestantism: The discourse On childhood*. State University of New York Press, Albany, New York.

—— (1990) *Constructing the child viewer: A history of the American discourse on television and children. 1950–1980*. Praeger, New York.

—— (1991) 'On reading the child: A feminist post-structuralist perspective', *Australian Journal of Reading 14* (2), pp. 109–16.

Moretti, F. (1992) 'The dialectic of fear', *New Left Review*, 136, pp. 67–85.

Nathan, P. (1995) 'The show biz angle', *Publishers Weekly*, 242, 13 March, p. 18.

Pike, C. (1995) *The cold one*. Archway Books, New York.

—— (1999) *The grave*. Forge, New York.

Rice, A. (1993) *The tale of the body thief*. Ballatine Books, New York.

—— (1993) *The queen of the damned*. Ballatine Books, New York.

—— (1993) *The vampire Lestat*. Ballatine Books, New York.

—— (1993) *Interview with the vampire*. Ballatine Books, New York.

Rose, J. (1984) *The case of Peter Pan*. MacMillan, London.

Shelley, M. (1831) *Frankenstein* (1965 reprint). New American Library, New York.

Standard & Poors (1995) *Register of corporations, directors and executives* (vol 1). McGraw-Hill, New York.

Steedman, C., Urwin, C. and Walkerdine, V. (eds) (1985) *Language, gender and childhood*. Routledge & Kegan Paul, London.

Stevenson, R.L. (1886) *The strange case of Dr. Jekyll and Mr. Hyde* (1967 reprint). Bantam Books, New York.

Stoker, B. (1897) *Dracula* (1965 reprint). Signet, New York.

Twitchell, J.B. (1985) *Dreadful pleasures: An anatomy of modern horror*. Oxford University Press, New York.

Verney, S. (1994) 'R.L. Stine', in K.S. Hile and E.A. Des Chenes (eds), *Author & artists for young adults*. Gale Research Inc, Detroit, pp. 211–17.

Walkerdine, V. (1984) 'Developmental psychology and the child-centered pedagogy: The insertion of Piaget into early childhood education', in J. Henriques, W. Holloway, C. Urwin, C. Venn and V. Walkerdine (eds), *Changing the subject: Psychology social regulation and subjectivity*. Methuen, London, pp. 153–202.

Goosebumps books used in this study

Note: all titles are by R.L. Stine and published by Scholastic Books.

A night in terror tower	(1995)	#27
Attack of the Jack o'-lanterns	(1996)	#48
Attack of the mutant	(1994)	#25
Bad hare day	(1996)	#41
Calling all creeps	(1996)	#50
Deep trouble	(1994)	#19

Eggmonster from Mars	(1996)	#43
Ghost beach	(1995)	#22
Ghostcamp	(1996)	#45
Go eat worms	(1994)	#21
How I got my shrunken head	(1996)	#39
How to kill a monster	(1996)	#46
Legend of the lost legend	(1996)	#47
Let's get invisible	(1993)	#6
Monster blood	(1992)	#3
Monster blood II	(1994)	#18
Monster blood III	(1995)	#29
My hairiest adventure	(1994)	#26
Night of the living dummy	(1993)	#7
Night of the living dummy III	(1995)	#40
One day at Horrorland	(1994)	#16
Piano lessons can be murder	(1993)	#13
Return of the mummy	(1994)	#23
Revenge of the lawn gnomes	(1995)	#34
Say cheese and die	(1992)	#4
Say cheese & die again	(1996)	#44
Stay out of the basement	(1992)	#2
The Abominable Snowman of Pasadena	(1995)	#38
The beast from the east	(1996)	#43
The cuckoo clock of doom	(1996)	#28
The girl who cried monster	(1993)	#8
The haunted mask	(1993)	#11
The headless ghost	(1995)	#37
The horror at Camp Jellyjam	(1995)	#33
The phantom of the auditorium	(1994)	#24
The scarecrow walks at night	(1994)	#20
The werewolf of Fever Swamp	(1993)	#14
The ghost next door	(1993)	#10
The haunted mask	(1995)	#36
Vampire breath	(1996)	#49
Welcome to Camp Nightmare	(1993)	#9
Welcome to dead house	(1992)	#1
Why I'm afraid of bees	(1994)	#17
You can't scare me	(1994)	#15

Fatal attractions:
death, femininity and children's literature

Kerry Mallan

For centuries, artists and writers have found the subject of female death of compelling interest, as have so many readers. This chapter takes as its focus the representations of death and femininity in children's literature with particular reference to the ways femininity is constructed in terms of sexuality and motherhood. The underlying presuppositions of this discussion are that death and femininity are inextricably linked in Western culture and that narrative and visual representations of female death draw from a common pool of culturally constructed images of the feminine body as an object of spectacle and a site of alterity. There is a perverse fascination about death, especially when it is the death of a beautiful, youthful woman. Another image, the death of the mother, also arouses curiosity. Maternity is crucially linked to female sexuality. It is sexuality's sign, a sign that makes sexuality manifest (Langbauer, 1990: 99). Consequently, the deaths of women are fatal attractions calling a crowd of onlookers and inviting close inspection.

Another reason for this fascination with female death lies in ways texts — literary and visual — provide a means for working through anxieties about death, subjectivity and female power. Death is one way of defusing or erasing female power both literally and metaphorically. Paradoxically, however, death can also be the means for restoring it. This paradox can be seen in the way the narrative moment or the visual stasis of death suggests the erasure of subjectivity, yet it may reaffirm or reinstate the subjectivity of others who exist both inside and outside the narrative frame. This instance of a reinstated or rearticulated subjectivity is a feature common to many young adult novels whereby maternal loss or absence is the plot device for enabling the protagonist to construct an independent selfhood away from maternal constraint. The ensuring *bildungsroman* often maps the child's journey away from and back to the domestic space. Dever (1998) sees the trope of maternal loss as a central element in this type of narrative as complex questions relating to sexuality and subjectivity are considered and given temporary resolution. When the narratives are concerned with the death of a female virgin (the 'death of the maiden') Martin suggests a contradictory reading is available in terms of female sexuality and patriarchal definitions and limitations:

> Death removes the virgin body from the sexual economy which defines it … Death or dying negates, as it stands in for, the dangerous sexuality of the female.

(Martin, 1997: 33)

I am conscious of the fact that, as this preliminary account suggests, there is ambivalence surrounding images of female death, and so, to speak of representation is to acknowledge misrepresentation. Representation is, therefore, Janus-faced, revealing and concealing at the same time. Two central questions inform my discussion: What are the ideological implications of femininity and death in children's literature? and What are the ambivalent compensatory structures that emerge in the wake of the female death?

As a way of framing the discussion, the following account situates the topic within a broader context by considering the ways death, as a general topic, features in children's literature and the possible reasons for the glaring absence of detailed critical discussion of femininity and death in this field.

Un/covering death in children's literature

The death toll in children's literature has been rising over the last three decades with numerous picture books and novels dealing with the twin subjects of death and dying (Gibson and Zaidman, 1991). Dead and dying bodies in children's books form a morbid catalogue comprising dead pets, parents, grandparents, siblings, friends and enemies. (See *The Literature Base* [1992] 3, 3, pp. 24–7 and White [1993; 1996] for lists of books on death and dying.) A corresponding range for the causes of death covers all possibilities: disease, accident, suicide, murder, execution, old age, childbirth, birth defects and so on. In removing death as a taboo of children's literature it now seems to be thriving as both topic and trope in terms of content and form.

Elizabeth Bronfen reasons that:

> the aesthetic representation of death lets us repress our knowledge of the reality of death precisely because here death occurs at someone else's body and as an image.
>
> (Bronfen, 1992: x)

It is the safety that comes with the vicarious experience that appears to inform many accounts of death in children's literature. Hunt states that adolescents have a 'love of books about death and dying' (1991: 241), and posits the view that the vicarious experience of reading about death provides readers with a prior knowledge that will help them when the death bell tolls — 'readers of these books feel that they know what to expect and that they can handle it' (p. 242). Such confident claims as to the empowering potential of books characterise much of the general academic writing about death in children's literature (see: Sutherland and Arbuthnot, 1991; Huck et al., 1997; Saxby 1993, 1997).

While Huck et al. (1997) suggest that children's literature now discusses the topic of death 'openly and frankly' (p. 562), Gibson and Zaidman (1991) feel that twentieth century children's books 'treat death more subtly' than their literary precedents. These contradictory approaches — open, frank, subtle — vary according to the subject (death of a pet or teenage suicide) and the age of the intended readers. For instance, picture books, while often dealing in a frank manner in words about the death of a pet or a grandparent, may convey through the illustrations a more subtle, symbolic image of the deceased. This visual trope then stands in for the dead loved one. For example, an empty chair symbolises Granpa's death (*Granpa* [1984] by John Burningham); the kindly spectral presence of Grandma comforts a grieving grand-daughter (*Grandma's shoes* [1994] by Libby and Elivia Hathorn); a skull-ring serves as a doubly encoded *memento mori* of young Lily's death (*Lily and me* [1996] by Moses Aaron). These revenants and symbols serve to reassure the grieving child (or adult) that the absent one is still present in a metaphorical sense and are more gentle reminders of death than the gruesome *memento mori* such as dancing skeletons, walking corpses, and opening graves that appear in horror fiction for older readers.

In some cases, the corpse is the object of viewing. In *Snow White and the seven dwarfs* the body of the beautiful young maiden is left intact and does not succumb to the natural decaying process:

> Now Snow White lay in the coffin for a long, long time, and her body didn't decay. She looked as if she were sleeping, for she was white as snow, as red as blood, and her hair was black as ebony.
>
> (Grimm/Jarrell, 1972)

The description of the dead body as a sleeping body is a euphemism employed by some adults (and writers) for explaining death to young children; the folly of this inappropriate trope in terms of children's fears about sleep and death is obvious. It also has a more sinister (and frightening) implication when the dead body is later reanimated as in the case of Snow White. This point will be explored in more detail later. The idea of a 'sleeping' corpse, however, is rejected by the young protagonist in *A taste of blackberries* (Smith, 1973) when he views the body of his dead friend at his funeral: 'There was Jamie. He was straight with one hand crossed over his chest. He didn't look like he was asleep to me. Jamie slept all bunched up. Jamie looked dead' (p. 36). Bronfen (1992) sees the preserved corpse as functioning as 'a kind of "auto-icon", signifying a representation that consists of the thing itself' (p. 96). While the auto-iconicity of the preserved body of Snow White means that she becomes the Prince's object of desire from the moment he sees her, for Jamie's friend, seeing the laid-out corpse of his friend is the point of severance. His 'seeing' is imbued with a rationality and an access to a truth of human mortality that the Prince is unable to experience.

Apart from the representation of death as sleep, the use of symbol or metaphor to substitute for the reality of death and decay is understandable, especially for young children. However, the demands of the metaphorical leap required to appreciate the significance of the substitute may not only be beyond the conceptual abilities of the age group, but seem to be at odds with the general consensus that children today should not be shielded from the reality of death and dying through euphemism and other ambiguous rhetorical (and iconic) devices. Thus, the interstice between realism, artistic/literary representation and reader response is a key point of ideological and creative negotiation and compromise.

In novels for older readers, the dead parent, grandparent or friend is often remembered through ordinary mementoes — clothes, jewellery, toys, books, photographs, and so forth. Often writers employ the motif of remembrance as a device for mediating grief and prompting recovery for the mourner. In *Thunderwith* (Hathorn, 1989), Lara's suitcase of items that accompanies her to her new home after her mother's death serves as a link with the past which is inextricably linked with the mother. In Diana Kidd's *I love you, Jason*

Delaney (1996) it is when Ali eventually gains access to the bedroom of her beloved (and dead) Aunty Mim and its contents — clothes, jewellery, a hat with a red rose, a box of photographs — that she and her family finally come to terms with their loss. It is here that Ali finds her aunt's final birthday gift for her, an opal ring, given to Mim by her first love. The ring becomes a memento of Mim's life and death. In both books, the mementoes serve to put reality on hold, and mitigate or assuage the pain of loss. They also open up a space between life and death for a revitalising storytelling which becomes a significant feature of mourning and recovery.

The focus on the mourning process that occurs in both novels and picture books involves an identification between the living mourners and the recently deceased in that each is entrapped between the world of the living and the world of the dead. The dead one continues to live in the thoughts of the mourner who remains lost to the world of the dead. Mourning plays an ambivalent game with the emotions of the mourner, in that the mourner both loves and hates the deceased (Bronfen, 1992). This is particularly apparent in books which involve the death of a friend where the living friend is angry with the deceased for dying and abandoning the friendship (see: *Bridge to Terabithia* [1980] by Katherine Paterson; *A taste of blackberries* [1973] by Doris Smith). The more common treatment in children's books is to reconcile these ambivalent feelings by showing the mourning character moving from a depressive sadness to a state of joyful remembrance and conciliation: a final coming to terms with loss. When this state of joy is not reached, the mourner may desire his/her own death (see: *John Brown Rose and the Midnight Cat* [1977] by Wagner and Brooks; *The very best of friends* [1989] by Wild and Vivas). When the mourner has an additional burden such as guilt, melancholy and self-loathing can turn suicidal (see *Dear Miffy* [1997] by John Marsden).

A similar feeling of hate or resentment is conveyed in books that deal with a dying parent (see: *Swashbuckler* [1995] by James Moloney; *Mullaway* [1986] by Bron Nichols; *Elephant Rock* [1983] by Caroline Macdonald). Each of these novels involves a kind of 'death-watch' (Tanner, 1996) as the child witnesses the slow death of a parent with a terminal illness. The 'gaze' which is often implicated in theories of gendered power relations and masculine visual pleasure is given a different treatment in this type of death-watch narrative. The gaze becomes both painful and confronting when it is shifted from its usual focus on the erotic fetish to a focus on the dying body. The consequences of the painful gaze are such that the body of the dying person becomes the object of the look and bears the visible marks of the illness. In *Elephant Rock*, Ann watches her mother's dying body and her gaze is a form of double-vision, of seeing simultaneously the living body before her eyes and the dying body that fades away: 'Mum was now too weak to sit out on the terrace, or even sit up in bed. Ann felt her mother was fading away even as she watched her' (Macdonald, 1983: 59). This 'fading away' resonates with the dissolution of an embodied subjectivity (mother-woman) as the dying object of sight succumbs completely to the absolute tyranny of the dis/eased body. This penultimate deathbed scene has a dual compensatory function as it serves to prepare the watcher for imminent death of the loved one and 'to close the gap in social relations produced by death' (Bronfen, 1992: 77).

In psychoanalytic terms, the normal trajectory from mourning to remembrance to commemoration is marked by a release of the focused energies on the deceased loved one, the first lost object, by a reinvestment of these energies in a second surrogate object, who may be perceived in the image of the deceased, but who is nevertheless different (Bronfen, 1992: 327). For some characters in children's fiction, this process becomes the narrative trajectory. Whereas a parent may remarry and thus reinvest libidinal energies in the replacement loved one, the child may go through an extended period of resentment or unhappiness before reaching a point of conciliation (see: *Me and Mr Stenner* [1977] by Evan Hunter; *Thunderwith* [1989] by Libby Hathorn). In fairy tales, the substitute or surrogate parent is normally female, and a wicked one at that. In the case of *Snow White and the seven dwarfs* the wicked Queen fails to reach the standard of the maternal ideal and for her abuse of her maternal power is punished by being forced to dance to her death in red-hot, iron shoes. (The irony of the 'shoe' as an erotic fetish works as a doubly encoded metaphor for a deadly female sexuality of the *femme fatale*.) Consequently, this serves as a powerfully instructive tale on motherhood for young female readers.

Given the plethora of books written for children and young adults which deal with the subject of death and the range that encompasses female deaths in particular, there are relatively few academic writings on the subject of death and femininity. An edition of *Children's Literature Association Quarterly* (1991) devoted a special section on the topic of death in children's literature, but the articles are descriptive accounts concerning: death in terms of old age (Gibson and Zaidman; Sadler); youth suicide (Apseloff); a focus text study of *The bridge to Terabithia* (Chaston); and a survey essay on dead athletes and other martyrs (Hunt). None of these articles approaches the topic through the perspectives of literary, feminist or other critical theories. There are, however, varying critical accounts of death, femininity and maternity in selected scholarly children's literature texts and journals (for example, Scutter, 1999; Beare, 1998; Silver, 1997; Zipes, 1997; Kertzner, 1996; Bradford, 1996). Overall, however, there appears to be very little critical engagement with the ways in which femininity and death in children's literature are represented in both iconic and rhetorical forms. The accounts of death in Victorian children's literature are the exception, but these are usually located in general literature texts (for example, Bronfen, 1992; Dever, 1998). It would seem that the lady has indeed vanished and there are only faint traces of academic inquiry into the circumstances of her death/disappearance and the effects of her loss in terms of feminist inquiry into questions of representation.

It is not the concern of this chapter to undertake a body count in terms of the frequency of deaths among women and girls compared with men and boys. As the preceding, brief overview illustrates, the causes of death for both male and female characters are not so vastly different. Rather, as the following discussion argues, it is the ways women are represented in the process of dying and in death that are often quite different from their male counterparts. A significant part of this difference in representation lies in the fact that there has been an almost universal identification of women and sexuality with the tendency to view the latter as woman's main or only function (Bassein, 1984). Women have been (and continue to be) represented as objects to be looked at (Mulvey, 1975).

Furthermore, such objectification of women is so pervasive in Western culture that any examination of feminine representation and its ideological effects necessitate critical enquiry into the ways in which the female body is the site of visual pleasure and sexuality, and the object of the gaze (de Lauretis, 1984).

The following discussion is a move from the general to the specific by considering the intersection of woman, sexuality and death in relation to specific texts written and illustrated for children and young adults. It also addresses the relation between desire and subjectivity as this too is inseparable from death.

Death becomes her: the erotics of female death

The death, then, of a beautiful woman is, unquestionably, the most poetical topic in the world.

(Poe, 1996 [1846]: 1379)

The woman is perfected./Her dead/Body wears the smile of accomplishment.

(Plath, 1981: 272)

Both Edgar Poe and Sylvia Plath write of the erotics of death. While their meanings as to the relationship between death, beauty, and femininity appear strangely to coincide, the ideological underpinning of their statements are vastly oppositional. To dismiss Poe's statement as a form of 'necrophilic misogyny' (Bronfen, 1992: 60) is to ignore the multiplicity of issues that are condensed and displaced in the image of the dead female body. A similar dismissal of Plath's words fails to recognise the subtle subtext that speaks of patriarchal constructions of 'woman' which, like Poe's observation, imply that she can only achieve perfection as a corpse — 'the closest approximation a woman can make to the "perfect" appearance of a lifeless mannequin' (Leonard, 1992: 73). In looking at deadly perfection in children's texts, attention is focused on the ways the 'feminine body in death' (or in the process of dying) is represented. Both Poe's 'most poetical topic' and Plath's 'perfection' are implicit in these representations.

The motif of the 'death of the maiden' is one which can be traced throughout the course of Western literature, including writing for children. Famous 'death scenes' such as those of Judy in *Seven Little Australians* (Turner, 1894) and of Little Nell in *The Old Curiosity Shop* (Dickens, 1972), with their prolonging of the inevitable demise, are on the whole largely absent from contemporary fictional deaths which seem to invert the old maxim of youth subcultures 'live fast die young' to 'live young die fast'. The effect of the lingering death was not so much to indulge in a prolonged form of morbidity (though this may have been a writer's intention), but to give more than adequate space to the atonement of the young girl's life. From a patriarchal perspective, both Nell and Judy must be sacrificed, because they are both motherless and therefore lack the appropriate forms of maternal guidance that would keep them controlled and in order. (Even Nell's name with its connotations of death [knell] can be read as a sign of impending demise from the beginning.) Judy is too feisty of spirit and Nell is a wanderer. Both are disruptive feminine presences and, therefore, need to be silenced and annulled. Both are also virgins. According to Langbauer, 'Nell seems the best example in Dickens, if not in English Literature, of the absolute denial of any active female sexuality' (1990: 143). It is somewhat ironic that her death scene is generally regarded by critics as being 'sexually charged' (see Langbauer, 1990: 144).

Snow White is another fictional female virgin who is motherless and dies not once, but three times. In one sense, Snow White's refusal to die suggests a certain victorious image of feminine resilience, but this is a ruse as it is through the efforts of others (males) that she is resuscitated time and again. When Snow White dies (for the third time) from eating a poisoned apple, the dwarfs decide that they 'can't bury her in the black ground' and so make a coffin of glass 'into which one could see from every side' and write 'her name on it in golden letters, and that she was a king's daughter' (Grimm, 1972). Snow White's beautifully preserved body encased in a glass coffin becomes the object of aesthetic and erotic viewing. She is showcased, watched over, and labelled 'like an art object' (Bronfen, 1992: 100) for male viewing pleasure. When the Prince sees her body, he is unable to be separated from it and demands it for himself so that he can 'honour and prize her as my own beloved' (Grimm, 1972). As Bronfen (1992) explains, it is the dead Snow White who becomes the Prince's erotic object/fetish. This recalls both Poe and Plath's comments on the poetics and perfection of feminine death. Both Snow White's body displayed in its transparent coffin and the watching Prince are the apotheoses of Western culture's constructions of woman as spectacle and man as the bearer of the gaze (see Mulvey, 1975).

Nancy Ekholm Burkert's illustrated version of *Snow White and the seven dwarfs* (Grimm, 1972) shows a side-on view of the coffin containing Snow White, who is depicted in a long white dress, with her arms crossed over her chest, as she appears to 'sleep' peacefully. (The virginal colour of her dress carries a coded message about her sexual innocence.) *Snow White in New York*, Fiona French's (1986) satirical 1920s version of the story, initially displays the dead body in the traditional side-on viewing position of the coffin in the funeral procession. However, the position shifts to a high viewpoint forcing the viewer to look down at the open coffin when it is at rest. Unlike Burkert's version, which does not show the moment of awakening, French juxtaposes two images of Snow White — dead and reanimated. This juxtaposing of images of death and life enables the viewer to witness Snow White's transformation from deathly pallor to healthy pink glow (and full make-up). The 'dead' Snow White with her crossed arms over her chest and pious, peaceful expression is an intertextual reference for the knowing viewer/reader who is invited to draw on a stock of artistic conventions of virgin sainthood in order to read its canonical significance. The adjoining illustration of the reanimated Snow White semiotically encodes her double 'awakening' from death and virginity in her sly smile, suggestive perhaps of her anticipated sexual pleasure (Plath's 'smile of accomplishment'?) and in the touch of her hand on her 'Prince' who acts as silent witness.

Another instance of the dead female body as spectacle is in Charles Keeping's illustrated version of the *Lady of Shalott* (Tennyson and Keeping, 1986). Keeping's version of this poem opens and closes with the repeated visual image of the dead Lady in her boat. The Lady wears a transparent dress that reveals her bodily shape and parts beneath its diaphanous outer layers. By drawing the Lady with swirling lines and transparent cover, the female body is offered as the object of the eroticised gaze through the ways it is both (un)clothed and posed. The lifted arm placed at the back of the head exposes and stretches the curve line of the breast and continues down to the undulating curves of the hip and leg. The arrangement of the hip and leg pulled to the centre gives an angle to the frontal pose, and explicitly emphasises a sensuous thigh. The right hand forms an awkward salute with its bent wrist suggestive of rigor mortis. The image, with its placement of arms, legs, supine posture, open-mouth, and half-closed eyes, cites other images of both the reclining nude and publicity shots of Hollywood female icons of the 1940s and 1950s.

Both the bodies of Snow White and the Lady of Shalott are contained within the boundaries of their physical enclosures — a coffin, a tower and a boat. Such containment acts as a trope for the limits placed on women in patriarchal societies. The trope of the 'enclosed woman' is one familiar to domestic romances and other genres. By viewing these dead females in their enclosed spaces, we can begin to understand Nead's point 'that the act of representation is itself an act of regulation' (1992: 9). The fictive bodies of Snow White and the Lady of Shalott are the subjects of the gaze and at the same moment they are sites of alterity: the objects of the sexual and social 'other'. Both women also have bodies which are contained within the idealised morphologies of feminine perfection — there is no excess of body fat. This double containment of the woman's bodily limits is necessary in terms of phallocentric views of woman's unruly body: 'the formless matter of the female body has to be contained within boundaries, conventions and poses' (Nead, 1992: 11).

The Lady of Shalott's sequestered life in the tower both protects and confines her. A similar containment of the woman in the 'home' is thematised in *Snow White* where the young woman's safety is guaranteed only if she remains inside the home of the seven dwarfs. Once she steps outside the domestic space she meets with her death. Similarly, after the Lady looks directly at Sir Lancelot as he enters the landscape beyond her confined space, she moves into the outside world and towards her death. Signifying a break from her mirror-mediated and narcissistic world 'the mirror crack'd from side to side'. By inscribing her name on the prow of the boat, the Lady of Shalott prepares her coffin-boat as a site for staging her (dead) body as a beautiful object of sight. This act of self-textualisation is similar to that undertaken by the dwarfs in inscribing Snow White's name on her coffin (Bronfen, 1992). Upon seeing her dead body when it arrives at the gates of Camelot, Sir Lancelot's comment, 'she has a lovely face', echoes Poe's contention that a dead beautiful woman is 'the most poetical topic'.

The discussion to this point has shown how the erotics of these texts is located in the body of a woman. Though chaste, Snow White and the Lady of Shalott are nevertheless portrayed as seductresses with their innocence and beauty making them endlessly desirable but unavailable. Ultimately, all except Snow White are sacrificed and annulled by what are constructed as their own desires — Judy's feisty nature, Nell's wandering, and the Lady of Shalott's sexuality. While Snow White is given a third chance at living, her disobedience and naivete nevertheless provide ample warning for young girls of the consequences of ignoring patriarchal advice with the implication that women need to become the property of men (the Prince's 'prize') so that they can be protected, and kept dependent.

Mummy dearest: maternity as a deadly game of power

The significance of maternal loss either by accident, abandonment or death is another feature of literature for young people. Starke (1998) notes quite candidly that in terms of realistic fiction 'dead mums are literally everywhere' (p. 3). In a sense, this recent trend appears to have taken up from where the Victorian period finished. As Dever observes, 'To write a life, in the Victorian period, is to write the story of the loss of the mother' (1998: 1).

Both Dever and Starke share the common observation that 'death of mother' is often used as a plot enabler. The maternal absence (either by death or abandonment) defines the parameters and dynamics of the domestic space and those who inhabit its spatial confines and configurations. As previously mentioned, the mother's absence is a means for the young protagonist to embark on a journey of self-discovery, the familiar *bildungsroman*.

It is in this focus on the maternal, that there appears to be a shift away from Lacan's Law of the Father to the Law of the Mother in that mothers and daughters supplant fathers and sons (see Kristeva, 1982). In some instances, as the following discussion will demonstrate, the 'phallic' mother is marked through both presence and absence. Hence, the space of the maternal is fluid, shifting and doubly charged. There is also the problem that such shifts and fluidity result in a partial rather than a complete representation. Such narratives run the risk of being categorised as 'women's stories' assuming that they are written only for women and girls and would have no interest for men and boys. This categorising, like the terms 'mother' and 'motherhood', implies an essentialism which denies or obscures the different bodily, sexual and cultural experiences of women. A further complication that Langbauer (1990: 105) considers is that recourse to the mother simply collapses the woman with the body, the reproductive body. This argument that representation and essentialism are always partnered is one which Mulvey (1975) also maintains. These are some of the tensions that occur in texts which feature maternal loss and are considered in this section.

In considering the conflicting images of the maternal, stereotypes emerge in terms of the saintly mother and the transgressive mother. These appear as opposites, yet both are found in the body of 'woman'. Fairy tales laid the foundation for these feminine extremes and their prototypes continue to emerge in contemporary children's literature. To return to *Snow White and the seven dwarfs*, the transgressive mother is given full treatment in the form of the wicked Queen, Snow White's stepmother. She provides the template for the out-of-control, jealous woman whom children come to recognise through films and cartoons such as Disney's versions of *101 Dalmatians* (1996) and *The Little Mermaid* (1989) (see Mallan, 2000). She is also recognisable as the 'hysteric', a familiar image of female transgressiveness which emerges in various literary and other cultural texts.

In constructing the mother as transgressive, the daughter is often constructed as her opposite — controlled and conforming, and most significantly 'good' and beautiful. The hysteric or evil mother is, therefore, 'a double', as Gilbert and Guber explain, 'the image of a double is often present, the other half, the woman beyond the mirror, the unconscious, the evil spirit of which to rid the self' (1984: 43). These evil women need to be eradicated so that order, especially patriarchal order, can be restored. In commenting on *Hansel and Gretel* (Grimm, 1984), Zipes argues that just as the children in the tale were 'drawn into accepting the rule of the father as more benevolent than that of the mother' the children who read these stories are also 'misled to conceive that order will always be restored through the intervention of God the father and a resolution that restores faith in the good father' (1997: 50–1). Herein lies a critical point for this discussion. As Zipes contends, these stories of evil stepmothers, witches, and hysterics have been so much a significant part of the Western cultural tradition that they are embedded in our consciousness. It is too difficult, outrageous even, to expect children to see other more positive possibilities for these demonised women, especially as they are continually re-presented to them through book, film and cartoon in their stereotypical evil form. Furthermore, goodness, beauty and youth are focalised through the young female protagonist, thus forming an alliance between the young protagonist and the young reader/viewer (see Stephens, 1992: 67–70).

The struggles that occur between the transgressive, hysterical woman and others in a text centre on an unsettling or usurping of power. While invariably loud cheers greet the demise of the evil (step)mother there is rarely the opportunity for humble atonement. However, as Langbauer notes, 'What distinguishes the hysteric is her refusal actually to become the mother, her insistence on separating herself from the very horizon that gives her meaning' (1990: 169). This resistance to motherhood is witnessed in both the wicked Queen in *Snow White* and in the stepmother in *Hansel and Gretel*. Making both women 'step' mothers rather than biological mothers suggests that biological or 'true' mothers are incapable of doing their children harm — a point which runs counter to the actions of some 'real' mothers. The evil stepmother/witch hybrid in these tales is an ogress who wants to eat her children — the wicked Queen asks for the lung and liver of Snow White to be served to her as a meal while the witch in *Hansel and Gretel*, who is conflated with the stepmother, wants to cook and eat the children. This 'silencing of the lambs' strategy emerges in contemporary literature in the form of the all-consuming mother who preys on her children's minds, seeking control of their thoughts and bodies. The devouring mother may not necessarily be evil; she could be the 'good' mother whose love for her children is voracious and insatiable. It is only when the mother is killed that the child becomes free and can live without fear of being swallowed up by maternal desires and needs.

Kerry, the absent mother in *A bridge to Wiseman's Cove* (Moloney, 1996), embodies a form of resistant maternity. She is always an absent presence in the novel and is therefore only given partial representation. The reader comes to 'know' her through the thoughts and memories of her son Carl and others: 'That mother of yours. She was always taking off' (p. 16). The reader is therefore aligned with these focalisers by accepting their versions of this aberrant mother. She is a woman who has never married, though she has had three children by three different fathers. Her transgressive sexuality marks her failure as a 'good' mother. She is also constructed in the image of the woman-as-victim, men love her and leave her, and she struggles to find a life for herself away from the confines of motherhood and domestic restraints and responsibilities. Her attempts to escape are always foiled. For example, she 'loses' her then 4 year-old son in a shopping mall only to have the police return him later in the day. Her other escapes, which her children euphemistically call 'Mum's holiday', usually entail only days away from the domestic environment. Kerry is also constructed in the image of the hysteric, though the reader is positioned to accept Carl's word for this as he is the one who hears her screams and recriminations even though the words are never actually spoken. The reader is also expected to view Kerry's hysterical body through Carl's eyes in order to 'see' how her body betrays her thoughts and emotions:

> There was the frantic mood, the screeching, the recrimination. *What are you doing here? You're mucking up my life. I can't stand it.*
>
> Kerry didn't actually say these words but Carl heard them. Or at least, he saw them shooting out of her mouth, straining upwards to form a speech balloon like frames from a comic book.
>
> (Moloney, 1996: 4)

Kerry's hysterical body is also a dangerous one capable of harming her children, if not physically then psychologically. When Carl describes Kerry's vitriolic attack of words like 'barbs … piercing his own flesh' (p. 4), the mother's word is strangely made flesh and the son suffers the consequences of her abjection and misery. The illusion of insight attributed to Carl privileges not only a masculine way of seeing, but also a masculine inscription of the hysterical mother's body. Kerry's body becomes a *tabula rasa* which permits her son (and the other men in her life) to write 'her' story, in their words, not her words. This masculine penetration into the female body and psyche reverberates back through the history of psychoanalysis and Freudian interpretation of the hysterical woman/mother (see Showalter, 1985).

By setting up from the outset the relationship between Carl and his mother as one of extreme tension, the novel's trajectory is established in that the problem of the mother is thus 'foregrounded' so that it can be eventually solved by her death. The ensuing *Bildung* maps Carl's journey away from the maternal and towards self-discovery and back to a re-configured domestic space with a new family who loves him. This story relies on the predicament of abandonment as its main narrative strategy. Carl can only achieve mature subjectivity (and sexuality) through negotiating maternal abandonment and loss, and by establishing a subject position independent of the mother. His final 'letting go' of his emotions by allowing 'the tears he craved' to flow, means that his tears not only wash away the 'longed-for ache of his mother's death' (p. 241), but also by implication his mother. This emotional release means that now 'at least he was alive to feel it' (p. 241). This rebirthing of the son relies on the maternal and points to the inescapable maternal presence, even in its absence. Kerry's death echoes with those of other transgressive women throughout history and literature. Kerry is not granted a peaceful end, nor is she given the opportunity for atonement as she dies in a bus crash (on her way back to Carl and the family). Furthermore, she is denied a final image of feminine perfection as Carl comes to see her brutalised dead body in a police missing person's file:

> … Kerry Matt's lifeless eyes stared up from the desk.
>
> He couldn't move, couldn't look away or cry out. Stared into the photograph, into the face of his mother. The face was severely bruised and swollen. He doubted that anyone who hadn't known his mother recently would have recognised her. But it was her.
>
> (Moloney, 1996: 226)

A significant element of *A bridge to Wiseman's Cove* is male powerlessness. The unstable domestic space is a highly charged maternal and feminine site in terms of Kerry's presence and absence and Carl's surrogate mother replacements — his sister Sarah and his Aunt Beryl (who is also constructed as an hysteric, and transgressive 'mother'). All three women abandon the family, though it is Carl's abandonment that the reader is expected to feel is the most intense and traumatic:

> Once again *he* was abandoned. They were all gone then. Dessie Matt, wherever he was, Kerry, his mother who would never come home, Sarah in Europe somewhere, Harley across the water, and now Beryl.
>
> (Moloney, 1996: 235, my emphasis)

Yet, this self-pitying state of abandonment brings its own compensatory reward: 'He was free to go anywhere — back to the city, further if he wanted. For the first time in his life he was free' (p. 235). The removal of the maternal means that the anxiety experienced by the male protagonist is eased and the contesting domestic power relations appear to be resolved.

In a related way, *love, ghosts & nose hairs* (Herrick, 1996) also tells of the absent mother and the impact her absence and 'presence' has on the lives of her family. Unlike Kerry, Jack's mother is the 'good mother' whom Jack constructs in terms of her continuing domestic servility and surveillance in his family's life:

> There's a ghost in our house
> in a red evening dress
> black stockings
> and Mum's slingback shoes
> her hair whispers
> over white shoulders
> as she dances through the rooms.
> In Desiree's
> she cleans under the bed
> folds the five pairs of Levi's
> Des wears for months without washing.
> In my room
> she flips through my poems …
> In Dad's room
> she sits at the dresser
> I can see her
> smiling at the mirror too scared
> to announce her presence.

(Herrick, 1996: 24)

As Jack's mother romances the home, her dance romances the mother's role as homemaker. Langbauer suggests that the metaphor of the dance 'domesticates, perhaps in order to trivialize, women's role, in the way it inserts the category of the body into questions of articulation' (1990: 177). Jack's mother's spectral dance could be a waltz or even a polka as she weaves through the rooms attending to her family's clutter, fossicking through private objects, and stopping to gaze at her reflection in the mirror. This scene articulates an image of happy, good motherhood and as such is in sharp contrast to a similar dance scene in *Snow White and the seven dwarfs*. The wicked Queen also dances, but not by choice. Unlike Jack's mother's carefree waltz, hers is a tortured hot-footing to her death, with her feet trapped in shoes that force them to leap and fall to their deadly rhythms. In other times, she too gazed into her mirror seeking affirmation of her (beautiful) presence. Both scenes mirror patriarchal notions of woman by representing opposing images of the silent domestic mother and the screaming beautiful temptress. Whereas the stepmother is forced into an hysterical death dance for being the 'bad' mother, Jack's 'good' mother is rewarded by being forever remembered as happy and carefree in her domestic and 'proper' place.

'The mirror' is a recurrent motif in children's literature as the examples in this essay have illustrated. It is invariably tied to woman's narcissism and her demise. Jack's sister, Desiree, also gazes at her reflection in the mirror. But her gazing is a surveillance of her feminine body, a body which appears complicitous in plotting her death:

Late at night
when Jack and Dad are asleep
I stand naked in my bedroom
in front of the mirror
I look at my breasts
in the surgery fluorescent light
of my Mother's death
I touch them
feel my nipples harden unwillingly
it can kill me
this thing, this woman thing.
I find a different lump every night
and lie awake
wishing it away.

(Herrick, 1996: 67)

Desiree's mirror is not unlike the wicked Queen's as both recall the sight of other women, and both judge their womanly bodies and name that which threatens them. Desiree's body is thus inscribed with symbolic value in that it is made in the image of her mother's body and, as such, is imagined to bear the signs that will force her body to duplicate her mother's dead body. Whereas Poe and Plath write of the poetics of feminine perfection in death, Desiree sees a fearsome sight of corruption and destruction. Unlike Carl's *bildungsroman*, which was a journey 'out' away from the maternal and towards self-discovery, Desiree at this moment imagines only a voyage 'in', and one turned towards the maternal and death.

Jack is ultimately able to dispense with his mother's presence and, like Carl, is on track in terms of an end to his prolonged mourning phase. His decision to bury the dead is part of his own independent subjectivity and sexuality. However, despite his newly found bravado in telling his mother's ghost 'no more visits' (p. 112), her 'visible' presence remains etched in his face, and in Desiree's hair and hands (p. 113). Furthermore, she will remain their muse 'in what we do in this world' (p. 113).

The women discussed in this section are not only drawn from familiar stereotypes, but they are enigmas, and, therefore, given only partial representation. In one sense, these mothers exert a totalising power over their children who have difficulty in separating from her. While these images of powerful women might suggest a form of 'phallic' motherhood, their law is short lived and their power is illusory. They are either punished for being controlling or they are dismissed into eternity. In the examples discussed above, the mother ultimately serves the male order. The wicked Queen exemplifies the consequences of feminine transgressiveness, yet her actions provide the route back to patriarchal order which is achieved by Snow White's marriage to the Prince. Kerry is the scapegoat for the men in Carl's life who are equally, if not more, culpable of blame. By resisting her primary caregiver role, Kerry disrupts the domestic order and is punished and made an example of poor mothering and its consequences. Jack's mother is always known in terms of her relation to someone else, she has no name, she is simply 'My Mum' and 'My wife'. Her elusive presence is reported by others and through the confines of her domestic space. While she achieves the standard of ideal motherhood — the all-giving mother who devotes herself to the care of others — she is denied within the narrative frame any claims to a subjectivity beyond her mother/wife position.

Conclusion

As I have argued, the female deaths in children's literature serve more than an enabling narrative strategy as they represent particular constructions of 'woman' which are imbued with a patriarchal ideology. As readers and viewers, the narrative strategies, rhetorical devices and iconic representations attempt to situate us within the texts' ideologies so that we come to 'see' the woman according to either the implicit or explicit focalising strategies of the narrator or artist. The women's deaths discussed in this chapter have provided compensatory structures, but as foreshadowed at the beginning of this paper such compensations are ambivalent. In the examples provided, the compensations are more consolations for the male characters and, as the previous section concluded, serve to shore up masculine power and restore patriarchal order. There are, nevertheless, other compensatory structures which emerge in discussions of death (male and female) in children's literature. These were considered in the earlier part of this chapter and were shown as providing closure to the social relations between mourner and deceased, and confirmation of the stages of the mourning–remembrance–conciliation process.

This chapter has taken a particular interpretation of the cultural paradigm that links femininity with death. This approach was intended to highlight the ways convention (narrative and artistic) comes to shape our consciousness about this dual subject and lower our resistance to reading and seeing from another perspective. Writers of children's literature and critics need to dismantle the conjunction of woman and death and seek other ways of telling their stories and drawing their images which will incite a paradigm shift calling a crowd of onlookers and inviting close inspection of a different tableau of fatal attractions.

Bibliography

101 Dalmatians (motion picture) (1996) Disney Enterprises.

Aaron, M. (1996) *Lily and me.* Random House, Milsons Point.

Apseloff, M. (1991) 'Death in adolescent literature: suicide', *Children's Literature Association Quarterly*, 16, 4, pp. 234–8.

Bassein, B. (1984) *Women and death: linkages in western thought and literature.* Greenwood Press, Westport.

Beare, D. (1998) 'Representations of the "absent mother" in Australian adolescent fiction', *Papers*, 8, 3, pp. 16–24.

Bradford, C. (ed.) (1996) *Writing the Australian child.* University of Western Australia Press, Nedlands.

Bronfen, E. (1992) *Over her dead body: death, femininity and the aesthetic.* Routledge, New York.

Burningham, J. (1984) *Granpa.* Jonathan Cape, London.

Chaston, J. (1991) 'The other deaths in *Bridge to Terabithia*', *Children's Literature Association Quarterly*, 16, 4, pp. 238–41.

de Lauretis, T. (1984) *Alice doesn't. Feminism, semiotics, cinema*. Indiana University Press, Bloomington.

Dever, C. (1998) *Death and the mother from Dickens to Freud*. Cambridge University Press, Cambridge.

Dickens, C. (1972) *The old curiosity shop* (1841). Penguin, Harmondsworth.

French, F. (1986) *Snow White in New York*. Oxford University Press, Oxford.

Gibson, L. and Zaidman, L. (1991) 'Death in children's literature: taboo or not taboo?', *Children's Literature Association Quarterly*, 16, 4, pp. 232–3.

Gilbert, S. and Guber, S. (1984) *The madwoman in the attic: the woman writer and the nineteenth-century literary imagination*. Yale University Press, New Haven.

Grimm, Brothers (1972) *Snow White and the seven dwarfs* (translated by R. Jarrell, pictures by Nancy Ekholm Burkert). Kestrel, Harmondsworth.

—— (1984) *Hansel and Gretel* (retold by R. Lesser, illustrated by Paul O. Zelinsky). Dodd, Mead & Co, New York.

Hathorn, L. (1989) *Thunderwith*. Heinemann, Melbourne.

Hathorn, L. and Elivia (1994) *Grandma's shoes*. Viking. Ringwood.

Herrick, S. (1996) *love, ghosts & nose hair*. University of Queensland Press, St Lucia.

Huck, C. Hepler, S. and Hickman, J. (1997) *Children's literature in the elementary school* (6th edn). McGraw Hill, Boston.

Hunt, C. (1991) 'Dead athletes and other martyrs', *Children's Literature Association Quarterly*, 16, 4, pp. 241–5.

Hunter, E. (1977) *Me and Mr Stenner*. Hamish Hamilton, London.

Kertzner, A. (1996) 'Reclaiming her maternal pre-text: Little Red Riding Hood's mother and three young adult novels', *Children's Literature Association Quarterly*, 21,1, pp. 20–7.

Kidd, D. (1996) *I love you, Jason Delaney*. HarperCollins, Pymble.

Kristeva, J. (1982) *Powers of horror: an essay on abjection* (translated by Leon S. Roudiez). Columbia University Press, New York.

Langbauer, L. (1990). *Woman and romance*. Cornell University Press, Ithaca & London.

Leonard, G.M. (1992) ' "The woman is perfected. Her dead body wears the smile of accomplishment": Sylvia Plath and Mademoiselle Magazine', *College Literature*, 19, 2, pp. 60–83.

Macdonald, C. (1983) *Elephant rock*. Nelson, Melbourne.

Mallan, K. (2000) 'Witches, bitches and *femme fatales:* viewing the female grotesque in children's films', *Papers*, 10, 1, pp. 26–35.

Marsden, J. (1997) *Dear Miffy*. Pan Macmillan, Sydney.

Martin, S.K. (1997) 'Good girls die, bad girls don't: the uses of the dying virgin in nineteenth-century Australian fiction', in K. Charmaz, Howarth, G. and Kellehear (eds), *The unknown country: death in Australia, Britain and the USA*, St Martin's Press, A. New York.

Moloney, J. (1995) *Swashbuckler*. University of Queensland Press, St Lucia.

—— (1996) *A bridge to Wiseman's Cove*. University of Queensland Press, St Lucia.

Mulvey, L. (1975) 'Visual pleasure and narrative cinema', *Screen*, 16, 3, pp. 6–18.

Nead, L. (1992) *The Female Nude*. Routledge, London and New York.

Nichols, B. (1986) *Mullaway*. Penguin, Ringwood.

Paterson, K. (1980) *Bridge to Terabithia*. Penguin, Harmondsworth.

Plath, S. (1981) 'Edge', *the collected poems*. Harper & Row, New York.

Poe, E.A. (1996) *Edgar Allan Poe: poetry, tales, and selected essays* (1846). Library of America, New York.

Sadler, D. (1991) ' "Grandpa died last night": children's books about the death of grandparents', *Children's Literature Association Quarterly*, 16, 4, pp. 246–50.

Saxby, M. (1993) *The proof of the puddin'*. Ashton Scholastic, Sydney.

—— (1997) *Books in the life of a child*. Macmillan Education, South Melbourne.

Scutter, H. (1999) *Displaced fictions: contemporary Australian books for teenagers and young adults*. Melbourne University Press, Carlton South.

Showalter, E. (1985) *The female malady. Women, madness and English culture 1830–1980*. Pantheon, New York.

Silver, A. (1997) 'Domesticating Bronte's Moors: motherhood in *The secret garden*', *The Lion and the Unicorn*, 21, 2, pp. 193–203.

Smith, D. (1973) *A taste of blackberries*. Crowell, New York.

Starke, R. (1998) 'Dead Mums', *Viewpoint*, 6, 1, pp. 3–4.

Stephens, J. (1992) *Language and ideology in children's fiction*. Longman, London and New York.

Sutherland, Z. and Arbuthnot, M. (1991) *Children and books* (8th edn). HarperCollins, New York.

Tanner, L.E. (1996) 'Death-watch: terminal illness and the gaze in Sharon Olds's', *The Father. Mosaic*, 29, 1, pp. 103–21.

Tennyson, A. (1986) *The Lady of Shalott* (illustrated by Charles Keeping). Oxford University Press, Oxford.

The Literature Base (1992) 'Books on Death and Dying', 3, 3, pp. 26–7.

The Little Mermaid (motion picture) (1989) Disney Enterprises.

Turner, E. (1894) *Seven little Australians*. Ward Lock, London.

Wagner, J. (1977) *John Brown, Rose and the midnight cat* (illustrated by Ron Brooks). Kestrel, London.

White, K. (1993) *Australian children's fiction: the subject guide*. Jacaranda, Milton, Queensland.

—— (1996) *Australian children's fiction: the subject guide update*. Jacaranda, Milton, Queensland.

Wild, M. (1989) *The very best of friends* (illustrated by J. Vivas). Hamilton, Sydney.

Zipes, J. (1997) *Happily ever after: fairy tales, children, and the culture industry*. Routledge, New York and London.

Chapter 12

The representation of suicide in adolescent literature as a site of 'crossing boundaries'

John McKenzie

The story he had told the man in the black greatcoat, meant to cheer him up, had ended up contributing to the man's depression, perhaps pushing him over the brink.

(Seidler, 1982: 23)

Introduction: the problem

Youth suicide is widely recognised as a major health issue which increasingly impacts on educational professionals (teachers, librarians, counsellors as well as writers and educational publishers), parents and families. Little attention has been paid to the nature and potential impact of representations of suicide in fiction as read by children and young people, especially materials sourced within New Zealand and Australia, and the professional implications in the use of such representations. This chapter seeks to explore some of the issues associated with representation, indicating thus the interdisciplinary focus, the crossing of boundaries, that needs to take place to enable practitioners to make informed decisions. The focus questions for this chapter are:

- Are writers absolutely free to *write at will about youth suicide*?
- Are librarians and teachers *absolutely free to disseminate at will any representation*?
- What are some of the issues that can inform the practitioners' use of this literature?

The intentional self-destruction of a young person is a devastating event. Clearly, the overwhelming and unbearable pain of the teenager exhibiting suicidal behaviour is part of this devastation. It is hard to accept the idea that a young person, on the brink of life and all its possibilities, felt it right to choose annihilation and non-being rather than choose the inevitable risks of being and becoming. Whilst the young person may have made mistakes, may have experienced powerful negative events in his or her life, may have suffered profoundly from clinical depression, and may have experienced acutely both the stressors and angst of being, there is no second chance in death. One gets one shot at life, as it were. There is also a tremendous sense of loss, bewilderment, guilt and anger within the wider community of family, peers and the school when confronted by the stark reality of this

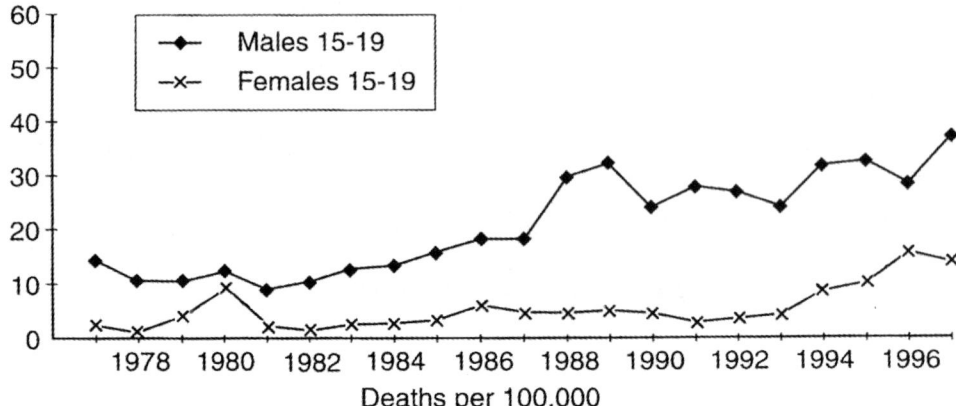

Figure 12.1 Youth suicide rates

choice. There wasn't time to say what needed to be said perhaps. The investment by the wider community in that young person's life, an investment perhaps of love, mutual companionship, education and hope, comes to nought. Even in the context of a life of abuse and despair, there is no possibility of transformation when suicide is chosen. Not only is life rejected, but also (intentionally or not) the hope that a community might bring. Youth suicide touches then on what it is to live in a community. Figure 12.1 shows the youth suicide rates spanning three decades.

Writers are not immune to the social issues that surround them. In broad terms, writers both respond to and help shape the social forces that operate in the reading event. In this sense, it is interesting to note the correlation between the total number of fictional representations of youth suicide and youth suicide rates.[1]

Whilst the 'respond to' would no doubt characterise all writer's *intentions* in the representation of suicide, is there any evidence that 'shaping' takes place? Whilst overt shaping in the form of the didactic voice has long since been critiqued and avoided by writers, it is also an accepted literary principle that there is no such thing as an innocent text; that the book is a site of ideology and therefore the possibilities of persuasion. Is there any evidence of fictional representations being a precipitating factor in a suicide event, a 'cause' as much as a correlation? Can writers (and, in terms of the food chain, teachers and librarians) claim immunity from the ethical implications of representation? On what grounds could a representation be considered ethically good or problematic? What arguments can be mounted to defend any representation to give weight to notions of immunity from book challenges?

Representations of suicide, especially as mediated in a pedagogical setting, are a site of complex questions involving a range of professional interests where practitioners, wittingly or not, must daily cross boundaries in making choices. There are a range of searching questions that could be asked of these representations from a variety of perspectives.

The health professional may well want to know:

- To what extent are these representations accurate or 'realistic' in terms of epidemiological data?
- To what extent are models of intervention and postvention representative of best practice and, if they are not, is this critiqued?
- To what extent are myths about suicide evident in these fictions and are these myths critiqued?
- Is there any therapeutic value in these representations for health professionals working with adolescents at risk? Is there any evidence that justifies a bibliotherapeutic approach?
- How are helping agencies positioned in these fictions and to what extent are the representations of such agencies life-affirming for the reader?

The ethicist may well want to know:

- To what extent are the ethical/philosophical/theological issues related to adolescent suicide represented?
- Do writers have an ethical obligation to the implied reader? Are there different obligations for publishers, teachers, librarians or parents?
- Should a writer be concerned about consequences in representing 'the real'?
- What useful ethical guidance can be given to practitioners in the use of representations?

The literary critic may well want to know:

- What patterns and themes emerge in the sub-genre as a whole, as well as in individual books?
- What discoursal features do these representations use and how is the reader positioned in the text to respond to the representations?
- What is the ideological impact of the discoursal features of the text? To what extent is suicide as represented in literature different to or the same as suicide in life?
- What criteria should be applied to evaluate these fictions and to what extent should non-literary criteria matter? What is the relationship of information to what is fictive?
- What is the relative nature and effect of fictional versus non-fictional representations in different media?

The social scientist may well want to know:

- To what extent are social theories of suicide represented?
- What cultural variants exist in the representation of suicide?
- Are the sociodemographic variables represented accurately?

The teacher/librarian may well want to know:

- Do fictional representations of suicide positively or negatively (or both) influence readers?
- What principles should underpin best practice in the use (storing, marketing, mediating) of this genre?
- How do I respond to a reader who is disturbed by a particular reading?

This chapter cannot obviously deal with all the complexities inherent in many of these questions. What these questions demonstrate is the necessity to cross the boundaries of different academic disciplines in order that the notion of 'informed decisions' for the practitioner can have some depth.

This chapter begins this journey. Narrow credentialism that insists on the power of the authoritative voice that is constructed through ownership of a specialised and privileged knowledge is, of necessity, being challenged. This writer makes no special claim on either theories or praxis in such diverse disciplines as health science, abnormal psychology, suicidology, normative ethics, sociology, literary representations, adolescent literature, librarianship or teaching and learning in the reading process. Crossing the boundaries inevitably involves moving outside of one's comfort zone and accepting conditionality and tentativeness as defining features of one's discourse. This chapter presents questions for the reader therefore, as much as answers.

An underlying assumption of this chapter is that the notion of suicide as a rational choice for an adolescent is untenable. If it could be argued that an adolescent has the right to choose death,[2] then there is a considerable limitation on the responsibility of the writers (and other practitioners) to that adolescent. It may be acceptable, for example, that a writer should demonstrate how to commit suicide painlessly for the adolescent who wishes to exercise that right, or to warn the adolescent about the awful consequences of not getting it right if an attempt was to be made. On the other hand, if an adolescent has not got the moral right to choose death, then a writer conceivably should not be in the business of aiding or abetting (by omission or commission) an adolescent's faulty belief that he or she has that moral right. Psychological necessity is not the same as moral rights.

That suicide is morally reprehensible in some situations cannot be denied. The pilot that commits suicide whilst flying, thus resulting in the deaths of many passengers, is acting amorally. The father or mother who commits suicide without any regard for the welfare of their children is acting amorally. That they do so is unarguable as a statement of psychological necessity and real world events. But the moral stance in so acting can be critiqued. In some of these fictions, ethical critiquing takes place through the adoption of a critical stance by the reader when the author uses irony, through comments from survivors and through the apportioning of blame, as for example, in Mahy's (2000) *Twenty Four Hours*.

Arguments for a rational decision to end life, and the right to make such a decision, can be illustrated from the following contexts:

- a person suffering extreme pain through terminal illness, having fulfilled social obligations, may be morally justified in choosing to hasten the inevitable;
- a captured soldier who, knowing that the enemy will kill him during torture, chooses death rather than 'spilling the beans' under duress and betraying his or her country, may be morally justified in ensuring the survival of personal dignity.

The principle in these cases seems to be that a person chooses death for himself or herself in order that a higher moral good (e.g. other people's lives) may be served.

As Brandt puts it:

The basic question a person must answer, in order to determine which world-course is best or rational for him to choose, is one which he would choose under conditions of optimal rise of information, when all of his desires are taken into account. It is not just a question of what we prefer now, with some clarification of all the possibilities being considered. Our preferences change, and the preferences of tomorrow (assuming we can know something about them) are just as legitimately taken into account in deciding what we do as the preferences for today.

(Brandt, 1975: 193)

He further points out that depression, like any severe emotional experience, tends to 'primitivise one's intellectual processes' and that the best choice simply cannot be known in the context of depression. Given that approximately 80 per cent of adolescents who commit suicide suffer from psychiatric disorders, dominantly affective disorders (like depression), substance abuse disorder and anti-social behaviours (Hider, 1998) there can be no argument for such adolescents having a moral right to choose. Indeed, most teenagers who attempt to suicide, having received appropriate help, do live full and productive lives, clearly negating the attempt as the 'best' option.[3] Given this assumption that adolescent right to choose suicide is untenable (though debatable), what is the writer's role? Can writers justify the freedom to *write at will about youth suicide*; what arguments can practitioners employ to be *absolutely free to disseminate at will any representation*?

Arguments for the representation of suicide

Firstly, it can be argued that the writer is simply 'telling it as it is' which is the primary function of a writer. The writer has little, if any, responsibility to the reader; the writer's responsibility is to the truth of the phenomenon as observed by him or her.[4] Social realism is the dominant genre in which these fictional representations are found, and is the genre which is grounded in contemporary or 'real life' or 'telling it as it is' in terms of plot, character, theme and setting that encapsulates change and (possibly) growth. However, there are both epistemological and literary issues in terms of this definition that are problematic. What do we mean by 'real', whose 'reality', how is 'real' authenticated and how does a text reinforce or subvert this authentication? What counts for real when art is an imitation? As Eagleton puts it:

> In some literary works, in particular realistic fiction, our attention as readers is drawn not to the 'act of enunciating', to how something is said, from what kind of position and with what end in view, but simply to what is being said, to the enunciation itself. Any such 'anonymous' enunciation is likely to have more authority, to engage our assent more readily, than one which draws attention to how enunciation is actually constructed.

(Eagleton, 1996: 147)

This stamp of authority, 'telling it as it is', as found in realistic and historical fiction, tends to position the reader to assume that form and function are coterminous, that fiction is not a lie (Hollander, 1996).

Stephens (1992) has noted that children's literature is constructed within two parameters in terms of a continuum; at one end there are those texts where readers are invited to consider the texts 'as if' they are a documentary transcription of events in the actual world, and at the other end there are those texts where conscious attention is drawn to the construction of the text and where readers are invited to be the author's playmate and become more aware how meanings are both linguistically and socially constructed. Stephens argues that in the first parameter, publishers pre-empt reader's subject positioning by identifying texts as 'real life dramas' and 'based on true stories' such that the reader is positioned to erase awareness of the surfaces of textuality and respond instead to the content of the transmission. Such texts dominate social realism and historical fiction as genres.

Realism, then, as a genre asserts a mode of authority that positions readers to accept the 'truth telling' of the author. However, there seems to be considerable critical confusion over the distinction between realism as establishing a one-to-one correspondence with the actual world (telling it as it really is) and realism as a *representation* where, finally, there is no absolute, determinate reality and what is presented is a 'shaped' reality. Rarely is this epistemological conundrum identified and considered in defining social realism as a genre, especially in novels that are grounded on a social issue.

In epistemological terms, the argument that the writer is ideologically neutral, reflecting simplistically the 'real world' cannot be sustained. Writers cannot escape their embedded world views. Literary techniques employed may be self-effacing and beguile the reader as it were to its truth-telling, but the concept of a representation asserts the idea of fiction as a take, a slant, a perspective. Thus it is that critical literacy as a curriculum seeks to empower readers to unlock the ideology embedded in representations. Kamler and Comber argue that:

> While critical literacy does not stand for a single approach ... we can identify some shared assumptions: that literacy is a social and cultural construction, that its functions and uses are never neutral or innocent, that the meanings that are constructed in text are ideological and involved in producing, reproducing and maintaining arrangements of power which are unequal.
>
> (Kamler and Comber, 1996: 1–5, 9)

Writers, for example, who are themselves depressed and suicidal may bring acute observation, courage and 'reality' to their work, but may not bring an 'equal' or 'balanced' perspective to the representation of suicide as a phenomenon (Berman, 1999). The representation is less reflective of all possible realities but is an artefact of the writer's schema. Thus the writer cannot ignore their bias and cannot ignore also the existence of the reader in bringing his or her bias: in the very construction of a text, a reader is envisaged and various readings possible. Various possible readings mean that predicting response is a problematic business. As Eagleton puts it:

> To understand a poem means grasping its language as being orientated towards the reader from a certain range of positions: in reading, we build up a sense of what kind of effects this language is trying to achieve ('intention'), what sorts of rhetoric it considers appropriate to use, what assumptions govern the kinds of poetic tactics it employs, what attitudes to reality these imply ... And such tactics and assumptions may not be mutually coherent: a text may offer several mutually conflicting or contradictory 'subject positions' from which to be read.
>
> (Eagleton, 1996: 104)

The operative question is the degree to which there is a responsibility, a form of social contract between writer and reader (and mediating professionals) as it were, especially in the representation of a social issue like suicide where the potentiality of the text for shaping unfortunate responses is both possible and unpredictable. In utilitarian terms, what is the 'right thing to do'? This is not simply an academic question. How is a reader at risk of suicidal behaviour positioned in the following novel?

Jed, known as Shoovy Jed by his sister India, is deeply depressed with his lot in life (*Shoovy Jed*, Stewart, 1997). From his zits to his ex-mates, Jed (15) is despairingly helpless in the face of life's challenges. Where his sister India (12) seems able to cope by switching out from parental conflict and find humour and meaning from singing Elvis songs in appropriate (and at times, inappropriate) contexts, Jed finds some solace in his journal. Teachers and counsellors, though well-meaning enough, are not able to reach through the tunnel vision that encompasses Jed's world, and the meticulous planning he engages in to end his life.

There is an inevitability in this narrative (self-mutilation, signs not understood, dysfunctional parents fixated on division of labour issues, being socially isolated) that leads up to the suicide event. His lack of self-esteem and hopelessness (even in his first fumblings in a sexual encounter) mean that there is little spark for the reader to grasp as a possibility for redemption or transformation. The ending is as sudden as the event itself: a change of voice and register in the final epilogue is stark and uncompromising. Clearly Jed miscalculated the depth of water under the bridge from which he has jumped with a tragic consequence: he ends up crippled. The cover from *Shoovy Jed* appears in Illustration 12.1.

There is no question with regard to the verisimilitude-authenticity of this narrative. It comes as close to the bone as one could get in terms of understanding the psyche of a

Illustration 12.1 The cover from *Shoovy Jed*

youngster intent on committing suicide. It is a superb evocation of the suicidal character. However, the ending invites a critical debate. If one believes in the efficacy of the awful warning cautionary tale (nineteenth century vintage), then perhaps it could be argued that it is a powerfully responsible book. The inside blurb lists appropriate helping agencies. However, to the extent that the book elaborates with mathematical precision on dying efficiently (but an unfortunate miscalculation at the end), the implied message, particularly for an unstable reader, is that if you are going to do it, think of all the variables and get it right. Such a rational conclusion undermines the inside blurb that resists the idea of the moral right to rationally choose to die. The ending of *Shoovy Jed* is at best ambiguous.

There is a dilemma then between 'telling it as it is' and the writer's implied ideology towards life, death and choice; and the didactic implications of that tension, especially for the unstable reader who is reading texts that are inherently unstable.

Secondly, it can be argued that fictional representations that present information about suicide as a phenomenon may be educative. The relationship of information and fiction, seemingly disparate entities, can be viewed from a variety of perspectives. Increasingly, fiction is used in educational practice as a source of information whereby young readers are encouraged to assume an efferent stance of 'taking away' (Latin *effere*) information using strategies based on the transactional theories of Rosenblatt (1978).[5] The following contexts reinforce this idea of an efferent stance:

- students often expect life likeness as a determinant of quality in their fictional expectations (Lowry, 1995);
- teachers position students to adopt this stance in many of their teaching strategies (Kaywell, 1994);
- writers assume a stance of authority in linking the fictive and the real by asserting a research basis for the fiction in the front blurb of the book, seeking expert endorsements in cover material, referring to research within the text, articulating expert opinion where irony is not signalled and by using the authoritative first person voice of the teenager;
- publishers frame the text as part of a series relating to the actual world and by endorsing helping agencies in the blurb;
- some health professionals use story as an adjunct therapy (Gladding, 1994);
- the development of 'faction' as a category of literature.

Such contexts reinforce the authority of realism as a narrative act, subverting the fictive component of the text so that what is 'real' and what is 'fictive' are increasingly seen as two sides of the same narrative coin. It is therefore reasonable to critique the nature of information provided and how it is mediated or represented in the fictive act. If the argument that fiction can present information that is educative is to be sustained, then accuracy and authenticity become critical concerns.

There is an uneasy relationship between the humanities and science in representing the phenomenon of youth suicide. This was succinctly put by Pritchard (1996) when describing his own methodological stance in describing suicide as follows:

There is a longstanding tradition in the humane services of an emphasis upon the personal and the individual. This 'qualitative' approach can lead to denial of the

The Real World as Setting

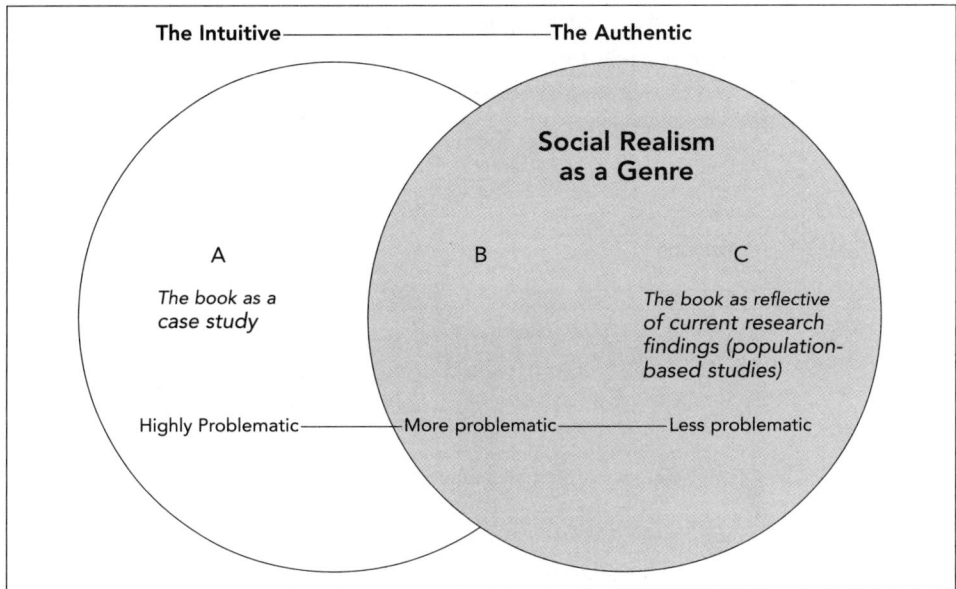

Figure 12.2 A model of social realism as genre

'quantitative', as if an empirical approach based on a series of studies is a disavowal of the individual, or we turn the person into a detached statistic. It is a feature of our approach that an essential synthesis is sought, because 'analysis' enumeration without 'empathy' is sterile and depersonalising, whilst empathy, without analysis can lead to confusion and chaos, as all are sucked up into the maelstrom of crisis and existential despair.

(Pritchard, 1996: 16)

There is a need for crossing the boundaries. If writers, publishers and practitioners are in the business of claiming the authority of realism, then the information so presented needs scrutiny. That scrutiny will lie outside traditional literary criticism (qualitative approaches) and will, in the case of youth suicide, utilise current research findings as found, for example, in epidemiological studies (the quantitative). The relationship between the fictive and the 'real' may be envisaged as per Figure 12.2.

The diagram in Figure 12.2 allows for the following evaluating texts in terms of the following dimensions:

A   Texts that have little or no evidence of being research-based. These texts tend to be more intuitive/speculative on the part of the writer or may be based on paradigms that are not reflective of current research findings in suicidology (as for example, in representing psychoanalytic theories as causes for suicide). They may be overtly ideological in representing a particular view of the act of suicide. Questions of verisimilitude may arise where the speculative element suggests fantasy as a genre. In epistemological terms, the information is less determinable.[6] To that extent, these texts are highly problematic as texts that fit within the genre of social realism.

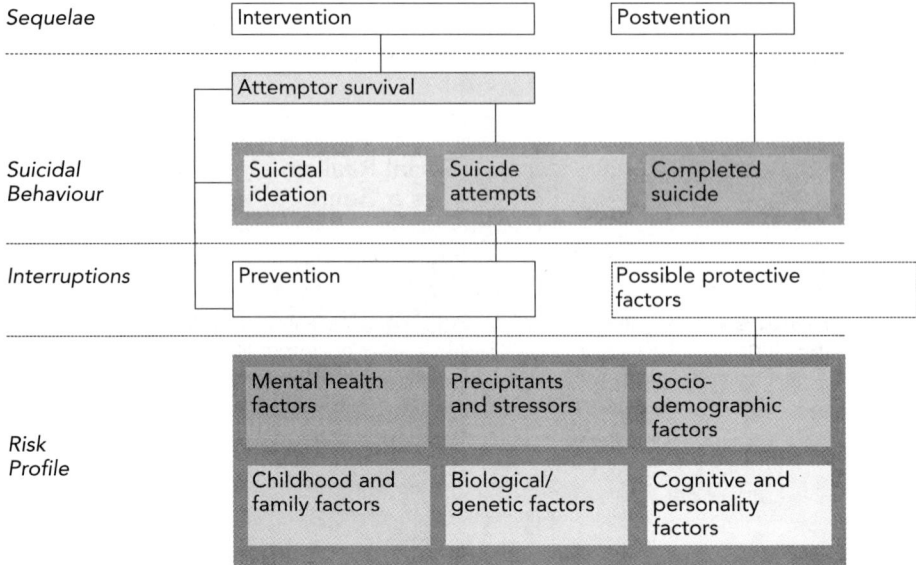

Figure 12.3 A model of youth suicidal behaviours

B   These texts are largely based on research findings but may have idiosyncratic aspects that indicate speculation on the part of the writer. Further, though there is evidence of research-based information, that information may be incomplete or indicate little depth. Ideological indeterminacy is possibly evident where information asserted and discourse features may be contradictory. Such texts are more problematic (than category C) as texts within the genre of social realism.

C   These texts are highly consistent with current research findings in terms of the social or psychological phenomenon in question where there is a high degree of correspondence ('authenticity') between the actual world and the represented world, and where there is sufficient breadth that a reasonably complete picture of the phenomenon is given. There are less problems in identifying the book as fitting within the genre of social realism. These books are highly suited to readers adopting an efferent stance of taking information about youth suicide.

Specifically in the case of youth suicide, representations, in order to be informative and hence educative, should encompass something of the complexity of the phenomenon as indicated in Figure 12.3.

This model of youth suicide asserts the following propositions that one could expect in a 'realistic' representation that purports to be educative:

- that a suicide event is multi-factorial. Suicide is a complex behaviour that is enclusive of a range of risk factors that predispose a person at risk to suicidal behaviour. A representation of suicide that identifies a singular stressor as 'cause' would be highly problematic.
- that some risk factors are more significant than others: there is a hierarchy of contributing factors where mental health factors are especially significant. One should be able to trace evidence of this hierarchy for a representation to be identified as 'realistic'.

Illustration 12.2 The cover from *Blindfold*

- that each risk factor generates a complex set of indicators based on clinical/research evidence. For characterisation to be identified as showing depth, one could expect that these indicators are detailed (see McKenzie, 1999c).
- that suicide is a process that emerges generally over time. Plot development should reflect a revelation of predispositions, a vulnerable history and precipitating events.

The book *Blindfold* (McCuaig, 1989), for example, arguably fits within the first dimension (A) of Figure 12.2 where texts have little or no evidence of being research-based. When two brothers, Benjii Goldstein and Joel Goldstein, commit suicide together, 15 year-old Sally O'Leary (who was loved by them both) gets the blame.

In the course of the story we see that Benjii and his blind brother have a highly dependent relationship where a protective mother obliges Benjii to put his brother first as 'he has suffered enough'. Whilst Sally is attracted to Benjii, both boys are attracted to Sally. Joel increasingly turns inward into psychic phenomena in order to make sense of his world including some fairly heavy spiritualist experiences. It is his interpretation of a horoscope message, invented by Benjii and Sally, that provides the final cause for (inexplicably) both jumping to their deaths from a lighthouse. To Joel, he is wanting to free his soul from his body; for Benjii it is almost an obligation in a co-dependent relationship. The story chiefly consists of the unravelling of the mystery of how the event came to be and Sally receiving counselling for her part in the mystery-thriller from a Dr Jago and a local hobo, Lifesaver. The cover from *Blindfold* appears in Illustration 12.2.

Though set in the real world, this novel lacks both verisimilitude and contains limited research as endorsement for the information found in the text. Firstly, we are asked to believe that Dr Jago will take a young girl to his private home ('Wanted you to see where I live … I only invite my friends here') as part of therapy and, when Sally explodes, he 'grabs

Illustration 12.3 The cover from *Tunnel Vision*

my arms, twists them behind my back, and holds me against all my strength' (p. 29). Professional ethics don't exist in this fiction.

Secondly, whilst it is possible to envisage the dependency/relationship between Benjii and his brother Joel relating to Joel's disability (even in the 1980s), the notion that one follows the other in a suicide stretches credibility, especially as the psychological realities of dependency–co-dependency are very lightly drawn in the story. There is no evidence of co-dependent relationships as a contributing factor in suicide in epidemiological research, especially in adolescence.

Finally, the trigger for deciding to jump (a misinterpretation of a horoscope reading) is so far beyond the normal risk profile/precipitating stress factors that credibility is lost entirely. Characterisation based on research of adolescents at risk in terms of Figure 12.3, especially for Benjii, is very weak in this story.

The problem is partly the confusion of genre: it is at once set in the real world, revolving around real world issues of disabilities, sibling relationships and suicide; but it is also an adventure story with something of a whodunit in the plot. Hence genre expectations are an essential component in a useful reading (Eagleton, 1996) of this text.

In contrast, *Tunnel Vision* (Arrick, 1980) reveals a degree of authenticity that is likely to provide much more useful information about youth suicide. The cover from *Tunnel Vision* appears in Illustration 12.3. When Anthony hangs himself in his bedroom with his father's ties, those who loved him struggle with their feelings of guilt and anger. There is Carl, his cousin, who admired the straight-A Anthony whose athletic prowess was legendary: there is Ditto, a friend whose wisdom surprises Carl; Jana, Anthony's girlfriend, a young Czech émigré who has herself experienced great loss in both her old land as well as the new; Denise, his younger sister, a dope addict who has struggled with low self-esteem in the shadow of Anthony; and his parents, especially his father Rand, a very busy businessman who was so ambitious for his son but had lost deeper more intimate connections.

Told through a juxtaposition of present narrative and flashbacks, what emerges is that Anthony was profoundly depressed and that, though his mother recognised the need for professional help, his father's self-confidence in being able to make sense of adolescent depression proves wanting. Though the signs of depression were evident in Anthony's 'tunnel vision', the lack of awareness of reading the signs proves catastrophic.

This fiction clearly reveals an understanding of the complexity of 'causation' that matches epidemiological data. We observe a dysfunctional family through a variety of relationships (childhood and family factors), we understand the nature of clinical depression (mental health factors), we can see the consequences of distorted thinking (cognitive and personality factors) and we sympathise for a youngster who, despite high potential, lacks self-esteem. The fact that the signs of suicidality are not seen by family and friends is entirely believable. This fiction gives insight to the realities of youth suicide. However, it is not simply a sociological treatise: it is also a powerful literary work.

Clearly, there is value for the critic to use epidemiological data as a means to evaluate the individual case studies of writers. The argument that fictional representations can present educative information about suicide as a phenomenon such that the reader learns, presupposes substantial critical scrutiny utilising current research findings in suicidology.

It can be argued that fiction can be a transformative experience and therefore representations can be a collective 'good'. Fiction not only touches the head ('information') but also the heart. The focus of this argument is on reader response and the efficacy of bibliotherapy. To the extent that a phenomenon is represented in the fictive, it can be argued that the experience of that phenomenon is safer for a reader in that attention is focused not on the personal life of the reader (as in counselling), but on the secondary created world where there is some degree of emotional distance. Emotions of the reader are focused outwards on characters rather than inwards on the personal. Class discussions may be more safe for the reader at risk of suicidal behaviour when focused on this secondary world.

Bibliotherapy has been defined in specific terms as a 'family of techniques for structuring interaction between a facilitator and a participant based on mutual sharing of literature' (Kortner, 1993). However, a distinction needs to be made between clinical bibliotherapy (a 'hard' form of the term) where a formal therapeutic situation is developed between a facilitator and client(s) with an identified presenting problem, usually as an adjunct therapy, as opposed to developmental bibliotherapy (a 'soft' form of the term) where, in a typical classroom situation, books are perceived to be helpful and illuminating and methodology is contextualised as normal pedagogic practice. The practice of bibliotherapy is based on an Aristotelian model of the reading process in terms of reader identification with protagonist, the catharsis of emotion in the denouement and insight into theme with self-reflection by the reader.

Scientific review of the efficacy of *clinical* or hard bibliotherapy, with case studies being the main form of methodology, has produced very mixed results, dominantly with a nil effect (Tillman, 1984).[7] However, it would be fair to say that a *developmental* or soft bibliotherapeutic view would be held by most children's literature specialists though they may well eschew the term bibliotherapy. That is, most writers of textbooks in children's literature extol the virtues of literature being a benefit to children though enthusiasm for bibliotherapy has spawned a type of story that tends to social thesis rather than literature, much to the chagrin of critics.[8] What needs to be noted is that developmental bibliotherapy works on the assumption that story has a positive effect on the reader, though clinical bibliotherapy recognises the need for not only a careful selection of materials but also the timely intervention of a skilled therapist in a one-on-one situation. This is not the context of classrooms.

Indeed, the argument that representations may have a transformative or bibliotherapeutic effect assumes that the text allows the possibility of transformation. The following nine discoursal features[9] potentially position the reader to assume an acceptance of, rather than resistance to, youth suicide as a choice behaviour and therefore a bibliotherapeutic intent or potential effect is likely to be subverted by these features.

The dominance of the first person narrative

The choice of first person to represent the angst of the alienated teenage narrator is no doubt an effective technique to enable close identification between narrator and reader; we see inside the situation from the inside point of view of the person exhibiting suicidal behaviours. We understand the pain, we trace the behavioural changes, and we expect perhaps the inevitable. However, we do not see the pain of the family or friends, and we do not see beyond the tunnel vision of the narrator unless an ironical stance is encouraged by the narrative. Irony, however, by drawing attention to textuality undermines emotional engagement and identification and consequently this is not the usual mode of narration in realistic fiction. We are generally not positioned to doubt the adolescent voice.

The connection between the first person and the unstable reader is at its most intimate in using the first person voice and without the wider perspective of the third person (or multiple first person voices), a false reading of the social pain and anguish of suicide may result.

The positioning of helping agencies as ineffective

Many narratives position potential helpers as ineffectual, unavailable and/or inimical to the needs of the person exhibiting suicidal behaviours. Of course it is a reality that many persons exhibiting suicidal behaviours do find that helping agencies (from parents to professionals) are woefully inadequate in terms of understanding their particular dilemmas (especially if the central issue is coming out gay in an homophobic world) and indeed may be central to the problem of the person exhibiting suicidal behaviours. However, for the unstable reader who has fixated on suicide, the result of negative positioning of helpers may well be to reinforce their own loneliness and helplessness in the face of their particular dilemmas. To the extent that the fictional hero commits suicide as a form of release, this may well be the lesson learnt. Nobody understands, and the protagonist's choice is therefore valid (and the reader's potential choice is validated too).

Hopelessness as a dominant theme

Again, the writer who vividly portrays the hopelessness of the alienated youngster in a society that rejects them (for example, the abused streetkid of colour) may well be reflecting reality. Given that hopelessness may be the final predictor of a suicide event (Simonds, McMahon and Armstrong, 1991), for the unstable reader his or her hopelessness (often an irrational feeling associated with an affective disorder) may be reinforced. If a bleak reading gives no hope within the parameters of the story (other than perhaps a publisher's blurb about helping agencies despite the narrative positioning of those helping agencies), then it could be argued that the book is highly problematic for the unstable reader.

For this reason, McKenzie (1997: 14) argued that both John Marsden's *Dear Miffy* and Margaret Clark's *Care Factor Zero* are problematic books in that the ending allows for little hope at all. Hope does not mean fairytale endings. Hope could mean:

- that sympathetic and helpful others (peer and/or adults) do exist and will be there for the protagonist;
- that despite the reality of life's unfairness and bleakness, life has it potentialities for joy and some signposts are given;
- that the processes of grief are acknowledged and enacted;
- that alternative coping strategies are given especially by characters who have been through the mill;
- that health professionals are positioned as being capable interventionists and that cognitive behavioural therapy or a variation, dialectic behavioural therapy (with anti-depressants), the therapies of choice, are detailed;
- that growth and maturation of the protagonist or the narrator is detailed as a result of the experience of the life events;
- that nihilism as a value system is critiqued within the novel;
- that some meaning can be derived from the death of a character;
- that there is a sense of transcendence beyond self when searching for meaning;
- that suicide is an irreversible tragic event for the person and the community, but, despite the pain, healing can take place, life continues; and
- that there is an ironical contrast between a character who is overcome by despair with another character, with a similar life-story who, having been through despair, begins to see transforming possibilities.

The placement of the suicide event in the narrative

The suicide event can be placed generally at three points in the story. Firstly it may be found at the beginning. The consequence of this is that, in the case of linear narratives, the book focuses on the aftermath and the impact of the event on those left behind. This enables the choice of suicide to be challenged in that the consequences can be delineated. However, in the case of fractured narratives (where flashbacks and multiple voices can explicate the past), the book that has the suicide event in the beginning may focus both on the causes as well as the consequences.

Secondly, the suicide event may be found in the middle. Such books are typically linear where causes and consequences are given in a sort of equal balance. However, in the third case of suicide event placement in linear narratives, where the suicide event is placed at the end of the narrative, the affective impact of the suicide is at its most powerful. Here the causes are given prominence; the consequences are minimised. It could be argued that the romanticisation of suicide in the form of an identification with a tragic hero is most likely in this form of the structuring of the narrative and that such structuring positions the reader to be less critical of suicide as a choice behaviour. Here lies a difficulty with Shakespearian tragedies.

The silencing of voices

When a comparison of the findings of epidemiological studies is used as a basis of examining risk profiles as found in fictional representations, what is remarkable is the silencing of some voices.

In the case of rural males (where access to more violent means is greater) and where rates are high, very few representations portray the particular problems of growing up in an isolated rural environment. Given the high number of Aboriginal and Maori males who commit suicide (especially in prison), there seem to be very few fictional representations. What is well represented in the genre (especially from American sources) is the pain of the upper/middle-class youth who find it too painful to meet the expectations of family and friends and choose to opt out. Yet research does not indicate that this is a likely scenario for suicide, at least within New Zealand. Rather, youth suicide is a reflector of social and educational disadvantage (Ministry of Youth Affairs). Through a process of bibliotherapy, where readers identify with a protagonist, many unstable readers will not find such identifications: their problems are not articulated.

Suicide as a normal stress response

Epidemiological studies suggest that the act of suicide is a complex interrelationship of a range of contributing factors (as detailed in Figure 12.3). Suicide is less a random event that strikes unawares as a result of a particular stressor and more a situation of an at-risk, predisposed individual who, at a given point, finally acts after an accumulation of trauma. If a suicide event is posited as a response to singularity rather than multiplicity, misleading signals may be given to the unstable reader.

Whilst it is unreasonable to say that adolescence is marked by stressors and that childhood is free of them (thus privileging only some childhoods), there are particular stressors that mark adolescence. For example, the loss of a loved one is a traumatic business when deep psychological needs of partnership, intimacy and sexual pleasure have been fulfilled for the first time. Equally though, it is fair to say that such events are common enough (but no less traumatic for the participants) and do not automatically lead to suicide. A book that details a suicide as a response to a relationship breakdown as *sole* cause misleads the reader into believing that this is a typical or normal response to extreme distress. Normalisation of suicide occurs when suicide is seen as a normal response to a normal situation. It isn't, and fictions are more problematic if they support such responses.

For this reason Fleischman's (1998) *Whirligig* is a problematic novel in that the attempted suicide of Brent as a result of a public humiliation from a potential but not actual girlfriend (basically a 'get lost' message) would no doubt strike fear in the heart of most adolescent boys in their first tentative steps in relating to girls, but is not a necessary or sufficient condition for suicide in terms of a research/clinical profile. He hears a voice that urges self-destruction which is suggestive of schizophrenia but this is not detailed at all in the development or resolution of the plot. Though partially drunk at the time (the public humiliation was at a party) there is no elaboration of substance abuse as a disorder. Shy, sensitive uncertainties about one's place in the world is common enough (though traumatic) but does not generally lead to attempted suicide.

The (re)construction and perpetuation of myths about suicide

Statements about the alleged myths of suicide abound, but are often simplistically understood and potentially misleading. For example, it is stated that 'talking about suicide will cause people to do it' is a myth. The contrary argument is that, by bringing the topic out into the open, there is a greater chance of identifying those at risk and giving appropriate intervention. However, there is equally the danger that constantly highlighting the issue normalises it such that suicide is seen as a normal event.

For example, although females attempt suicide nearly four times more than males, males succeed because of the 'lethality' of the methods chosen. To talk about this may not cause a suicide attempt, but may make it more lethal if females begin to change methods as a result of such talking. Equally, it is stated that suicide as a response is a long-term solution to a short-term problem and that intervention and alternative strategies will enable the suicide ideator/attemptor to work through these problems such that the person will be able to go on and live a normal life. There is evidence to support this. However, for the gay person exhibiting suicidal behaviours in a homophobic community, the person exhibiting suicidal behaviours may believe that suicide is a long-term solution to a long-term problem, and such feelings may be unfortunately true ('better dead than gay'). Fictions that are not grounded on the complexity of the issue or reinforce common myths are arguably ethically problematic.

The lack of verisimilitude in representations of suicide

Where the reader's credibility in the narrative is stretched, manipulated or undermined, there is a danger that the issue of suicide is made simplistic and trivialised. For example, the issue of assisted suicide is developed in Barbara Gilbert's *Stone Water* (1998) where Grant, the protagonist, is confronted by his grandfather's wish to die when terminally ill. Having suffered from a stroke and progressively deteriorated over time (not being able to perform basic body functions without assistance), his grandfather is able to both whisper 'Now' and hold the cup of poison, thus exonerating his grandson. This extremely unlikely turn of events shifts from Grant the enormity of the act of assisted suicide and its emotional/ethical/legal effects. It would seem that the author finally lost faith in the inevitability of the narrative and resorted to an unlikely *deus ex machina* to tie up the loose ends.

The sensationalisation of suicide as a plot device

There are some fictions that do not purport to be realistic but belong to a different genre; for example, detective thrillers or ghost stories. The use of a suicide event is less an attempt to understand suicide as a biopsychosocial phenomenon and more a catalyst to excite interest in the plot. Suicide in another genre other than realism (or future realism) can present the issue of trivialisation where little understanding of suicide results. For example, in Laura Solomon's (1997) *Nothing Lasting*, the protagonist is an arsonist who, in killing a farmhand in his first arson, attempts suicide by self-immolation. From there develops a bizarre tale of anger, cruelty and moral depravity as the narrator (egged on by the spirits of his dead parents) attempts to immolate his foes (middle-class yuppies) and thus allow his parents to enter the pearly gates. A surrealistic thriller, a roman noir, this novel gives little understanding of suicide, its causes and consequences.

Thus, the notion of the transformative possibilities of representation can be powerfully limited by textual features. What needs to be noted is, as Berman (1999) discovered, even *positive* mediations are not a necessary and sufficient condition to produce a positive effect in students; that in terms of current research of the impact of fictional representations, individual responses are unstable and unpredictable. Conditionality and tentativeness need to be hallmarks of the connection between representation and reader response.

Finally, it can be argued that intellectual freedom, even to espouse unpopular ideas, is the highest good and that therefore writers are free to represent 'at will' and publishers free to publish. This is *the* moral high ground that, for university lecturers, is a freedom that, in New Zealand, is enshrined in law (1989 *Education Act*, Part Four). This law is designed to ensure that the pursuit and dissemination of knowledge is independent of the governance of tertiary institutions (the development of which is the chief function of the Act). However, that freedom is not absolute: the law requires such freedoms to be exercised 'within the law' thus bringing other laws (from defamation to criminal negligence) as considerations in the exercise of intellectual freedom.

This notion of freedom is central to librarianship as a profession such that arguments for the exercise of discretion (not censorship) invoke accusations of professional ignorance and possibly malpractice.[10] However, balanced against intellectual freedom as an ethical proposition are other ethical 'absolutes' such as the medical/counselling ethic of 'do no harm'. Claims of intellectual freedom have little currency in the deliberations of research ethics committees where any form of intervention that affects human or animal subjects are scrutinised for potential harm to the individual. Claims of 'the greatest good for the greatest number' have little currency either, as research committees come under public and legal scrutiny by individuals who have been affected by decisions made. For writers (and others in the food chain) to claim intellectual freedom as an absolute is tenuous indeed.

Thus far, this chapter has identified some (by no means inclusive) arguments *for* the representation of youth suicide in fictional form and has indicated that those arguments are not simplistically clear-cut. There are some strong caveats. What are some of the arguments for the non-representation of youth suicide in fiction?

Arguments for the non-representation of suicide

Firstly, there is the argument that a representation may produce imitative behaviour on the part of the reader in what is known as the contagion or Werther effect. Is there any evidence for a media experience being in itself a cause or precipitating factor in a reader's suicide or suicide attempt?

At a level of anecdote, a father within the community in which this writer lives indicated that he viewed the suicide of his stepson was, in part, a consequence of the reading material the adolescent had become obsessed with and that 'you English teachers have to take some responsibility'. Apparently the stepson had left an open copy of Shakespeare's *Romeo and Juliet* on his bed. This link between life and art as it were was confirmed when this writer approached a professional working with suicidal adolescents in a hospital setting who stated that one of her current clients was profoundly troubled by the text by J.D. Salinger entitled *Catcher in the Rye*. What evidence is there in terms of research other than anecdote?

Velting and Gould (1997) have provided a recent review of the research. They noted in the period 1986–1997 a methodological shift from descriptive, ecological and inferential studies to laboratory-based, experimental designs and psychological autopsies. With specific reference to the potential contagion effect of fictional representations of suicide, they note contradictory findings where both affirmation and rejection of an imitation effect have been determined. Controversy seems to be the rule in that of the eight published studies; three provide evidence consistent with an imitative hypothesis, three find no such support and two studies report mixed findings.

The following are the pertinent issues that have emerged from this research:

- repeated doses (eg. a multi-program series on suicide or repetition of a suicide scene or motif) is more directly associated with a rise in suicide rates;
- imitation following a celebrity suicide has a positive effect on suicide rates;
- the closer the match (age, gender) between the 'dose' or the suicide and the reader, the greater the risk;
- contagion arising from non-fiction is more conclusive than fiction;
- the more publicity given to the story, the greater the increase in suicides thereafter;
- the increase is proportionally larger for teenagers, but is also evident in other demographic groups;
- males seem to be more susceptible to contagion than females; and
- research into fictional suicides as found in books has yet to be done. What is to be noted is that all of the studies refer to fictional stories as mediated by film and television. There seems to be little recognition within the research where an analysis of discoursal features of the fiction (as indicated by this chapter) needs to take place as a central factor in determining possible differing connections between the stimulus and the response.

The need for caution by practitioners was clear, in terms of crossing the boundaries of media, when Stack, Gundlach and Reeves (1994) examined the effect of Heavy Metal subculture (music, lyrics themes) on youth suicide and found a positive correlation. They noted that a content analysis of lyrics may be divided into two categories: firstly the theme of Dionysian excess where, for example, sexuality is marked as hot and sweaty, without commitment and a symbol of male power; and secondly, chaos of both an individual nature (the dark or sad side of relationships) and a societal nature (pollution, war, political corruption, disaster and injustice). Both themes were linked by pessimism with hopelessness as a character trait. They further noted that devotees of Heavy Metal were more inclined to engage in life-risking behaviours, with 50 per cent of lyrics about killing. Further, devotees were dominantly from working-class backgrounds.

Stack et al. (1994) hypothesised that metal subculture could foster suicidal tendencies. Given epidemiological studies that showed higher suicidal risk from the working class, they sought to determine if Heavy Metal had an impact beyond the problematic living conditions of the working class. Using subscription rates to a Heavy Metal magazine and factoring in other social chaos indicators (divorce rates and migration rates), they compared suicide rates and subscription rates across 50 States of the USA. A control group was a different age cohort. Though the study was limited by the lack of data such as drug use and individual psychopathology, the data being unavailable, they concluded that the findings showed that the greater the extent of Heavy Metal subculture, the greater the suicide rate. They contend that Heavy Metal is less a cause than a precipitating factor in susceptible youth (Stack, Gundlach and Reeves, 1994: 15–23).

Berman (1999) struggled with this question of the efficacy of literary representations of suicide when he delivered two university graduate courses on 'Literary Suicide'. Using action research methodology, this is the most substantial 'data' that investigates the effect of fictional representations on reader response to date. He posed the questions 'does a fictional character's suicide awaken the same emotions within us as a real character's suicide? What are the conditions in which a reader's identification with a suicidal character may lead to heightened vulnerability?' He implemented an institutionally approved program of literary study whereby reader-response journals became the main focus of intervention in the study of a range of adult texts that incorporated a suicide event, including those authored by writers who themselves committed suicide. The response of a majority of students found the process of reading and discussing honestly both the literature and their response to it cathartic of ambivalent feelings and experiences of suicide. But not possibly in the case of Mary. Berman's conclusions were equivocal:

> Did the course plant a 'seed' of suicide that had not existed before? Was her suicide attempt an imitation of Dorothy Parker's drug overdose? As we have seen, both real and fictional characters sometimes find themselves at risk as a result of reading accounts of suicide. Was Mary one of these people? Do certain students experience at the end of a semester feelings of disconnection or abandonment that some patients feel at the end of therapy? I cannot answer these troubling questions. Nor could I have predicted Ultra's or Mary's responses.
>
> (Berman, 1999: 260–1)

It must be noted that an elective course at university is a different proposition to the compulsory element of a high school. One writer who has come to recognise this is Fleur Beale who would not now write a story like *The Rockman* (1996), having experienced three youth suicides in the school in which she works. To quote from the article in which Fleur Beale is reviewed:

There is one issue that Fleur would walk away from now. When I interviewed Fleur, I asked her if there was any issue in the social realism genre that clearly was her forte, that she would not want to write about. After experiencing three youth suicides at the secondary school where she teaches, Fleur indicated that she was now much more uncertain about the representation of youth suicide in teenage fiction and what would make appropriate writing. In *The Rockman*, for example, Ambrose (a staunch socially isolated teenager who maintains rigid control over his life and feelings) attempts suicide when pressure of events overtake his ability to control. His experience of violent fathering and fear of vulnerability is the breeding ground for suicidal behaviour. Fleur is now less certain that she would want to include suicidal episodes in her novels. 'I don't think we really know how to handle it. Reading about suicide encourages kids to think of that theme. Having experienced suicides at our school, I have seen how tricky it is.'

(McKenzie, 1999b: 35–40)

It does need to be noted that the contagion effect is pertinent as a potential issue in a limited range of suicide events — approximately 5 per cent at most (Beautrais: personal communication). Clearly, with regard to the contagion effect in fictional representations, the jury is out. Given the complex range of variables that operate in the production, distribution and reception of books as well as the ethical impossibility of an experimental design, evidence through case studies and ecological studies is, by and large, likely to be indicative. The evidence suggests however, that caution is the better part of valour.

An argument for the non-representation of suicide is the issue of normalisation. This is the idea that overexposure to suicide as a phenomenon in the media gives the impression that phenomenon is a common event when, statistically speaking, it isn't. The consequence

Illustration 12.4 The cover from *The Hour of the Wolf*

of this impression may mean that an adolescent at risk of suicidal behaviours may see suicide as a common and therefore reasonable response to life's stressors. This sense of suicide as a common 'natural' response to life's stressors could be reinforced by a reading of Calvert's (1983) *The Hour of the Wolf*. The cover from *The Hour of the Wolf* appears in Illustration 12.4.

Jake, the protagonist, finds that the expectations of his father to follow on in his footsteps, the most successful defence attorney of the Mid West, too much to cope with. Coupled with low self-esteem where nothing he does seems to be competent, he attempts suicide by using his grandfather's pistol. Lucky to survive, he goes to Alaska to stay at the home of his father's old schoolmate, Doc, a veterinarian. There he is given the responsibility of looking after the husky dogs where, at the same time he is befriended by Danny, an indigenous Indian. Danny seems so very capable and is looking forward to running the longest dog sled race in the world, the Iditarod Trail, named after a significant moment in Alaskan history. However, the pressure on Danny to succeed in another culture is too much and he commits suicide. Jake contacts Danny's sister Kamina to borrow the team of dogs so that he can run in the race in memory of Danny as a rookie. Kamina seems a tough young woman sure of her future (getting in touch with the Old Ways) and embarks on the same adventure. A misadventure brings them close together and Jake discovers deep resources within his own character. The father loses an important case and begins to reassess his relationship with Jake.

Though Jake's rehabilitation from his suicide attempt is very much 'the story', the catalyst is the suicide of Danny Yumiat, an Athabascan Indian boy. The personality profile of Danny, up to the moment of his death, was that of a capable youngster, achieving well at school, popular with girls, sure of what he wanted in life, a well-rounded personality who in all respects had his life together (in contrast to Jake). He had an immediate goal of winning a major international dog sledding event, had planned carefully for it, and had every chance of success. He had a longer-term goal: to be a lawyer for his people. In following in Danny's footsteps, Jake atones for both his attempt and Danny's death. What process is elaborated on in terms of Danny's death? The sister Kamina intimates that there were two Dannys: one that was an outgoing character ready to achieve; the other that few knew who 'didn't know that he could hack it'. Period.

There is little attempt in the narrative to develop a risk profile of a suicide event in terms of epidemiological studies: depression, co-morbidity, personality traits, hopelessness, external locus of control. Danny is simply a type, a foil for Jake's development: an indigenous person out of his depth. There is little hope for Athabascan Indians reading Danny's story. The lack of depth leading up to Danny's suicide reinforces some of the myths associated with youth suicide: that suicide is unexpected and that there are no warning signs. Ironically, the more that is known about suicide by youngsters at risk of suicidal behaviour, the more possibilities there are that warning behaviours will be subverted and hidden deliberately to avoid rescue. This is the end product of normalisation: representations that propose that suicide is a simple response to life's stressors.

The contrary argument to the idea of normalisation is that ignorance is not bliss, that knowledge empowers. It was precisely this idea that motivated Berman (1999) to develop his course on Literary Suicide. Course evaluations suggested that for most people on the course, literary representations were illuminating of real-life dilemmas. To quote one student of Berman's who was relating fictional texts with life experience where silence (the opposite of normalisation) meant that 'rescue' of youth at risk was not possible:

> But of course I feel guilty. Was I just the straw that broke the camel's back? Should I have said I would do it just to help him out of his depression? Should I have known that he was suicidal? When I had been told of his severe depression no-one mentioned the S word. Damn! How can we eliminate the fear of this word?
>
> When I once worked as a volunteer on help line, we all had to be trained to be able to say the word suicide to our depressed clients. This was a country wide line that dealt with many problems aside from suicidal clients, but the big phone calls, the scary ones, were from suicidal people. I did learn to say 'Have you been thinking about suicide?' I probably surprised the client as I surprised myself by saying the word. As a society we have to learn that words don't kill people.
>
> (Berman, 1999: 34)

As has been noted, in terms of current research unpredictability of response is the key issue : what might be illuminating to one reader encouraging distance and resistance, may to another be self-reinforcing.

An argument for the non-representation of suicide is that representations of suicide as a strategy for suicide prevention is too negative: suicide prevention is now loss-focused on whole class population-based programs specific to suicide prevention and is now more focused, in school contexts, on reducing risk factors and building resiliency without the label 'suicide prevention'. School programs (including literature-based units) that focus specifically on suicide prevention risk the normalisation and contagion effect and have been shown to be ineffective and indeed, counterproductive (Hider, 1998: 59). National prevention strategies both in Australia and New Zealand intend to accentuate the positive in terms of 'promoting wellbeing' through the strengthening of families:

> This goal is based on reducing the likelihood that young people will develop suicidal behaviour, by changing the ways we relate to and treat young people within families and communities. Young people at increased risk of suicidal behaviour are likely to have experienced social disadvantage, negative childhood experiences and family hardship. Through strengthening families and communities to support the positive development of young people, many of those risk factors can be overcome.
>
> (Ministry of Youth Affairs, nd: 14)

That is, the target of 'suicide prevention' is on improving mental health services for the youngster at risk, rather then education programs. Therefore, exposure to a substantial resource of literary representations where hopelessness, nihilism and negativity may be perceived could be counterproductive to the national goals of suicide prevention for some readers.

Thus, there are compelling arguments for the non-representation of suicide in adolescent literature, especially in unmediated settings. Simply put, we do not know in any substantive way what the impact of a story may be for readers, especially for those at risk of suicidal behaviour. There are no current assessment instruments for suicidal risk that are efficacious (minimising false positives), nor given the complexity of the phenomenon, are there likely to be in the near future.

Implications for practitioners

The representation of suicide in adolescent literature is therefore a site of contradictory intentions, claims and possible consequences. What then is the writer, the publisher, the reviewer, the librarian, the teacher, the parent to do? What about the classics of the literature classroom? What principles should inform practitioner's use of these fictions?

This question was posed by Cline (1989: 21–3) when a parent asked him:

> Are you trying to kill my daughter? To depress her? Can't you give her something less deadly to read?

Challenged, this teacher examined what was being taught by the particular school system and had to acknowledge that, in some ways, the mother was right. Whilst most youngsters in the class were able to cope by distancing themselves and rationalising what was happening in the fictions, Cline was disturbed by one girl's response:

> I do not enjoy violent novels because, though I realise they are fiction, the characters and the plots remind me of all the violence that does exist in the world … I forget that the characters and plots are fictional, and I often cry. It depresses me to know that sometimes life is so bad that a person feels there is no outlet but death.

However, Cline recognised that censorship was out of the question: these texts were part of our great literary tradition and were not only required as preparation for further education, but were of value in and of themselves. He recognised the need to:

> counterbalance (the gloom and despair) with at least some happiness and hope. We must be certain not only to differentiate between the fictional world of the work and the real world but also ensure that the students can differentiate. And most important, we must make certain that nothing we teach legitimises or condones the taking of anyone's life. We can't forget the 2 of 100 comments. Your call, then, has changed my teaching!

Here lies the central dilemma for the English teacher and the librarian as a supplier of resources and an intermediary between the inquiring youngster and those resources. On the one hand, there is the call of the classics. On the other hand, there are the very clear guidelines of the Ministry of Education (New Zealand) which state, on the basis of research (and some of the arguments outlined herein):

> It is recommended that school-based programmes aimed at increasing the awareness of young people about youth suicide are NOT undertaken.
>
> (Beautrais et al., 1997: 13)

The following principles/practices may begin to point the way forward.

- Teachers and librarians should know their books and be thoroughly familiar with the detail of books that contain suicide. Reviewers should identify plots that contain suicide as an aspect of the review to signal to teachers and librarians the need for appropriate scrutiny. Selection criteria should include issues of authenticity and discourse features that may be problematic.

- Individual novels that offer little hope (or what hopefulness in the novel is obscure and not readily perceived by a reader at risk of suicidal behaviour) should go through an established book selection process where a written caveat placed inside the book may be appropriate. Even if the publishers have not included helping agencies, such information could be identified in the book cover.
- No publicity should be given to books with suicidal themes/episodes in order to attract readers, either in the form of book displays or book talks. The issue of normalising/romanticising suicide is pertinent here.
- There is no room for a unit on youth suicide as a thematic study. The problem of repeated doses in terms of contagion research would indicate that a deleterious effect is likely for suicidal class members.
- The cataloguing of fiction as youth suicide with cross referencing and multiple accessing should be seriously reconsidered in a school-based library.
- Where a student fixates on books on suicide (indicated by multiple issues), a school counsellor should be notified. The issue of confidentiality is less important than a student's mental health/physical survival.
- The use of classics should not be used as a means of highlighting youth suicide. The English teacher should demonstrate how the writer critiques suicide as a heroic choice (or if necessary challenge the writer). The experience of such literature should be counterbalanced with life-affirming literature. Such literature would reveal that there is finally hope and acceptance through a grieving process as we all experience the stressors of grief and loss in life.
- Teachers and librarians ought to be well versed in the best of these fictions (as case studies) as a means for them to gain understanding and empathy for the adolescent in distress. The best of these fictions could well form the basis for effective staff development (mindful of the fact that suicide is not just a phenomenon of youth) in order to remedy the known deficits in understanding of teachers (and clergy!) about youth suicide, even among those who had taken courses or had experience of a close friend or relative who had suicided (Leane and Shute, 1998:165–73).
- Finally, it may be the librarian, who in accessing information about youth suicide and motivating the staff to be prepared, is the one who has thought through the issues in terms of a crisis management policy (McArthur, 1997: 45–6).

Bibliography

Abrahamson, R. (1978) 'The Ultimate Developmental Task in Adolescent Literature', unpublished paper. ED 161 075.

Apseloff, M. (1974) 'Death in Current Children's Fictions: sociology or literature?', paper presented at the Forum on the Criticism of Children's Literature of the Midwest MLA, Ed 101 371.

—— (1991–1992) 'Death in Adolescent Literature: suicide', *Children's Literature Association Quarterly* vol 16, no 4, pp. 234–8.

Arrick, F. (1980) *Tunnel Vision*. Bradbury Press, Scarsdale, New York.

Bailis, L. (1997-8) 'Death in Children's Literature: a conceptual analysis', *Omega* vol 8, no 4, pp. 295–302.

Baume, P. (1996) 'Suicide in Australia: do we really have a problem?', *The Australian Educational and Developmental Psychologist* vol 13, no 2, pp. 3–39.

Beale, F. (1996) *The Rockman*. Harper Collins Publishers, New York.

Beautrais, A. (1995) 'Youth Suicide', *NZ Annual Review of Education* 5, pp. 3–21.

—— (1997) 'Suicidal Behaviour in Young New Zealanders', *Social Work Now* no 8, December, pp. 18–25.

—— (1998) 'Risk Factors for Serious Suicide Attempts among Young People: a case control study', in Kosky et al. *Suicide Prevention*. Plenum Press, New York.

Beautrais, A., Coggan, C., Ferguson, D. and Rivers, L. (1997) *The Prevention, Recognition and Management of Young People at Risk of Suicide: development of guidelines for schools*. Ministry of Education, Wellington, p. 13.

Beautrais, A., Joyce, P. and Mulder, R. (1998) 'Psychiatric Illness in a New Zealand Sample of Young People Making Serious Suicide Attempts', *NZ Medical Journal*, 27 February, pp. 44–8.

Berman, J. (1999) *Surviving Literary Suicide*. University of Massachusetts Press, Amherst, pp. 260–1.

Bernstein, J. (1979) 'Literature for Young People: non-fiction books about death', *Death Education*, vol 3, pp. 111–19.

Brandt, R. (1990) 'The Morality and Rationality of Suicide', from Donnelly, J. (ed.) *Suicide: Right or Wrong? Contemporary Issues in Philosophy*. Prometheus Books, New York, p. 193.

Calvert, P. (c1983) *The Hour of the Wolf*. Scribner's, New York.

Carr, R. (1973) 'Death as presented in Children's Books', *Elementary English* vol 50, no. 5, pp. 701–5.

Cline, R. (1989) 'A Killer Curriculum: Violence and Death in Literature', *Pointer* vol 32, no 4, pp. 21–3.

Cohen, R. (1992) 'Descriptions of Psychiatric Conditions in Literature', *British Journal of Psychiatry* vol 161, pp. 280–1.

Crain, H. (1972) 'Basic Concepts of Death in Children's Literature', *Elementary English* vol 49, no 1, pp. 111–15.

Danielson, K. (1995) 'Death: Realism in Children's Books', paper presented at the Annual Meeting of the Plains Regional Conference of the International Reading Association, ED 270 785.

Davis, G. (1986) 'A Content Analysis of Fifty-seven Children's Books with Death Themes', *Child Study Journal* vol 16, no 1, pp. 39–54.

Deats, S. and Lenker, L. (1989) *Youth Suicide Prevention: lessons from literature*. Insight Books, Plenum Press, New York.

Dehart, F. and Bleeker, G. (1988) 'Young Adult Realistic Novels: model for information transfer?', *Journal of Youth Services in Libraries*. Fall, pp. 64–71.

Delisle, R. and Woods McNamee, A. (1981) 'Children's Perceptions of Death: a look at selected picture books', *Death Education* vol 5, pp. 1–13.

Diekstra, R. (1989) 'Suicidal Behaviour in Adolescents and Young Adults: the international picture', *Crisis* vol 10, no 1, pp. 16–35.

—— (1995) 'The Epidemiology of Suicide and Parasuicide', from Diekstra, R., Gulbinat, W., Kienhorst, I. and de Leo, D. *Preventative Strategies in Suicide*. E.J. Brill, New York.

Drummond, W. (1997) 'Adolescents at Risk: causes of youth suicide in New Zealand', *Adolescence* vol 32, no 128, Winter.

Dukes, R. and Lorch, B. (1989) 'The Effects of School, Family, Self-Concept, and Deviant Behaviour on Adolescent Suicide Ideation', *Journal of Adolescence* vol 12, pp. 239–52.

Eagleton, T. (1996) *Literary Theory: an introduction* (2nd edn). Blackwell Publishers, Oxford, p. 147.

Ellis, J. and Lane, D. (1993) 'Attitudes towards Child Suicide', paper presented to South Eastern Psychological Association, ED 359 476.

Ellis, T. and Newman, C. (1996) *Choosing to Live: how to defeat suicide through cognitive therapy*. New Harbinger Pubs, Oakland, CA.

Ferguson, D., Horwood, J. and Beautrais, A. (1999) 'Is Sexual Orientation Related to Mental Health Problems and Suicidality in Young People?', *Arch Gen Psychiatry* vol 56, pp. 876–88.

Fleischnizan, P. (1999) *Whirligig*. Laurel-Leaf, New York.

Gilbert, B. (1998) *Stone Water*. Laurel-Leaf, New York.

Gladding, S. (1994) 'Teaching Family Counselling through the Use of Fiction', *Counsellor Education and Supervision* vol 33, no 3, pp. 191–201.

Greene, D. (1994) 'Childhood Suicide and Myths Surroundings It', *Social Work* vol 39, issue 2, pp. 230–4.

Grolman, E. (1988) *Suicide: Prevention, Intervention, Postvention*. Beacon Press, Boston.

Harvey, C. and Dowd, F. (1993) 'Death and Dying in Young Adult Fiction', *Journal of Youth Services in Libraries*. Winter, pp. 141–54.

Hassan, R. (1995) *Suicide Explained: the Australian Experience*. Melbourne University Press, Carlton South, Vic.

Hawton, K. and van Heeringen, K. (2000) *The International Handbook on Suicide*. John Wiley & Sons, Chichester, UK.

Hazell, P. (1991) 'Postvention after Teenage Suicide: an Australian experience', *Journal of Adolescence* vol 14, pp. 335–42.

Heckler, R. (1994) *Waking Up, Alive: the descent, the suicide attempt and the return to life*. Ballantyne Books, New York.

Hendin, H. (1995) *Suicide in America* (revised). W.W. Norton & Co, New York.

Herrell, R., Goldberg, J., Truw, W., Ramakrishnan, V., Lyons, M., Eisen, S. and Tsuang, M. (1990) 'Sexual Orientation and Suicidality', *Arch. Gen. Psychiatry* vol 56, October, pp. 867–74.

Hider, P. (1998) *Youth Suicide Prevention by Primary Healthcare Professionals: a critical appraisal of the literature*. New Zealand Health Technology Assessment Clearing House, Christchurch.

Hill, K. (1995) *The Long Sleep: Young People and Suicide*. Little Brown & Co, UK.

Hollander, J. (1996) 'The Shadow of a Lie: poetry, lying and the truth of fictions', *Social Research* vol 63 no 3, pp. 643–62.

Kamler, B. and Comber, B. (1996) 'Critical Literacy: not generic — not developmental — not another orthodoxy', *Changing Education: A Journal for Teachers and Administrators* vol 3 no 1, March pp. 1–5, 9.

Kaywell, J. (1994) 'Using Young Adult Problem Fiction and Non-Fiction to Produce Critical Readers', *Alan Review* vol 2 no 2, pp. 29–32.

Keinhorst, C. Wolters, W. Diekstra, R. and Otte, E. (1987) 'A Study of the Frequency of Suicidal Behaviour in Children aged 5 to 14', *Journal of Child Psychology and Psychiatry* vol 28 no 1, pp. 153–65.

Kimmel, E. (1980) 'Beyond Death: children's books and the hereafter', *The Horn Book*, June, pp. 265–73.

Kortner, A. (1993) 'Bibliotherapy', *ERIC Digest, Report No EDO-CS-93-05*.

Leane, W. and Shute, R. (1998) 'Youth Suicide: the knowledge and attitudes of Australian teachers and clergy', *Suicide and Life-Threatening Behaviour* vol 28 no 2 pp. 165–73.

Legge, K. (1997) 'Life Sucks, Timmy', *The Australian Magazine*, 8–9 March, pp. 10–18.

Lester D. (1990) 'Depression and Suicide in College Students and Adolescents', *Personal Individual Differences* vol 11 no 7, pp. 757–8.

Lester, D. and Miller, C. (1990) 'Depression and Suicidal Preoccupation in Teenagers', *Personal Individual Differences* vol 11 no 4, pp. 421–2.

Lowry, L. (1995) *Dear Author: students write about books that changed their lives*. Conari Press, Berkeley, California.

Maltsberger, J. and Goldblatt, M. (1996) *Essential Papers on Suicide*. New York University Press, New York.

Marshall, R. (1975) 'The Concept of Death in Children's Literature', paper presented at the Annual Meeting of the Illinois Association of School Librarians, ED 111 431.

Marsich, A. and McKenzie, J. (2000) 'Talking about William Taylor's *Jerome*', *Talespinner*, May, pp. 44–7.

Marttunen, M., Henriksson, M., Isometsa, E., Heikkinen, M., Aro, H. and Lonnqvist, J. (1998) 'Completed Suicide among Adolescents with no Diagnosable Psychiatric Disorder', *Adolescence* vol 33 no 131, pp. 669–82.

McArthur, J. (1997) 'When an 11-year-old wants to take his own life', *American Libraries* vol 28, no 11, December, pp. 45–6.

McCuaig, S. (1990) *Blindfold*. Holiday House, New York.

McKenzie, J. (1997) 'To Be or Not to Be? Don't be a Wuss: Life Sucks! Moral responsibility and suicide in children's literature', *Access* vol 11, no 3, August, pp. 10–13.

—— (1998) 'Letter to the Editor', *Orana* vol 34, no 3, pp. 3–6.

—— (1999a) 'Youth Suicide: should writers and publishers develop a code of ethics?', *Talespinner*, May, pp. 34–8.

—— (1999b) 'Fleur Beale: Writing for Teenagers Today', *Talespinner* no 8, September, pp. 35–40.

—— (1999c) *Guidelines for Primary Care Providers: detection and management of young people at risk of suicide*. Wellington: The Royal New Zealand College of Practitioners.

—— (2000) *The Representation of Youth Suicide in Adolescent Literature Published from 1990 to 2000* (Ph D research in progress). Wellington: Victoria University

Ministry of Youth Affairs (nd) *In Our Hands: New Zealand Youth Suicide Prevention Strategy*. Ministry of Health, Wellington, Te Puni Kokiri, p. 14.

Molnar, N., Shade, S., Kral, A., Booth, R. and Watters, J. (1998) 'Suicidal Behaviour and Sexual/Physical Abuse among Street Youth', *Child Abuse and Neglect* vol 22 no 3, pp. 213–22.

Moore, T. and Mae, R. (1987) 'Who Dies and Who Cries: death and bereavement in children's literature', *Journal of Communication* vol 37, no 4, pp. 52–64.

Moss, J. (1972) 'Death in Children's Literature', *Elementary English* vol 49, no 4, pp. 550–32.

Muehrer, P. (1995) 'Suicide and Sexual Orientation: a critical summary of recent research and directions for future research', *Suicide and Life-Threatening Behaviour* vol 25, Supplement, pp. 72–81.

Nimon, M. (1998) 'Finding the Acceptable Boundaries: the challenge of young adult literature', *Orana* vol 34, no 2, pp. 18–24.

O'Neale, Z. (1987) 'Books to Help Kids Deal with Difficult Times', *School Library Media Quarterly*, Spring, pp. 165–7.

Philips, D. and Carstentensen, L. (1986) 'Clustering of Teenage Suicides after Television News Stories about Suicide', *The New England Journal of Medicine* vol 315, no 11, pp. 685–9.

Platt, S. (1993) 'The Social Transmission of Parasuicide: is there a modelling effect?', *Crisis* vol 14 (1) pp. 23–31.

Plotz, J. (1988) 'The Disappearance of Childhood: parent-child role reversals in *After the First Death* and *A Solitary Blue*', *Children's Literature in Education* vol 19, no 2, pp. 67–79.

Pritchard, C. (1995) *Suicide: The Ultimate Rejection?* Open University Press, Buckingham, Philadelphia.

Queralt, M. (1993) 'Risk Factors Associated with Completed Suicide in Latino Adolescents', *Adolescence* vol 28, no 112, pp. 831–51.

Radley, G. (1999) 'Coping with Death in Young Adult Literature', *The ALAN Review* vol 27, no 1, pp. 14–16.

Romero, C. (1974) 'The Treatment of Death in Contemporary Children's Literature', unpublished Master's theses, ED 101 654.

Rosenblatt, L. (1978) *The Reader, the Text, the Poem: the transactional theory of a literary work*. Southern Illinois University Press, Carbondale.

Rosenthal, L. (1988) 'To Be or Not to Be: suicide in literature for young people', *The Lion and the Unicorn* vol 12, no 1, pp. 19–27.

Runeson, B. (1989) 'Mental Disorder in Youth Suicide: DSM axes I and II', *Acta Psychiatry Scandanavia* vol 79, pp. 490–7.

Seidler, T. (1982) *Terpin*. Andre Deutsch Ltd, London, p. 23.

Shaffer, D., Garland, A., Gould, M., Fisher, M. and Trautman, P. (1988) 'Preventing Teenage Suicide: a critical review', *Journal of the American Academy of Child & Adolescent Psychiatry* vol 27 no 6, pp. 675–87.

Shafi, M., Steltze-Lenarsky, J., Derrick, A., Beckner, C. and Whittinghill, J. (1988) 'Co-morbidity of Mental Disorders in the Post-mortem Diagnosis of Completed Suicide in Children and Adolescents', *Journal of Affective Disorders* vol 15, pp. 227–33.

Shiltz, P. (1985) 'Suicide in Books for Children Age 11-14', unpublished Doctoral Dissertation, University of Akron, Ohio.

Simonds, J., McMahon, T. and Armstrong, D. (1991) 'Young Suicide Attemptors Compared with a Control Group: psychological, affective and attitudinal variables', *Suicide and Life-Threatening Behaviour* vol 21, no 2, pp. 134–51.

Smith, K. (1990) 'Suicidal Behaviour in School-aged Youth', *School Psychology Review* vol 19 no 2, pp. 186–96.

Solomon, L. (1997) *Nothing Lasting*. Tandem Press, North Shore City, NZ.

Stack, S., Gundlach, J. and Reeves, J. (1994) 'The Heavy Metal Subculture and Suicide', *Suicide and Life-Threatening Behaviour* vol 12, no 1, pp. 15–23.

Stefanowski-Harding, S. (1990) 'Child Suicide: a review of the literature and implications for school counsellors', *School Counsellor* vol 37 no 5, pp. 328–36.

Stephens, J. (1992) *Language and Ideology in Children's Fiction*. Longman, New York, p. 170.

Stewart, M. (1997) *Shoovy Jed*. Random House Australia, Milsons Point.

Sullivan, A. (1993) 'Death in Literature for Children and Young Adults', *Focused Access to Selected Topics*. ED 356 485.

Tillman, C. (1984) 'Bibliotherapy for Adolescents: an annotated research review', *Journal of Reading*, May, pp. 713–19.

Velting, D. and Gould, M. (1997) 'Suicide Contagion', from Maris, R. and Canett, S. (eds) (in press) *Annual Review of Suicidology*, Guilford, New York.

Walker, M. (1978) 'Last Rites for Young Readers', *Children's Literature in Education*, vol 9, no 4, pp. 188–97.

Warner, L. (1980) 'The Myth of Bibliotherapy', *School Library Journal*, October, pp. 107–111.

Westefled, J., Range, L., Rogers, J., Maples, M., Bromley, J. and Alcorn, J. (2000) 'Suicide: an Overview', *Counselling Psychologist* vol 28, Issue 4, pp. 445–511.

Endnotes

1   McKenzie, J. (2000). *The Representation of Youth Suicide in Adolescent Literature Published from 1990 to 2000* (PhD research in progress). Victoria University, Wellington. For a bibliography of over 200 titles where suicide as a behaviour is represented in adolescent fiction, readers are invited to contact the author at john.mckenzie@cce.ac.nz. It is to be noted that the total number may be an artefact of bibliographic technology over time, but the trend as indicated is significant.

2   For an overview on the morality of suicide see Battin, M. & Maris, R. (1983) 'Suicide and Ethics' *Suicide and Life-Threatening Behaviour*, vol. 13 (4), Winter, a special issue. A timely reminder for clinicians that the issue of rationality is more complex than pure philosophy is in Pritchard, C. (1995) *Suicide: The Ultimate Rejection?* Open University Press, Buckingham, Philadelphia: where intervention by attemptors have been initially resisted by the patient, but remission for illness made the rationality of the earlier attempt of suicide doubtful. Battin, M. (1982) *Ethical Issues in Suicide*. Prentice-Hall, Englewood Cliffs, New Jersey explores the dominant paradigms that inform ethical discussions.

3   Cullberg, et al. (1988) in a ten year follow up of adolescent and young adults who had attempted suicide found that 6 per cent eventually died by suicide whilst 94 per cent did not. Cullberg, J., Wasserman, D. and Stefansson, C. (1988). *Acta Psychiatrica Scandanavia*. Vol. 77, pp. 598–603. Quoted in Pritchard, C. (1995). *Suicide: The Ultimate Rejection?* Buckingham, Philadelphia, Open University Press, p. 77.

4   For example, note the following excerpt from an interview with Sonya Hartnett with regard to her novel *Sleeping Dogs*, a Children's Book Council short-listed title. The book thoroughly deserves high praise for its skilful use of language to create character and setting. However, in response to concerns about its classification as a 'young adult' book (let alone winning a children's book award), Hartnett replied, 'What gives them authority to tell me what I can't write for young adults and why is their opinion any more right than mine which says I can? I refuse to let anything stand in my way when it comes to what I want to write about. I would have no hesitation about writing anything that I wanted to write because I thought it was for young adults.' Quoted in Hillel, M. (1996) 'Sonya Hartnett', *Reading Time* vol 40. no 2. p. 3.

5   See also Dehart and Bleeker (1988) for an example of realistic novels being used specifically to teach information skills.

6   Determinancy here meaning based on empiricist/rationalist approaches. This chapter does no assert an absolutist truth value placed at either end of the determinancy/determinancy continuum. It simply problematises non-scientific understandings of biopyschosocial phenomenon. That is, more problematic is not, of necessity, less true. This is demonstrable in terms of the more subjective 'truth' of case study methodology where generalisability is limited. For a fuller discussion on research methodologies and issues of reliability and validity with regard to youth suicide, see Hider (1998) pp. 101–103.

7   A more polemic article (rather then a scientific review) can be found in Warner (1980) 'The Myth of Bibliotherapy', pp. 107–111.

8   See Egoff, S., Stubbs, G. & Ashley, A. (1969). *Only Connect: readings on children's literature*. Toronto, p. 437.

9   Acknowledgments to Darnell, D., editor of *Talespinner*, who allowed much of the article the researcher wrote for Issue No. 7 (May 1999, pp. 33–8) to be included here.

10 See Nimon (1998) 'Finding the Acceptable Boundaries: the challenge of young adult literature' (*Orana*, pp. 18–24) followed by the rejoinder: McKenzie (1998) 'Letter to the Editor' (*Orana*, pp. 3–6).

Not telling it straight

Ray Misson

It's hard to talk about love in a classroom. It's beyond the limits of what can be treated seriously. Students, however young, are conditioned to find it embarrassing, and teachers are inclined to consider love, serious love, outside the emotional range of the child and adolescent.

It's hard to talk about desire in a classroom. Any acknowledgment of the disruptive power of libidinal drives undercuts the primacy of rational control that so much of education is designed to inculcate. One is forced either to moralism or to a coy defensiveness.

It's hard to talk about sex in a classroom. Suspended between the clinical aridity of anatomical talk in biology and the pious irrelevance of 'relationship' talk in much of the humanities, the physical actuality of bodies pleasurably together is occluded.

Think then, how hard it is to talk about homosexuality, about gay and lesbian people, who are defined by, whose very identity is constituted by, whom they desire, whom they have sex with, by whom they love.

Of course, if it is true that homosexual people are defined by their sexual object choice, it is no less true of heterosexuals: they too gain a significant aspect of their identity from their sexual identification. But heterosexuals can (and overwhelmingly do) treat their orientation as natural, and it becomes so invisible that they seem to themselves to have no 'orientation' at all. They just are 'natural', 'normal' 'human' beings. Lesbian and gay theory is concerned to undercut that feeling of naturalness, or at least of exclusive naturalness. If heterosexuality is natural, then homosexuality is no less natural, if somewhat less common and mundane.[1]

If we are concerned with 'crossing the boundaries', bringing sexuality into the classroom is a considerable boundary to cross . Few of the other boundaries transgressed in this book are so fraught with danger, but none is so important to breach. We are only just beginning to recognise the terrible damage and the appalling waste of lives and potential that heterosexism and homophobia are causing. The image of Matthew Shepard — a battered scarecrow, left for dead, tied to a rough wooden fence in Wyoming — captured the media's imagination and undoubtedly galvanised action in some quarters against gay-bashing. But it is even more potent as a terrible, accurate metaphor for the daily psychic damage caused by heterosexist bullying, by the power of mainstream society to make people feel dislocated from their basic affects. Schools have a responsibility to educate the community away from inflicting such damage.

If one wants to address homosexuality in text-based work in the literacy or English classroom — and one should, because there are too many homosexual people in the world for anyone reasonably to ignore it — then there are two kinds of text that particularly need to be addressed. The first kind are the texts that are everyday creating the students' familiarity with things gay and lesbian. Virtually all students know about homosexuality and have been subject to various views of it. The obvious place to begin on work in schools is with this current knowledge, and this is most easily achieved by looking at the representation of lesbian and gay people in the popular media. These representations are by no means all bad, so it is not a matter of generating horror at the appalling quality of the media or of hounding out stereotypes. It is rather a matter of raising consciousness that the images given *are* representations and that they are drawing on particular social understandings, popular 'myths' about lesbian and gay people, and that they are doing it with particular ideological effects.

The second aspect of work in the classroom (and this is the easier one) is to introduce texts that help deepen understanding of what it is to be lesbian or gay. This will give lesbian/gay students access to texts in which they can recognise themselves positively, and give straight students access to texts that might hopefully make them less inclined to treat homosexual people (or those they wish to think are homosexual) badly.

However, as important as it is, I do not want to argue that the only (or even the main) reason for acknowledging homosexuality in the classroom is an anti-discriminatory one, to try to change prejudicial attitudes towards gay and lesbian people. In a very real way, this simply perpetuates the notion that homosexuals are somehow weak and dependent on mainstream pity for a place in the sun. There are other lessons to be learnt from dealing with representations of homosexuality, lessons about the way our subjectivity is constructed, the way society operates on individuals, and the ways in which narratives work to produce a particular ideological standpoint. In highlighting minority sexuality and the ways in which — and purposes for which — texts represent it, we are teaching students more generally about the relationship between themselves, their ways of thinking and being, the society they live in, and the texts they read.

I want to look at both kinds of textual work outlined above: first of all, representations of homosexuality in readily available popular texts, and then representations in books specifically written for children and young adults that might deepen understanding. However, before starting to look at particular texts, it will be useful to make a brief foray into lesbian and gay theory, and establish one or two of the basic insights given there. We need to begin with Michel Foucault.

Lesbian and gay theory

The work of Michel Foucault is central to lesbian and gay studies: a great deal of the writing takes him as a starting point, particularly his *History of Sexuality*, of which he had completed three volumes before his death in 1984. If one were to isolate a particular founding moment for gay and lesbian studies as a major intellectual field, it would be Foucault's writing of the following passage in the first volume of *The History of Sexuality* (entitled *La Volonté de Savoir* [*The Will to Knowledge*] in its original French publication). He is talking about the move to enshrine heterosexuality as the one true way during the nineteenth century:

> This new persecution of the peripheral sexualities entailed an *incorporation of perversions* and a new *specification of individuals*. As defined by the ancient civil or canonical codes, sodomy was a category of forbidden acts; their perpetrator was nothing more than the juridical subject of them. The nineteenth-century homosexual became a personage, a past, a case history, and a childhood, in addition to being a type of life, a life form, and a morphology, with an indiscreet anatomy and possibly a mysterious physiology. Nothing that went into his total composition was unaffected by his sexuality. It was everywhere present in him … It was consubstantial with him, less as a habitual sin than as a singular nature … The sodomite had been a temporary aberration; the homosexual was now a species.

Foucault points out that the word 'homosexual' was only first used in the latter part of the nineteenth century, and its coining he sees as a sign of the shift from thinking in terms of someone who performs certain kinds of sexual act to thinking in terms of a particular kind of person. Building on this insight, gay and lesbian studies have centrally investigated how homosexuality is constructed socially and what purposes this construction serves within the power matrices of society.

Foucault is not denying that there were people who engaged in same-sex acts before the nineteenth century, nor even that there were people who *preferred* same-sex acts to different-sex ones — one remembers Marlowe's perhaps/probably apocryphal remark, 'He who likes not tobacco and boys is a fool!' — but what he is concerned to point out is that these acts meant different things in other times and people who performed these acts were perceived differently, and perceived themselves differently. They did not see their sexual activity as defining their identity, as being the most important thing about them.

Sexuality was not felt as central, or central in the same way as today, permeating the whole of the being. To use a very crude example, in some earlier times (the Middle Ages, for example) one might have seen one's identity as being defined by a Christian binary: one was either a good person or a sinner, one was either damned or saved. Sexuality might be related to this (all but the most polite sex tends to go with damnation), but one didn't see oneself as defined by the sex itself. A person might have various sexual inclinations and perform various sexual acts, but in constituting the self, these were only significant as far as they placed one on either side of the great binary: good/evil. These days, we might see the people who perform sex as good or bad, but we don't define them, or they don't define themselves, according to their goodness or badness. There are just good or bad acts. On the other hand, we do define and categorise people according to the homosexual/heterosexual binary, by whether they are attracted to having sex with others of the same sex or not. We would never these days think of saying about one of our acquaintances, 'She's a sinner', whereas we think it perfectly reasonable to say 'She's a lesbian'. And what's more, we say it as if it explains something. Indeed, we often say it as if it explains *every*thing.

One must be careful on this point about the social construction of a homosexual identity, since it could seem to play into the hands of those who wish to 'cure' homosexuality.

If the homosexual identity as we know it is a relatively recent construct, then homosexual people might be reconstructed into another identity. This is, of course, dangerous and naive nonsense. Sexuality is a fundamental part of life: how we experience ourselves as sexual beings may be socially governed, but it is not something susceptible much at all to *conscious* external management. There is no doubt that for most people in Western society these days, they feel profoundly that their sexuality is an ineradicable part of their identity, and they are right. They have constituted themselves by performing their sexuality in certain ways that make it central.

Another facet of Foucault's legacy is an awareness that such profound changes in the systems through which we come to know ourselves as particular kinds of people are bound up with the ways in which power circulates within society: they are the iceberg tip of profound shifts in how the social system operates. Power is bound up with knowledge, and the power/knowledge nexus operates through discourses. Foucault has made us profoundly aware that we live out our lives and understand ourselves through the images and narratives made available socially, and that we use these to construct a self. Our knowledge of ourselves and the world is governed by the ranges of language — discourses — that are available to us for representing ourselves and the world. If sex has become centrally important as a defining characteristic of people, it is because discourses through which we can actually think and talk about sex have become available. Whether these discourses talk about sex negatively and are geared to controlling it (as in the Victorian era), or whether they talk about it positively and aim to promote it (as, say, in the hippy discourse of the sixties/seventies) is less relevant than the fact that there is a discourse that makes it visible and important. If we constantly talk about sex with the aim of proscribing and limiting it, we are as surely affirming its existence and significance as if we are talking about it to promote free love.

Homosexuality has never been more talked about than it is at present: this article would probably not have been published in a book like this ten years ago. Much of the talk is outsider talk: homosexuality as insult to police perceived deviance ('God, you're gay!'), homosexuality presented as a threat to life-as-we-know-it in order to shore up the status quo (family values), homosexuality as social problem (discrimination, gay-bashing), homosexuality as pathology (AIDS), homosexuality as gossip ('Is Celebrity X gay?'). However, even for lesbian and gay people, the closet door is opening, and it is no longer quite so much 'the love that dare not speak its name'. Homosexual people are gaining visibility and a voice.

But, of course, it is the visibility and voice of the minority outsider, defined in opposition to mainstream heterosexuality. If heterosexuality is perceived as normal and natural, homosexuality will always be marked. It will always carry along with it a burden of particular oppositional images. There will always be a 'meaning' and an attitude conveyed. It will never just be. And one will always read it differently as one reads from a homosexual or heterosexual positioning.

Homosexual and lesbian representation in mainstream media

In Cameron Crowe's film, *Almost Famous* (2000), there is a climactic, comic scene in which the rock band Stillwater is on a light plane when they hit an electrical storm. They are terrified, think they're going to die, and come out with a desperate series of anguished confessions of sexual and other misdemeanours, reaching its climax when one of the band who has been silent up to this point, blurts out 'I'm gay!' just as they pass through the storm and peace descends. The rest of the band are stunned into silence: the newly confessed gay man shrinks down in his seat. The audience laughs: the poor guy has made this confession thinking he was going to die, and he will now have to live with it. One does not want to get prim about this, but it is predicated on the assumption that we all know it's preferable to be closeted. Under ordinary circumstances, nobody in their right mind would confess they were gay.

Let me outline three reactions. The first is that of the majority of the audience, which I have outlined above. For these people, it is their heterosexual subject position that is being appealed to and affirmed. They are the ones who laugh, because the moment is structured within the heterosexual discourse to create laughter. (Some heterosexual people in the audience might resist that, because they subscribe to anti-discriminatory discourses, and, it's true, they are another group.)

The second reaction is mine, and I presume the reaction of many of the other gay and lesbian people in the audience. I don't laugh. I am not particularly offended, because if I were offended by this kind of thing, I would go around in a constant rage, but I notice that once again homosexuality is the source of an easy joke, once again the assumption is that homosexuals are a lesser kind of life. But I have a certain power: I can talk about my reaction in an article I'm writing. I can assert my resistance to this kind of negative representation.

The third reaction, and this is the one that I am particularly concerned about, is that of the homosexual person in the audience who hasn't got my institutional position and my sense of personal security — perhaps the young woman or man who is still uncertain about her/his sexuality, or the lesbian or gay man who is still subject to those dominant discourses that make them feel guilt and self-loathing. I don't imagine that they react particularly strongly outwardly. They probably laugh. But the laughter has a particular quality: it's the laughter of the outsider. This is not an incidental over-in-a-moment joke for them: it's an assertion or a confirmation that something is wrong with the way they are. They laugh to affirm their 'normality' — to themselves as much as to others — but in doing that, they are denigrating very deep impulses within themselves, impulses which, as Foucault has shown us, are felt to be constitutive of identity at the present time.

Such a moment in a film is fairly incidental, and not likely to prove a major trauma for anybody in this third group. But that is actually the point. It is just one of the myriad moments that gay and lesbian people live through in the average week that suggest that heterosexuality is central and okay, while homosexuality is not central and a bit suspect. Being lesbian or gay is not something that can just be accepted. In most texts it will be, as mentioned before, 'marked'. It will always be there for some purpose, drawing along with it some attitude.

Narratives are all about attitudes. They are structured to make us see the world they show in particular ways . Everything in a narrative is there for a purpose, for a particular effect it will have. Narratives also necessarily draw on categorisations of people — types, if not stereotypes — so as to be able to tell their story economically . They activate common social attitudes and understandings. This is what was happening in that moment in *Almost Famous:* Cameron Crowe knows that the audience will understand the full import of the situation because of the social framework they bring to their functioning as viewers.

It's often particularly interesting to look at moments like that, because the attitudes and assumptions are very nakedly displayed, not covered over by a lot of circumstantial detail. One can often learn more about how homosexuality is constructed within society, and what narrative uses it can be put to, in these almost incidental moments.

Take Sam Mendes' *American Beauty* (1999), another excellent film, and deserving of its Academy Award. It's not a film 'about' homosexuality, but homosexuality is used in it both as an absolutely crucial plot device, and for satiric purposes. The next-door neighbours on one side of the Burnhams (the Kevin Spacey/Annette Bening household) are a gay couple, and they are a perfect parody of suburban contentment, talking about their pet and the garden, bringing gifts to the new arrivals on the street. Their conventional 'coupledness' is underlined by the fact that they are both named 'Jim' (so that the cast list actually designates them 'Jim#1' and 'Jim#2'). Unlike the heterosexual families, they are living out the middle-class, middle-American domestic dream, seemingly oblivious to all the undercurrents of discontent, disturbance and despair around them. The satiric element comes from, or at the very least gains most of its impact from, the fact that they are a gay couple. Their homosexuality provides an instant parody of every suburban move they make, because it is set against heterosexual norms. In embodying the fantasy domesticity in same-sexed bodies, the domesticity is seen as performance. One could liken the effect to that which is often claimed for drag in relation to femininity: that it uncovers the ways in which women perform femininity and makes us realise how much femininity *is* a performance, a construct. The cheeriness with which this gay couple live out the suburban dream actually makes them look silly, but I doubt anyone would get very upset over this particular representation, even though, it is true, the heterosexual couples are considered to be much more seriously interesting.

The main use of homosexuality in the film is a different matter. The gay couple play a structural role in the narrative, as well as providing parody of suburbia. They are the occasion of Colonel Fitts, the military father on the other side, displaying his profound homophobia (and, incidentally, his way of relating to his son). The climax of the film is generated out of this homophobia. When he thinks his son has been having sex with Lester (Kevin Spacey), he descends on the garage, and the audience expects violence — after all, we know Lester is going to be killed — but the expected violence is deflected into his making a pass at Lester, which Lester rejects quite gently and gracefully. The rejection channels the violent passion back into homicidal fury and does, in fact, later, lead to the murder. The motivation in the Colonel draws on a widespread conception, that homophobia stems from repressed homosexuality. The 'phobia' element in the very term homophobia suggests this kind of an explanation, that the hatred of homosexuality stems from fear of it, the fear being usually fear of its unacknowledged existence in the self. When I saw the film, the audience in the cinema gave a giggly gasp at the moment when Colonel Fitts kissed Lester, but there seemed to be no incredulity, since the pop-psychology explanation was ready at hand. It was a very convenient stereotype that the film-makers could draw on to precipitate the climax. There is a trope of homosexuality as psychopathology, homosexuality as a force twisting the personality to violence, and it just needed to be activated in an economical shorthand for the motivation that leads to Lester Burnham's death to be covered.

It is worth considering *American Beauty* in the light of our earlier discussion about Foucault. The homosexuality of the characters isn't incidental: these people are homosexual first and foremost, homosexual through and through. They only have purpose within the film as far as they are homosexual because they would not 'work' in the film if they weren't. The satire developed out of the gay couple is totally dependent on their gayness: the plot development at the climax is totally dependent on the Colonel's repressed homosexuality. I am not saying that these purposes could not have been achieved in other (heterosexual) ways — quite clearly they could have been — but the fact of the matter is they weren't: the homosexual types were activated. One can imagine the father with a different psychopathology — trauma from the Vietnam war, for example — or one can imagine a heterosexual couple being set up as a bourgeois parody. But in these cases, their heterosexuality would not have been spotlighted — it would have been totally incidental, a matter of no concern — whereas homosexuality is almost always a matter of concern, because it is the minority binary opposite of the invisible mainstream heterosexuality.

There is always the risk that one will be seen as making too much of such elements in a film, of being paranoid about unintended implications, and indeed one does not want to appoint oneself as a member of the thought-police, searching out and castigating every negative image of homosexuality one might come across. However, it is worthwhile returning again to our third group in the audience, this time watching *American Beauty*. The choices confronting them as images of themselves seem to be either inane conformity or pathological psychosis. It is not that heterosexuality comes out of the film particularly well (although it certainly comes out as having a greater range of nuanced pleasures and possibilities). Rather, it's that heterosexuality in itself is not made an issue in the film — it is just what most people are — whereas homosexuality is viewed from the outside, as something to be manipulated by the authors for particular effects, as something to be noted and responded to by the audience, as what most people are not.

Given all of this, if any writer or film-maker wants to give a positive image of homosexuality — and there is a great and welcome desire to do this today — they have to position the lesbian or gay characters very carefully. It is probably significant that I have chosen to talk about two films in which the homosexuality isn't central. It would be almost impossible for anyone to make a consciously anti-lesbian/gay mainstream film these days. In films in which homosexuality is central, it is either affirmed in the end after being comically suppressed (*The Birdcage*, *In and Out*), or the discrimination against it that has produced the social drama is well and truly condemned (*Philadelphia*, *Priest*).

Coming down to the texts that almost all school students access, many television series by now have their resident gay character, particularly sitcoms, since we know that gay people are wonderfully witty and come out with fantastic down-putting one-liners (a myth I would quite like to subscribe to). Also gay people make fuddy-duddy conventional people comically upset, and it is felt, at the moment in the sitcom world, that it is worse to be un-hip than gay. In fact, gay characters are undeniably fashionable, in all senses of the word. But again, note, that the gayness is central: these characters are gay before anything else. And, on the whole, gay, not lesbian: gender discrimination is more alive in representations of homosexuality than almost anywhere else, 'Ellen' notwithstanding.[2]

'Ellen' was famous as the first television show in which the central character came out — with disastrous results for the ratings after the initial excitement. The show wasn't constructed to accommodate a lesbian central character, and the necessary adjustments weren't made, or weren't made quickly enough. 'Will and Grace' has been more successful, but then it has been predicated from the beginning on Will's homosexuality. The positioning of Will has obviously been a very delicate operation. Part of the balancing is the relationship with Grace that shows he can operate in a heterosexual world. However, as in most sitcoms, the most significant thing is the flanking of the main character by refracting images of what he is not. In 'Will and Grace', we get two other regular male characters who by contrast define and affirm Will's status as sitcom hero. On one side, there is Jack, who is the kind of stereotyped, feather-headed, camp gay man one could not possibly take seriously: by contrast he shows Will's 'normality'. On the other side is Will's boss, who is the epitome of all that is awful in egotistical masculinity: by contrast he shows Will's (quite masculine) niceness. Thus Will seems far preferable and more attractive than the other men, and the audience is positioned to accept his homosexuality.

Something else may be going on here too. I happened to mention to two people that I had watched 'Will and Grace' in case I wanted to refer to the program in this chapter, and both said to me, 'He's not really gay, you know,' referring to Eric McCormack, the actor who plays Will. When watching the show, I had no idea whether he was 'really gay' or not, but quite clearly the word was around that he wasn't, and one could only suppose that the marketing machine had spread the word because the character becomes that much more acceptable if we know the actor is just pretending.[3] There is often a close connection between the actor and the character in sitcoms: note how often the main character has the same first name but not the same surname as the actor. In this case, the actor's known heterosexuality makes the character's homosexuality more palatable: he's 'not really gay, you know'. It is probably no accident that his surname is Truman (true man!). Poor Ellen made the mistake of conflating her coming out as a person and as a character.

It probably seems to straight viewers that homosexuality is everywhere these days, although the actual instances (in film and theatre) are not that many and rarely central. Still, young people come to school with a broad acquaintance with homosexual characters. 'Friends' is still leading the ratings, and Ross's (first) ex-wife left him when she came out as a lesbian. There is Jack in 'Dawson's Creek', following in the footsteps of Matt in 'Melrose Place' in that the makers of the program don't seem to know quite what to do with him. (It's very hip to have a gay character, but no way comfortable actually to show him emotionally and sexually engaged: Jack could never be involved in a gay relationship that was elaborated and physcialised as much as the straight ones that Dawson and Pacey engage in.) 'South Park' often plays with homosexuality, as in the amazing episodes where we have the Satan/Saddam/Chris triangle, or the one in which Stan's gay dog, Sparky, finds happiness at Big Gay Al's Big Gay Sanctuary for Gay Animals. Even very young students will tell you that

Smithers in 'The Simpsons' is gay (he's written a musical!). If students happen to be home in the middle of the day, Ricki Lake and Jerry Springer's television shows provide an array of 'real-life' homosexuality. Jerry Springer, in particular, in his extraordinary unfolding of a complex narrative of relationship patterns, will often have a homosexual element as a particular climax: we will discover that a wife has been having an affair with her sister-in-law, or some guy with his girlfriend's father.

The representations of homosexuality in the literature written for young people is rather limited compared with this, although much more uniformly positive.

Homosexual representation in literature

If one wants to study texts that present positive images of homosexuality that young people might relate to, there are films that could be used, such as *Beautiful Thing*, *Edge of Seventeen*, or *Show me Love*. Ang Lee's *The Wedding Banquet* or Stephen Frears/Hanish Kureifi's *My Beautiful Laundrette* are rather more complex films about older people that could also be studied interestingly (both of them incidentally having significant things to say about ethnicity as well as sexuality). One needs to avoid simplistic films (like *The Sum of Us*), that are so obviously and simple-mindedly well-intentioned (not to mention inherently heterosexist) that they are almost enough to turn one straight for life.

However, it is more likely that English/Literacy teachers will want to use prose narrative. I have no intention of allowing this chapter to degenerate into a listing of relevant books — there are bibliographies that give that information — but rather I will suggest the qualities that I would want to see in a book or story to be used in the classroom, and the things that I would want to bring out in my work on it with the students.

Predictably, many of the stories and novels written around homosexuality are coming-out stories. Either the main character is unsure whether she/he is lesbian/gay and the novel deals with the realisation that they are, and/or the main character is aware of their homosexual orientation, and the story is of how their family and friends accommodate themselves to the fact. Given that these stories are written for people in the teenage years, and it is in those years that people often do come to terms with their sexuality, this is understandable and probably all to the good. One would like, however, to see more stories that didn't treat homosexuality as the source of angst, but simply accepted it as inevitable.

The book that has brought more discussion of homosexuality into Australian classrooms than any other, undoubtedly, is Morris Gleitzman's *Two Weeks with the Queen* (1989). The main homosexual character, Ted, is not the central character in the book — indeed he doesn't appear until page 80 in a book that is only 127 pages long — but he has a considerable effect when he does appear. Ted turns the story around, because he is the one adult who takes an interest in Colin and takes his quest to find a cure for his brother's cancer seriously; that is, seriously as an expression of an emotional need that has to be worked through.

Ted is a remarkable piece of characterisation, and a considerable triumph for Gleitzman. The basis of the character is very much the stereotypical camp gay person, such as one might deplore in many other narratives. However, here the flamboyance and the heart-on-sleeve openness of the emotional swings are tremendously positive. This is achieved through having the book told almost exclusively from Colin's point of view (although it is not a first-person narrative). We have suffered with Colin the greyness and the emotional constriction of his life with Uncle Bob and Aunty Iris. The reader, like Colin, is feeling an intolerable narrowing-down of possibilities and, beyond sympathising with what Colin feels, is feeling *for* Colin as he suffers from the total lack of understanding of those around him and the misguidedness of his quest to find a cure for his brother's cancer.

The one weakness of the book, and it always surprises me that it doesn't totally wreck it, is that Colin seems unbelievably naive for someone who is round about 13 years old. I know he comes from up the country somewhere, but even so … I expect the book still works because the emotional material about cancer early on is so strong, and many of the jokes are so good, that one turns a blind eye to the basic unbelievableness of Colin's character for the emotional and comic pay-off.

Ted enters the book like a ray of light in the London gloom. He is established very economically. We first see him sitting in the gutter, crying. Then, immediately afterwards, we see him handing out chocolate frogs in the canteen to make people feel better. The range of his character and its dominant traits of free emotion and flamboyance are thus quickly established. Homosexuality has liberated him from the kind of conventional constriction that limits most of the other characters in the book. He thus enables Colin to see the importance of facing up to emotionally demanding facts, and of acting independently as seems intuitively right.

Colin doesn't at first realise that Ted is gay. It dawns on him after Ted has been the victim of homophobic vilification and gay-bashing:

> He looked at Ted, and saw that Ted was watching him carefully.
> 'Is that why they bashed you up,' said Colin, ''cause you and Griff are in love?'
> Ted's face relaxed and he nodded.
> Pathetic, thought Colin. All the blokes in the world doing really mean and cruel stuff and getting away without even a smack round the ear and here's a bloke getting totally bashed up for being in love with another bloke.
>
> (Gleitzman, 1989: 103)

Although it's predicated on Colin's almost literally incredible innocence, and although it seems insufficiently responsive to the social outrage of gay-bashing, the passage provides something of an ideal, a model of what one would wish the attitude towards homosexuality to be.

Two Weeks with the Queen is in most ways a conventional novel, although an amazingly tactful (and successful) one. The other two pieces of writing I want to look at are less technically conventional, but instead make use of a battery of narrative techniques to create the experience of their young gay protagonists.

The first is a short story by Dean Kiley, that first appeared in his excellent collection *and that's final* (1995), but was then republished in the anthology *Hide and Seek*, edited by Jenny Pausacker (1996). The story is called 'Staying In', and it tells of a gay (but not yet out) boy, John (nickname Worm), on a Year 11 geography excursion to examine the geological layers in a cliff that happens to be at a nude beach, even, by rumour, a *gay* nude beach. He feels it is a place of danger where something might happen that will trigger his classmates into making the associative leap and discovering he is gay. Actually, that makes him sound too pathetic.

What is so good about the story is that the thread of tension about being discovered doesn't dominate and turn him into a quivering terrified blob. His other reactions continue as normal, and the story captures brilliantly the mundane reality of a boring geography excursion, the dynamics of relations among classmates, and the kinds of normal media-based sexual fantasy with which teenagers (and most other age groups) pass the time when there is nothing else to occupy the mind. In fact, much of John's inner life is structured around, and like, film. This is undoubtedly true of many teenagers (indeed, I would think, most people) these days: the main (leisure) textual input in our society is film and TV, so it's no wonder that we live out our fantasy lives as if we were part of a TV program. One of the reasons for the success of 'Dawson's Creek' is that it works with this, and plays its postmodern referential games. Dean Kiley's story is clearly Australian, and much tougher than anything in 'Dawson's Creek', but students who know 'Dawson's Creek' will recognise the territory. (Any student who is alive in the early years of the twenty-first century will recognise the territory!)

The writing captures the rough-and-tumble complexity of the situation and John's thoughts, through an easy-flowing, fractured, highly referential language. The class have just been moving through the nude beach:

> In hissed exchanges the boys tot up their tit totals but it's fast losing its appeal. Bit of a fizzer really. No-one seems to be embarrassed or guilty or sexy or on the prowl. They're all just sitting around like they've got their everyday clothes on. The Emperor's old clothes. BorrrrrrrrrrRING. Something'll have to be done about this.
>
> Kosta's hand shoots up Heil Hitler *Scuse me! Sorry! Sir? Mr McKenzie?* John thinks *Here it comes.* The geology tape (Side B) in Mr McKenzie's mouth clicks off. He glares at the kid, as close to hatred as teachers are trained not to get.

The writing has enormous energy, and the basic perception is comic, which totally removes from John's anxieties any taint of sentimentality. John is as much exasperated by the whole venture as scared of exposure, as much nascent film-maker as potential gay victim. By not overplaying the sympathy for John, and by lodging him in such a commonplace world that he perceives with such incisive, disillusioned liveliness, Kiley has managed to write a story that gives the experience of a boy fearing outing that, I think, even potential 'outers' would relate to.

Kiley manages to catch the multiple levels of experience on which one lives and the disjunctions between them extraordinarily well. One does not, of course, want to claim any kind of exclusivity for gay and lesbian people in living on multiple levels, but gay and lesbian people do experience more radically than most the disjunctions between the inner and the outer world, the private and the public domains, between what can be expressed readily and what can not.

The best book for young adults about a homosexual relationship that I know is Aidan Chambers' *Dance on my Grave* (1995). There is not space here to talk much about its complexities, but it is remarkable for two things. Firstly, homosexuality is treated as normal in the book and not seen as 'a problem'. Secondly, the book constantly reminds the reader, even more than the Kiley story, of the complexity and 'multi-layeredness' of experience.

The homosexuality in the book is purely accepted. The characters themselves are perfectly comfortable, and the book doesn't create it as any sort of an issue. Neither Hal nor Barry seem to have had any crisis of identity about entering a same-sex relationship. There is no outside ostracism either, although, by the same token, there is no support. The social context of the seaside resort of Southend is sketched in well, but one is not conscious of the boys being part of a functioning community that might have an attitude to their relationship. The narrative cocoons them from any people who might pry and be outraged. It is the summer holidays, and we only see one of their friends from school, who is gay or bisexual himself. Barry's mother is eccentric and on sleeping pills, so the boys are free to sleep together. Hal is distant from his parents, and they are pleased that he has got a vacation job (in Barry's store) and presumably also pleased that he has found such a good friend in the boss.

Chambers uses a whole battery of narrative techniques that help create the complexity of the story, and help him avoid sentimentality, although the book gives a tremendous sense of a strongly passionate relationship. The title page tells us it is:

A Life and a Death
in Four Parts
One Hundred and Seventeen Bits
Six Running Reports
and Two Press Clippings
With a few jokes
a puzzle or three
some footnotes
and a fiasco now and then
to help the story along

Hal is the main narrator, but even his narration is constantly circling on itself and revealing new perspectives, new revelations of what is going on beneath the surface. The main influence is again cinematic. There are 'Action Replays', 'Retakes', even a section in which he moves to a third person account 'starring Henry S. and Kari Norway'. The effect is often to make one extraordinarily aware of how the vivid depths of feeling have been bleached out and displaced as the feeling realises itself in surface action. The narration of the first part is a good example.

Barry and Hal meet when Hal, out sailing, is caught in an unexpected storm and the boat capsizes. Barry comes to his rescue and then takes him home to get cleaned up. We have various action replays of bits of this, and we are very aware that Hal is feeling attracted to Barry, and Barry may be encouraging this. Finally we get a 'Retake' in which version we learn that Hal had noticed Barry before that day, had been attracted to him, and this influenced the way he played out the morning's events. There is nothing exceptional about this: men and women (and men and men and women and women) have been having such experiences since time immemorial. And yet, as I say, because the experience of disjunction between unspoken desire and surface expression is extreme for gay and lesbian people, the book creates it with particular power.[4]

To return to an earlier point, *Dance on my Grave* might help some students achieve a more understanding attitude towards homosexuality by giving them the narrative entry into a world in which same-sex love is treated as normal, but it will perhaps have an even greater effect in making them aware of the complex ways in which people become and act out what they are, and in giving them an inkling of the complexity of interpersonal experience.

Conclusion

Several years ago, I gave a seminar at a Young Adult Literature conference on novels about lesbian and gay young people. A quite well-known young adult novelist was in the audience. We were talking afterwards, and he was very seriously (and I think honestly) saying that he had found the session interesting and it had made him think how important it was that such books were written. Then he went on to say something like, 'Of course, I couldn't write one: you'd have to be gay to do it properly'. I made some non-committal noise because he was a keynote speaker, a writer and a guest, and I was but a lowly seminar presenter. However, what I wanted to say was that many a gay and lesbian novelist over the years has actually done a rather good job of writing about heterosexual relationships, and it was perhaps about time that the imbalance was redressed. If he felt it was so important, he shouldn't excuse himself so easily.

I would say much the same thing to teachers. It is difficult to cross this particular boundary, and it's difficult whether you are lesbian/gay or straight. The difficulty is different in each case. For the homosexual person, it can be tantamount to coming out, and that always brings with it tensions and dangers. For the heterosexual teacher, the dangers are still there. Students can become unruly; all kinds of unwanted personal attitudes and issues can erupt; people might even think you're homosexual ('not that there's anything wrong with that,' as Jerry Seinfeld would say). But to keep silent on sexuality is, in the end, to be complicit in the heterosexist denigration of gay and lesbian people.

Turning the tide so that all kinds of love can be accepted and talked about in the classroom is as much the responsibility of each heterosexual teacher as of homosexual ones. Making the world better and safer for homosexual people is too important, if we want to live in a just and humane society, to be left only to the lesbian and gay teachers who feel strong enough to take the battle on unsupported.

Bibliography

Almost Famous (motion picture) (2000), Cameron Crowe (dir and scr). Dreamworks Pictures.
American Beauty (motion picture) (1999), Sam Mendes (dir) and Alan Ball (scr). Dreamworks Pictures.
Britzman, D. (1998) *Lost Subjects, Contested Objects: Towards a Psychoanalytical Inquiry of Learning.* SUNY Press, Albany.
Butler, J. (1990) *Gender Trouble: Feminism and the Subversion of Identity.* Routledge, New York.
Chambers, A. (1995) *Dance on my Grave.* Red Fox, London.
Cohan, S. and Shires, L. (1988) *Telling Stories: A Theoretical Analysis of Narrative Fiction.* Routledge, New York and London.
Davis, L. (1987) *Resisting Novels: Ideology and Fiction.* Methuen, New York and London.
Epstein, D. and Johnson R. (1998) *Schooling Sexualities.* Open University Press, Buckingham and Philadelphia.
Epstein, D. and Sears, J.T. (eds) (1999) *A Dangerous Knowing: Sexuality, Pedagogy and Popular Culture.* Cassell, London and New York.

Foucault, M. (1981) *The History of Sexuality: Volume 1: An Introduction*. Penguin, Harmondsworth.

Gleitzman, M. (1989) *Two Weeks with the Queen*. Pan, Sydney.

Jagose, A. (1996) *Queer Theory*. Melbourne University Press, Melbourne.

Kiley, D. (1995) *and that's final*. BlackWattle Press, Sydney.

Letts, W.J. (ed.) (1999) *Queering Elementary Education: Advancing the Dialogue about Sexualities and Schooling*. Rowman & Littlefield, Lanham, Maryland.

Medhurst, A. and Munt, S.R. (eds) (1997) *Lesbian and Gay Studies: A critical introduction*. Cassell, London and Washington.

Misson, R. (1995) 'Dangerous Lessons: Sexuality Issues in the English Classroom', *English in Australia* no 112, pp. 25–32.

—— (1996) 'Character Building', *Idiom* 31(2): pp. 88–97.

—— (1996) 'What's in it for me?: Teaching against Homophobic Discourse', in *Schooling and Sexualities: Teaching for a Positive Sexuality*, L. Laskey and C. Beavis (eds). Deakin Centre for Education and Change, Geelong, pp. 117–29.

—— (1998a) 'Telling Tales out of School', in *Literacy and Schooling*, F. Christie and R. Misson (eds). Routledge, London and New York, pp. 104–28.

—— (1998b) 'Will and Story, or The Ultimate Metanarrative', *English in Australia* no 121, pp. 24–32.

Pausacker, J. (ed) (1996) *Hide and Seek: Stories about Being Young and Gay/Lesbian*. Mandarin, Melbourne.

Sedgwick, E.K. (1990) *Epistemology of the Closet*. University of California Press, Berkeley.

Endnotes

1   I have made a number of decisions about terminology in this article that will undoubtedly brand me as old-fashioned, if not reactionary. First of all, I have opted to talk about Lesbian and Gay Theory rather than Queer Theory. The two things, of course, cannot be conflated, but then, they do coincide in many ways. I made this particular decision because the political agendas of Lesbian/Gay Theory and Queer Theory seem to me to be rather different, the former being more concerned with fighting against discrimination, the latter more concerned with achieving a postmodern freedom from the constraints of categorisation and social expectation. Temperamentally I find myself more comfortable engaging with the mainstream and trying to turn it around than in celebrating a kind of transcendent carnival that largely ignores it.

Another decision I have made is to confine myself to talking about lesbian and gay people, rather than opting to use the nowadays common acronym LGBT (Lesbian, Gay, Bisexual, Transgender). This decision was made on two grounds, the first being that the acronym is not immediately meaningful to the wider audience I hope will read this chapter, the second being that, in fact, I don't say anything about transgender and bisexual people. The issues surrounding them are rather different (and in fact more congenial to discussion in a Queer Theory framework), as well as being very different from each other, and so I thought it best to limit the discussion to lesbian and gay people alone. For readers wanting to read into the area of Lesbian/Gay/Queer Theory (if I may conflate them), I would suggest beginning with Medhurst (1997) and Jagose (1996). After that, the indispensable central text is Sedgwick (1990).

2   I am very aware that in this article I too am concentrating on gay males rather than lesbians for most of my examples, and so perpetuating this trend. My only defence is that I needed to work with texts that were either well-known or fairly readily available, and these sorts of texts do tend to be male-centred.

3   I subsequently looked up the 'official' website, *http://www.nbci.com/LMOID/*, and there, at the end of Eric McCormack's bio we read:

> McCormack and his wife divide their time between their permanent home in Los Angeles and a second home in Vancouver. His birthday is April 18.

One can almost hear the sighs of relief echoing around the world: not only a wife but *two* houses, and a birthday we can feel free to celebrate as well.

4   Deborah Britzman (1998) has an interesting psychologically oriented discussion of another text that works in a similar way.

Part four

Social, cultural and linguistic effects on books for children

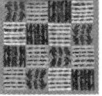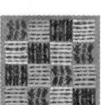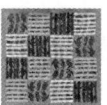

Chapter 14

Writing *by* children, writing *for* children: schema theory, narrative discourse and ideology

John Stephens

When readers read, their understanding of a text is a combination of the text and the prior knowledge, experiences and cultural situation of those readers. What readers bring to the act of comprehension results in variations in interpretation, but the process of interpretation is based on a large body of shared knowledge. If it were not, nobody would understand anything. With relatively young and inexperienced readers, we are perhaps on more uncertain and unstable ground, given some inevitable limitations in their knowledge and experience. At the same time, though, it can also be argued that, especially for young readers, the conceptual frames, or schemata, made available through shared cultural and linguistic knowledge are a key enabling element in the construction and decoding of narrative discourse. Cognitive research carried out with children as young as three and four has indicated that they already organise their knowledge and experience of the world and their understanding of typical narrative forms by means of such schemata (Thorndyke and Yekovich, 1980; Mandler, in Hudson and Shapiro, 1991; Crawford and Chaffin, 1986), though it is much later before they are able to use schemata to generate their own fictive stories.

In an earlier study I argued that:

A narrative without an ideology is unthinkable: ideology is formulated in and by language, meanings within language are socially determined, and narratives are constructed out of language.

(Stephens, 1992: 8)

As elements of discourse, schemata inevitably bear an ideological freight, but one which is focused far less significantly in the writing of young children than in adult writing for children. In particular, young writers may be apt to elaborate the components of a schema for reasons which do not accord with notions of adult significance, so that ideological loading may seem more a matter of accident than substance. In order to explore this difference, this paper will examine two examples of writing by children (Bridget, aged seven, and Raphael, aged eleven),[1] looking at how they manipulate both broad narrative schemata (macroschemata) and more specific narrative or social schemata (microschemata). I will then go on to compare these with Anna Fienberg's chained collection of stories, *The Magnificent Nose and Other Marvels* (1991).

Simple stories conform to a common macroschema which children recognise and reproduce after a couple of years of schooling, and which is evident here incipiently in Bridget's text and fully developed in Raphael's. The schema is:

- an onset (or orientation) in which the main characters are introduced;
- a complication, usually in the form of a goal to be achieved or problem to be overcome, which is dealt with in one or more episodes — episodes may be linked causally or sequentially, and characteristically pivot on new problems for the main characters to overcome;
- a resolution.

The stories we give to or read to young children present a cognitive model which accords with this macroschema, but which also invariably inscribes within it particular moral structures grounded in social ideology. Both examples of writing by children follow the conventional structure of story schema, but with a crucial difference. When children tell or write their own created stories, they tend to draw on other factors: personal experience of everyday life; television; video; imagination and fantasy. Schemata are employed more eclectically in Bridget's story than in Raphael's, and — most importantly — although she uses schemata to frame her narrative discourse her macroschema lacks the clear ideological shaping evident in his story. Below is the opening segment of Bridget's story.

The Ireland Treasure

Long, long ago in Ireland, before people, there were such things as leprechauns. Leprechauns are little, little people that disappear so quickly that you don't notice them! These leprechauns always have treasure, and this story is about pirates stealing the leprechauns' treasure. The leader of them all is … CAPTAIN HOOK!!! Now let's begin.

One morning a leprechaun skipped across the wet sand near the sea. Then, a pirate jumped out and grabbed the leprechaun, and then he tied the leprechaun up. Poor old Happy. Happy is his name. Happy was brought to the pirates' awful ship. Captain Hook walked towards Happy. Happy got very scared! Don't know how he could take it.

Meanwhile, back inside a rock where Happy lived, all the leprechauns in Ireland were together inside that main rock. The leader of the leprechauns said, 'Where is Happy?' Everyone stopped and stared at the King of the leprechauns. Then suddenly the entrance flew open. Happy rushed in. Happy had escaped from Captain Hook's awful, awful ship. But a pirate was chasing Happy! So that is why he ran. The King of leprechauns said, 'Where have you been?' 'Captain Hook tied me up and then he took me to his ship and I ran because a pirate was chasing me,' replied Happy. The Queen of leprechauns heard what happened and said to Happy, 'Oh dear, Happy! Let's get you to bed,' said Queen leprechauns. 'But, dear,' said the King, 'he hasn't had his dinner.' 'Oh, all right, but go right to bed when you have finished,' the Queen said. So Happy ate his dinner and went to bed (which was a pile of gold). Then all the other leprechauns did the same.

Meanwhile, inside Captain Hook's ship, Captain Hook was walking around saying, 'Why didn't you get him?' Sme replied, 'Captain, we will get all the leprechauns in Ireland.' 'Well, Sme, if we are going to do that we will have to find their rock,' said Captain Hook. 'Captain,' said Sme, 'I have already found their rock.' 'Really?' said Captain Hook. 'Yes, really,' said Sme. 'Here is my map, or could I say, plan. Here it is. Do you like it?' asked Sme. 'Like it? Like it? I love it!' said Captain Hook. 'Let's go to bed, Sme,' said Captain Hook. So they went to bed.

In the morning, Sme and Captain Hook got ready for their plan ...

When this chapter was written, Bridget's story was as yet unfinished, still generating its complication as a long series of episodes. It is, however, not important that an audience lacks a perspective from the close, since each episode has its own narrative integrity and any anticipated outcome is only implicit as a story function, not as a thematic or ideological teleology. Thus the propensity for the story to unfold as a sequence of localised moments has implications for the functioning of schemata because it reinforces a process whereby ideological effects are already randomised.

As knowledge structures which provide the framework for understanding, schemata shape our knowledge of all concepts, from the very small to the very large, from the material to the abstract. Within this range some schemata are minimally marked ideologically. The object schema 'the wet sand near the sea', for example, serves as a 'boundary' schema, situating the leprechaun on the boundary between land and sea, between leprechaun and pirate territory, though it may actually originate in the practical, everyday knowledge that this firm, smooth surface is the best place to skip on a beach. The schema specifies spatial and functional relationships, and has few if any ideological overtones. Schemata shaping our knowledge of personal and social relationships are much more obviously marked, as in Bridget's assumption that societies are hierarchies of authority, whether these are leprechaun or pirate societies. As is suggested by the incident in which Happy is sent to bed, these societies are here implicitly mapped onto notions of everyday human behaviour. In contrast to this tacit inscribing of ideology, in representing the literary schema 'pirate' Bridget is quite overt in confirming that it is marked for villainy:[2] narrative point of view is sympathetic with the captured leprechaun, and the repeated descriptor 'awful' indicates an appropriate audience attitude. Each of these three schemata illustrates a variation on how schemata function as aspects of memory, whether experiential (as in the first), textual (as the third), or the second's more complex assimilation of textual to experiential. A schema normally consists of a network of constituent parts, and when, as audience, our memories activate part of a schema the stimulus evokes the network and its interrelations, especially what is normal and typical about that network. Schema theory suggests that as we read we call up schemata which are likely to be the most salient fit for the data we're processing. Bridget evidently builds her schemata in a similar, associative way, but is apt to combine isomorphic schemata, thereby transferring ideological freight from one to another.

Ideological variation can also occur within a schema because of the propensity for schemata to have both constant and variable components. Bridget begins her story by specifying a number of components or 'slots' which make up the 'leprechaun' schema:

'Leprechaun' schema
    Irish
    little
    rarely seen (disappear quickly)
    treasure keepers

objects of empathy
monarchic social structure

The first four components are constant attributes, derived from textual memory; that is, the slots are always filled in the same way and constitute the fundamental schema. Audiences may already be able to supply these components or 'subschemata' as *default values* in response to the simple cue *leprechaun*. On the other hand, any reader without previous knowledge of leprechaun stories would now have a fairly well-developed leprechaun schema. Bridget's first two components are not especially salient to the story which is about to unfold, but some redundancy is acceptable in an orientation. The last two components are variables, introduced perhaps in part by analogy with fairies, who are normally represented as having a monarchic hierarchy, and in part by analogy with social structures in *Peter Pan*. Crucially, however, they replace normal subschemata of the 'leprechaun' schema — unsociability and deceptiveness — and so frame the narrative as an unambiguous conflict between heroes and villains.

A fascinating narrative aspect of Bridget's story is her varied use of the 'going to bed' schema. A reader constantly makes and evaluates hypotheses about the most plausible interpretation of a text — that is, decides which possible schemata are the most salient possibilities. Readers are then said to have understood the text when they are able to find a configuration of schemata that offers a coherent account for the various aspects of the text. The process is made obvious here in the *en*coding when Bridget writes that 'Happy ate his dinner and went to bed', and we would normally respond by defaulting to some kind of typical 'bed' schema. In this case, however, Bridget promptly cancels the general schema network by defining the bed as 'a pile of gold', an unusual subschema more salient for a leprechaun network. On the other hand, in her uses of the 'going to bed' schema as an action, Bridget relies entirely on default values, presumably because the schema is so experientially familiar. At the level of specific subschemata, we might activate concepts such as undressing, teeth-cleaning, turning out the light, and so on — a host of actions implicit in the 'going to bed' schema which we might randomly assume or think of. But the schema also has several mutually exclusive subschematic variants of a more conceptual kind:

'Going to bed' schema
a) everyday occurrence
b) response to illness or stress (Happy)
c) punishment for transgressive behaviour (children in general)
d) to refresh oneself in preparation for the next day (Hook)
e) to make time pass faster (Hook?)
f) (for sexual purposes)

These tend to be more thematically salient than the action subschemata, so when the Queen insists that Happy should go to bed, and subschema *b* is thus implicitly activated, the schema is grounded in complex social assumptions. Subschemata *b* and *c* are a subset which express power relations, specifically the authority of a 'parent' over a child, and as such are ideologically marked. The King's insistence that Happy have dinner first suggests that Bridget is constructing *b* as the appropriate subschema here rather than *c* (though *c* itself may be further broken down into the variants 'without dinner' and 'straight after dinner'), in which case the ideological burden is embedded as a sub-subschema — that is, well below the surface level of text.

Stories by young writers may not develop a strong thematic or teleological structure because they tend to favour temporal markers rather than cause and effect as elements of text cohesion, and this is another use to which Bridget puts the 'going to bed' schema: as a temporal transition, it closes off episodes of the story. She does this at the end of the third paragraph and again at the end of the fourth. When Captain Hook says 'Let's go to bed, Sme', readers might therefore simply activate a narrative schema ('time passes'), or in addition they may activate subschemata *d* or *e*. Adult readers, however, may read transgressively, reading against the text and activating subschema *f*. In normal reading we might treat that particular schema as a rejected hypothesis.

The randomness of ideological marking is clear in the operation of default values, because a young writer will still be feeling her way with this principle. An example where a schema is over-specified rather than evoking its default value is seen in Bridget's use of a 'pursuit' schema. Both the narrative and the dialogue explain that Happy ran because he was being chased by a pirate, though of course most readers would postulate a 'pursuit' schema from the context — the previous capture, and the information that Happy 'rushed in' and that a pirate was chasing him — and so the fact that Happy was running would be part of the schema's default value. Hicks (1990: 99) has observed that in oral storytelling children tend to use a higher proportion of phonological stress than in other genres, and perhaps the tendency to over-articulation here is a written equivalent. Nevertheless, the emphasis remains a story function and does not have special thematic or ideological implications. It might thus be said of Bridget's use of schemata that:

- the 'leprechaun' schema is quite fully articulated because it is new, interesting, plot-implicated and part of the story's opening movement;
- the 'pursuit' schema is over-articulated because of a narrative urge to express tension and excitement; and
- the 'going to bed' schema is *not* articulated because it is an aspect of everydayness with accessible default values.

Schema theory envisages any particular schema as a pyramid, hierarchically organised so that the more inclusive and more abstract concept is at the top and subcategories of more specific information are embedded at lower levels. It does not follow, however, that ideological aspects of text are organised into a comparable hierarchy, because they may be inscribed at various subschematic levels. Nevertheless, a narrative which moves to a highly thematised resolution may organise ideological effect more hierarchically, and this seems to be the case with Raphael's story.

The general structure of Bridget's story follows the macroschema for stories outlined above: she begins with an orientation, and formally closes it off with 'Now let's begin'. The next three paragraphs are episodes which develop the complication. Each begins with a temporal marker — 'One morning', 'Meanwhile', 'Meanwhile' — and each is clearly closed off: the first by authorial intrusion, 'Don't know how he could take it', and the next two when the respective characters go to bed. On the other hand, though, the repeated 'going to bed' motif draws on aspects of everyday experience rather than conventional narrative schema. This is one reason why adults may find its use here disruptive. Within a few years, a skilful young writer will have assimilated the adult schema, as seems evident in Raphael's story.

Shivers! It's My Turn

I usually like swimming because I'm the best in my class, but I hate diving …oh dear, I'm getting carried away with myself. My name is Frederick — not Fred because Fred is too boring. My friends call me Freddy the Fish because I'm a good swimmer. My friend is Jake. He isn't a very good swimmer, but he's very clever. My worst enemy is Martin Mashagan. We call him Martin Orang-outang, because he looks like one. He is the second best swimmer in the class and he's getting better … fast! Pretty soon he could be better than me. My girlfriend is Suzie Studebaker, and I always show off in front of her so that she'll like me. Anyway, enough of orientation. Let's get on with the complication.

It was the school swimming carnival and I had been trying for weeks to try and perfect my diving. I already knew Martin Orang-outang was very good at diving, so I had to polish up.

Anyway, the big day came for the swimming carnival, and when I looked at the order of age races I saw all the 12 year olds were last — and I am 12!

We waited for hours watching all these people from younger classes swim. Then came the 12 year olds' turn for the diving. You didn't have to try it, but I knew that if I didn't try everyone would call me a chicken and Suzie wouldn't like me, so I *had* to do it.

We waited in a queue and Martin Orang-outang was before me and did the best dive ever. I was going to need a lot of help. Suddenly it was my turn. I broke into a cold sweat. I knew I couldn't do it, but maybe I could. Just then I saw Martin Orang-outang laughing at me. He knew I couldn't do it, but then I saw something else: it was Jake and Suzie holding hands. I was so shocked I slipped off the diving board and did a triple somersault into the water. It was the best dive the judges had ever seen from a 12 year old. I won the diving medal, but then I saw Suzie. She walked up to me and said, 'I don't like show-offs.'

The End

In Raphael's classroom stories are already pre-shaped by the tenets of a genre theory based on a functional model derived from systemic linguistics. Part of his narrative sophistication is his ability to play with the conventional form he has been taught, and he flags this playfulness by citing two of the key technical descriptors as a way of ending the first paragraph. The story is very self-consciously organised around the narrative schema of orientation–complication–resolution, a point made immediately obvious by the way the opening sentence declares itself to be a wrong move because the contrast between 'like swimming' and 'hate diving' has propelled the story straight into a complication, and the storyteller overtly interrupts and redirects the discourse. Sentence two thus begins with a classic orientation utterance, 'My name is', and continues by introducing several characters and defining their essential qualities and relationships. From the perspective of the end, of course, we see why Jake's cleverness and relationship to Frederick are specified and then not activated until called on to prompt the resolution — 'I saw … Jake and Suzie holding hands'.

Arguably, the narrative self-consciousness functions as an important cue for readers to grasp that the narrator is constructed as an object of gentle ridicule.

The link between orientation and resolution is only one element in a tightly woven narrative form. Other crucial elements are the pervasive use of temporals to effect narrative cohesion throughout the complication — 'for weeks', 'the big day came', 'We waited for hours … Then', 'We waited', and 'Suddenly' — and the climactic sequence dealing with Frederick's sense of how to impress Suzie, which motivates all three parts of the structure:

> *Orientation:* I always show off in front of her so that she'll like me.
> *Complication:* if I didn't try … Suzie wouldn't like me.
> *Resolution:* [Suzie] said, 'I don't like show-offs.'

Finally, Frederick's improbable victory in the competition is both undeserved and Pyrrhic, and these factors combine not just as a comic effect but to draw attention to the moral schema which frames the narrative: it is socially undesirable to flaunt innate gifts. That this articulation of a particular social ideology as story closure is achieved through an apparently conscious awareness of schemata seems evident when Raphael proposes and dismantles an 'overcoming fear' schema: 'I broke into a cold sweat. I knew I couldn't do it, but maybe I could.' That is, this schema is evoked in order to challenge an ideological principle especially applied to boys, that they must face up to and overcome the fears associated with risks and danger. It does so by subsuming the schema first into the contrary 'accidental accomplishment' schema, which is more characteristic of broad comedy, and then into the final narrative twist. The story's relationship to social ideology is thus quite interrogative, able simultaneously to question and affirm the ideological freight of various schemata.

I remarked earlier that Bridget's manipulation of the 'going to bed' schema indicates that she draws on aspects of everyday experience rather than conventional narrative schemata. Raphael's writing shows how a slightly older writer has fully assimilated the adult narrative macroschema in both its expressive and ideological functions, and is at least intuitively aware of the ideological freight of particular microschemata, whereas Bridget's articulation of the components (or subschemata) of any particular schema appears to be independent of the story schema.

In contrast, adults writing for children around Bridget's age employ schemata very elaborately, both as structural and as ideological aspects of text. In composing the linked stories in her collection, *The Magnificent Nose and Other Marvels* (1991), Anna Fienberg addressed a common challenge in writing for a younger audience: how can narrative form be employed to convey abstract concepts which are only vaguely, if at all, recognisable to the audience? The themes expressed in the first, framing story, 'Lindalou and her Golden Gift' — themes which recur in different ways in the subsequent stories — are the transformative power of the creative imagination and the social necessity of allowing and enabling each individual human being to cultivate to the full the capacities she or he is born with, even — or especially — if this entails nonconformist behaviour. Summarised in these rather crude terms, the themes indicate a heavy investment in certain ideological positions pertaining to subjectivity and society which are commonly expressed in literature for children, but which also might be perceived as under threat in the contemporary world, whether from the economic rationalist desire to channel knowledge into narrow vocational ends (as in 'Ignatius Binz and his Magnificent Nose'), or from the anti-humanist rejection of the concept of unified, self-present subjectivity (as in 'Valentina Lookwell and her Surprising Portraits').[3]

While each of the stories in *The Magnificent Nose and Other Marvels* is a self-contained narrative, they are cross-referenced by the appearance in each of Aristan, a golden spider whose narrative function is to be a catalyst and turning point in the unfolding story, and are brought together in a brief concluding segment when the four protagonists from stories two to five happen to meet when travelling to Kathmandu, and go together to visit Lindalou. In addition, Fienberg is able to 'narrativise' abstract concepts by accessing both actual-world and folktale schemata. The stories draw on a common pool of structures, themes and motifs which Fienberg has largely derived from folktale; the repetition of these as narrative elements from story to story constitutes them as a set of schemata which a child audience aggregates through reading the group of stories. For example, each of the protagonists has a unique gift, either innate or acquired, which enables an individual self-fulfilment that also makes the world a better place. Thus what I will refer to as a schema for 'the creative individual', a schema grounded in the difference signalled by some unusual character attribute, is realised by distributing its components across the story so that their aggregation in itself imparts a sense of shapeliness and completeness, and articulates the underlying ideological effect.

The subschemata which comprise 'the creative individual' schema that a child would construct from *The Magnificent Nose and Other Marvels*, and its distribution across the stages of the narrative schema, are set out in Table 14.1.

Table 14.1 Schema for the 'creative individual'	
Narrative stage	**Subschemata of the 'creative individual' schema**
Orientation	1. the protagonist is distinguished by an unusual quality
Complication	2. the primary unusual quality may be enhanced by a second quality 3. the protagonist's unusual quality either poses a problem to family or community or is used to solve problems 4. the unusual quality is instrumental in the protagonist's development of subjective agency
Resolution	5. the unusual quality proves to be a general boon to humankind.

The major schematic difference amongst the five stories occurs with subschema 3, where 'Lindalou' is unique because her gift impacted adversely upon her family — her constant hammering had the effect that 'Her mother bought a set of earplugs. Her father wore a pillow around his head' (p. 7). Apart from this exception within the opening frame story, each story employs a common configuration of the five subschemata as a narrative scaffold.

It also, simultaneously, functions as an ideological orientation by powerfully affirming the value of heterogeneity.

Because the stories are principally about subjectivity in a state of becoming, the protagonist's unusual quality, which is pivotal for the narrative, constitutes the orientation. The revelation or acquisition of an enhancing second quality is an aspect of complication because it is its addition that enables the protagonist to make a difference:

- Lindalou acquires additional woodworking tools;
- Andy Umm's introspectiveness is enhanced by an ability to converse with animals;
- Ferdinand's inexhaustible curiosity is enhanced by a chance gift of magic spectacles with which 'he could see right through skin and flesh to the dark, pumping world below' (p. 23);
- Ignatius Binz's delicate power of smell seeks a larger arena than the perfume factory because of his urge to be part of the wider world; and
- Valentina Lookwell not only has the gift of being able 'to look right into people, and see them as they really were' (p. 37), but has the gift of painting things in a lifelike way — by combining these, she 'made a change in the world' (p. 45).

The stories' affirmation of heterogeneity is grounded in the protagonist's unusual quality and particularly in its instrumentality in enabling the development of subjective agency in the forms of self-constitution, moral integrity, and a combination of altruism and self-awareness that enables meaningful interpersonal relations. This latter aspect is perhaps seen most clearly in the story of Andy Umm, when he volunteers to take over as Lion Tamer after the expert had quit because the lion had become too fierce. Andy's understanding of the lion's need for a deep intersubjective relationship prompts him to risk his own life and eventually to be acknowledged by the lion as 'The best Lion Tamer in the history of the world' (p. 20). Thus the fourth subschema — the protagonist's development of subjective agency — functions as an emergent theme in the complication of the narrative and drives it on to its resolution, in which the unusual quality is recognised as a general boon to humankind.

The intertwining of the narrative schema and the 'creative individual' schema in itself imparts a sense of narrative shapeliness and completeness. In contrast to Bridget's multiple, diverse episodes, and more like Raphael's simpler structure, each story follows the orientation–complication–resolution schema either with only one substantial episode in the complication ('Ignatius Binz') or a sequence of similar incidents functioning as preludes to a pivotal event ('Andy Umm', 'Curious Ferdinand' and 'Valentina Lookwell'). It is much denser at any given point, though, as the framing story well illustrates.

As remarked above, 'Lindalou and her Golden Gift' does not completely actualise 'the creative individual' schema, but it does lay the ground for its subsequent ideological significance. The book begins with Lindalou's birth, and immediately introduces a significant variation into the 'birth of a child' schema:

When Lindalou was born, her mother and father were surprised.

Her aunt fainted.

The cat's whiskers fell off.

> For curled in each of Lindalou's little fists were two strange and beautiful things. In her right hand lay a tiny golden hammer. In her left lay a golden nail.
>
> Lindalou was a quiet baby. She smiled when her mother filled her cradle with teddies and ducks and woolly tigers. But she didn't play with them.
>
> Lindalou played only with her tiny golden hammer and tiny golden nail.
>
> (Fienberg, 1991: 5)

There are three key, if obvious, variations of the underlying schema here. First, the text invokes the expected joy at the birth of a child by displacing it by the 'surprise' of the parents and the more extreme responses of aunt and cat. The situation is more like a birth in a folktale where the parents have breached some dire interdiction. Second, the fantastic element of the child born holding mysterious objects is a minor folktale schema — for example, in the Norwegian story 'Tatterhood' the eponymous heroine is born riding a goat and waving a wooden spoon (see Asbjörnsen and Moe: 1969: 240).[4] Third, Lindalou's creative gift is so strong that from the outset she resists the interpellative socialisation (signified metonymically by the catalogue of stuffed toys) that would make her just like any other child, although at this stage the symbolic significance of the hammer and nail is more potential than actual. The important effect of evoking the 'birth of a child' schema here is to emphasise the tension between individual and normative behaviours.

I suggested earlier that a young writer's narrative is apt to be linked by temporal relationships rather than by causality. The sequence of events in 'Lindalou' is, of course, marked by temporals, but its various episodes also tend to be linked by an underlying causal succession rather than by simple temporal succession. Thus Lindalou's first creative products are three small boxes. After they have been completed, she dreams of a house in the trees and wakes to find inside her boxes the woodworking tools requisite for going on to build the more complex structure. A key omission from the story is any suggestion about how the tools got there, and so they are most readily understood within a schema for creativity, as one creative act enables the conception of a greater act, and this act in turn produces the means for its actualisation. In other words, the whole procedural sequence is the product of Lindalou's imaginative processes. When at the close of the story Lindalou uses her flying boat to take her family and neighbours on a trip to Kathmandu (a place simultaneously actual and mythical), the 'flight' of the imagination is fully figured. Although Fienberg comes close to spelling out the metonymic significance of Lindalou's golden tools when the narrative declares her parents' acceptance of her difference by posing the question, 'how could they take away the golden gifts that came into the world with Lindalou?' (p. 7), this remains a mere hint towards the significance implied by interplay of schemata that comprises the story's very fabric. The contrast between the highly patterned elements from which the story's significance is woven and Bridget's randomly occurring ideological significances is, needless to say, vast.

Fienberg, no doubt, is not consciously using schema theory. It can be easily identified in what she does because it is a convenient way for talking about how we organise knowledge and narrative. When we do look at the story in the way I have, we can see that it is very schemata-driven in a balance of familiarity and newness which offers a young audience three things: familiar objects, situations and structures; models for thinking in new ways about the familiar, as with Lindalou's hammer and nail; and models for constructing new schemata. In this sense, schemata render a narrative more readily accessible to a young audience and facilitate their movement through it. At the same time, to note the articulation of a schema in a framing story, and the repetition of a version of it in four following stories, emphasises how very ideologically marked the procedure is. Like most other representational strategies in children's literature, this one is intrinsically double-sided: it enables texts to be written and read; it also tends to inscribe ideological significances within the process itself.[5]

Bibliography

Adams, M.J. and Collins, A. (1979) 'A Schema-Theoric View of Reading', in *New Directions in Discourse Processing*, R.O. Freedle (ed.). Ablex, Norwood, NJ, pp. 1–22.

Asbjörnsen, P.C. and Moe, J.I. (1969) *Popular Tales from the Norse* (translated by George Webb Dasent). The Bodley Head, London.

Cook-Gumperz, J. and Green, J.L. (1984) 'A Sense of Story: Influences on Children's Storytelling Ability', in *Coherence in Spoken and Written Discourse*, D. Tannen (ed.). Ablex, Norwood, NJ, pp. 201–18.

Crawford, M. and Chaffin, R. (1986) 'The Reader's Construction of Meaning: Cognitive Research on Gender and Comprehension', in *Gender and Reading: Essays on Readers, Texts, and Contexts*, E.A. Flynn and P.P. Schweickart (eds). The Johns Hopkins University Press, Baltimore, pp. 3–30.

Fienberg, A. (1991) *The Magnificent Nose and Other Marvels*. Allen & Unwin, North Sydney.

Hicks, D. (1990) 'Narrative Skills and Genre Knowledge: Ways of Telling in the Primary School Grades', *Applied Psycholinguistics* 11, pp. 83–104.

Hudson, J.A. and Shapiro, L.R. (1991) 'From Knowing to Telling: the Development of Children's Scripts, Stories, and Personal Narratives', in *Developing Narrative Structure*, A. McCabe and C. Peterson (eds). Lawrence Erlbaum Associates, Hillsdale, NJ.

Phelps, E.J. (1978) *Tatterhood and Other Tales*. The Feminist Press, New York.

Rumelhart, D.E. (1980) 'Schemata: The Building Blocks of Cognition', in *Theoretical Issues in Reading Comprehension*, R.J. Shapiro et al. (eds). Lawrence Erlbaum, Hillsdale, NJ, pp. 33–58.

Stein, N.L. and Glenn, C.G. (1979) 'An Analysis of Story Comprehension in Elementary School Children', in *New Directions in Discourse Processing*, R.O. Freedle (ed.). Ablex, Norwood, NJ, pp. 53–119.

Stephens, J. (1992) *Language and Ideology in Children's Fiction*. Longman, London and New York.

Taylor, S.E. and Crocker, J. (1981) 'Schematic Bases of Social Information Processing', in *Social Cognition. The Ontario Symposium. Volume 1*, E.T. Higgins et al. (eds). Lawrence Erlbaum, Hillsdale, NJ, pp. 89–134.

Thorndyke, P.W. and Yekovich, F.R. (1980) 'A Critique of Schema-based Theories of Human Story Memory', *Poetics* 9, pp. 23–49.

Endnotes

1 Both are 'found' stories, in the sense that they were independently written for pleasure, not elicited as a task of any kind. I owe special thanks to Bridget and Raphael for permission to quote and discuss their stories.

2 The inspiration is 'literary' in the sense that Disney movies are obvious and evoked pre-texts for Bridget's story. *Peter Pan* is not only the source for Captain Hook but also for the conceptualisation of the leprechauns' subterranean hall and the conflict between pirates and leprechauns. Empathy with Happy is established through the association with the 'lovable' dwarfs of *Snow White*.

3 The latter stance is characteristic of various strands of poststructuralist thought, but the main strands are generally associated with the work of Louis Althusser and Jacques Lacan. In 'Valentina Lookwell …', Valentina's ability to perceive an individual's innate subjectivity enables her to free them from false interpellation, so that a character can 'just be himself' (p. 40).

4 In a note to her retelling of 'Tatterhood', Phelps suggests that the tale 'deals with the themes of individuality and nonconformity' (1978, p. 163). As such, it seems a significant pre-text for 'Lindalou and her Golden Gift'.

5   An earlier version of this chapter appeared in a paper — *Revue Belge de Philologie et d'Histoire* 73, 3(1995): 853–63.

Chapter 15

Sociocultural background as a factor in acquisition of narrative discourse skills

Myrna Machet

It is often assumed that stories as a form of text can cross any border and be accessed by children irrespective of their background. However, an important element of accessibility within a multicultural environment is the underlying text structure. There are specific requirements for understanding and accessing Western narrative discourse structure. In this chapter I will examine the ability of African children from a predominantly oral background to access this form of discourse, and then discuss some interventive strategies which might further assist them to do so.

Narrative discourse structure

Stories are reflections of social values, beliefs and goals that underlie and involve human interaction. At the centre of the story is a sequence of events that records the dilemmas people encounter and the methods used to resolve these dilemmas. Each culture will have its own stories with themes that are relevant to that particular social group (Stein, 1988: 282–3). Stories are a particular category of text and as such have a conventional structure that is familiar to the general reader. This helps the reader to comprehend and remember the text. Researchers who have examined the story as a particular category of prose have developed story grammars or schemata which attempt to define the prototypical structure underlying simple stories. A story schema may be defined as:

> a set of rules specifying the structural units present in a story and the manner in which they are logically ordered and related to one another. Thus, the grammar specifies the ideal form of what the reader/listener expects in a story (i.e. the schema) as well as what might be directly experienced (i.e. heard or read).

> (Buss et al. 1983: 22)

On the basis of research into what is regarded as a story, Stein (1988: 291) concluded that the ideal form of a good story for a Western adult is a goal-based story with the inclusion of an obstacle and an ending. A coherent goal-oriented story includes the following elements: a setting; an initiating event and/or an internal response that includes a goal; an overt attempt to attain the goal; a consequence and a reaction. The use of linguistic connectives such as *and*, *then*, *because* is important for establishing causality and goals as is the use of internal state information (Benson, 1996: 230). Younger children (5 to 7 years old) think a descriptive sequence, an action sequence and a reactive sequence is a good story. Adults, however, make clear distinctions between narratives that are causally structured and those that are not; and non-causal sequences are not rated as stories by Western adults (Stein, 1988: 289, 295). Most formal definitions of stories require that both temporal and causal relationships connect events. This is reflected in the various story grammars that have been developed, which are all based on the assumption that the behaviour described in stories is goal-directed and motivated (Glenn, 1978: 229). Readers or listeners use the story grammar to guide comprehension during encoding and as a retrieval mechanism during recall (Mandler and Johnson, 1977: 111). When a long text is read, the difficulty of comprehension is determined not only by the syntax, vocabulary and concepts at the level of sentences or paragraphs, but also by the overall organisation of text.

In order to understand stories the child needs a large body of knowledge about human 'intentionality' and the social context in which events occur, and, in addition, must be able to use that knowledge to infer implicit aspects described by the story. The child must infer the goals of the protagonist(s), determine the reason a goal is present, infer the strategy that the protagonist is using to achieve his goals, infer how an action is part of the plan, determine the consequences of the action, and infer the emotional reactions on the part of the protagonist(s) to the events determining the goals and to the consequences (Stein and Trabasso, 1982: 184). As the reader tries to represent the incoming textual information in a well-defined structure, inferences serve two main functions: first, to fill in the missing slots in the structure, and second, to connect events in the structure with other events in order to provide a higher level organisation.

As stated above, the schema acts as a general framework within which detailed comprehension processes take place during encoding. This framework performs several functions. First, it directs attention to certain aspects of the incoming material, for example, the words 'once upon a time' indicate that the story will be a traditional folk-story. Second, the framework helps the audience keep track of what has gone before and increases the predictability of what is coming. Finally, the framework indicates when a section of the story is complete and can be stored, or is incomplete and must be held until further material is encoded (Mandler and Johnson, 1977: 111–12). Although the schemata used to encode a story and retrieve it are related, they are not identical. Recall will be influenced by the extent to which the story matches the reader's ideal schema of a story (Mandler and Johnson, 1977: 113). As a result, readers who come to a story without the necessary experiential background or schema may alter stories to fit their expectations when restructuring and remembering them (Machet, 1992). An important factor which influences the understanding and recall of stories is that a story schema may be particular to a specific culture (Kaplan, 1988). A schema for stories from a Western cultural background may diverge greatly from schemata from other cultural backgrounds (Kintsch and Greene, 1978).

Another important aspect of a reader's or listener's ability to access the story is cohesion. The two types of cohesion, temporal and causal, reflect two distinct narrative orientations:

one of linearly sequencing events and the other as indicating the consequences and meaning of such events. A major component of comprehension involves determining how the episodes in a story are connected. According to Goldman and Varnhagen (1986: 402), events that have a more direct causal relationship with other events will be more readily retrieved than those that have weaker connections to other events. Therefore, it can be assumed that in a summary the causal links should be strongly represented.

When elaboration is not provided in the story, readers will add information which is consistent with that given in the story. Glenn's research (1978) indicates that inferences are a normal part of the comprehension process and that people are capable of making numerous inferences even from very short passages. Inferences in narratives are based mainly on three identifiable sources of information: logical relations between events specified in the texts; informational relations between events specified in the text; and the reader's world knowledge about the objects, actions and events specified in the text. Relevant inferences specify information about what happened and why.

Children's internalisation of narrative structure

In order for a child to understand a story, the world of story must be fully assimilated into his or her general view of the world, and made sense of on the child's own terms (Applebee, 1978: 44). Children learn to construct a story schema from two sources: from listening to stories and learning how they are typically constructed, including aspects such as typical beginnings and endings; and from experience which includes knowledge about causal relationships and various kinds of action sequences. The units which form the final story schema will either condense or ignore many aspects of logical and experiential knowledge about the world. Only those perceptions, feelings, actions and events which are essential to the plot will be represented in the final schema, even though they may subsume other logical and psychological conditions (Mandler and Johnson, 1977: 111–12). In narrative every detail must be relevant to the story and contribute to its development.

Research on early acquisition of causal connectors shows that Western children as young as three years connect references to a psychological or mental state with whatever else they know about the events around it — particularly with precipitating and consequent actions of the participants involved. This may be a common communicative convention in Western-European languages (Bamburg and Damrad-Frye, 1991: 697). Older children are more likely to impose a causal structure on their narratives and to tell stories with causally embedded episodes (Stein, 1988: 290). It can, therefore, be assumed that children from Western cultures will include causal connectors in their summary of a story from a relatively young age.

Parents or caregivers, when they start to tell or read stories to a child, teach the particular narrative structure used within their culture. In Western mainstream societies this usually involves training children to listen for the essential elements of a story in a procedure which closely replicates what happens in a conventional Western school environment. Children coming from an oral environment will have been taught different structures and as a result listen and look for different elements (Heath, 1982, 1983, 1984). Oral story structure may be cyclic or episodic, with stories seldom having a formal beginning or ending. It does not have the controlled temporal and causal chain ordering the conventions of Western literate narrative (Michaels, 1986), but is episodic and utilises a topic-associating style, which consists of a series of sections or episodes implicitly linked together by emphasising some person or theme. It has no plot in the way it is understood in literate societies; that is, a climactic linear structure (Ong, 1982).

Protagonists in the oral tradition are reactive; that is, the events happen to a person, whereas in Western stories protagonists are proactive, initiating and in some way controlling the action. The listeners often act as a chorus encouraging and responding to the storyteller, but there is no interactive questioning to highlight important elements of the story. Adults do not separate the elements of the environment around the child to focus his or her attention selectively, so children do not have elements of their experience isolated for them. Adults do not simplify their language, or label items or features of objects either in books or the environment at large. Children must themselves select, practice, and determine rules of production and structuring from an almost continuous stream of communication. They appear to develop connections between situations or items by configuration links, rather than by specifying labels and features in the situations (Heath, 1982: 64–70). Thus they can answer questions such as 'What's that like?' but they can rarely name the specific feature(s) which make two items alike.

Western narrative structure places certain demands on readers which may not be met by readers from different cultures. My research on African children from a predominantly oral culture in South Africa indicates that particular aspects of Western literate story structure are not accessible to these children because their indigenous story structure differs in essential elements from that of the Western story (Machet, 1993). The following differences were identified through empirical research as having an effect on accessibility.

Differences in narrative discourse structure between Western literate stories and oral stories

Form of story

In my study, the respondents had a problem seeing logical and causal connections in a story (Machet, 1993). Whereas Western children will recall incidents which are linked causally better than other aspects of the story (Applebee, 1978: 58–72; Stein, 1988: 290) this was not the case with these children. Their recall of the stories was random. Many of the structural elements that Westerners take for granted were not understood or perceived by these children. They recalled the stories according to an episodic structure rather than the linear structure and as a result often missed the point of the story altogether. In contrast, in her research with Western children Glenn (1978) found the opposite: those elements of the story that form the causal centre around which the story is organised were better recalled than other types of information. One must conclude that the African children did not organise their story around a causal centre. They also seldom indicated temporal or causal connections or motivation. A large percentage of the respondents (who were all 11 years or older) did not include a goal, which is an essential element of a Western story (Machet, 1993). Research with Western respondents indicates that by the age of nine the vast majority of respondents include goals (Berman 1988; Trabasso and Nickels, 1992).

Channel constraints

A reader who comes from an oral background lacks familiarity with the conventions used in written discourse to convey emotions or physical movement, to group together pieces of information so as to emphasise certain sections and to downplay others, to indicate a shift in theme or subject, and to establish and maintain perspective within a topic (Collins and Michaels, 1986). These would be conveyed by an oral narrator through facial expression, movement and intonation. The children from a predominantly oral culture did not have the schemata to enable them to understand or perceive the connections or structures in a piece of written text. They were unable to perceive shifts in the text indicating psychological changes in characters. For example, they were able to understand anger when it was displayed through physical aggression but not as an internal reaction or state of mind (Machet, 1993).

They were also unable to identify important sections of the text and separate these from less important aspects. They failed to centre on a single topic or series of closely related topics and there was little thematic development or lexical cohesion. Their summaries had few lexicalised markers besides 'and' between topics which made them difficult to follow if one was expecting the summaries to focus on a single event or object.

Formulaic

Oral 'literature' is made up of formulas or cliches which have accumulated meaning within the society. Although an oral storyteller will tell the story differently each time, the story will be composed of set formulas which already exist in the culture. The individuality lies in the storyteller's ability to combine these formulaic elements effectively and dramatically rather than to display literary originality, as would be expected in a literate society (Opland, 1983: 52, 164). Redundancy is closely related to the use of formulas. The elements of oral thought and expression tend to be groups of similar or antithetical terms, phrases or clauses (Bowerman, 1981). For example, in oral discourse the soldier will be the brave soldier, the princess will be the beautiful princess.

These factors are important when considering accessibility of text because in a culture with a high residue of orality it is possible that readers will relate better to works that display a formulaic character with familiar cliches they can recognise. This proved to be so in terms of cliches and structure. Fourteen children were interviewed and all except one preferred traditional trickster tales or fairytales to other forms of storybooks even though they were between 11 and 14 years old, well past the age that most Western children have stopped reading fairy stories. They also used redundant expressions, such as the wicked wolf, in their own summaries (Machet, 1993).

Emphasis on action

Because of the relatively short attention span of the listening audience, in oral literature the emphasis is on telling the story through actions, incidents and dialogue. The narrative style concentrates on presenting a clear visual picture of outward appearance and movement (Ho, 1990). In literate stories the emphasis is often on character development rather than action.

My respondents better remembered the elements of the story that had a higher level of activity than descriptive elements (Machet, 1993). The characters in oral narrative are usually flat, heroic and stereotypical as these types of characters are easier to remember (Bowerman, 1981: 162). This differs from the more rounded character typically used in literate stories. The respondents saw characters as one-dimensional and no attempt was made at differentiating characters from each other in any meaningful way (Machet, 1993).

Ending

In the Western framework no story would be considered complete without a final event that ties all the threads of a story together and indicates the relevance of the other events. However, this may not be an essential element of an oral story framework. Although all stories in oral tradition have a dramatic structure (Fischer, 1963: 237), they do not necessarily include some form of resolution of conflict. Conflict may be created and deliberately not resolved (Finnegan, 1967: 30). Thus a number of traditional African stories have unsatisfactory endings from a Western reader's point of view.

The respondents failed to include a cogent resolution or to provide evaluative comments, both of which have been identified as a common trait of Western narrators (Michaels, 1986). The children did not see a final resolution as an essential part of a story, and did not use devices that would have enabled them to evaluate, interpret and conclude the stories adequately by Western standards. They did not attempt to make their summaries of the stories meaningful but simply listed those events they could remember. Many omitted the last event or failed to complete the sequence as they did not see its relevance. Because they did not understand the underlying meaning of the story they failed to recognise and remember which elements were important. The emphasis of the summaries was on action and there was no attempt at evaluation or interpretation (Machet, 1993).

It can be concluded that Western story structure is largely inaccessible to children from an oral environment. It is important that children master this structure as not only are stories structured this way but most forms of Western exponential discourse reflect elements of this structure. For example, in history one of the first things that is taught is the reasons for things happening and the result. This is not to imply that Western discourse structures are superior to other forms, but it must be recognised that children who have not learned this discourse structure will be marginalised in terms of higher education and long-term employment opportunities. This marginalisation is reflected in South Africa by high failure and drop-out rates. For example, the average failure rate of Grade 1 in the West Coast region in 1996 was 21 per cent. In some rural areas (where the majority of children come from an oral environment) it was as high as 50 per cent (Pretorius, 2001: 13).

Although text is still the predominant means whereby individuals acquire subject knowledge it has been postulated that it is possible that nonlinear hypertext will be a closer approximation to the oral method of communication and that children from an oral culture might find information in this form easier to understand. The tendency during linear text processing is for readers to operate in a more private individualistic manner. Linear texts favour more individualistic cognition during the reading act whereas nonlinear hypertexts seem to encourage more social cognition. However, learners situated in these nonlinear text environments still need to have the microprocessing strategies to make sense of print (Alexander, Kulikowich and Jetton, 1994: 216). Learners require the ability to build a conceptual map or schematic representation of what they are reading and this is likely to be more difficult with hypertext which offers multiple possibilities than with traditional linear text which already has guidelines in place to help inexpert readers. This is particularly true when learners are working in a field where their domain knowledge is poor. In these cases learners rely on general text-processing strategies which may not work effectively when working with nonlinear hypertext.

The following interventive strategies are suggested as an attempt to address the problem of children lacking a story schema.

Interventive strategies

There are many negative factors in African children's literacy environment. Many parents do not have the discretionary income to enable them to afford to buy books for their children and libraries are often not easily accessible as they have been built predominantly in areas that were traditionally white areas. Black parents frequently opt out of the child's education not because of disinterest but because they feel that they have nothing to give the child that will be of value. Many children are no longer experiencing the rich oral culture of storytelling — an important pre-literacy experience. Parents are too busy and too tired in the evenings to spend time telling young children stories. Also, many parents feel that their oral culture of storytelling does not have a value in today's high-tech world. Thus children are deprived of any form of storytelling. This has a serious negative affect as children start school without any story schema and also tend to develop a negative feeling towards their own indigenous culture as they feel it is inferior to a Western culture (Machet and Olën, 1997a).

This background is not usually taken into account when teaching children to read. Children are taught to read in a way which does not assist them to develop a meaningful concept of text or reading because teachers assume that children will be aware of this. Reading is taught as a bottom-up process and its interactive nature is ignored. Even once it is learnt, reading requires both top-down and bottom-up processing. This is important with children who have no preliterate experience and are not exposed to books in the home. Any teaching system that focuses on one level at a time diminishes the possibility of producing competent readers (Cole and Griffen, 1986: 119).

In South African education the predominant paradigms are Western. However, an important factor is that the literacy codes and texts selected for use in schools will be interpreted and mediated by the teacher in the classroom in the process of transmission. This is significant as, although books may be selected that reflect a linear causal structure, it is probable that within the school situation the causal structure will not be transmitted or mediated to the child due to the fact that many of the African teachers do not perceive it themselves. On the other hand, white teachers take it for granted that by the time children come to school they will have internalised this schema, so they also fail to mediate it.

My research showed that teachers who were trained to actively mediate books for learners, helped learners understand and internalise this discourse structure. Direct instruction in text structure and use of organisational devises promotes comprehension.

The use of questions related to elements of story structure is an effective technique that teaches learners to organise and retain important information. Teachers need to be provided with support packages for the most popular stories to enable them to do this, as many of them have not internalised this discourse structure. These packages consist of a background poster, figurines and activity cards which assist the teacher in teaching the child linear story structure as well as causal and temporal structures. The teacher will show a picture from the story and then ask the children questions such as: 'What comes next?'; or 'Why did this cause that to happen?' Although these activities were primarily developed to teach language skills, through them the children are also taught how Western story structure works. These interventions should start as early as Grade 1 to have maximum effect.

A number of other studies substantiate this finding and show that teaching learners about story grammars will have positive effects. Various types of story mapping instruction may be used to enhance multiple dimensions of learner's comprehension such as their ability to recognise central story ideas, to recall important story elements, to compose well-formed narratives, to make predictions and to organise their thinking (Baumann and Bergeron, 1993: 409–10; Fox and Wright, 1997: 387). Teaching schema which are culture-specific helps both story comprehension and recall (Mahoney, Hull and Shillaw, 1997: 67). Children are able to transfer this knowledge of story structure to unfamiliar stories and are better able to comprehend narrative features (Baumann and Bergeron, 1993: 431). Explicit instruction in story grammar and drawing up story maps can result in positive effects on reading comprehension skills as the emphasis on story structure serves as a framework to highlight important relations which in turn lead to a deeper understanding of the story. Stories are mapped by identifying important information about the characters and events in the story. Story maps should include character, time, place, problem, goal, action and outcome. They are visual tools that delineate the most important ideas and reflect the linkage of concepts and facts within a passage and help learners generate questions about narrative stories (Gardill and Jitendra, 1999: 2).

An important means of increasing children's understanding of the underlying structure is through retelling stories. Research shows that learner's knowledge of story structure is increased when they retell the stories they read. Retelling helps children develop greater insight into how to use the structure of stories to organise their thinking and helps them recall more information (Fox and Wright, 1997: 398).

Through use of story schema, learners' ability to tell stories will also progress more rapidly to include narrative detail, descriptive contextualisation and evaluative devices. By bringing the structural frameworks to their conscious awareness, learners are more able to focus on the mechanics of production (Liskin-Gasparro, 1996: 283). An approach to teaching storytelling skills might be to have learners build their own stories from the bottom up, first plotting the narrative line, then pinpointing where contextualised detail would be effective and finally inserting both internal and external evaluative devices at appropriate points (Liskin-Gasparro, 1996: 283). Another approach which may be useful in a multicultural classroom is to allow learners to analyse their own oral narratives and identify the underlying structure.

In higher grades a free voluntary reading program can help learners internalise story structure. Most children in South Africa have limited access to storybooks as few schools have libraries and public libraries are often not easily accessible. In addition, homes may not have storybooks for children. Children's experience of stories is thus frequently limited to the few readers they are given at school. In a research project on the effect of free voluntary reading on children's comprehension of English (the participants were all African children who were second-language English speakers) it was found that the improvement over an eight-month period was significant. Exposure to storybooks and time spent reading can help children to internalise a Western story structure (Machet and Olën, 1997b). However, in the project the emphasis was on the number of books children read and children were thus discouraged from re-reading books. Re-reading books is important as this gives children more time to internalise the structures which are unfamiliar to them. It is thus not a good idea to have readathons where children are rewarded for the number of books that they read. It is preferable to allow children to read at their own pace and to re-read stories if they wish to.

Children need to be actively motivated to read and provided with books which reflect their own culture and which will help to give them pride in their cultural heritage. There are very few books available which contain information, attitudes and values that the African child can take back home and use. One of the reasons for this is that in South Africa publishing is still largely controlled by whites. Although there are an increasing number of African publishers and authors there is still a dearth of children's books that reflect alternative text structures. Part of the problem is that writers have frequently been through the educational system and internalised Western discourse structures. In addition there is growing pressure for education in English rather than the indigenous languages. It is estimated by the READ Educational Trust that as many as 80 per cent of schools are teaching in English (Roberts, 1999) whereas only 9 per cent of the population speak English as a first language (*South African survey 1995/6* 1996: 16). Most books available in English reflect Western structures. Publishers have tried publishing children's story books in the other nine official indigenous languages but the market for these books is very limited and they have found, in general, that it is not financially viable.

Although many South African publishers perceive the need to make children's books more Afrocentric, they seem to feel that this is achieved by making the main protagonist a black child, giving the book a South African setting or having black children in the illustrations. The books are still Eurocentric in terms of values, text structure and world view.

Another pertinent issue is that many of the causal and temporal connections that are present in a Western story are implicit, because they are so much part of a Westerner's schema that they are taken for granted. However, this is not the case for African children from an oral environment who do not share a Westerner's framework. An effort should be made to make these connections as explicit as possible. Further, causal connections tend to lengthen sentences, and so are frequently taken out in an attempt to simplify text for second language readers and make them, superficially at least, easier to understand. For many African readers, however these causal structures are not self-evident and need to be highlighted.

In their studies with children from an oral environment Heath (1983) and Michaels (1986) found that although these children did not have linear cognitive structures they were able to see metaphorical connections that teachers themselves were unable to see because they were limited by their linear thought processes. This has been substantiated by anecdotal evidence in South Africa. African children are often very sensitive to the underlying symbolic meaning, particularly in stories with a traditional structure.

In a multicultural environment teachers should broaden their teaching base. Instead of teaching only one narrative structure that is implicitly assumed to be superior, children should be exposed to a number of alternative structures. This increases sensitivity and understanding of other cultures as well as extending cognitive skills.

Conclusion

Western research and education systems are based on a primarily technological world view which places great value on clarity and precision in the framework of a rigorously logical system (Kaplan, 1988: 290). Western thought structures are often perceived as superior to those of other cultures and it is therefore perceived as right to impose these structures on other cultures as an improvement. Western paradigms, however, should not simply be imposed on African children, who may have alternative cognitive structures which may be more creative than the linear Western models.

Literacy must be culturally specific in order to be culturally meaningful. Western children, when going to school, have their cultural value and patterns reinforced, giving them pride in their culture. African children experience the opposite. School denigrates traditional ways of doing things and makes these children feel incompetent and inadequate. Every child has the right to feel a pride in his or her own cultural heritage. When the child is alienated from this culture, he or she is placed in the impossible situation of either rejecting home or the school. Unless the teacher adapts his or her teaching methodology to take this into account and to begin from where the children are, these children soon become disillusioned with school as they are unable to adapt to the demands of the teacher or relate to the teaching methodology. Research on education in South Africa (Macdonald, 1990) indicates that the teaching methods used in schools are often inaccessible to African children and alienate the child from the system.

The school curriculum should build on the children's strengths. By starting from where their students are, teachers can increase their students' abilities. This does not mean that Western methodologies should not be taught, as these methodologies are essential for disciplines like science and mathematics, rather that they should not be taught at the expense of the children's indigenous thinking patterns. By teaching children additional narrative structures their repertoire is broadened; by replacing one paradigm with another, their abilities are reduced.

Bibliography

Alexander, P.A., Kulikowich, J.M. and Jetton, T.L. (1994) 'The role of subject-matter knowledge and interest in the processing of linear and non-linear texts', *Review of Educational Research*, 64, 2, pp. 210–52.

Applebee, A. (1978) *The Child's Concept of Story: Ages two to seventeen*. University of Chicago Press, Chicago.

Bamburg, M. and Damrad-Frye, R. (1991) 'On the ability to provide evaluative comments: Further explorations of children's narrative competencies', *Journal of Child Language*, 18, pp. 689–710.

Baumann, J.F. and Bergeron, B.S. (1993) 'Story map instruction using children's literature: Effects on first graders' comprehension of central narrative elements', *Journal of reading behavior*, 25, 4, pp. 407–37.

Benson, M.S. (1996) 'Structure, conflict and psychological causation in the fictional narrative of 4- and 5-year-olds', *Merrill-Palmer Quarterly*, 42, 2, pp. 228–47.

Berman, R. (1988) 'On the ability to relate events in narrative', *Discourse Processes*, 11, pp. 469–99.

Botvin, G. and Sutton-Smith, B. (1977) 'The development of structural complexity in children's fantasy narratives', *Developmental Psychology*, 13, 4, pp. 377–88.

Bowerman, M. (1981) 'Language development', in *Handbook of Cross-Cultural Psychology: Developmental psychology* vol 4, H. Triandis and A. Heron (eds). Allyn and Bacon, Boston, Mass.

Buss, R. et al. (1983) 'Development of children's use of a story schema to retrieve information', *Developmental Psychology*, 19, 1, pp. 22–8.

Cole, M. and Griffen, P. (1986) 'A Sociohistorical Approach to Remediation', in *Literacy, Society and Schooling: a Reader*, S. de Castell, A. Luke and K. Egan (eds). Cambridge University Press, Cambridge.

Collins, J. and Michaels, S. (1986) 'Speaking and writing: Discourse strategies and the acquisition of literacy', in *The Social Construction of Literacy*, edited by J. Cook-Gumperz. Cambridge University Press, Cambridge, Mass.

Cook-Gumperz, J. (ed.), *The Social Construction of Literacy*. Cambridge University Press, Cambridge, Mass.

Finnegan, R. (1967) *Limba Stories and Story-telling*. Clarendon Press, Oxford.

Fischer, J. (1963) 'The sociopsychological analysis of folktales', *Current Anthropology* 4, pp. 235–95.

Fox, B.J. and Wright, M. (1997) 'Connecting school and home literacy experiences through cross-age reading', *Reading teacher* 50, 5, pp. 396–403.

Gardill, M.C. and Jitendra, A.K. (1999) 'Advanced story map instruction: effects on reading comprehension of students with learning disabilities', *Journal of Special Education* 33, 1, pp. 2–17, 28.

Glenn, C. (1978) 'The role of episodic structure and of story length in children's recall of simple stories', *Journal of Verbal Learning and Verbal Behaviour*, 17, pp. 229–47.

Goldman, S. and Varnhagen, C. (1986) 'Memory for embedded and sequential story structures', *Journal of Memory and Language*, 25, pp. 401–18.

Heath, S. (1982) 'What no bedtime story means: Narrative skills at home and school', *Language in Society* 11, pp. 49–76.

—— (1983) *Ways with Words: Language, life and work in communities and classrooms*. Cambridge University Press, Cambridge.

—— (1984) 'Oral and literate traditions', *International Social Science Journal* 99, pp. 41–59.

Ho, L. (1990) 'Chinese narrative theory and readers in English as a second language (ESL)', *International Review of Children's Literature* 5, 1, pp. 29–38.

Kaplan, R. (1988) 'Contrastive rhetoric and second-language learning: Notes towards a theory of contrastive rhetoric', in *Writing Across Languages and Cultures: Issues in contrastive rhetoric*, A. Purves (ed.). Sage Publications, Newbury Park, California.

Kintsch, W. and Greene, E. (1978) 'The role of culture-specific schemata in the comprehension and recall of stories', *Discourse Processes* 1, pp. 1–13.

Liskin-Gasparro, J.E. (1996) 'Narrative strategies: a case study of developing storytelling skills by a learner of Spanish', *Modern Language Journal* 96, pp. 271–86.

Macdonald, C. (1990) *Crossing the Threshold into Standard Three in Black Education. The Consolidated Main Report* of the Threshold Project. Human Sciences Research Council, Pretoria.

Machet, M. (1992) 'The effect of socio-cultural values on adolescents' response to literature', *Journal of Reading* 35, 5, pp. 356–62.

—— (1993) 'Mediated libraries' effect on black South African children's ability to access western story structure', Ph.D. thesis. Rand Afrikaans University, Johannesburg.

Machet M.P. and Olën, S.I.I. (1997a) 'Literacy environment of pupils in urban primary schools', *South African Journal of Library and Information Science* 65(2), pp. 77–84.

—— (1997b) 'Free voluntary reading', in *Journeys in Language and Learning: ESOL students in elementary classrooms around the world*, M. Lewis (ed.) ITP Nelson, Canada.

Mahoney, D., Hull, J. and Shillaw, J. (1997) 'Storing simple stories: narrative recall and the Chinese student', *Language, Culture and Curriculum* 10,1, pp. 66–85.

Mandler, J. and Johnson, N. (1977) Remembrance of things parsed: Story structure and recall. *Cognitive Psychology,* 9: 111-51.

Michaels, S. (1986) 'Narrative presentations: An oral preparation for literacy with first graders', in *The Social Construction of Literacy*, J. Cook-Gumperz (ed.). Cambridge University Press, Cambridge, Mass.

Ong, W (1982) *Orality and Literacy: The technologising of the word*. Routledge, London.

Opland, J. (1983) *Xhosa Oral Poetry: Aspects of a black South African tradition*. Cambridge University Press, Cambridge.

Pretorius, C. (2001) 'And they all learned happily ever after', *Sunday Times* 21, 13 January.

Roberts, B. (1999) READ Educational Trust, 20 April, personal communication.

Rumelhart, D. (1977) 'Understanding and summarising brief stories', in *Basic Processes in Reading: Perception and comprehension*, D. Laberge and S. Samuels (eds). Lawrence Erlbaum Ass, Hillsdale, New Jersey.

South African Institute of Race Relations (1996) *South Africa survey 1995/96*. Johannesburg.

Stein, N. (1988) 'The development of children's storytelling skill', in *Child Language: A reader*, M. Franklin and S. Barten (eds). Oxford University Press, New York.

Stein, N. and Trabasso, T. (1982) 'Children's understanding of stories: A basis for moral judgement and dilemma resolution', in *Verbal Processes in Children: Progress in cognitive development research*, C. Brainerd and M. Pressley (eds). Springer-Verlag, New York.

Trabasso, T. and Nickels, M. (1992) 'The development of goal plans of action in the narration of a picture story', *Discourse Processes* 15, pp. 249–75.

Popular as a dirty word:
investigating literary and cultural biases through a study of Paul Jennings

Jeri Kroll

Introduction

'According to a survey of the reading habits of 17 000 Australian children aged 5 to 12 years, kids today are more likely to turn to *Bumface*, *Gizmo* and *Wicked*' (Walker, 1999: 5). But turn to those contemporary books in preference to what — classics such as *Alice in Wonderland* or *Treasure Island*? What about Enid Blyton and popular series of the more recent past? Writers such as Paul Jennings and Morris Gleitzman dominate the preteen and early teen market in Australia. Word of a new release streaks through playgrounds and schools like a high-speed train and some adults fear that the roar obliterates thoughts of reading anything else.

Whether we like it or not, publishing has succumbed to the pressures of globalisation, and is now one cog in the wheel of multinational machines that spin at their own heady speed. Books targeting the lowest common-denominator reader often become bestsellers. The cultural conscience that some publishers supposedly had in the mid-twentieth century has all but vanished, squeezed out by the pressure to placate company accountants. Does this mean that there is little that qualifies as 'literature' published any more? As Ken Gelder has said of the paranoia that accompanies this debate, 'Popular fiction is literature's Other, the thing literature despises even though it needs it to be, well, literary' (2000: 34). Yet modern publishing has always been entwined with commercial imperatives. In fact, back in 1744, John Newberry, the publisher of *A Little Pretty Pocket-Book*, knew that he must temper 'instruction with delight' (Susina, 1993: v). As Jan Susina suggests, 'perhaps children's literature should be viewed as a test case for all literary texts in that children's books are a more open and obvious mix of artistic, educational and commercial ideologies' (1993: vii).

This chapter will examine what is meant by a children's book, then consider the cultural and literary implications of the term 'popular', before setting Paul Jennings' work in context. A related issue that I will discuss is whether the popularity of one type of book might so overwhelm the market that other types will suffer. In 1992, the theme of the First National Conference of the Children's Book Council of Australia was *At Least They're Reading* and the titles of two panels indicate specific areas of debate: 'Are There Books Children Should Not Be Reading?' and 'What's a Good Book? A Panel on Awards and Reviewing'. Many educators do not agree with the 'At Least They're Reading' principle — fearing that young people will not graduate to more challenging material.

Astute publishers know that children do read differently from their parents, however, and this has inevitably affected what books children make popular. Back in the 1970s, commentators were noting that 'the current media — TV and movies — were already changing children's brains in ways that video games and computers would later accelerate' (Krull, 1999: 567). Jennings is a writer committed to holding young people's attention amidst the buzz of competing technologies. As he says:

> We need to share our stories in order to work out who we are and where we are going. Cultures across the world have always used stories to regulate themselves. Right now I believe that our own culture is turning its back on stories. Never have we had so many badly told, trivial, gratuitous tales served up to us. And children are the main sufferers.
>
> (Ricketson, 2000: 297)

Paul Jennings: the kids' choice

Paul Jennings has been catering for Australia's 'middle-aged' (Foster and Nimon, 1995: 178) children since the 1980s.[1] He is a bestselling star in international terms with the kind of financial success that most Australian writers for adults could only achieve in their imagination — as characters in an airport novel perhaps. To maximise his exposure, Jennings had the added help of three award-winning television series based on his fiction; *Round the Twist*, aired in the 1990s,[2] rated remarkably well both here and overseas (Ricketson, 2000). Any publisher will tell you that is the equivalent of winning a lottery. With the release of Jennings and Morris Gleitzman's collaborative serial novel *Wicked!* his sales in toto have no doubt skyrocketed. *Wicked!* has sold over a million copies to date (Cazzulino, 2000: 10). These figures do not take into account the inevitable boost that the broadcast, in late 2000 in Australia, of the twenty-six part animated television series of *Wicked!* (which is due for release overseas soon) will generate.

Sales figures aside, Jennings has dominated the various states/territories' Children's Choice Awards for years in both the younger and older readers' categories: the BILBY, the COOL, the CROW, the KOALA, the KROC, the WAYRA and the YABBA.[3] Jennings came to understand just what young people enjoy (and what they need) by a circuitous route, however. Trained as a schoolteacher, he eventually did postgraduate study and became a Senior Lecturer at the Warrnambool Institute of Advanced Education ('now part of Deakin University' — Ricketson, 2000: 68). His first stories grew out of his determination to write something enjoyable as well as appropriate for one of his sons, who had reading difficulties.

Serious critical recognition by adults came slowly to Jennings. His first award was not for a book, but for the *Round the Twist* series — an AWGIE (Australian Writers' Guild) Award for Best Children's Adaptation (TV) in 1990 and another AWGIE in 1993 for episode five in series two (pauljennings.com.au/awards/htm). Book reviewers have always emphasised Jennings' accessibility, which allows TV-numbed, computer-hyped children, especially reluctant readers, to persist with stories long enough to enjoy his trademark clever twists. Praise of Jennings' fiction as exuberant fun and admiration of his plotting were often undercut by those who decried the abundant lavatory humour in his collections as well as the sameness of his narrators (mostly Anglo-Celtic males). It was really after the publication of his ninth collection of stories, *Unseen!*, which won the inaugural Queensland's Premier's Literary Award for Best Children's Book in 1999, that Jennings felt he had been accorded the critical approval of his peers (Ricketson, 2000: 194-95). He said in his acceptance speech: 'The real prize is that the children read books, but this is the first time I've won a literary award from adults and I'm incredibly honoured' (quoted in Ricketson, 2000: 195).

Previously, some had perceived the collections of quirky tales as uneven. The Queensland judges noted that here they were 'of equal merit' (Ricketson, 2000: 194–95). Earlier in the year, Pam Macintyre had made a similar evaluation in her critique of *Unseen!* in *Australian Book Review*: 'Apart from 'Piddler on the Roof', which appears to have been included for those who are fixated on the scatological, the collection is uniformly strong' (1998/–1999: 42). She concludes with a summary of Jennings' strengths that can apply to his best work generally:

> Jennings offers a lot to young emerging or tentative readers: fun, suspenseful, accessible, well crafted narratives, themes that echo the concerns and experiences of his young readership without ever preaching, a compassionate view of the world where awful things might happen and do, but in which the individual finds reassurance.
>
> (Macintyre, 1998–1999: 42)

What is the secret of Paul Jennings' ability to attract young readers? Is it that his books are similar to each other, so that children encounter a familiar experience each time? That is one factor behind the success of much popular fiction and series, like *The Baby-Sitters Club*, *Teen Power Inc.*, *The Saddle Club*, *Point Horror*, *Goosebumps* and *Creepers*. Is Jennings now so well known that he has been transformed into a product like adult blockbuster personalities? 'As Stephen King has said, he himself is a brand name like Ivory soap or a Hershey bar — the "Green Giant of horror fiction" ' [Jolly Green Giant — food logo] (Twitchell, 1992: 103–4). Is it that his uncomplicated style as well as his weird mix of fantasy and grossness appeal to both skilled and reluctant readers? I will consider all of these questions in an attempt to demonstrate that Jennings, while writing popular fiction, can also produce complex work that merits scrutiny. This chapter next investigates, therefore, what we mean by 'serious' and 'popular' children's literature.

The conundrum of children's literature

> A children's book is a primer… It's welcome to society, kids, here's how it works.
>
> (Lurie, 1991: 2)

Although critics still argue about what literature is, until the late twentieth century they have usually agreed that books produced for children do not merit inclusion. The dominant Anglo culture's vision of what constituted 'great', 'serious' work (T.S. Eliot, F.R. Leavis, et al.) avoided authoritative definitions, but stemmed from a particular socio-cultural bias (Hunt, 1991: 48–9). Literature designed for those who, by virtue of their age and inexperience, must be deficient in discrimination did not merit critical attention.

Rebecca Lukens, however, one of the advocates for the study of children's literature, argues that in fact this dismissal is ludicrous, because although children are not 'little adults'

(Lukens, 1990: 7), they are still of the same species, simply less knowledgeable. By extension, their literature will deal, albeit in a less sophisticated way, with some of the same themes as adult books. Children's literature should be judged, therefore, using the same critical standards as those applied to work for adults. Morris Lurie makes this point satirically in his 1991 novel *Madness*, where his artist-hero, Tannenbaum, defines 'Kiddie Lit':

> A children's book is a primer. It's a guidebook. It's a standard of behaviour. It's a map. It's welcome to society, kids, here's how it works. It's welcome to avarice, welcome to deceit, welcome to injustice, welcome to the pursuit of happiness and other false goals, welcome to hypocrisy, welcome to toe the line, welcome to never growing up, welcome to insecurity, welcome to terror, welcome to the quashing of the human spirit, welcome to madness, welcome to fear. Did I miss anything out? A goblin somewhere? A wicked witch? A good fairy?
>
> (Lurie, 1991: 70)

In other words, children's literature is not divorced from life but a part of it. If we accept this analysis, then the arguments propounded about the worth of popular versus serious adult literature can apply to popular versus serious children's literature. In his study of cult fiction, in fact, Clive Bloom connects disparaging views about adult pulp with certain critical positions about popular children's material:

> It is a fact that all the arguments here rehearsed regarding adult reading matter can be applied to, or have already been applied to, children's reading matter; debates over quality, taste, the canon, morality and ethical acceptability as well as questions of content and style mirror such debates elsewhere regarding literature, its cultural significance and social importance.
>
> (Bloom, 1996: 6–7)

First, we need to survey some of the characteristics claimed to belong to 'serious' and 'popular' literature. Peter Hunt notes that serious work is often 'thought to be "higher", "denser", "more highly charged", "special", "apart", and so on; it is also thought to be the "best" that a culture can offer', Hunt says, adapting Matthew Arnold's ideas (Hunt, 1991: 50). Dense work, of course, invites readers to revisit it and critics, in their purest form, are passionate readers who (think that they) approach a work 'with no strings attached'. We know, however, that in crucial respects literature for young people has 'strings attached'. As Peter Hunt explains:

> We read literature in a different way from non-literature; we extract from the text certain feelings or responses. Yet with children's books, we cannot escape from the fact that they are written by adults; that there is going to be control, and that it is going to involve moral decisions. Equally, the book is going to be used not to entertain or modify *our* views, but to form the views of a child.
>
> (Hunt, 1991: 51)

We come then to the question of functionality. Children's literature might be appreciated in an aesthetic way by a child alone, but we have no clear indications as to when this happens. We do know, however, that teachers, librarians and relatives choose books for young people for particular reasons; for example, 'when the book is an end in itself' and when 'books are means to ends' (Kirk, 1992: 149). Two common uses of literature, then, are to teach children how to evaluate aesthetic objects and to acquire knowledge at the same time. Louise Rosenblatt has coined the term 'efferent' (Lukens, 1990: xi) to explain an experience that involves 'the acquiring of information through … reading' (1990: xi). Certainly this process happens in both nonfiction and fiction, for in novels, let alone fairytales, children can, as Lurie puts it, be 'welcome[d] to society' and find out 'how it works' (Lurie, 1991: 70). In other words, they learn specific information as well as the more abstract cultural norms of their society. An educative purpose, thus, seems to be on the minds of most adults and determines how they evaluate what is published: 'Children's books are defined as much by "good for" as by "good"; and again, by definition, that which is useless cannot be good for the child-reader' (Hunt, 1991: 56).

Yet when children make books popular — that is, when they seek books out, lend them, want to buy more of the same — they follow a different process from seeking out what is 'good for' them. They are usually not thinking (at least in the first instance) about learning. The culture of children is not necessarily understood by adults, or not in the same way as children. Is there (or should there be) what Jeffrey Garrett calls 'a separate and independent poetics of childhood'? (1995–1996: 2). This point leads to a discussion of what we mean by popular, because paradoxically the popular can be both part of the dominant culture and also something subversive — part of the culture of childhood.

Popular as a dirty word

Let's face it: the adjective 'good' is conferred upon children's books by adults. Children, on the other hand, can never make a book 'good,' only popular.

(Garrett, 1995–1996: 2)

Children's books have become big business and in some cases, like the food that is served in many fast food restaurants, children's literature has evolved into a kind of educational junk food, a sort of 'kiddie lite'.

(Susina, 1993: vii)

Popular literature for adults as well as children has received both good and bad press, depending on how 'popular' is defined. Dominic Strinati canvasses the various ways we can understand this term, ranging from opinions engineered by an elite to expressions of genuine widespread belief (1995: 2–3). Berger notes simply that 'some define it as the culture of the ordinary person' (1995: 161). The most relevant definitions are those that refer to 'inferior kinds of work (cf. popular literature, popular press as distinguished from quality press); and work deliberately setting out to win favour … as well as the more modern sense of well-liked by many people, with which … in many cases, the earlier senses overlap' (1995: 2–3). It is this overlapping phenomenon that can often confuse when educators or critics want to assign value to texts.

For example, take the *Harry Potter* novels. Certainly these books are incredibly popular (i.e. well-liked), but are they original and well-crafted or 'popular' in the sense of formulaic? Are they derivative and designed to win favour by being so, as some reviewers have suggested? Perhaps in part they are original and in part formulaic? Which aspects make them 'popular' (well-liked)?

The rush to assign literary value is inevitably bound up with the cultural values a text upholds, whether consciously or unconsciously. As John Fiske explains, 'culture (and its meanings and pleasures) is a constant succession of social practices; it is therefore inherently political, it is centrally involved in the distribution and possible redistribution of various forms of social power' (1989: 1). According to Fiske, the texts of a dominant culture, which are meant to serve both economic and social goals, can also serve the interests of the powerless. 'Children', Paul Jennings maintains, 'have no power. And the powerless always develop ways of mocking those who control them' (Ricketson, 2000: 299).

So literature that children embrace (sometimes against the advice of the moral gatekeepers, sometimes with the coaxing of advertisers) might at times be a form of rebellion for them: '… popular culture … is obvious and superficial … tasteless and vulgar, for taste is social control and class interest masquerading as a naturally finer sensibility' (Fiske, 1989: 6). Fiske goes on to argue that popular texts are by nature ephemeral, because 'as the social conditions of the people change, so do the texts and tastes from which relevances can be produced' (1989:6). Whereas educators want to pass on the classics that they found valuable, the mass of adults as well as children crave some immediately relevant gratification — at least *some* of the time. The extreme position some might take is that what they as adults choose is literature, whereas what most children today would choose, given the chance, is not. But what is it? The confusion here derives from the fact that the word 'popular' can be synonymous with mass-market trash.

It is impossible in the new millennium to discuss what constitutes good and bad literature without briefly considering what has happened to publishing. In a word, as James Twitchell asserts, it has become part of 'showbusiness' (1992: 1), that postmodern melange of cultural industries (including high and low art) that controls all the words we read and the images we see in protean forms, whether on old-fashioned page, advertising billboard, TV, film or computer as well as the associated tie-ins (T-shirts, postcards, lunch boxes and even food). The ultimate goal of every global corporation involved in 'entertainment products' (Twitchell 1992: 6) is to score a blockbuster.

The preferred format for these megaconglomerates with insatiable appetites for product is an endless series or a bestseller that turns the author into a commodity. Most of this work will have little redeeming value. In other words, it is rubbish. But who decides what that is? In his article, 'A Defence of Rubbish', Peter Dickinson talks about 'all forms of reading matter which contain to the adult eye no visible value, either aesthetic or educational' (1976: 74). But, as Dickinson goes on to argue, what some describe as rubbish 'may not be rubbish after all. The adult eye is not necessarily a perfect instrument for discerning certain sorts of values' (1976: 75–6). He believes that 'bad' writing does not necessarily disturb children, who gloss over imperfections and extract what they want or need.

Interestingly, the terms used both to support and berate lowest common-denominator writing are similar. The battleground is the body popular and the prize is health. Consider the frequency of food metaphors. Like nutritionists, some advocate a balanced diet of the 'literary' and the 'popular,' which means for Dickinson 'pap or roughage' (1976: 75)[4] some of the time. Co-creator of the Australian *Creepers* series, Bob Condon, talks about his 'baked bean humour' (1996: 68). Jenny Pausacker describes popular work as 'chips and chocolate' (1998: 115). The fear is, of course, that children will gorge, leaving no room for anything else. That fear has grown as our limited leisure time shrinks and reading competes with the razzle dazzle of other media. Books that do succeed on a global scale tend to be packaged. Twitchell creates an apt analogy, calling trends in adult formula fiction 'franchise entertainments — McGenres — books aspiring to the condition of hamburgers' (1992: 124), which could easily apply to the *Sweet Valley High* or *Goosebumps* series.

A formula for what?

So what characteristics do popular books have? Ken Gelder sets up the cultural oppositions in general terms:

> Literature is creative; popular fiction is about production … Literature has genius; it will grudgingly concede that popular fiction, at its best, is ingenious. Literature has 'style'; popular fiction is functional. Literature is meandering, defiant and complex (like 'life'); popular fiction obediently follows a few simple 'formulas'. On the other hand, literature is 'understated' and evocative, while popular fiction is excessive, exaggerated.
>
> (Gelder, 2000: 34)

Let us look now in particular at what attributes an 'inferior' children's book has. Analysing popular and series fiction, Foster and Nimon list a number of characteristics that begins with 'a dependence on formula', then goes on to list 'commercialization to be more obviously than usual the primary aim … little or no extension of the reader … and actual popularity with children or adolescents' (1995: 177). Finally, these books offer no challenges because of 'unchanging characters' as well as a 'controlled vocabulary' (Foster and Nimon, 1995: 186). The language itself tends to cliche; familiarity makes the prose flow as do uncomplicated sentence structure and short paragraphs.

Another point worth making is that many children's series could be set anywhere in the developed world. In this sense, they do not exalt the ephemeral — they are bland, located, as Tom Engelhardt says, in 'the Great Here–predominantly a land of suburban, middle-class malls, or at best a rural area' (1991: 56). The geography, therefore, cannot add anything to characterisation or plot; children have been globalised out of their individuality.

Perry Nodelman perceives value, however, in some popular books that are not only pleasurable but beneficial precisely because they follow familiar patterns and are therefore 'similar enough to other books to fulfil young readers' expectations' (1996: 167). If these children eventually move on to complex material (but many do not), we can see that they have been able to absorb from formula books 'the basic patterns that less-formulaic books diverge from' (Nodelman, 1996: 168). John Cawelti speaks of the 'special delight' (1976: 1) that young and adult readers find in popular genres that are constructed for the comfort and resonance that come from the 'embodiments of archetypal story forms in terms of specific cultural materials' (1976: 6). In other words, resurrecting these forms for each generation means recasting them in relevant (perhaps ephemeral) terms.

Predictability has another dimension, however. Genre or series' fans seek to identify with a group just as children want to join clubs; sometimes this identification reflects class and educational lines (Bloom, 1996: 5). Like adults, children desperately want to belong. The 'stamp of consumer approval' (Sheahan-Bright, 1999: 12) is often given to what makes children feel accepted, to feel 'acceptably "normal" ' (Nodelman, 1997: 118), whether that means owning a bestseller by Paul Jennings or Morris Gleitzman, or owning a complete set of *Goosebumps*, a series that 'exploits the deep-seated need of the human psyche to belong to a tribe' (Coppell, 1998: 5).

Does popular fiction really damage young people?

> Equal trash for all.
>
> (Silver, 1995: 95)

Is this type of popular work truly damaging? Let us clarify the most significant arguments for and against, which focus on social control, literacy and manipulation of the child as consumer. The first focal point, social control, involves exercise of power. Obviously, our culture's priorities determine how we use all literature. Strinati's questions about the ideology of popular culture could be raised as well about writing for young people:

> Is popular culture [popular children's fiction] there to indoctrinate the people, or to get them to accept and adhere to ideas and values which ensure the continued dominance of those in more privileged positions who thus exercise power over them? Or is it about rebellion and opposition to the prevailing social order?
>
> (Strinati, 1996: 3–4)

Whereas Roald Dahl's anarchic texts, for example, demonstrate challenges to authority characteristic of youth, the *Goosebumps* series' support of the patriarchal order, as analysed by Vicki Coppell recently, demonstrate the goal of 'continued dominance' (Coppell, 1998: 9). Our perception of how damaging this process is will fluctuate with whether we want to support the status quo. John Fiske suggests that many popular texts, although produced by the dominant powers, allow 'the subordinate' a release by 'making do within and against the system, rather than of opposing it directly' (1989: 11). For instance, certain types of romances (including those for teens), might give positive models of relationships to women and, thus, gradually help to change readers' views of what is acceptable.

James Twitchell and Noël Carroll both observe that the horror genre causes the release of tension and aggression, although the dominant society's values are re-established at the end of films or books. Bob Condon discusses this cathartic experience in relation to children, who in reading about monsters experience 'the triumph of facing fears head on', which leads to 'the empowerment of the disempowered' (Condon, 1996: 68). His partner in the *Creeper* series, Robert Hood, clarifies how children's engagement with horror texts substitutes as rebellion:

> Children love pushing the boundaries, eating forbidden fruit (or at least forbidden lollies) and being allowed in some measure to indulge in bad attitudes. It's a way of testing the limits, of coming to understand the ethical chaos through which we're all forced to find our way. Why shouldn't we let them be naughty, here where it's safe?
>
> (Hood, 1996: 81)

According to Nodelman, R.L. Stine, in particular, makes reading 'itself an act of rebellion … The power structure is safe from any actual efforts to change it' (Nodelman, 1997: 119).

The second focal point in the debate about the damaging effects of lowest-common denominator fiction is literacy. Many educators fear the 'dumbing down' of young people. The National Statement on English for Australian Schools divides literature into three sections, including the popular. Teachers can certainly exploit it to provoke discussions about 'the ways that writers use particular linguistic structures and features' (Love, 1994: 77), among other strategies. But how impoverished is young people's understanding of linguistic structures if they read predominantly popular fiction?[5]

Strinati canvasses this problem in general by admitting that popular literature, as identified with 'mass culture', not only 'trivialises', but encourages 'the loss of the skills and abilities required to appreciate and understand high culture' (Strinati, 1995: 15). The fear is that if young people do not develop skills that will enable them to read more complicated literature, they will grow up into adults who will not be able to evaluate, let alone value, what they read. The cliches of the hack impoverish the reading experience. Too many children's books 'have been stripped down to the generic … in fact, to something like a single formulaic literature of anxiety and reassurance, the reassurance sometimes lying only in the fact that another book just like the first is still to be purchased' (Engelhardt, 1991: 56).

Language affects how we think about the world, as George Orwell cogently argued in his still relevant 1945 essay, 'Politics and the English Language'; unfortunately, 'the slovenliness of our language makes it easier for us to have foolish thoughts' (Orwell, 1945) and for others to manipulate us. So mass culture (and its inferior literature) is dangerous because it 'destroys all values, since value judgments imply discrimination' (Strinati, 1995: 16). How could children reared predominantly on this kind of diet develop? Engelhardt foresees that for the majority, 'the only exit increasingly being offered from such a world is into infantilized best-selling genres for adults' (1991: 62).

Few educators would desire the above scenario. Young people might be visually sophisticated, but they are certainly, compared to their parents and grandparents, linguistically deprived, according to recent studies. Twitchell quips:

> One picture may well be worth a thousand words, especially if the audience doesn't understand many words. The average number of words in the written vocabulary of a six- to fourteen-year-old American child in 1945 was twenty-five thousand; the average number today [1992]: ten thousand.
>
> (Twitchell, 1992: 256)

Australian youth literature advocate Agnes Nieuwenhuizen is one of those who attacks the 'At Least They're Reading' principle by insisting that we are 'insulting [young people's] sensibility and intelligence if we assume that all they want to read or are able to read is generic, plot driven, one dimensional shock/schlock/humour/horror fiction' (Nieuwenhuizen, 1996: 74). But it is not simply this reading diet that bothers Nieuwenhuizen so much as the context of its production. This brings us to the third point of contention — the child as consumer rather than reader. When content and style have other than literary motives, popular literature is demonised by profit. For example, the *Goosebumps* series has TV and merchandising tie-ins; the first Jennings-Gleitzman collaboration, *Wicked!*, has followed suit, while their new novel, *Deadly!*, offers postcards and mouse mats.

Ironically, numerous articles in the popular press in recent years have railed against the media giants who have saturated the market and altered concepts of profit. With the growth of chain books stores in developed nations, the ability of a few publishers and distributors to control what young people have access to is terrifying. As Professor Joel Taxel complains, '... this trend will virtually assure the proliferation of the worst of the series and other mass-market books that take up all but a fraction of the space in mall book stores and supermarkets' (Jones, 1995: 9).

Where do we situate a global bestselling writer such as Paul Jennings? He exploits humour, irresistible to children, but humorous books rarely win literary awards. He seems to understand the preoccupations of his target audience and can embody them in texts that are linguistically accessible. In the next sections, I will discuss Jennings' treatment of plot and character as well as his style in order to investigate how he manages to be highly individual and yet widely appealing.

Paul Jennings: weird plots but familiar patterns

I will concentrate on the short story form that made Jennings' reputation because it clearly reveals his strengths and weaknesses as well as how aspects of his plotting follow the pattern of some formula fiction. His favourite authors suggest why his forte is the short story that usually incorporates a moral consciousness: these include 'Ray Bradbury, Somerset Maugham, Chekhov ... I think 'The Gift of the Magi' by O'Henry is the best twist I have read in a short story' (Paul Jennings File, 2000). He admires Charles Dickens, that master of moral melodrama, and in the majority of Jennings' stories he devises an appropriate payback for transgressors.

In this respect, Jennings' work bears comparison with the type of formulaic fiction that has 'a preference for tangible results, clear cut rewards and punishments, plots that work out' (Tucker, 1976: 180). His protagonists, who do not inhabit an ideal world (they might be orphans, they might have embarrassing families, they might be shy or 'unsporty'), generally do not deserve the treatment that they receive from bullies or unscrupulous adults. Nicholas Tucker notes Piaget's opinion about the unimportance, if not direct threat, of the concept of chance in the psyche of children: '... for him [sic] to admit of chance or coincidence is for him to admit that the universe is in fact an unordered, amoral place' (1976: 18). A standard tactic in fairy tales is to provide a fitting end for the wicked, and John Marsden has described Jennings as a writer of contemporary fairytales (Ricketson, 2000: 319).

In Jennings' work, therefore, examples abound of poetic justice, both major and minor. In his first collection, *Unreal!*, Giffen in 'The Strap Box Flyer' pursues profit at the expense not only of people's feelings, but of their lives. Giffen's Great Glue only lasts four hours and so he, too, appropriately falls from grace by falling from the sky, when Flinty uses Giffen's glue to join together his flying invention. The narrator of 'Smart Ice-Cream', full of intellectual superiority, thinks he will outsmart Mr Peppi by stealing his magical ice-cream. But he has no sense of irony; when he eats the 'SMART ICE-CREAM for smart alecs' (1985: 91) he wakes up 'the nekst day' and he 'don't feal quite az smart' (1985: 92). Sometimes a lesson has to be taught on behalf of other creatures. In 'Smelly Feat' (*Unbearable!*), the narrator overcomes Horse and his gang who want to destroy the eggs of Old Shelly, the turtle, by turning a failing into an asset — the pungent smell of his adolescent feet make others narcoleptic.

More recently in *Unseen*, Jennings offers 'One-Finger Salute', where the protagonist has no middle fingers. After swallowing his droptail lizard's tail, he finds he can grow new ones that, unfortunately, detach. Despite the embarrassment this causes, their detachability so horrifies the bully Gumble and his mates that they never insult the narrator again. In 'Piddler on the Roof', Weesle pees out a second-story window and so pollutes the water tank of his obsessively clean aunt and her son Ralph (an extortionist-in-training) who have done nothing but criticise his habits. Whether the transgressions are criminal, morally reprehensible, environmentally irresponsible or merely schoolyard torture, Jennings tries to devise an appropriate response. Once young readers have absorbed the reward-and-punishment structure, they anticipate the twist in the next story. What is truly original in Jennings' best fiction, however, is the nature of the twist.

In one of the most successful tales, 'Inside Out' (*Unbelievable*), the twist achieves a resonance that derives from Jennings' parody of the horror genre as well as from his exposure of adolescent bravado. This story provides an excellent example not only of how horror functions in juvenile fiction but of Jennings' originality. Before discussing it, however, I want to consider how his tales in general exhibit a range of conventional images that children will recognise as hallmarks of horror.

Ghosts usually lurk in isolated places. In Australia, we have shadowy backyard dunnies ('Skeleton on the Dunny' — *Unreal!*) and an outback populated by indigenous spirits. Jennings invents his own; for instance, the beneficent Wobby Gurgle made out of water ('You Be the Judge' — *Undone!*) and the voracious Spirit of the Forest ('Guts' — *Unseen*), which has politically correct appetites. It only devours what might harm it — miners, introduced species like cane toads and 'developers of the worst sort' (1998: 93) who want to build casinos in rainforests. In addition, we have haunted lighthouses instead of Gothic castles. In 'Lighthouse Blues' (*Unreal!*), the resident musical ghosts turn out to be benign, only wanting to protect their home. Sometimes Jennings' ghosts are agents of retribution, punishing the guilty (something Charles Dickens favoured). For example, in 'Spooks Incorporated' (*Quirky Tales*), two young men exploit horror for the pleasure they derive from psychological cruelty as well as for material gain. Using the obligatory chains, flickering candles, and a skeleton's hand, they scare people into selling their homes cheaply. But the real ghost of a headless chicken (they had constructed a mechanical one) so terrifies them that they drown.

James Twitchell qualifies our understanding of the way in which these images work: 'Horror art is not, strictly speaking, a genre; it is rather a collection of motifs in a usually predictable sequence that gives us a specific physiological effect — the shivers' (1985: 8). Jennings' audience enjoys these effects in and for themselves, but in 'Inside Out' (*Unbelievable*), they are turned more to characterise the narrator and then to teach him a lesson.

Jennings focuses here on the 'I dare you' aspect of juvenile horror, a standard motivation in the *Goosebumps* series. The protagonist Gordon typifies this obsession plus a number of other teenage traits. He lords it over his younger 'sook' sister; he rebels against having to babysit. Full of adolescent male aggression, he craves the most graphic horror films to prove his superiority. His choice of video, against his sister's wishes (she wants a love story), is *Chainsaw Murder*. (Jennings has fun making up summaries of Gordon's favourites.) In a culture deficient in tradition, these young 'connoisseurs of gore … may be using the fictions as macho rites of passage' (Carroll, 1990: 193). This belief is confirmed by Twitchell, who maintains that 'a fascination with horror clusters around adolescence' (1985: 66) and then dissipates.

Gordon taunts his sister with the fact that their parents won't be home until two. When 'the little monster' (1987: 35) nicks the video, his outrage as well as his sense of power drive him to abandon her to take a long walk, where he pumps himself up by remembering horror films and deciding that even real terrors wouldn't faze him. The rest of the story is cast in the mould of tests for the young hero. But the nature of the hero becomes part of the twist. When Gordon finds a derelict house, he decides to kill time there so that he can really 'teach Mary a lesson' (1987: 37) by coming home only just before their parents. Jennings cleverly maintains the surface bravado by having Gordon fantasise that he is 'the hero out of *Dark House of Death*' (37). And then the cliched motifs begin: floating candles, clinking and clanking, green ghostly hazes, suspended lips. But Gordon is an aficionado of horror and it's all old hat to him: 'Halitosis' (39), he taunts the disgusting mouth. The ghost is obviously insulted, but Gordon continues his critique of technique — a dancing skeleton doesn't cut it if it can't do rap.

This last insult forces the spectre to materialise; he's a teenager, too, but a leather-jacketed, mohawked punk with a safety pin in his nose. Tough in life, but not tough enough in death. Gordon seems to have the upper hand until the ghost explains that if he fails his spook exam, his test case — Gordon — will have to remain in suspended animation for a year until the re-sit. Jennings manipulates the suspense well when the Senior Spook arrives, with readers wondering if the punk ghost will really be able to scare the supremely confident teenager. The spook's few 'conjuring tricks' (43) with his pink power that turns things *inside out* seem incredibly lame — until he turns to throw the pink power over Gordon. Result? The Senior Spook as well as Gordon faint and the punk ghost receives an A plus. Formerly macho Gordon staggers home, knees knocking, to take refuge in his bed, afraid even to watch his sister's Muppet Caper movie. Jennings leaves it open as to whether the ghost set Gordon up by dragging out all the old horror conventions to make him complacent. But the fright of his life is a consummate stroke.

In Jennings' collections as well as in the *Gizmo* series (which are really extended illustrated stories rather than novels), we find, then, a moral dimension to the twist in the plot. Bullies are stereotypes who either receive their just punishments or precipitate a moral crisis for others. 'Do unto others' lies behind *The Gizmo Again* (1995), where Jack's concern with his own welfare (and his lunch) force him to treat another child badly, even though he can empathise with the new boy in school. He begins to shrink and is only released from the gizmo's power when he apologises.

In *Come Back Gizmo* (1996), Jimmy learns that looks are indeed only skin deep (in this case, the cliched blue-eyed blonde's) and that animals have feelings, too. Jennings combines these maxims with the 'first kiss' scenario, since it is a peck from the egocentric Samantha that clouds Jimmy's judgment. His hormones lead him to lock his dog, Biscuit, in the car boot since Samantha complained that he harasses her cat. 'I have sold my dog down the river for a kiss' (18), he laments. When the gizmo gradually turns Jimmy into his dog, he experiences the truth about doggy feelings. Appropriately, at the conclusion, Samantha's training (as a cat) is just beginning.

As Ricketson phrases it, 'the magical, mysterious gizmo represents a child's conscience' (2000: 195). Perhaps more explicitly, it forces the protagonists to confront their failings and makes them listen to that conscience. The trials in the form of embarrassing situations and the reparations that the child has to make are very much set within the context of their adolescent world. One way in which Jennings has been able to avoid a sententious tone is by having unexplained magic drive the plot. The other is by creating an easy-to-read style laced with humour.

Humour

Humour has never been very popular with critics of children's literature, although it is a positive attribute, not simply because it attracts children to books or because laughter supposedly has health benefits. What young people find funny is often ephemeral, the product of a particular culture, as much humour is. An article in the *Weekend Australian* (24–25 Feb 2001) by Rachel Grunwell has the headline, 'Children's authors flush with success of toilet humour', suggesting a scatological resurgence. Yet Roald Dahl certainly knew that mention farting, or 'whizzpopping' as he terms it in *The BFG* (1982: 68), and most preteens will laugh.

Grunwell sees this return to 'poo, snot and wee' (2001: 3) as an attempt to hitch a ride on the runaway success of *The Simpsons* and *South Park*. These TV shows are certainly satiric as well as humorous. The publishers she interviewed waxed rhapsodic about getting 'fun' back into kid lit. Academic Greer Johnson noted that children's books had become 'less conservative' (2001: 3), only mirroring social changes. The success of writers like Gretel Killeen (*My Sister* series), Catherine Jinks (*The Stinking Great Lie*) and Kaz Cooke (*The Terrible Underpants*) testify to this trend. In fact, humour that relies on a fascination with the scatological, the disgusting and the grotesque facilitates a safe form of rebellion. It has formed 'a pact of the private lore of childhood. Adults enamoured with the innocence of childhood won't admit it, however, and other adults don't approve … ' (Klause, 1987: 35). Bob Condon specifically describes his horror series as 'a suppository of toilet humour' (1996: 68); reading it gives children the power to annoy adults.

Paul Jennings has been exploiting the humorous and the disgusting since the mid-eighties. Take a story such as 'Licked' (*Unbearable!*), where a boy horrifies his father in front of his boss by licking a fly swat that he has smeared with licorice and currants; or 'Little Squirt' and 'Piddler on the Roof', which both deal with urinating; and 'Ringing Wet', which deals with bed-wetting.[6] In 'Spaghetti Pig-Out' (*Uncanny!*), Guts Garvey gets his comeuppance when a magic video remote control allows him to eat (at fast forward speed) forty bowls of spaghetti at a contest. But he loses by spewing it up, and the narrator from whom he has stolen the remote presses REWIND, forcing the river of sick back into him. In these examples Jennings relies on exaggeration and sheer grossness which is, in fact, the basis of much classic comedy. Some of his humour is linguistically based, however; he likes punning or playing with colloquial expressions. Note his story titles ('Wunderpants', 'Smelly Feat', 'Frozen Stiff', 'Tonsil Eye 'Tis', 'Batty').

Humour is also positive because it can help children at a particular point in their lives to cope more effectively. As Klause suggests, 'the reasons that adult and child humor can differ so much is that appreciation of humour is tied in with the developmental stages, those steps in physical, psychological, and cognitive ability through which all humans go, and which greatly influence their relationship with the world' (Klause, 1987: 34). So a child's sense of humour will alter not only with their cultural circumstances (and each culture has a particular habit of mind),[7] but with their developmental context.

Jennings relishes incorporating black humour, too, which allows children, he believes, not to take their fears too seriously (Kroll, 1989: 24). One of his earliest stories, 'Without a Shirt' (*Unreal!*), concerns a boy who lives with his widowed mother in a cemetery. His dead father's dog, Shovel, eventually digs up (on the beach) the bones of a drowned ancestor. Part of the humour in this serious tale about laying a ghost to rest lies in a comedy of situation: 'Kids always laugh when I say it's not a good idea to live in a cemetery if your dog digs holes' (Kroll, 1989: 24).

For Jennings, humour is not so much about rebellion as it is about recreating the ambience of the child's world. It is humour in the service of inclusion, demonstrating that Jennings understands the quality of young people's minds. His readers empathise with his characters, even though they might laugh at them. As he says, 'Just because a hero or heroine is humorous does not mean they are stupid or without values or unable to set an example' (Ricketson, 2000: 145). More to the point, an adult consciousness is not present to criticise what the characters (and their readers) find funny; it is simply given.

Accessibility and the reluctant reader

It is Paul Jennings' appeal to the reluctant reader that has, on the one hand, made him incredibly popular and, on the other, supported the view that his work does not merit scrutiny. The reading problems of his adopted son spurred him to write initially:

> One particular evening, I had brought home a story about a motorbike for him ... he was about eleven. And he threw it across the room, he had tears in his eyes. He said, 'I'm sick of these piddly little books'. I felt really ashamed that I'd insulted him with a book that looked as if it was really meant for younger kids ... I looked at it and thought, oh, I could write a better plot than that, I'm sure I could.
>
> (Kroll, 1989: 24)

At this time Jennings was a Senior Lecturer in education and so threw himself into the project, researching for six months how to create an easy-to-read book that also had a strong storyline. He settled on about 30 strategies (Kroll, 1989: 24); these include short sentences and paragraphs as well as a restricted vocabulary. In addition, the text's layout needs to be user-friendly, especially 'so that it's obvious who has spoken' (McQuade, 1998: 68). Colloquial idioms and cliches, which some might consider inappropriate in a 'literary' book, help problem readers along. It is, of course, his quirky twists that Jennings thought critical:

'Plot is everything to me to keep kids hooked in' (Kroll, 1989: 24). Consistent surprise offers a kind of predictability. Formulaic fiction and idiomatic expressions, then, can be beneficial to the struggling reader.

In the afterword to *Wicked!*, Jennings praises his audience's tenacity in persisting through six volumes: 'Altogether the six *Wicked!* books contain over seventy-thousand words. That's a lot of writing. And a lot of reading.' Jennings has always been adamant, however, that he wants to appeal to more than the reluctant: even 'if you write for kids who don't like to read, the kids who do like to read have got to find it good, too' (Kroll 24). He has always supported 'literature-based approaches to teaching reading … with real stories by the best writers that we can find' (Kroll, 1989: 24).

The panic about the prevalence of literature for reluctant readers is not that it does not have its place, but that it is in danger of swamping the market: 'By the mid-1990s it had become common for publishers to produce books aimed squarely at the average reader' (Ricketson, 2000: 193).[8] Does 'average' now imply 'reluctant'?[9] Does 'reluctant' now include competent readers who choose to spend their leisure time engaged with other media? In this environment, the problem is reluctant publishers, who hesitate to commit to more challenging books that will attract a smaller audience and, hence, generate less profit. This fact might affect some critics' estimation of Jennings' work.

Character: 'How come you know what it's like to be me?'

Quoted in Ricketson's biography and reported by Jennings at many writers' festivals:

> [Children] have their own culture. When I write I enter this culture, the biggest homogenous group to be found anywhere. Children across the world have more in common with each other than they do with parents and other adults who surround them.
>
> (Ricketson, 2000: 299)

Paul Jennings' typical child displays no outstanding talents or weaknesses. Usually an Anglo male,[10] he simply wants to enjoy the basic pleasures — TV, a pet, sweets, a walk with a girl — that are possible in a world constrained by adults. It is often other children, however, that deprive him of friendship and love. 'I want to save them [children] from the terrors of the schoolyard' (Ricketson, 2000: 298), Jennings said in the Afterword to his biography.

Given this desire to help children to face peer as well as adult pressure, Jennings has developed a formula that I have already discussed. I want to clarify here how that formula affects his portrayal of character, because one criticism of popular books is that there is little character development. In Jennings' fiction the children triumph through fantastic or magical forces, not through their own agency. This wish-fulfilment often allows the underdog to be accepted as part of the group; to become, in effect, popular.

For example, David, the narrator of 'Wunderpants' (*Unreal!*), manages not only to win the mouse race with Swift Sam, but to triumph over the cheating Scrag Murphy (who has entered a rat), using the source of David's earlier mortification — the magical fairy underpants — which have already taught him a lesson about cheating and complacency by shrinking on him. A similar pattern is followed in 'Spaghetti Pig-Out' where the source of mortification becomes the source of revenge and retribution. In both cases, the protagonists demonstrate typical childhood weaknesses. The challenge in Jennings' fiction is for the hero to survive long enough to acknowledge those weaknesses and to turn the tables.

In many stories, characters need to modify their behaviour from the beginning or to learn to appreciate what they have, but their insights result from external (magical or supernatural) forces specifically designed to enlighten them (for example, in 'Lucky Lips', 'Inside Out' and 'Wake Up to Yourself'). If they change, it is not because of conscious moral decisions that come from introspection. As contemporary children's authors know, the more description and introspection, the harder it is to hold the average reader's attention.[11] Jennings' characters are usually from the same generic family then; individuals only in so far as their hair colour or family structure differs. Their names or personalities are not memorable, but the twists in their stories are.

Jennings is interested more in the kinds of effects that come from non-realistic narratives, such as fables and fairytales, where character is not a focus.[12] In addition, his narrative structure has affinities with the picaresque, where unchanging protagonists are common. The *Gizmo* series and Jennings' latest short fiction, *Sucked In ...* (2000), as well as his longer short stories, owe something to this old popular tradition. The picaresque, a precursor to the modern novel, flourished in Spain in the sixteen hundreds (Abrams, 1993: 130); Cervante's *Don Quixote* is the most famous example. Its influence permeated many of the eighteenth-century's popular novels. The 'Picaro' or 'rogue' (Abrams, 1993: 130) is the hero (or anti-hero) who resorts to his native intelligence to survive; but he 'shows little if any alteration of character through a long succession of his adventures' (1993: 130), partly because the thrust of the picaresque was to satirise literary and social conventions.

Jennings' longer fictions are in the line of picaresque narratives because of their episodic structure. The incidents are usually not arbitrary, but part of a chain designed to make the protagonist realise something about himself. In Jennings' latest, *Sucked In ...* , however, the escapades of the hungry appendix that wants to be reunited with Trevor seem to be there solely for the grotesque humour, like an extended joke. The refrain, 'We must always be together' (62), sends up romantic notions of togetherness, but in the most obvious way. Jennings' longer fictions, then, do not develop as novels do by integrating character and incident.

To summarise, in the majority of Jennings' work character has been at the service of plot as it is in much popular formulaic fiction, where the emphasis is on pace and the seductiveness of incident. There are exceptions to this sketchy technique, however, which I do not have space to discuss here. 'Nails' (*Unbearable!*) and 'Shadows' (*Unseen*) both treat character in a more complex — but not realistic — way, hence they invite multiple readings. The first leans towards the mythic and the other towards the symbolic, but both delineate psychological states quite successfully.

In *Unseen* as a whole Jennings has begun experimenting with other ways of portraying his protagonists and with content that reflects more accurately the mid-teen years. For example, in 'Seeshell' Alan battles with his desire for Shelley. Although she takes the initiative to kiss him, she is a worthy object of his affections (unlike other Jennings' snobby objects of desire) and Alan is ultimately not punished for wanting her. 'Ticker' depicts a boy facing his fears, but despite the Gothic atmosphere the supernatural is not involved. It is his love for his deceased grandfather and his mourning grandmother that allows him to brave alone a terrifying bridge over a gorge and thus to mature.[13]

Conclusion

> Thirty years ago, readers read 'down' through layers of meaning, now they 'surf', gathering understanding from powerful surfaces …
> BUT: is that all that we should expect?
>
> (Hunt, 1998: 4)

Paul Jennings' career took off near the end of the twentieth century when the written word was placed under unique pressures. His quirky tales mix traditional structures, conservative moral values and highly original — zany, outrageous, bizarre — incidents. He began with an educative purpose, but one that was inextricably bound up with the suspicious concept of 'fun'. He believes that reluctant readers need particular strategies, but as well that all readers need to enjoy themselves. In order to make his stories entertaining and good reading practice, he concentrates on tight plots delivered with humour, especially of the gross or scatological variety.

His uniqueness lies in his ability to come up often enough with twists that keep his predictable structure of reward and punishment fresh. As opposed to the lowest level series book, which has limited ways of being read, Jennings' texts sometimes do ask to be understood in multiple ways, and so begin to demand more of his audience. Certainly he writes popular fiction in the sense of being 'well-liked', in fact wildly loved, by young people. His stories in many cases possess some of popular formulaic fiction's attributes and there is a sameness in strategy and unevenness in execution in many collections as a whole. A lack of gender balance bothers some critics; his male characters at times appear interchangeable. There is too much lavatory humour for most adult tastes, but not too much if one postulates a 'poetics of childhood' for a certain developmental stage. Both competent and reluctant readers might outgrow some stories, but not others.

If we consider how prolific Jennings is, he has produced a reasonable number of outstanding stories where plot, style and tone (including humour) create the aesthetic balance critics seek in adult literature; some are postmodern by being self-conscious and playing with convention. Many authors for adults would have published a 'best of' at this point in their careers, on which their reputations might rest.

If it is true that, as Tucker suggests, 'a popular book should have some sort of connection with the tasks of childhood' (1976: 92), then Paul Jennings has zeroed in on what matters most to average children in the developed world — the humiliations and terrors that confront them at home and at school, the inevitable trials of puberty. Through fantasy and horror, humour and scatology, he enables them to laugh off or confront some of the constant pressures in their lives by sharing his protagonists' embarrassments as well as triumphs. In this sense his work is escapist, but it is also cathartic and, thus, empowering. When they recognise themselves, as Jennings does when he admits, 'The boy in the story is always me' (Ricketson subtitle, 2000), they can perhaps bear their powerlessness more easily.

Bibliography

Abrams, M.H. (1993) *A Glossary of Literary Terms. Sixth Edition.* Harcourt Brace College Publishers, Fort Worth, San Diego, pp. 130–31.

Berger, A.A. (1995) 'Cultural Criticism: A Primer of Key Concepts', *Foundations of Popular Culture* vol 4. Sage Publications, Thousand Oaks, California; London; New Delhi.

Bloom, C. (1996) *Cult Fiction: Popular Reading and Pulp Theory.* Macmillan, Houndmills/London.

Carroll, N. (1990) *The Philosophy of Horror.* Routledge, New York and London.

Cawelti, J.G. (1976) *Adventure, Mystery, and Romance: Formula Stories as Art and Popular Culture.* University of Chicago Press, Chicago and London.

Cazzulino, M. (2000) 'Deadly double', The *Daily Telegraph* (Sydney), 11 April, W 10.

Children's Book Council Proceedings (2000) *The Third Millennium: Read On!,* B. Alderman and S. Page eds. CBC, Canberra.

Childs, K. (1996) 'Do boys and books mix?', The *Age,* education section, 19 March, p. 3.

Condon, B. (1996) 'Balancing the Books: A Place for Reading in Popular Culture', *Claiming a Place: Proceedings from the Third National Conference of the Children's Book Council of Australia.* Thorpe, Melbourne, pp. 67–70.

Coppell, V. (1998) 'The "Goosebumps" in Goosebumps: Impositions and R.L. Stine', *Papers,* vol 8 no 2, pp. 5–15.

Dahl, R. (1982) *The BFG.* Puffin Books, London.

Dickinson, P. (1976) 'A Defence of Rubbish', in *Writers, Critics, and Children: Articles from Children's Literature in Education.* G. Fox, G. Hammond, T. Jones, F. Smith, K. Sterck (eds). Agathon Press, New York, pp. 73–6.

Engelhardt, T. (1991) 'Reading May Be Harmful to Your Kids: In the Nadirland of Today's Children's Books', *Harper's,* June, pp. 55–62.

Fiske, J. (1989) *Reading the Popular.* Unwin Hyman, Boston.

Foster, J. and Nimon, M. (1995) *Australian Children's Literature: An Exploration of Genre and Theme.* LIS Press (Literature and Literacy for Young People: An Australian Series), Wagga Wagga.

Garrett, J. (1995–1996) 'To the Reader', editorial, *Bookbird: Special Double Issue: 'Bad' Books, 'Good Reading?'* vol 33, no 3/4, Fall-Winter, pp. 2–4.

Gelder, K. (2000) 'The Obscure(d) World of Australian Popular Fiction. *Australian Book Review* no 222, July, pp. 34–7.

Grunwell, R. (2001) 'Children's authors flush with success of toilet humour', The *Weekend Australian,* 24–25 Feb, The Nation, p. 3.

Hodge, D. (1999) 'Perspective: Childness: is it "scary?" ', *Viewpoint,* 2, pp. 9–14.

Hood, R. (1996) 'A Playground for Fear: Horror Fiction for Children', *Claiming a Place: Proceedings from the Third National Conference of the Children's Book Council of Australia.* Thorpe, Melbourne, pp. 76–81.

Hunt, P. (1991) *Criticism, Theory, & Children's Literature.* Blackwell, Oxford and Cambridge.

—— (1998) 'Perspective: Slouching towards the millennium: business as usual in british ya literature', *Viewpoint* vol 6, no 3 (Spring) pp. 3–4.

Jennings, P. (1985) *Unreal!* Puffin Books, Ringwood.

—— (1987) *Quirky Tales.* Puffin Books, Ringwood.

—— (1987) *Unbelievable!* Puffin Books, Ringwood.

—— (1988) *Uncanny!* Puffin Books, Ringwood.

—— (1990) *Round the Twist.* Puffin Books, Ringwood.

—— (1990) *Unbearable!* Puffin Books, Ringwood.

—— (1993) *Undone* Puffin Books, Ringwood.

—— (1995) *The Gizmo Again.* Puffin Books, Ringwood.

—— (1996) *Come Back Gizmo.* Puffin Books, Ringwood.

—— (1998) *Unseen.* Puffin Books, Ringwood.

—— (2000) *Sucked In ...* (illustrations by Terry Denton). Puffin Books, Ringwood. (Text copyright, 1995. First published as 'Together Again' in *The Paul Jennings Superdiary 1996.*)

—— website: http://www.pauljennings.com.au

Jennings, P. and Gleitzman, M. (1997) *Wicked! (part 6) Till Death Us Do Part.* Puffin Books, Ringwood.

Jones, C. (1995) 'Pulp Fiction Threatens Children's Literature', The *Weekend Australian,* 15–16 July, p. 9.

Kirk, J. (1992) 'What's a Good Book?', *At Least They're Reading: Proceedings of the First National Conference of the Children's Book Council of Australia*. DW Thorpe, Melbourne.

Klause, A.C. (1987) 'So What's So Funny, Anyway?: The differences between children's and adults' humor', *School Library Journal* vol 33, no 6, Feb, pp. 34–5.

Kroll, J.(1989) 'Plot is Everything: Paul Jennings Talks with Jeri Kroll', *Lowdown: Youth Performing Arts in Australia*, June, p. 24.

—— (1997) Interview with Morris Gleitzman, Adelaide, SA.

Krull, K. (1999) 'Revisiting Eleanor, Marshall, and Roald: or, Having a Sense of Humour in the Millennium', *The Horn Book Magazine 75th Anniversary Issue* Sept/Oct, pp. 564–71.

Love, K. (1994) 'The Pleasure of the Popular: Popular Culture as Valid School Literature', *Making the Hard Decisions*. Conference Papers. Melbourne University, Melbourne pp. 77–90.

Lukens, R. (1990) *A Critical Handbook of Children's Literature* (4th edn). HarperCollins, Oxford, Ohio.

Lurie, M. (1991) *Madness*. Collins/Angus and Robertson, Sydney.

Macintyre, P. (1998–1999) Critique of *Unseen!* in *Australian Book Review* no 207, December–January, p. 42.

McQuade, E. (1998) 'Finding the Right Book for the Right Child', *School Librarian* vol 46, no 2, Summer, pp. 68–9.

Nieuwenhuizen, A. (1996) 'Balancing the Books: A Place for Reading in Popular Culture', *Claiming a Place: Proceedings from the Third National Conference of the Children's Book Council of Australia*. Thorpe, Melbourne, pp. 71–5.

Nodelman, P. (1996) *The Pleasures of Children's Literature* (2nd edn). Longman, New York.

—— (1997) 'Ordinary Monstrosity: The World of Goosebumps', *Children's Literature Association Quarterly* vol 22 no 3, 118–24.

Orwell, G. (1966)'Politics and the English Language', *Writer to Writer: Readings on the Craft of Writing* (F.C. Watkins and K.F. Knight eds), first published in 1945, Houghton Mifflin, Boston, pp. 193–207.

Paul Jennings File (2000) 'The Man and His Nonsense: An Interview with Paul Jennings Taken from the Puffin Post', http://www.pauljennings.com.au/teachers/ppi.htm, November.

Pausacker, J. (1998) 'A Balanced Diet', in *Time Will Tell: Fourth National Conference of the Children's Book Council of Australia*. (S. van der Hoeven, ed.). CBC, pp. 114–16.

Rabus, S. (1995–1996) 'Pop Author Triumphant: Austria's Thomas Brezina', *Bookbird: Special Double Issue: 'Bad' Books, 'Good Reading?'* vol 33, no 3/4 (Fall-Winter), pp. 8–14.

Ricketson, M. (2000) *Paul Jennings: 'The boy in the story is always me.'* Viking, Penguin Books Australia, Ringwood.

Ridge, J. (1999) 'Perspective: "The Latest Big Thing." ', *Viewpoint* vol 7 no 3, Spring, pp. 3–4.

Ryan, J. (1998) 'Little book of horrors: a blessing or a curse?', The *Sunday Age*, p. 9.

Sheahan-Bright, R. (1999) 'It's a Supermarket: Children's Publishing and the mass market', *Magpies* vol 14 no 2, May, 10–13.

Silver, M. (1995) 'Horrors! It's R. L. Stine!', *U.S. News & World Report*, 23 October, pp. 94–5.

Sorenson, M. (1992) 'From the Word Go: Books for Younger Readers', *Australian Book Review* no 138, Feb/March, p. 58.

Strinati, D. *An Introduction to Theories of Popular Culture*. Routledge, London.

Susina, J. (1993) 'Editor's Note: Kiddie Lit(e): The Dumbing Down of Children's Literature', *The Lion and the Unicorn* vol 17 no 1, June, pp. v–ix.

Sykes, C. (1995) *Dumbing Down Our Kids: Why America's Children Feel Good About Themselves But Can't Read, Write, or Add*. St Martin's Press, New York.

Tucker, N. (1976) 'How Children Respond to Fiction', in *Writers, Critics, and Children: Articles from Children's Literature in Education*, G. Fox, G. Hammond, T. Jones, F. Smith, K. Sterck (eds). Agathon Press, New York, pp. 177–88.

Twitchell, J.B. (1992) *Carnival Culture: The Trashing of Taste in America*. Columbia University Press, New York.

—— (1985) *Dreadful Pleasures: An Anatomy of Modern Horror*. OUP, Oxford, New York.

Walker, J. (1999) 'Bestselling *Bumface* new kid on the book', The *Australian*, 20 May, p. 5.

Welch, B. (1994) 'If it's funny, you can't take it seriously', *Making the Hard Decisions*. Conference papers. Melbourne University, Melbourne, pp. 58–71.

White, K. (1999) 'A Look at Series Fiction: Sinister Artifices?', *Magpies* vol 14 no 2, May, pp. 20–1.

Williams, H.E. (1987) 'Characterizations in High-Interest/Low-Vocabulary Level Fiction', *School Library Journal* vol 33 no 6, Feb, pp. 31–3.

Endnotes

1   Paul Jennings' short fiction was originally aimed at an adolescent audience (the majority of his protagonists are adolescents). Jennings has gained a younger readership over the years for his story collections, which win both the younger readers' and older readers' categories in the children's choice awards. I do not have space here to look at his collaborative joke and riddle books, his other illustrated stories or his picture books.

2   Jennings drafted all of the scripts for series one, wrote nearly all for series two (with Esben Storm as script editor and director in both cases), but had no direct involvement in series three. The first *Round the Twist* series aired in 1990, series two in 1993 and series three in 1998. Produced by Patricia Edgar and the Australian Children's Film and Television Foundation, the first series collected seven awards, both in Australia and overseas, and the second another batch including a Prix Jeunesse for one episode (Ricketson, 2000: 171 and 'Going Round the Twist' chapter, pp. 130–50). Jennings writes about the creation of series one in *Round the Twist*.

3   Information about Jennings' awards is available on various websites. He won his first children's choice award in 1987. The awards are as follows: BILBY (Books I Love Best Yearly — Qld); COOL (Children's Own Outstanding Literature — ACT); CROW (Children Rate Outstanding Writers/Illustrators — SA); KOALA (Kids' Own Australian Literature Award — NSW); KROC (Kids' Reading Oz Choice — NT); YABBA (Young Australians' Best Books Award — Vic); WAYRA (West Australian Young Readers' Award — WA).

4   The Austrians have a similar term to describe food for the youthful herd — '*Lesefutter* ('reading fodder')' (Rabus 9) — which some use about the work of Thomas Brezina, 'who is not only Austria's current best-selling author for children, but the best-selling Austrian writer of any category' (9). He resents being considered a "yuck-author" (*Pfui-Autoren)*' (11).

5   In his study, *Dumbing Down Our Kids: Why America's Children Feel Good About Themselves But Can't Read, Write, or Add*, Charles Sykes connects the decline of literacy and numeracy to what young people are reading — but he doesn't accuse popular fiction. He blames the books that are supposed to teach children in the first place — readers and textbooks. He asks, 'has the long-term dumbing down of the texts assigned to students had a cumulative effect in eroding not only their base of knowledge, but also their vocabulary and other reading skills?' (1995: 128).

6   Jennings' recent experiences in therapy perhaps account for his fascination with scatology. He has said of toilet training: 'It is the one thing you do as a child where you have power. Your parents really want you to do it and you don't do it' (Ricketson, 2000: 164). Meg Sorenson's discussion of 'Little Squirt' in *Australian Book Review* (Feb/March 1992) made explicit the reservations of many educators at the time about this aspect of his humour — the disposable, and very male-oriented toilet humour that certainly appeals to cliched gender roles and that might push away some girl readers.

7   Penguin's Robert Sessions has described Jennings' humour as:

> essentially English … It is the sort of eccentric, outrageous comedy that the English delight in, but the Americans are prim and proper. They find it hard to understand and even offensive. American children do love Paul's work but the gatekeepers in the US — librarians and critics — have been blocking the way.
>
> (Ricketson, 2000: 268)

A good parallel to 'Spaghetti Pig-Out' would be the glutton scene in Monty Python's film *The Meaning of Life*, where the man 'pigs out' and explodes.

8   The most recent Children's Book Council Proceedings, *The Third Millennium: Read On!* (Belle Alderman and Sue Page, eds, Canberra: CBC 2000), includes a paper by Libby Gleeson entitled 'Marketing Forces: Living in the Age of Marketing', where she confirms that today it is extremely hard to convince publishers to take on anything that is challenging. She uses her own experience with her picture book, *The Great Bear* (1999), illustrated by Armin Greder, to prove her point.

9   There is no one profile for the reluctant reader, but current research indicates that girls more than boys seem to be 'getting into reading' (Childs, 1996: 3). Furthermore, 'teachers of working class boys are up against bigger problems' (Childs, 1996: 3), explains Professor Bob Connell of Sydney University. Covers can be an immense help in attracting readers to books, and Jennings 'insists on covers that no boy would be embarrassed to carry around' (McQuade, 1998: 68).

10 The lack of female protagonists has been noted by reviewers and Jennings has attempted to include more females in stories. He was certainly aware when writing the *Round the Twist* television series that

popularity also demanded a range of characters with whom a potential worldwide audience could identify. On the surface, his stories do not seem to deal with issues that pertain to one sex more than another, except for those, such as 'Little Squirt' and 'Piddler on the Roof', where the narrator requires the requisite equipment. One could say, however, that the type of bullying dependent on force (or its threat) often described is more common among boys; girls tend to use subtler techniques to torment their peers. 'What a Woman' (*Undone!*) is an exception, with Sally, the lone girl in a country school, tormented by her redneck classmates because she is hopeless at sport. This is perhaps too obvious a cliche. Sally does have a role model — her deceased Aunt Esso. Whether it is her dead aunt's toe or her positive thinking that allows Sally to triumph in the end, Jennings leaves open, but this equivocation makes the story uneven. In general, the failings of Jennings' other male characters are never the result of their sex per se but arbitrary — an accident of birth or the result of some specific incident (for example, putting one's hands underneath a lawn mower as in 'One-Finger Salute').

11 Morris Gleitzman has admitted that 'young readers don't engage that much with a more reflective style of writing and I think that's regrettable … ' (Kroll, 1997). Yet he still believes that 'there is continually an interior life and an interior kind of dialogue with the self going on for all of my characters … in a way that's totally absent from much popular fiction for young people' (1997).

12 In comparison, *Goosebumps* books have little characterisation but for no particular purpose other than to allow Stine to spend as much space as possible increasing the shocks. Stine admits, 'I have no crying, no hugging, and the kids never learn anything about themselves' (Nodelman, 1997: 12).

13 In Jennings' two collaborative novels with Morris Gleitzman, *Wicked!* and *Deadly!*, he has space, for the first time, for extended character portraits. Since they are the result of collaborative efforts, I will not discuss them here. It is worth mentioning , however, that in addition to being serial novels, they are also a mixture of conventional genres: horror, domestic problem novel, science fiction and pubescent romance. The authors have coined the term 'Gothic realism' (Ricketson, 2000: 248) to describe their creations.

Chapter 17

At the crossroads:
the market for children's publishing media

By Robyn Sheahan-Bright

Introduction

Children's publishing is situated in a busy marketplace, and at a conjunction between many forces which both promote and make complex the business of the production, marketing, distribution and consumption of literature for young people. Curiously, publishing in general has always been slow to recognise itself as part of several sectors, now most obviously of the media and entertainment industries, but traditionally as part of both the manufacturing and the cultural industries which have obvious conflicts inherent in their allegiance to differing priorities. Where a business must adhere to commercial principles, publishers have always preferred to adhere publicly to 'cultural' principles, though in private they have tended to pursue this objective with extremely diverse strategies. The presumption that 'books are different' has also created an implied superiority for books over other cultural mediums, a belief which ironically stems from the 'businessman' publisher's recognition that publishing books can be easily characterised as a non-profitable venture and therefore both worthy of special consideration and of positive discrimination which has the potential to advantage it in a highly competitive marketplace.

In Australia the entire publishing industry has been slow to develop, and extremely slow, as elsewhere, to conduct any analysis of the forces contributing to its development. This sort of analysis, therefore, provides some new insights with which educators may arm themselves to better understand the production and consumption of children's literature. This chapter will explore these developments in an Australian landscape observed in a global context, and demonstrate that in focusing on the views of educational theorists, there has grown a misunderstanding of, and over-simplification of, the forces which will drive the further development of publishing for young people. It will seek to isolate children's publishing strategies which may constitute likely trends in the future.

Children's publishing overview

Publishing is said to be a 'hybrid' combining both craft industry, and the more bureaucratic characteristics of mass industries (Coser et al., 1982: 7; 1984: 5). Though publishers are clearly in the business of making products, the nature of both the product and of the production process is unlike that of most other manufacturing industries. Corporate managers find publishing 'unusual'. It is not easy to monitor employee or product performance:

> when each title is unique, few authors have reliable track records, market research is scorned (or in a primitive state), profits are frequently dependent on the sale of subsidiary rights rather than the sale of the product, your brand name means nothing to the consumer, and no one can even agree on the definition of a 'good' book. Small wonder that new management becomes so attentive to the bottom line! Everything else is too slippery to grab hold of.
>
> (Luey in Kobrak and Luey, 1992: 6)

These observations are complicated in children's publishing media industries by the diverse factors and 'social implications' (Raugust, 1997: 5) not shared by producers of books for adults. Of course, children's literature theorists and educators share common understandings that the production of and reception of children's books can be influenced by four factors:

1 theories of childhood;
2 literary theories;
3 educational theories;
4 ideology.

Theories of childhood

Theories of childhood proposed by theorists such as Philippe Aries (1973), Lloyd De Mause (1974), Neil Postman (1983) and David Buckingham (2000) have caused us to re-evaluate childhood, viewing it as an adult 'invention'. Postman stresses that the invention of printing gave adults the right to keep 'secrets' from children:

> From print onward, adulthood had to be earned. It became a symbolic, not a biological achievement. From print onward, the young would have to become adults, and they would have to do it by learning to read, by entering the world of typography. And in order to accomplish that they would require education … therefore European civilisation reinvented schools. And by so doing, it made childhood a necessity.
>
> (Postman, 1983: 33–6)

With the advent of the media, this artificial boundary between adult and child was effectively difficult to defend. His term the 'childified adult' describes the media influence on fashions which has blurred the boundaries between age-groups in our society's desperate pursuit of youth. Kociumbas suggests that we are now experiencing a backlash, by adults who fear that 'unbridled sexuality and juvenile 'crime' (Kociumbas, 1997: 215) will become the order of the day, as a direct outcome of the 'self-expression' encouraged in our youth in recent decades. (Hence the growth of school-based parent groups censoring literature, and of other forms of more subtle censorship.) Hunt posits that childhood is, because it's less fixed in its development, 'more adaptable' and 'more open to genuinely radical thought' (Hunt, 1991: 57); both factors which incur adult interference by either trying to restrict children, or to demote them to a lower status than adults. He also points out how changeable notions of childhood are, and thus how this might impact on what we consider to be a children's book in any given era.

Literary theories

Literary theories have been applied less rigidly to children's literature, for its critics were slower than their counterparts, in the 'adult' English departments, to take theory on board. Recently, though, the range of theories have proliferated, influencing the reception of children's literature; for example, Feminist (Lissa Paull), Childist (Peter Hunt), Marxist Ideological (Jack Zipes), Postcolonial (Clare Bradford), Reader Response (Aidan Chambers and Hugh Crago) and Visual Literacy (Michèle Anstey, Geoff Bull, Perry Nodelman and Jane Doonan).

Children's books are now beset by a change in the theoretical frameworks through which we view them. From the Leavisite tradition which set up a divide between texts which were automatically 'good' and those which were 'inferior' — a division which privileged certain readers (i.e. academic ones) over those without those skills — we have moved to a situation now where we acknowledge the individual reader's capacity to interpret a text and just as importantly, we acknowledge the context in which that reader is reading the text. Leavis promoted a close reading of a text, a 'practical criticism' which allowed a reader to take a passage apart and thereby adduce its ' "greatness" and "centrality" ' (Eagleton, 1983: 43). This theorising led to the idea of treating a text without a context, and the idea of a 'canon or hierarchy' (Hunt, 1991: 2). We have moved since through various stages of theory, though, as John Stephens (1996) has pointed out, the research which has appeared has remained relatively traditional and theoretically superficial. He says that cultural studies may present a new way of approaching these texts, and breaking down some of the incorrect assumptions and the simplification of texts, based on the imagined 'needs' of the readers, for 'children's texts are produced within a cultural ideology that expects they will be about identity politics (or at least subjectivity) and social issues — especially issues relating to ethnicity, gender, and ecology and the environment' (Stephens, 1996: 166–7). Stephens also suggests that 'popular' writers like Paul Jennings who are regarded as 'less literary' are positioned as such by children's literature critics, 'because they don't thematicize social issues (1996: 167).' He suggests that 'intertextuality' (or examining texts in relation to other texts) has proved a very useful way of approaching texts in that it 'opens windows' and 'poses questions about the relationships between high culture and low culture' (Stephens, 1999: 11).

Educational theories

Educational theories have been applied to children's literature from its inception, when 'instruction' was seen as the key feature of books for the young. Consequently it has been assumed that books, often problematically, must be 'good for' children. Hence, they have been classified, for example, by relating them in an educative way to the various stages of development, a fact which has also influenced the marketing of books as we will see in later discussion. Children's literature has been analysed according to Kohlberg's (1967) 'Stages of Moral Development' to 'Preconventional, Conventional and Postconventional' child readers; or books have been assigned according to them being suitable for stages of reading ability

— a Pre-Reader, Beginning, Competent and Advanced or Adolescent Reader. Some of those who judge books for their educational value also apply rigid aesthetic considerations when they critique children's books — based on their perceived literary, artistic and design merits. Awards often hinge upon this, which is why the CBCA awards rarely feature 'popular' authors, and perhaps why kids' awards often fail to acknowledge those with this sort of merit.

Ideology

Ideology is another influence of which educators are keenly aware, in that it besets the analysis of children's publishing, including not only 'class, gender or ethnicity' but also the incursions of globalism (Sarland, 1996: 40).

It is not so widely recognised, though, that the production of children's publishing media is also subject to five other forces:

1   questions of audience;
2   the tension between commerce and culture;
3   the division of publishing products into specific markets;
4   the isolationist culture of children's publishing;
5   the pricing of children's books.

Questions of audience

Questions of audience have complicated the reading of, and therefore the production of, children's literature since its very inception. The reading of a children's book is always vexed by the fact that books for young people are generally bought by adults. These adult buyers are 'schizophrenic' in their approach in that they variously assume a protective, didactic and occasionally an empathetic approach to what they read. Whereas children read as adults do, in order to make some 'connection' with the work in question, adult perceptions of children's books are often obscured by their desire to have the book either instruct or improve.

Peter Hunt explains this as 'a tension between what is "good" in the exploded abstract, what is good for the child socially, intellectually, and educationally, and what we really, honestly think is a good book' (Hunt, 1991: 15). For publishers, and other members of the book trade, it constitutes a major marketing problem.

The tension between commerce and culture

This tension also imbues the entire publishing industry, and is a source of misunderstanding of the imperatives of publishing books which further complicates the children's publisher's role. The publisher's responsibility to the author and reader is necessarily also as much due to the other partners in the process and the necessity to recompense all those partners is often inadequately appreciated by critics of the publishing industry. There is also a failure to perceive that risks taken on cultural product, sometimes called 'non-commercial' product, are only made possible where, for example, the sale of other products is subsidising that loss. This issue of 'culture versus commerce' demands even closer consideration when discussing children's publishing issues, because of the claims of ideology and the questions of audience outlined above.

The division of publishing products into specific markets

This division is another significant factor which influences both the production of and the consumption of books for young people. Children's books have traditionally been produced for several distinct markets — educational, library, literary or 'quality' trade, mass-market trade and a category which has been described as 'Middle Market' (Ingram, 1987: 340). This leads to a certain 'expectation' of a book if, for example, it's purchased from the checkout at a supermarket. Significantly, though, this sort of division — between high and low culture, and concurrently, between types of book-selling outlets — is breaking down very rapidly, as a result of changing social and literary values, and the increase in the range of non-traditional book-selling outlets offering children's books as merchandise. There can be no doubt that the gradual growth of the mass market has altered the predominance of a bourgeois reading public, and hastened the transformation of the industry.

Though we readily accept that our 'material' (Gedin, 1975: 97) tastes have been altered by economic and social changes over the last 40 years, we are not so readily accepting that our consumption of 'cultural products' will necessarily change too. The predominance of popular cultural art forms is a factor which is altering the publisher's marketing strategies and increasingly their publication strategies, too. Furthermore, in the children's industry there has traditionally been a distinct separation between the two client groups represented by the library market and the trade. The 'library market' has wielded significant influence in the development of children's publishing, though, since the 1970s, there has been a decline in both the buying power and the influence of that market in children's publishing. In 1978 Turow predicted the growth in the mass marketing of children's books, as a result, (Turow, 1978: 3) and his predictions have proven correct. The pattern of 'mutual exclusivity' which has grown up is being challenged today by enterprises which recognise that their livelihood depends on taking advantage of the overlapping markets for books which might exist if these distinctions are not so rigidly adhered to.

The isolationist culture of children's publishing

The isolationist culture of children's publishing also differentiates it from adult publishing, a distinction created historically by:

- the relatively late development of institutionalised structures in children's publishing; for example, the first US children's editor was appointed in 1919 by Macmillan and in 1963 in Australia by Angus & Robertson;
- the importance of women, educationalists and librarians in the field contributing to the marginalisation of the industry, which conversely has created both a sense of isolation and 'freedom' giving it some advantages in developing a strong culture unimpeded by some of the restrictions placed on adult publishers;

▪ dismissive attitudes to children's culture which have determined that children's departments in publishing houses have generally been treated as 'less important' despite the fact that they have often contributed substantially to company turnover.

The pricing of children's books

The pricing of children's books is the final factor which makes this sector different. For there has been an expectation that books for young people must necessarily be 'cheaper' than books for older people. This stems from the desire to make books accessible, but also from notions that they are shorter, easier and 'less worthy' of the purchase price applied to adult books.

The growth of the children's market

The publisher for young people, then, sits at a conjunction of all these factors. How have these forces been managed? A selective examination of children's publishing isolates a number of historical landmarks which demonstrate that far from having become more susceptible to market forces as many educators suggest, the children's book has always provided an excellent example of the interplay between cultural and market forces, and that publishing trends have been produced by this dynamism. Where risk-taking and conducting business in an environment which is partially driven by non-business-like factors are 'norms', the children's publisher has often achieved the nearly impossible in marketing, extremely successfully, in such a volatile environment. Children's publishing has developed into a 'stand-alone industry' only in the last 50 years. This was during a revolutionary publishing period in which the trajectory of worldwide publishing growth was hastened and dramatically contributed to by Allen Lane's inspired creation of Penguin Books in 1935. That act 'changed the face of the book trade and made book ownership a possibility and a reality for all manner of men, women and children everywhere' (Morpurgo, 1979: 384). The changes this paperback revolution heralded were further hastened by electronic media development, contributing to the growth of the mass-structure which is publishing today.

First, though, it should be noted that the eighteenth-century origins of the children's publishing industry occurred in a climate of opinion which was firmly oriented towards instruction for young minds. Nevertheless, it's significant to note that 'pioneers' like John Newbery (1713–1767), when he published *The Little Pretty Pocket Book* (1744), quickly recognised the value of the niche market he was cultivating, and exploited it thoroughly. If critics of the media's influence on young people's literature are to be challenged, it is by the very history of the children's book itself. For, as Kline has noted, far from being 'contaminated' by twentieth-century marketing, the children's book was specifically invented and then manufactured by publishers in the nineteenth century who had begun to perceive a market, and who encouraged writers to produce for this market — 'Children's books were in fact the first "products" of any kind to be designed with children's special status and needs in mind' (Kline, 1993: 81–2). Children's books in this theoretical schema are the first mass-market products targeting children as consumers! They thus begin a tradition which has been exploited only recently by the very media industries which are said to be threatening the hegemony of the children's book. Nineteenth-century Australian precedents such as the bookseller/publisher E.W. Cole's commercial successes, and the 'Reward Books' marketed so successfully by companies such as the Religious Tract Society, provide ample evidence that publishers took the baton offered by the burgeoning children's market and ran with it. I will examine children's publishing, then, by demonstrating that despite the ostensibly 'improving' nature of these books, they have always been subject to an ambiguous conflict between commerce and culture, and that the forces of global culture have simply made the interplay a little more explicit. Instead of deriding globalisation, let's view it as part of a continuum, and try to more fully understand it.

Global media and children's books

Books are not only part of the mass-communication arena, but indeed the history of the book was a 'forerunner' of many of the trends we observe today with other communications media. Because of the predominantly library-oriented analysis to date, we have not fully recognised the need to position books within this schema. The book is not the product of an isolated creative artist, as it is mythically supposed to be, but rather, the product of a range of interconnected decision-makers and producers including managers, editors, designers, printers, booksellers and distributors (Coser, 1982: 5). Furthermore, most power roles in mass-media industries are filled by organisational players (Turow, 1992a: 22). The various institutions with a stake in book publishing are all similarly influenced by globalisation which is the 'expansion of the fragmentation and conglomerization phenomena across national borders' (Turow, 1992: 161) so that several national companies have consolidated into huge international conglomerates such as Time Warner, Disney, Bertelsmann, News Corp, Sony and Matsushita. The production of 'symbolic and material products' is therefore influenced in some significant ways, for such globalisation concentrates power over three areas in the production of mass media — structure, content, and technology (Turow, 1992b: 211).

Global or mass media features

Structure

Company structures are growing larger, and the world market for children's books has also grown enormously, with US sales leaping from $336 million in 1985 to $1.35 billion in 1995 (Raugust, 1997c: 80). In the UK titles rose 'from 4510 in 1986 to 7080 in 1994, and a turnover in the region of 215 million' (Reynolds, 1998: 38); in Australia children's book sales representing $134 million were recorded in 1997–1998 (Department of Communications Information Technology and the Arts, 1999: 3). It is also enlightening to examine the numbers of books entered for the CBCA awards each year, which rose from 183 in 1992, to 343 in 1998, and 326 in 2000 (CBCA, 1992, 1998, 2000). Massive takeovers and mergers, such as Paramount's of the prestigious old firm Macmillan in 1997–1998, have been matched by the absorption of Australia's first publisher, Angus & Robertson, into Murdoch's News Corporation Limited, as Harper Collins. Golden Books Family Entertainment commanded 19 per cent of the market with sales of $260 million in 1995 (though it has since experienced financial problems) (Raugust, 1997c: 83) and Scholastic (which has a large presence in Australia) was a close second. Disney has a share of 30 per cent of the US market when its in-house and licensed publishing are taken into account (Raugust, 1997c: 83). Such mass-market companies are philosophically directed towards mass audiences, so that US institutional children's sales were reduced from 80–90 per cent in the mid-1980s to 50–60 per cent in the mid-1990s (Raugust, 1997c: 80) The growth of the worldwide market has led to what some have called over-production and to a need for the industry to 'shake out'.

The rationalisation of US lists such as Little, Brown and Kingfisher (Raugust, 1997c: 81) was matched in the UK with the purchase of Andre Deutsch's list in 1991, by Scholastic (Reynolds, 1998: 24) and in Australia with the new imprints of the 1980s — Omnibus Books, Margaret Hamilton Books — becoming part of Scholastic, and Walter McVitty Books being sold to Lothian Books in the 1990s. Nevertheless one of the fascinating aspects of publishing is its ability to regenerate, and the ease with which a list may be established creates a pattern of renewal which is cyclical. As Long has pointed out, mergers have always characterised publishing, and 'the tendency towards concentration is offset by a tendency towards formation of new companies' (Long, 1992: 98). In the US 240 imprints could be identified in 1996 (Raugust, 1997c: 83), and the 1998-1999 APA directory identifies 23 Australian children's imprints. In Australia in the 1990s, new companies such as Working Title Press have been established, and lists such as Pan Macmillan Australia have begun to expand their children's lists as well. The most successful publishers here are not just the multinationals such as Scholastic Australia and Penguin Books Australia, but also Allen & Unwin, Era and Lothian Books. How they fit within this structure and, moreover, how they are adapting to these changes is enlightening. For these changes effect all companies, whether they be large or small, local or international, in a variety of ways and to different degrees.

The *five key structural features of global mass media* are:

1 vertical integration;
2 reducing competition;
3 market penetration;
4 exploiting territorial rights;
5 niche marketing.

Vertical integration

Vertical integration, or the practice of creating 'synergies', involves two strategies aimed at allowing companies to extend their profits by creating related materials via creative or subsidiary rights or to increase the product's attractiveness by offering value-added incentives (Turow, 1992b: 245–51.) US bestseller lists indicate an increasing tendency for books derived from other media properties to predominate (Raugust, 1997c: 87). Such product synergies come about via:

- cross-merchandising;
- supermarket and 'non-traditional book sales outlets';
- joint food and book promotions.

Cross-merchandising

Cross-merchandising is another strategy employed by children's publishers from the beginning — the toys John Newbery sold with his *Little Pretty Pocket Book*, Kate Greenaway's almanacs, and Beatrix Potter's many enterprises (Sutton, 1997). The growing supremacy of the merchandising property over the book, though, is a difference, as is the fact that the book itself may be a form of merchandise spawned by another media property; for example, Pokemon, Bananas in Pajamas, Teletubbies, Nickelodeon's Rugrats. The cross-merchandising practised by toy manufacturers has taught publishers two important strategies — how 'to capitalise on short term trends' and on 'cross-promotional opportunities' (Raugust, 1997b). Where publishing traditionally relies on predictable series, and on slow but steady selling properties, now publishers are more aware of techniques enabling them to capitalise on 'fads'. The type of products generated by such cross-marketing (apart from film, audio and TV tie-ins) are: *paper engineering, dolls, toys, board books, domestic accessories and clothing items*, all created to complement the book.

Paper engineering describes a range of products including pop-ups, lift-the flaps, cut-outs and other manipulative books which, once again, have been a 'constant' in the children's industry since the Victorian era with Ernest Nister and Dean & Co producing harlequinades and other such 'toy books'. The difference, though, is that their numbers have grown. Whereas in the past, the specific expertise needed and the high production costs tended to limit them, now they are produced with the benefits of concentration of production and mass-market production. This trend was advanced largely by one company — Intervisual Communications Inc in Los Angeles. Founder Waldo Hunt sold the concept to publishers in the UK in the 1960s, forming Graphics International (Fox, 1998: 97) but by 1975 had founded his own enterprise Intervisual Communications in Los Angeles, later changing its name to Intervisual Books Inc. It was estimated in 1991 as 'the world's major producer of pop-up books — over $500 million ... about 60% of the total world market in pop-ups' (Taylor, 1991). They estimate that 'from 1850 to 1965' only '10 million pop-ups' were produced, but by 1991 '10-15 million were ... produced each year' (Taylor, 1991). Their success was founded on their packaging for publishers (said to have numbered at least 30 majors amongst their clients) but they also owned a considerable volume of their product.

Early successes included the ground-breaking works by Jan Pienkowski which have sold millions. They produced via production-line assembly of book parts in countries such as Columbia, and were thus able to produce these labour-intensive works at a lower cost. They also set about diversifying and expanding product lines and, by 1991, had 'introduced 27 different formats ...' (Taylor, 1991). These range from electronic books with music and twinkling lights, to books with cloth finger puppets, carousel-shaped books, revolving and disappearing picture books, and a host of others. By 1997, they were experiencing troubles and Intervisual Books Inc. (IB) began to diversify into its own distribution of backlist titles, and direct-selling arrangements. It seems as the new century approached that IB was confronted by publishers and artists reserving the right to package their own books, having learned from the successes of this company. One such artist is the creator of the 'big title' in the US in 2000 *The Wonderful Wizard of Oz: A Commemorative Pop-Up* by L Frank Baum, illustrated by Robert Sabuda (S&S/Little Simon) which was promoted with a 'giveaway' of Emerald City green 3-D eyeglasses, and had sold 138 000 copies in a few months (Maughan, 2001). Sabuda handles his own production and negotiates his own packaging.

Toy-related imprints include both books generated by the toy, such as Power Rangers, Star Wars and Pokemon, and toys derived from books — notably, many *dolls* such as Winnie the

Pooh, Paddington Bear, Maisie and Madeline. Angelina Ballerina celebrated her tenth birthday in 1993, by which time 'there were nine picture books, two board books and doll-and-book package' (Bodin, 1993).

Board Books have diversified too, in that there are board book adaptations of picture books, which are said to have first appeared on the market in 1991, when Harper Collins published a *Goodnight Moon* board book (Raugust, 1998). Those which work are obviously those suitable for under three year olds, and those whose artwork can be converted to the format, without loss of its integrity. Whilst there has been a proliferation of some board books which are inappropriate to the format, they will no doubt be 'weeded out' by slowing sales.

Domestic Accessories are everywhere — Winnie the Pooh has his own exclusive collectable crockery and stationery lines; *Goosebumps* has spawned everything from stationery to sneakers that feature 3-D soles that allow wearers to make skeleton footprints (Benezra, 1996); Tomie De Paola, the US illustrator, releases his own catalogues and does proprietary deals with department stores on Christmas coffee mugs and other merchandise.

Clothing decorated with images made popular by Peter Rabbit and Paddington Bear are used as 'branding' labels on clothing for babies and toddlers. Some books generate all these spin-offs. One of the most successful of blanket promotions has been in conjunction with *Guess How Much I Love You* by Sam McBratney, which has now generated dolls, calendars and a range of other merchandise. DK Ink's Neal Porter summed up Bologna 97 'It's guess how much I love my teddy bear who's missing his button eye and looking for a new owner, with Sara Fanelli-like art and a value-added plush toy' (*A Sharper Focus*, 1997).

Sales through supermarket and 'non-traditional book sales outlets'

The growth of sales through supermarket and 'non-traditional book sales outlets' enables publishers to capitalise on this cross-merchandising via the sales of related non-book products. In 1996 an American survey estimated that 'independent and chain book stores accounted for only 15% of the total consumer market for children's books' (Rosen, 1997b). Discount stores (K-Mart and Wal-Mart) were reported in 1996 to be selling 30 per cent of all children' s books in the US (Latrobe, 1996). These outlets sell all the properties relating to the book — clothes, toys, stationery and crockery — whereas bookshops can rarely take the risk in stocking such a wide variety of non-book materials. In essence, this is another instance of how 'The dividing line between trade and mass market as product is blurring' (Lodge, 1997). Toy stores, too, are increasingly selling books. This has implications for the publishing trade, because of the different buying patterns of what one buyer described as 'impulse buyers', so that 'low-end' products with recognisable names are sought. Buyers seek 'the unusual', and stock 'one-off' items, rather than keeping a full range of a publisher's output (Rosen, 1997a).

The market potential of these new selling outlets is large, but requires a different concept of what might constitute 'viable product'. Firms with traditionally strong institutional lists have also entered mass-market publishing, and conversely 'literary' authors 'such as the Provensons started out as mass-market authors' (Donovan, 1991). In Australia, larger publishers such as Random House and Penguin have targeted this wider market with writers such as Christine Harris and Margaret Clark (Macleod, 1998), and illustrators such as Craig

Smith (Watts, 1994). But this pattern is not confined to larger companies. For even locally owned companies such as Lothian Books pursue 'special sales', exploring the potential for such synergies to be developed. Robert Ingpen, winner of the IBBY Medal 1986, produced the classic *Idle Bear* and sequels, later successfully merchandised to include cards, bookmarks and other materials. Lothian is currently investigating properties to be developed to market the work of new author/illustrator Lorette Boekstra's *Baby Bear* series.

Joint food and book promotions
Another way of cross-merchandising is with food, which is the ultimate consumer product! Book producers have latched onto the synergies which might be made between food and 'brain food'. Cereal has been offered with Little Golden Books ('Get your Kix', *Publishers Weekly*, 1997). Pritchard Marketing met with Smith's and Scholastic in 1997 with an idea which led to the creation of 'a 100 piece Goosebumps lenticular series' (known as 'tazos') to be inserted in Smith's Snack Foods and which led to 'the 59.8 % increase in snack-food sales' in 1997 (Pritchard, 1997: 39). Scholastic said they were 'the best licensing application they had for their product, the hottest children's property in the world' (1997: 39) and has since introduced it across the globe. They appear in a range of packaging for crisps and corn chips, and are linked to properties as diverse as Star Wars and Disney cartoon characters.

Goosebumps has also been marketed with fast food, and in joint promotions with 'Pepsi, Hershey Chocolate and Frito-lay' ('Goosebumps with Every Gulp', *Publishers Weekly*, 1996) and in 2000 'more than 25 licensed titles tied to food brands' (Raugust, 2000a) were available in the US. In Australia 'shelves are stacked with Rugrats Milk Smoothies Fruit Snacks, Pokémon crazy lollipops and The Wiggles Spaghetti Shapes' (McGilvray, 2000: 4).

Reducing competition
Reducing competition is another globalised production aim and so companies focus enormous promotion on a limited number of products; a fact bemoaned by opponents of monopolies, though a reduction in a surfeit of mass-media properties may not, in itself, be such a bad thing. But, moreover, as well as a reduction in the range and variety of products, prices in a monopolised market tend to be less subject to market forces. Children's books, as we've noted, are generally cheaper, so that publishers will increasingly aim to decrease competition and in a small market like Australia that is an even more significant concern.

Market penetration
Market penetration is the third structural feature, evinced by Disney's 1995 $19 billion takeover of Capital Cities/ABC in the US which gave it ownership of 'all four key distribution channels; filmed entertainment, cable television, broadcasting and telephone wires' ('Media Monopoly Makers', *Multinational Monitor*, 1995). This sort of practice is evident, to some degree, in Australia with companies like Scholastic and ABC Books.

Exploiting territorial rights
Exploiting territorial rights is another key issue since the influence of worldwide ownership and technology is changing patterns of access to copyright, making exclusive licensing difficult and 'contributing to the breakdown of traditional publishing practices' (Milliot, 1998). This has been an ongoing issue for countries like Australia and Canada, traditionally at the mercy of UK trade practising regulations, 'the next couple of years will probably see

the biggest change in territorial rights since the world was carved up by the Brits and the Yanks after World War II' (Milliot, 1998). Australia 'could very well become an open market before too long' (Milliot, 1998).

Niche marketing

Niche marketing identifies a niche, which 'refers to a distinct combination of resources that can support organisations with similar goals, boundaries and activities' (Turow, 1992b: 25). Because of the increasingly fragmented nature of our media industries, producers are attempting to target niche groups. The face of future publishing may lie in this sort of targeted marketing, which at its best can give each of us what we want in the exact format we request it to be delivered in. The publishing industry has adopted this approach in its increasingly age-based and audience-based approaches to children's publishing. Children's marketeers have been aware for some time of the various markets represented by children.

> There are babes and toddlers (0–2), preschoolers (3–5), kids (5–7), the tweens (8–12) and teens (13 plus). The industry is talking about even further segmentations to cater for the new online generation.
>
> (McGilvray, 2000: 4)

Such 'micro-targeting' can address specific genders, lifestyles and attitudes' (McGilvray, 2000: 4). Examples of niche markets currently prevalent are:

- book club marketing;
- proprietary deals;
- targeted 'brand' publishing for age or interest groups;
- the magazine market;
- direct marketing and mail-outs.

Book club marketing

Book club marketing in the US is controlled by three big players — Scholastic, Pages and Troll — with Scholastic the biggest. In Australia Scholastic has no competition for the school trade, having taken over Troll and a number of other short-lived enterprises. Its success can be attributed to the fact that it 'became part of the school fabric in the country where we were located' with 'Sales growing 20% in 1997 alone' (Milliot, 1998). It sometimes also forms 'strategic partnerships' (Sanislo, 1995) with other publishers and produces special products for the book fair markets. In the US, Pages Book Fairs has also begun to create 'niche fairs' (Milliot, 1996) for schools with a particular ethnic clientele.

Proprietary deals

Proprietary deals are those struck with non-traditional outlets (e.g. Target) to produce an edition solely for their market. Though a useful way to supplement sales, one publisher called it 'a relatively terrifying development. When bookshops start creating their own imprints, it's not too far a stretch that it might affect our core business' (Lottman, 1998). Often these deals are non-exclusive; that is, the book is available elsewhere but not in the special format created for the deal — for example, 'A Rainbow Fish journal (created by North-South) for Barnes and Noble' (Rosen, 1996) The advantage, as with book clubs, is the exposure to large markets frequented by non-book buyers.

Targeted 'brand' publishing for age or interest groups

Targeted 'brand' publishing for age or interest groups refers to books identified by a 'brand' which:

> connotes many things in the children's book industry. It can refer to a more traditional corporate brand, such as LEGO, which has become associated with a book series. It can be used to describe a licensed property, such as the Muppets. It can even be a synonym for a character, imprint or series, such as DK's Eyewitness line.
>
> (Raugust, 1997a)

One of the most successful brands in recent times has been Pokémon, whose mass-sales 'helped save Golden Books' (Raugust, 2000b), which had been experiencing financial hardship. Scholastic, which holds the trade rights to the name has also recorded massive sales. An author's name, too, can assume the nature of a 'brand', and R.L. Stine is as much an identifier as is his creation, *Goosebumps*; Australian Paul Jennings has similar brand value. The market has become increasingly segmented with age categories and interest groups being assigned their own series and publishing programs. Despite concerns that series can be less challenging, the 'up' side is that 'the right touch can bring out bookworms in any market … especially for boys who are so often disenchanted with reading, horror is doing the job'(Dunleavey, 1993). Stine's *Goosebumps* and *Fear Street* books have spawned a whole plethora of series for older readers; for example, *Bonechillers, Dead Time, Animorphs*. The 'library market' is also influenced by such segmentation, with, for example, the recent move towards adding another award to the CBCA awards for older teenagers. Another outcome is the potential for capturing multiple markets by different packaging for the same title; for example, Philip Pullman's *The Golden Compass* was released by Random House Audiobooks, Ballantine Books Fantasy Imprint, and Knopf Books for Younger Readers at the same time, with a $250 000 marketing budget (Alderdice, 1995).

The magazine market

The magazine market, too, has become increasingly niche-oriented, targeting teenage girls or sports or computer fanatics. It is said that:

> print will increasingly play a role as a mass-market branding tool, which will provide advertisers with a vehicle to reach highly targeted audiences when they need to communicate more complex information.
>
> (Chipperfield, 1996: 25)

For example, some magazines in the US are being produced in different editions for different target markets.

Direct marketing and mail-outs

Direct marketing and mail-outs are increasing, aided by the facility offered by electronic technology and databasing. Many advertisers, tired of the vagaries of a diverse market, are actually targeting niches via such direct mail; for example, 'Time Life education … mails its catalogues to 100 000 librarians and 50 000 school administrators' (Milliot, 1995) and companies such as Dymocks' chain of booksellers in Australia send out regular newsletters. Automated inventory systems have enabled some 'highly segmented, targeted marketing'

(Miller, 1999) so that book-selling chains can develop a profile of their users and their previous purchases and target them accordingly with incentives to buy more of similar products.

Content

Content is influenced by structural features which are indeed designed to control content. 'Many times, the book is the beginning in the content chain that leads to other products' (Milliot, 1998).

The five key content features of global mass media are:

1 global views;
2 content 'unknown';
3 censorship;
4 exploitation of intellectual property and copyright;
5 minimising risks.

Global views

Global views or the globalisation of content is sometimes described as the 'coca-colarisation' of the book. For, if one company owns and markets its product into a wide range of markets it is less likely to produce culturally specific rather than non-specific product. For example, Disney aims to 'avoid political controversy' and to create product easily translated into many languages (*Multinational Monitor*, 1995). Such homogenous programming will inevitably decrease local product and its diversity. There is a possibility that the regional and local may be fortuitously celebrated though, in this huge marketplace. For example, books reflecting the unique aspects of Australian life have 'gone global'; for example, *Possum Magic, Animalia* and *Where the Forest Meets the Sea*. One of the most vital factors in recent publishing has been the expansion of both culturally diverse publishing and indigenous publishing. In Australia the growth of companies such as Magabala Books and IAD Press and the willingness of publishers such as University of Queensland Press to establish indigenous lists has contributed to a new diversity of output. The eager reception of authors such as Ian Abdullah, Bronwyn Bancroft, Boori Monty Pryor and Melissa Lucashenko as exports seems to challenge the globalisation of culture. There seem to be two conflicting forces contributing to another source of dynamism in publishing. But it's not exactly an equal competition though, for 'Globalisation is hot and strong … the impulse to localise is cool and weak' (Rosen, 1995: 32–3).

Content 'unknown'

Content 'unknown' is a concept which describes the volatility of book format and delivery mechanisms, which have publishers in a state of flux, with product being produced for an increasingly complex marketplace, and new forms of media being developed, which may present a challenge to both their sales and copyright control. Instead of the book itself having primacy, it is the *exposure* the book receives in other non-print marketing mediums, and the possible *translation* of it into other media which are driving book production. 'For the moment, no new form is on the horizon, only the anxiety that precedes it … traces of today's anxiety-ridden mood can be found in publishing's ur-documents, which are not books but book catalogues and book contracts' (Engelhardt, 1997). Uncertainty about a book's likely future leads to some books not being published at all, to some very opportunistic promotion, and to some scurrilous contracting of authors, aimed at protecting publishers' rights rather than exploiting them on behalf of an author. *Catalogues* 'bear a growing resemblance to The Midday Show guest list' (Haigh, 1996: 55) in that they are 'offering almost-movies, soon-to-be-riveting television performances, market-blanketing radio interviews, interactive Web site moments and charismatic personalities' (Englehardt, 1997).

Content is no longer enough. For example, an Australian advertisement for Puffin Books shouts 'Pick of the Pack! Hook Into a Book With Puffin. Don't miss the chance for your students to win Puffin books for themselves and their school … Closes Oct 16, 1998' (Penguin Books Australia, 1998: 2) and the plot summary is in small print! *Contracts* too, indicate how fraught with doubt publishers are, as they resort to painstakingly detailed descriptions of possible electronic formats such as 'any other device or medium for electronic reproduction, publication, distribution or transmission, whether now or hereafter known or developed' (Englehardt, 1997). The limitless potential for transformation of the product is becoming increasingly difficult to describe.

Censorship

Censorship is another possible outcome of the power of these global companies which have the ability to censor content. For example, publication of 'Marc Eliot's Walt Disney: Hollywood's Dark Prince was aborted suddenly by Bantam in 1991' just before Bantam's Disney Library series went on sale in supermarkets, 'a deal worth far more than his book would have been' (Miller, 1997). Similarly, Harper Collins reneged on a contract to publish Chris Patton's memoirs because it was said that Murdoch feared a decrease in Chinese sales of Murdoch publications. Most censorship, though, is less overt, more subtle, though equally the result of the nature of the client relationships between producer and buyer.

Exploitation of intellectual property and copyright

Exploitation of intellectual property and copyright is a huge risk for writers in this new environment. How can they protect their intellectual property, in a media environment which makes Pocahontas into a simpering B-grade movie starlet whose Native American origins are just as obscured as the cultural origins of Aladdin in another equally popular animated feature? How do they ensure that bland and unsympathetic treatment is not meted out to their content? (As a purely personal view, the Robin Williams' high-camp Mrs Doubtfire is to my mind a pale shadow of the character created in Anne Fine's book *Madame Doubtfire*.)

Minimising risks

Minimising risks involves 'risk management' strategies or balancing change and continuity as a key publishing task. Because producers of books are in the business of producing one-off items whose sales rely on 'innovation', limited by cost and efficiency factors, they try to respond via measures aimed at reducing the vagaries of the market; for example, formulas, track records, stereotypes, series and serials, market research (albeit limited), and book sales statistics. 'Products' with proven track records include:

- name authors;
- series publishing;
- bestsellers;
- special event/personality promotions and tie-ins;
- award-winners;
- reprints of classics;
- the teacher/literature-based market;
- books without authors.

Name authors

Name authors are those whose consistent popularity can ensure 'saleability', and become the subject of intensive publicity campaigns; for example, signings, tours, media saturation. The name on the cover assumes more importance than the title, the blurb, or the image; for example, J.K. Rowling; R.L. Stine; Paul Jennings; John Marsden. Authors assume 'personalities' and the facts of their lives are 'enhanced' by marketing imperatives. They have interesting pastimes and pasts, and assume roles and responsibilities to their readers. For instance — Marsden as seer to angst-ridden teenagers; Mem Fox as celebrity author of Australiana for preschoolers.

Series publishing

Series publishing is another way in which publishers try to minimise risk. They may be age-based; interest-based or brand-name-based. For example, Penguin's *Aussie Bites* and *Aussie Nibbles* series is a recognisable brand, complimented by the 'bites' taken out of each cover; University of Queensland Press' (UQP) Young Adult fiction series relies on its identity as a series for teenagers; *After Dark* (Lothian) is for readers of horror; Omnibus's *Solos* are illustrated non-fiction for children. Individual authors have also been commissioned to write series featuring the same characters; for example, Margaret Clark's *Aussie Angels* (Hodder), Libby Hathorn's *Ghostop* (Hodder) and Brian Caswell's *Alien Zones* (UQP) series. Another experiment has been the serialised stories co-written by Paul Jennings and Morris Gleitzman entitled *Wicked* and *Deadly!* (Penguin).

Bestsellers

Bestsellers are another predictable technique in that there are topics, genres or formats which dominate the powerful bestseller lists, used as marketing tools in themselves. These lists are often the subject of specialised promotion; for example, TV personalities such as Rosie O'Donnell, or Oprah Winfrey's Book Club, are known to 'increase sales by more than 1,000 percent' (Miller, 1997). Mark Macleod's regular appearances on the Australian Midday Show in the 1980s were also known to influence buyers.

Special event/personality promotions and tie-ins

These categories of books rely on specific marketing or sales points which may be either *short-term and opportunistic* or *longer-term, predictable or anticipated events.*

Examples of *short-term and opportunistic* points are Lady Diana's death; current celebrity profiles such as Leonardo di Caprio and the Spice Girls; current celebrity authors, such as the Duchess of York's 'Budgie' books, and books by Michael Bolton and John Travolta.

Warner Books picked up Travolta's 'Propeller One-Way Night Coach' and printed 250 000 copies (Luscombe, 1997)

Examples of *longer-term, predictable or anticipated events* are the Olympics, the end of the Millennium, or Christmas, which also spawn bestsellers. Each month's bestseller list both reflects current fads and more lasting public pre-occupations.

Award-winners

Award-winners also represent safer publications, ensuring demands for reprints, and even offering some publishers an insight into likely future winners. Such 'second guessing' or predicting 'award-winning style' books based on previous choices has been suggested as a possible outcome of the CBCA's short-listing, which commentators note often features a predominance of 'issues-based' books, and may have led to the increased production of them.

Re-prints of classics

Re-prints of classics both suit the aspirations of baby-boomer parents to introduce their children to the 'canon', and meet the economic needs of publishers, since no royalties are involved. They sometimes suffer from the inferior reproduction of original illustrations, from excessive abbreviation (Hunt, 1998) or from censorship, with, for example, their offensive racism or sexism being excised, effectively destroying much of the historical value of the works. *The Story of Little Black Sambo* (1899) has been re-released in several versions and has gone from being 'One of the most controversial books in existence ... to the interpretation by different creators' (Hochwald, 1996). The longevity of Australian classics like *Little Mother Meg* by Ethel Turner, is partly reliant on their repackaging in eye-catching new covers, and even on some revision. For example, Mary Grant Bruce's *Billabong* series was edited by Collins/A&R some years ago to erase their more racist passages. Sometimes it is the publisher's *imprint and style* which is promoted as the unique feature of a classic reprint. 'Knopf's Everyman's Children's Classics' were re-released and described as, 'books to own rather than merely read. Each book has a silk ribbon bookmark ... two-colour illustrated endpapers, and printed bookplates ... unjacketed cloth covers, spines are gold stamped' (Schwartz, 1992). 'Modern' *classics*, such as *Madeleine, Babar* and *Thomas the Tank Engine* books, have all reappeared with dolls and other items to accompany them. At the 2001 Toy Fair in the US, there were prominent displays of *Eloise, Curious George* and *Clifford* toy lines (Raugust, 2001).

The teacher/literature-based market

This market has been both a surer and an ever-regenerative market to target. 'Promotions people want information about the ways books are used with children and children's reactions to old and new titles' (Van Orden, 1997: 26). But the schools or educational market can also be a minefield of variant demands and practices. Its power is evinced by the rapid growth in the production of *teachers' resources such as notes and kits* to complement books and other media. '*Big*' Books are another phenomenon which has resulted from the recognition of teacher needs. The '*Bibliotherapeutic*' approach often taken to books, in using them as 'tools', can be seen in *reviews* which describe books as being 'useful; for various purposes. *Textbooks* are often rigorously defined in order not to offend particular parent groups. Schools may 'de-select' or be forced to discard materials, at the behest of powerful parent groups. *Censorship*, therefore, often occurs even before the selection of material, and in the preparation of reading materials; for example, the New South Wales Government 'targeted for removal or non-purchase' Judy Blume's *Forever* in 1989 (Williams and Dillon, 1993: 77). Illustrators have been known to abandon their work, frustrated by publishers' efforts to be everything to everybody. Australian illustrators bemoan the fact that they can be asked to change virtually anything — to avoid risk-taking, and to avoid stereotypes, violence and naked bodies. These prohibitions have a lot to do with the fact that our books must also suit the US educational market which is far more conservative (Blaxland, 2000: 27).

Books without authors

These products can include several categories manufactured to order for a specific market, such as mail-order, fiction factories, novelisations, packaging, managed texts (Coser et al., 1982). This sort of conservatism is an extreme example of how publishers seek to minimise risk in markets leading to excessively rigid content control.

Technology

Technology is influenced by structure as much as is content, for media owners are understandably keen to control technology and its effect on products.

The three key technology features of global mass media are:

1   convergence of media;
2   electronic media in book production and distribution;
3   the influence of media on literacy.

Convergence of media

Convergence of media is where the media of carriage (telecommunications, computing, the electromagnetic spectrum) and media of content (newspapers and other print media, broadcasting) are being brought 'closer and closer together' (Cunningham and Turner, 1993: 324). '*Bundled*' *media* aims to produce a work capable of being converted into as many other forms as possible; that is, to be delivered in the format required by the user. Such 'digital convergence' (Hilts, 1997) can deliver in one format and be completed in another, if so desired. In future the marketeer 'will demand a media package that promises to deliver his target audience — not just any audience' (Levine, 1990). Content remains, though, the seed from which other projects spring.

Film and TV tie-ins and re-releases are the most obvious manifestation of how media owners seek to bundle rights and offer their content in varied formats. Movies are often jointly released with new or re-released book titles with covers featuring the movie stars; for example, *Stuart Little* and Geena Davis. Books create movies, but movies also create books. The Oscar-nominated film *Billy Elliot* is to have a book release adapted from the screenplay into a novel by Melvin Burgess, to be released by The Chicken House in the UK and by Scholastic in the US (Eccleshare, 2001: 4). There have been few greater phenomenons than James Cameron's movie *Titanic*. 'No single film has ever inspired sale for so many books from so many publishers' (Maryles, 1998). For example, *A Night To Remember* by Walter Lord, first published in 1958, is up to 2,777,000 copies in print after 71 printings (Maryles, 1998).

Electronic media in book production and distribution

Starting with the arrival of the manuscript on disk, computerization has transformed book production, billing, distribution and bookstore management. With Amazon.com, the online bookstore, it has even changed the way books are bought.

(Engelhardt, 1997)

Publishers have viewed the influence with some disquiet, though they have also begun forays into establishing electronic divisions in their companies, with the awareness that:

For the first time in half a millennium, 'publishers may lose control of their own package' ... for any new, booklike electronic format will not be invented by a publisher. What, then, will a publisher control? Perhaps ... only a holder of copyrights, a 'content provider' for others.

(Engelhardt, 1997)

The difficulties of adjusting to this challenge are apparent in the fact that some publishers have opened and then closed their new media divisions. Predictions are dangerous, mistakes are costly and the 'use by date' of new technology is often mercilessly imminent.

Internet selling

Internet selling and the growth of Amazon Com and Barnes and Noble's book-selling sites poses a potential threat and an opportunity to booksellers and publishers. The suggestion that 'London's demise as a major English language book publishing centre' (Kiely, 1994: 2) is imminent if publishers and booksellers do not begin to embrace electronic marketing methods, makes Australia even more vulnerable. To combat this development some sellers have resorted to the creation of superstores, with 'about 100,000 titles compared with an average independent's range of between 8000 and 12,000', the first of which was opened by Collins in Sydney (McGuire, 1998: 32). The idea is that an enormous range will compete with the Internet by offering instant delivery of the product.

Internet promotion

Internet promotion is being used by publishers and authors, too, with sites which are used for a range of functions including:

- *catalogue information* — it's better than the print format because it allows a consumer to 'sample' product, via text and illustrations;
- *cheaper 'targeted' promotion* aimed at special interest audiences;
- *individual writer promotion* with sites featuring biography or chapters online, or even characters from their books; for example, *The Paw* by Natalie Prior;
- *searching facilities*; for example, Scholastic allows kids to search by title or character and to read samples of *Babysitter Club* titles;
- *Online teachers' notes* are offered by companies too; for example, Bantam Doubleday Dell has a site including interviews with authors and illustrators; and
- the interactive nature of the Internet makes a lot of *publishing functions* more efficient and responsive — many publishers and authors now get direct feedback from their readers via email; for example, Eric Carle's site (*www. eric-carle.com*) allows those readers and booksellers to interact with each other.

Unsolicited manuscripts are also being accepted by publishers via the Internet. Some publishers and even authors are using it to direct sell their books. Future developments should include more direct communication and faster connections with booksellers, which will make the Internet even more effective.

Media influence on topics in fiction

Media influence on topics in fiction was dramatically demonstrated by the appearance of Gillian Rubinstein's *Space Demons* which used technology as both plot and thematic device, and works like Toby Forward's marvellous retelling of Peter Pan in *Neverland*.

Electronic publishing

Electronic publishing 'is going to be the most significant industry of the 21st century. The new internet environment — the demand for intellectual property in lots of different guises' (Hilts, 1997) will drive the further development of electronic books, which are just beginning to appear in formats such as 'handheld' books or those developed by MIT Media Lab. An electronic book looks like a book — with blank pages made of an 'electronic paper' which you charge with text, then unplug and take away to read. You can later plug it back in, suck out the text images and download new text (Hilts, 1997: 6). Such 'electronic ink' makes it possible, for example, to 'make the type larger for easier reading' (Vizard, 1997). It also makes it possible to release an online version before a printed copy. Both Stephen King and Bryce Courtenay in Australia have recently released books like this. The *Lurker Files* series began as a 'cyber soap' before it was printed (Rosen, 1997a). Some see the potential for producing 'hard-to-publish' books with a limited market, such as translations, on the Net.

Dual publishing — the hard copy with either an online or a CDRom version — has been applied successfully, particularly with picture books. 'The most successful are those that make the best use of the medium's potential for movement, action, sound and music — a potential it shares with video' (Butler, 1997). 'The CD has had its day already. It's static' (Hilts, 1997), whereas 'Electronic encyclopedias have been the fastest growing segment of the multimedia industry' (Milliot, 1995) and Scott Flanders of Macmillan says that '70% of their computer titles have an electronic component now' (Hilts, 1997). One of the most exciting things about the Internet is that a reader can get not only the content of a book online, but its context as well, by hyperlinking the book's content to related sources' (Hilts, 1997).

Media influence on packaging and production

Media influence on packaging and production of the book means competition with advertisements and computer games, featuring 'Attention Deficit Design' (Stevenson, 1997) with covers being brighter, bolder, more sophisticated and hipper; using new techniques such as computer graphics, embossing, foil, matte laminations, holograms; photographic images; series designs to make whole series readily identifiable; more mass-market covers to widen appeal; and targeting an ambiguous age of market to widen appeal. The interior of the illustrated book has changed too — typography, layout, design and structure feature mixed media and an infinite range of variables now, with fewer rules governing what can and can't be done within a picture book's confines.

The influence of media on literacy

Media influence on literacy is undeniable and has both the 'potential for encouraging at their simplest level, passive involvement and reception, and at their most sophisticated level, an ability to immerse youngsters in worlds created by large entertainment corporations' (Somers, 1995: 208). There are a range of aspects of the media which influence young people's reading habits. One is the concept of *virtual reality* where 'the boundary between "real" and "virtual" experiences will disappear' (Somers, 1995: 203), making this new generation very adept at entering into and even inventing their own stories. Another is *visual literacy* which has developed in new readers who are used to 'reading' pictures and to concepts such as interactivity, mixed media, complex visual texts and 'scriptlike' texts. This sort of 'nonlinear, nonhierarchical means of communication in the digital environment' (Dresang, 1996: 3) has made a different type of reader. The marketing manager for Nickelodeon says that 'Kids as young as four are going on to the website and we have a database of 93,000' (McGilvray, 2000: 5). Their demands are different, for:

> the discipline in screenwriting is to reveal the thoughts and feelings of characters through speech and action primarily, and secondarily through photography and through the expressionistic presence on the screen of certain visual and aural moods.
>
> (Gleitzman, 1992: 5)

These skills are being applied by book writers to their literature for young people, changing the book itself in a range of ways. Kids today spend their leisure time reading highly illustrated magazines, playing video games, watching music and being assaulted by sophisticated advertising campaigns. They don't turn the TV off when visitors arrive because:

> It would be like telling one of my friends to shut up and sit in the corner … Kids don't so much watch the box as interact with it … Their education and their media experience are framing their view of the world and of the products being marketed to them.
>
> (McCaughan, 1994: 15–16)

All this watching means that children are sophisticated consumers, aware of issues kids in previous generations were not supposed to know anything about. It is difficult to target the youth market because of its rapid change.

> Teenagers have a cultural cycle of between four and six months … They are impulsive … But they … have disposable dollars and they are willing to spend.
>
> (*Marketing*, 1994: 36)

They are not easily fooled, they are brand and image conscious, they're highly visually literate. The remote control rules in their worlds, leading to publishing responses such as Harper Collins' *Master Piece* series, launched in 1995, and picture books for older readers such as Gary Crew and Steven Woolman's graphic novel *Tagged* (1997) and Isobelle Carmody and Shaun Tan's *Dreamwalker* (Lothian). Publishers will continue to respond and to evolve as a response to the changing demands of these visually literate readers.

Conclusion

One of the scintillating things about publishing is that predictions can often be overturned by unforeseen occurrences. In 1993, a review of British children's publishing made two very reasonable suggestions that 'Despite his death Roald Dahl will probably continue to dominate the bestseller lists for several years to come ... Texts are tending to become much shorter' (Fisher, 1993: 113). Who could have predicted that several very 'long' books featuring a boy named Harry Potter would consign Dahl to a lower rung on the bestselling ladder? If Harry Potter has taught us anything, it's that children are a market in themselves. 'The similarity in children's consumer development suggests that children are a mass market' (McNeal, 1993). If the *New York Times* felt it necessary to create a separate Children's Bestsellers list for the first time in 2000 (Boloknik, 2000) in order to get Harry off the hallowed adult bestsellers list after a year of monopolising it, then kids' power has finally asserted itself, even in this revered literary forum.

The book, the publishing market, and how publishers and writers interact have all changed — dramatically! Books are media products, and publishers are in the business of not only producing them but also selling them. Bemoaning the manufacture of books by celebrities such as Julie Andrews, Jamie Lee Curtis, Jane Seymour or George Negus, must be contextualised by an acknowledgment of the tradition begun by Newbery, Greenaway, Alcott, Turner and Gibbs, all of whom helped to invent a genre and then went about producing for the market *they* had created. We call these books 'classic' now, though they were the pulp fiction of their day, just as Dickens was in the nineteenth century. The so-called 'mass-market title' has begun to cross the great divide and can be simultaneously literary and mass market; for example, *Haunted House*, a pop-up book by Jan Pienkowski (Schulman, 1982: 218), won the Kate Greenaway Medal in 1979. Popular culture has changed the way we view things, as evinced by the now legendary ALA campaign featuring Miss Piggy (Schulman, 1982: 219), now succeeded by recent posters featuring Antonio Banderas. Mass-media influence has determined that producing and marketing children's properties is now an even more complex mixture of commerce and culture.

Selling children's properties involves the negotiation of a blurring in the distinction between trade and institutional selling; a rapidly growing and bewildering range of technological developments; and the growing supremacy of marketing over the production of the work. There can be no doubt that the influences noted in this chapter have changed the complexion of publishing lists generally. But it is important to qualify these comments. For discerning publishers though, they are aware of these trends, and will continue to take them into account, and not base their publishing decisions on them. The best of publishers do not approach their tasks with any less idealism or passion. Rosalind Price of Allen and Unwin, says that what she looks for when she publishes is:

All the big, important things, of course — the hard and the soft. I look for intelligence, humour, honesty and compassion; affection and respect for children; intensity; love of language — prose that's both muscular and delicate; the ability to affect the reader ... A good laugh is always welcome.

(Sheahan-Bright, 1999b: 10)

Publishers do, nevertheless, find themselves increasingly aware of these influences, and can often use them astutely to promote the books they are publishing.

Children's publishing houses and their structures, the content of what they produce and the technologies they employ, have changed. But they are also very much the same as they ever were. Publishing has several continuous characteristics, one of which is that it has always been subject to bewildering forces, and those who produce these properties must be careful at the crossroads, for it is a busier place than it has ever been.

Bibliography

Alderdice, K. (1995) 'RL Stine: 90 Million Spooky Adventures', *Publishers Weekly[Online]* vol 242 no 29, 17 July, 2 pp. Available: InfoTrac Searchbank, Expanded Academic ASAP International Edition, Item 28 [accessed: 11 May 1998].

Aries, P. (1973) *Centuries of Childhood*. Jonathon Cape, London [1st edn: *L'enfant à la vie familiale sous l'ancien régime*, 1960].

Benezra, K. (1996) 'Scholastic's Cool Ghouls', *Brandweek [Online]* vol 37 no 23, 3 June, 2 pp. Available: InfoTrac Searchbank Expanded Academic ASAP International Edition, Item 24 [accessed: 11 May 1998].

Blaxland, W. (2000) 'What about the Wobbly Bits?', *Classroom* issue 3, pp. 26–9.

Bodin, M. (1993) 'Angelina Ballerina Leaps Into Bestsellerdom', *Publishers Weekly [Online]* vol 240 no 45, 8 November, 2 pp. Available: InfoTrac Searchbank, Expanded Academic ASAP International Edition, Item 16 [accessed: 9 May 1998].

Boloknik, K. (2000) 'A list of their Own', *Salon. Com*, August 16, 4 pp. Available: http: www.salon.com [accessed: 22 September 2000].

Bourdieu, P. (1993) *The Field of Cultural Production*. Polity Press, Cambridge.

Buckingham, D. (2000) *The Death of Childhood*. Polity Press, Cambridge.

Butler, T.P. (1997) 'Tale Spinning: Children's Books on CD-ROM', *The Horn Book Magazine* vol 37 no 2, 6 pp. Available: InfoTrac Searchbank, Expanded Academic ASAP International Edition, Item 161 [accessed: 29 April 1998].

Carmody, I. (2001) *Dreamwalker* (illustrated by S. Tan). Lothian, Melbourne.

Children's Book Council of Australia (1992) 'Annual Awards 1992 Judges Report', *Reading Time* vol 36, no 3, July, pp. 3–6.

—— (2000) 'Annual Awards 2000 Judges Report', *Reading Time* vol 44 no 3, August, pp. 2–12.

Chipperfield, M. (1996) 'In Pursuit of Print', *Marketing*, October, pp. 14–25.

Coser, L. (1984) 'The Publishing Industry as a Hybrid', *Library Quarterly* vol 54, January, pp. 5–12.

Coser, L. Kadushin, C. and Powell, W. (1982) *Books the Culture and Commerce of Publishing*. Basic Books, New York.

Crew, G. (1997) *Tagged* (illustrated by S. Woolman). Era Publications, Adelaide.

Cunningham, S. and Turner, G. (eds) (1993) *The Media in Australia*. Allen & Unwin, Sydney.

Curtain, J. (1993) 'Book Publishing', in *The Media in Australia*, Cunningham, S. and Turner, G. (eds), Allen & Unwin, Sydney, pp. 102–18.

Department of Communications Information Technology and the Arts (1999) *Cultural Trends in Australia No 9. Australian Book Publishing 1997–98*. Department of Communications Information Technology and the Arts and the Australian Bureau of Statistics, June.

De Mause, L.(ed.) (1974) *The History of Childhood*. Psychohistory Press, New York.

Donovan, J. (1991) 'Children's Book Publishing on the Ascent', *Publishing Research Quarterly[Online]*, vol 7 no 3, Fall, 8 pp. Available: FastDoc [accessed: 2 November 1998].

Dresang, E. (1997) 'Influence of the Digital Environment on Literature for Youth: Radical Change in the Handheld Book', *Library Trends* vol 45 no 4, Spring, 25 pp. Available: InfoTrac Web, Expanded Academic ASAP International Edition [accessed: 25 November 1999].

Dunleavey, M.P. (1993) 'Books That Go Bump in the Night', *Publishers Weekly[Online]* vol 240 no 27, 5·July, 2 pp. Available: Available: InfoTrac Web, Expanded Academic ASAP International Edition [accessed: 18 May 1998].

Eagleton, T.(1983) *Literary Theory: An Introduction*. Basil Blackwell, Oxford.

Eccleshare, J. (2001) 'Letter from London', *Publishers Weekly[Online]*, vol 248 no 10, 9 pp. Available: InfoTrac Web, Expanded Academic ASAP International Edition [accessed: 18 March 2001].

Engelhardt, T. (1997) 'Gutenberg Unbound: Publishing Execs No Longer Feel the Book, as a Freestanding Entity, is Sustainable', *The Nation [Online]* vol 264 no 10, 17 March, 9 pp. Available: InfoTrac Searchbank, Expanded Academic ASAP International Edition, Item 4 [accessed: 16 May 1998].

Fisher, C. (1993) 'Trends in the Publishing of Children's Books in the UK', *International Review of Children's Literature and Librarianship* vol 18 no 2, pp. 105–14.

Fox, G. (1998) 'Movable Books' in Reynolds, K. and Tucker, N., *Children's Publishing in Britain Since 1945*. *Scolar Press*, Aldershot, pp. 86–109.

Gedin, P. (1975) *Literature in the Marketplace* (translated by G. Bisset). Faber, London.

Gleitzman, M. (1992) 'Writing for Children', *Magpies* vol 7 no 1, March, pp. 5–10.

Haigh, G. (1996) 'Bloody Publishers', *The Independent Monthly*, March, pp. 50–5.

Hilts, P. (1997) 'The Road Ahead: Publishing Visionaries Look at the Changes that Digital Technology Might Bring', *Publishers Weekly[Online]* vol 244 no 31, July, 4 pp. Available: InfoTrac Searchbank, Expanded Academic ASAP International Edition, Item 4 [accessed: 18 May 1998].

Hochwald, L. (1996) '*Little Book Big Controversy*', *Publishers Weekly[Online]* vol 243 no 31, 29 July, 2 pp. Available: InfoTrac Searchbank, Expanded Academic ASAP International Edition, Item 8 [accessed: 30 May 1998].

Hunt, P. (1991) *Criticism Theory and Children's Literature*. Blackwell, Oxford.

—— (ed.) (1996) *Encyclopedia of Children's Literature* (associate editor, S. Ray). Routledge, London.

Ingram, A.B. (1987) 'From Manuscript To Marketplace', in Saxby, M. and Winch, G. (eds) *Give Them Wings: The Experience of Children's Literature*. Macmillan, South Melbourne, pp. 339–52.

Kiely, M. (1994) 'Big Money in Ethnic Marketing', *Marketing*, June, pp. 10–14.

Kline, S. (1993*) Toys, TV and Children's Culture in the Age of Marketing*. Verso, London.

Kobrak, F. and Luey, B. (eds) (1992) *The Structure of International Publishing in the Nineties*. Transaction, New Brunswick.

Kociumbas, J. (1997) *Australian Childhood: A History*. Allen & Unwin, Sydney.

Kohlberg.L. (1967) *The Philosophy of Moral Development*. Harper & Row, San Francisco.

Levine, J. (1990) 'The Last Gasp of the Multi Media?' *Forbes[Online]* vol 146 no 6, 17 September, 4 pp. Available: InfoTrac Searchbank, Expanded Academic ASAP International Edition, Item 9 [accessed: 16 May 1998].

Latrobe, K. and Schwartz-Porter, C.(1996) 'Bodies Corporate', *Emergency Librarian[Online]* vol 24 no 1, 14 pp. Available: FirstSearch, ArticleFirst, Item 14 [accessed: 2 November 1998].

Lodge, S. (1997) 'Children's Mass Market Business', *Publishers Weekly [Online]*, 1 December, 16 pp. Available: http:// www. bookwire com; http://www. publishers weekly.reviewsnews. com [accessed: 3 March 1998].

Long, E. (1992) 'The Cultural Meaning of Concentration', in Kobrak, F. and Luey, B. (eds) *The Structure of International Publishing in the Nineties*. Transaction, New Brunswick, pp. 93–117.

Lottman, H.R. and Roback, D. (1998) 'A Buzz-less Bologna', *Publishers Weekly[Online]* vol 245 no 17, 27 April, 4 pp. Available: InfoTrac Searchbank, Expanded Academic ASAP International Edition, Item 44 [accessed: 18 May 1998].

Luey, B. (1992) 'Introduction: The Impact of Consolidation and Internationalism', in Kobrak, F. and Luey, B. (eds) (1992) *The Structure of International Publishing in the Nineties*. Transaction, New Brunswick, pp. 1–22.

Luscombe, B. (1997) 'Not Your Regular Pulp Fiction', *Time[Online]* vol 150 no 4, 28 July, 1 p. Available: InfoTrac Searchbank, Expanded Academic ASAP International Edition, Item 1 [accessed: 6 May 1998].

Macleod, M.(1998) 'Marketing Books for Young People', *Viewpoint* vol 6 no 3, Spring, pp. 5–7.

Marketing (1994) 'From Homeys to Cool Bitches', *Marketing*, May, pp. 34–6, 38.

Maryles, D. (1998) 'A Ship-Shape Windfall', *Publishers Weekly[Online]* vol 245 no 6, 9 February, 1 p. Available: InfoTrac Searchbank, Expanded Academic ASAP International Edition, Item 242 [accessed: 18 May 1998].

Maughan, S. (2001) 'Moving on Up', *Publishers Weekly[Online]* vol 248 no 9, 26 February, 9 pp. Available: InfoTrac Web, Expanded Academic ASAP International Edition [accessed: 19 March 2001].

McCaughan, D. (1994) 'Kids Stuff', *Marketing*, October 1994, pp. 14–17, 21, 57.

McGilvray, A. (2000) 'This Little Kiddie', *The Weekend Australian Review*, 23–24 September, pp. 4–5.

McGuire, M. (1998) 'Buy the Book', *The Australian*, 5 June, p. 32.

McNeal, J. and Yeh, C-H.(1993) 'Born To Shop', *American Demographics[Online]* vol 15 no 6, June, 6 pp. Available: InfoTrac Searchbank, Expanded Academic ASAP International Edition, Item 2 [accessed: 21 August,1998].

Miller, L. (1999*)* 'Cultural Authority and the Use of New Technology in the Book Trade', *Journal of Arts Management, Law and Society[Online]* vol 28 issue 4, Winter, 28 pp. Available: InfoTrac Web, Expanded Academic ASAP International Edition [accessed: 19 March 2001].

Miller, M.C. (1997) 'The Crushing Power of Big Publishing', *The Nation [Online]* vol 264 no 10, March 17, 7 pp. Available: InfoTrac Searchbank, Expanded Academic ASAP International Edition, Item 1 [accessed: 5 June 1998].

Milliot, J. (1995) 'Libraries Opening Up Again', *Publishers Weekly[Online]* vol 242 no 22, May 29, 3 pp. Available: InfoTrac Searchbank, Expanded Academic ASAP International Edition, Item 31 [accessed: 16 May 1998].

—— (1996) 'Battle of the Book Fairs', *Publishers Weekly[Online]* vol 243 no 8, February 19, 4 pp. Available: InfoTrac Searchbank, Expanded Academic ASAP International Edition, Item 20 [accessed: 9 May 1998].

—— (1997*)* 'New Initiatives from Struggling Intervisual Books', *Publishers Weekly[Online]* vol 244, no 12, 24 March, 2 pp. Available: InfoTrac Searchbank, Expanded Academic ASAP International Edition [accessed: 19 March 2001].

—— (1998) 'Scanning the Globe for Growth', *Publishers Weekly[Online]* vol 245 no 1, 5 January, 3 pp. Available: InfoTrac Searchbank, Expanded Academic ASAP International Edition, Item 17 [accessed: 18 May 1998].

—— (2000) 'Intervisual Books Exploring Options', *Publishers Weekly[Online]* vol 247, No 48, 27 November, 2 pp. Available: InfoTrac Web, Expanded Academic ASAP International Edition [accessed: 19 March 2001].

Morpurgo, M. (1979) *Allen Lane — King Penguin.* Hutchinson, London.

Multinational Monitor (1995) 'Media Monopoly Makers', *Multinational Monitor[Online]* vol 16 no 9, September, 2 pp. Available: InfoTrac Searchbank, Expanded Academic ASAP International Edition, Item 17 [accessed: 18 May 1998].

Penguin Books Australia (1998) '[Advertisement]', *Magpies* vol 13 no 4, September, p. 2.

Postman, N. (1983) *The Disappearance of Childhood.* Delacorte, New York.

Pritchard, B. (1997) 'Enough To Give You Goosebumps', *Marketing*, July, pp. 38–9.

Publishers Weekly (1996) 'Goosebumps with Every Gulp', *Publishers Weekly[Online]* vol 243 no 36, 2 September, 1 p. Available: InfoTrac Searchbank, Expanded Academic ASAP International Edition, Item 22 [accessed: 11 May 1998].

—— (1997) 'Get Your Kix with Golden Books', *Publishers Weekly[Online]* vol 244 no 42, 13 October, 1 p. Available: InfoTrac Searchbank, Expanded Academic ASAP International Edition, Item 55 [accessed: 6 May 1998].

—— (1997) 'A Sharper Focus at Bologna Fair', *Publishers Weekly Interactive [Online]* 12 May, 9 pp. Available: http://www.bookwire com; http://www.publishersweekly.reviewsnews.com [accessed: 3 March 1998].

Raugust, K. (1997a) 'Branding: Benefit or Buzzword?', *Publishers Weekly[Online]* vol 244 no 19. 12 May, 2 pp. Available: InfoTrac Searchbank, Expanded Academic ASAP International Edition, Item 11 [accessed: 31 July 1998].

—— (1997b) 'Managing Fads: What the Toy Industry Can Teach Book Publishers', *Publishers Weekly[Online]* vol 244 no 35, 25 August, 2 pp. Available: InfoTrac Searchbank, Expanded Academic ASAP International Edition, Item 5 [accessed: 11 May 1998].

—— (1997c) *The Market for Children's Media and Entertainment.* EPM Communications, New York.

—— (1998) 'Board Book Editions Approach Saturation', *Publishers Weekly[Online]* vol 245 no 19, 11 May, 1 p. Available: InfoTrac Searchbank, Expanded Academic ASAP International Edition, Item 2 [accessed: 6 June 1998].

—— (2000a) 'Food for Thought', *Publishers Weekly[Online]* vol 247 no 18, 1 May, 8 pp. Available: InfoTrac Web, Expanded Academic ASAP International Edition [accessed: 18 March 2001].

—— (2000b) 'Talking Trends', *Publishers Weekly[Online]* vol 247 no 23, 5 June, 8 pp. Available: InfoTrac Web, Expanded Academic ASAP International Edition [accessed: 18 March 2001].

—— (2001) 'Toy Fair Exhibitors Adopt Conservative Approach', *Publishers Weekly[Online]* vol 248, no 9, 5 June, 8 pp. Available: InfoTrac Web, Expanded Academic ASAP International Edition [accessed: 18 March 2001].

Reynolds, K. and Tucker, N. (eds) (1998) *Children's Publishing in Britain Since 1945*. Scolar Press, Aldershot.

Rosen, J. (1996) 'Books Made to Order', *Publishers Weekly[Online]* vol 243 no 2, 24 June, 2 pp. Available: InfoTrac Searchbank, Expanded Academic ASAP International Edition, Item 45 [accessed: 2 May 1998].

—— (1997a) 'Beyond the Bookstore: Buyers Describe the Expanding Role that Children's Books are Playing in their Merchandising Mix', *Publishers Weekly [Online]* vol 244 no 7, 17 February, 4 pp. Available: InfoTrac Searchbank, Expanded Academic ASAP International Edition, Item 174 [accessed: 29 April 1998].

—— (1997b) 'They're Everywhere You Look', *Publishers Weekly[Online]* vol 244 no 29, 21 July, 4 pp. Available: InfoTrac Searchbank, Expanded Academic ASAP International Edition, Item 1 [accessed: 6 May 1998].

Rosen, M. (1995) 'Raising the Issues', *Signal* vol 76, January, pp. 26–44.

Sanislo, G. (1995) 'Scholastic Inc ... 75 Years Strong', *Publishers Weekly[Online]* vol 242 no 46, 2 pp. Available: InfoTrac Searchbank, Expanded Academic ASAP International Edition, Item 18 [accessed: 8 May 1998].

Sarland, C. (1996) 'Ideology', in Hunt, P. (ed.) *Encyclopedia of Children's Literature* (associate editor, S. Ray). Routledge, London, pp. 41–57.

Saxby, M. (1996) 'Challenging the Young Reader', *Orana* vol 32 no 2, May, pp. 76–91.

Saxby, M. and Winch, G.(eds) (1987) *Give them Wings: The Experience of Children's Literature*. Macmillan, South Melbourne.

Schulman, J. (1982) 'A Look Inside Those Shiny Covers', *Top of the News* vol 38 no 3, Spring 1982, pp. 216–220.

Schwartz, J.D. (1992) 'Alfred Knopf Revisits the Classics of Children's Literature', *Brandweek [Online]*, vol 33 no 45, 30 November, 2 pp. Available: InfoTrac Searchbank, Expanded Academic ASAP International Edition, Item 509 [accessed: 27 May 1998].

Sheahan-Bright, R. (1999) 'It's A Supermarket', *Magpies* vol 14 no 2, May, pp.10–13.

—— (1999) 'Publishing Profile 1: The Children's Books Publisher Robyn Sheahan-Bright Interviews Rosalind Price of Allen & Unwin', *Magpies* vol 14 no 3, July, pp. 8–10.

—— (1999) 'This Little Piggy Went To Market: Some Perspectives on Australian Children's Publishing Since 1945' in *Something to Crow About: New Perspectives in Literature for Young People*, S. Clancy and D. Gilbey (eds). Charles Sturt University, Wagga Wagga, pp 15–38.

Somers, J. (1995) 'Stories in Cyberspace', *Children's Literature in Education* vol 26 no 4, pp. 197–209.

Stephens, J. (1996) 'Children's Literature, Interdisciplinarity and Cultural Studies' in Bradford, C. (ed.) *Writing the Australian Child*, University of Western Australia Press, Nedland, pp. 161–79.

—— (1999) ' Children's literature, Text and Theory: What are We Interested in Now?' in *Something to Crow About: New Perspectives in Literature for Young People*, S. Clancy and D. Gilbey (eds). Charles Sturt University, Wagga Wagga, pp. 1–14.

Stevenson, N. (1997) 'Hipper, Brighter and Bolder: Publishers Struggle to Make the Book Jackets Stand Out on Ever More Crowded Shelves', *Publishers Weekly[Online]* vol 244 no 7, February 17, 3 pp. Available: InfoTrac Searchbank, Expanded Academic ASAP International Edition, Item 76 [accessed: 29 April 1998].

Sutton, R. (1997) 'Editorial (Children's Books and Merchandising)', *The Horn Book Magazine [Online]* vol 73 no 5, Sept–Oct, 2 pp. Available: InfoTrac Searchbank, Expanded Academic ASAP International Edition, Item 87 [accessed: 29 April 1998].

Taylor, S.A. (1991) 'Intervisual Communications: Popping Up All Over', *Publishers Weekly [Online]* vol 238 no 33, July 26, 2 pp. Available: InfoTrac Searchbank, Expanded Academic ASAP International Edition, Item 1 [accessed: 3 June 1998].

Turow, J. (1992a) 'A Mass Communication Perspective on Entertainment Industries' in *Mass Media and Society*, J. Curran and M. Gurevitch (eds) Edward Arnold, London, pp. 160–77.

—— (1992b) *Media Systems in Society: Understanding Industries, Strategies, and Power*. Longman, New York.

—— (1978) *Getting Books To Children: An Exploration of Publisher-Market Relations*. American Library Association, Chicago.

Van Orden, P.(1997)'Librarians and Publishers', *School Library Journal* vol 24 no 4, December, pp.24–6.

Vizard, F. (1997) 'Electric Tales', *Popular Science [Online]* vol 250 no 6, June, 3 pp. Available: InfoTrac Searchbank, Expanded Academic ASAP International Edition, Item 55 [accessed: 18 May 1998].

Watts, J. (1994)'From Little Acorns … The Growth of an Australian Children's List' in *Creative Connections: Writing Illustrating and Publishing Children's Books in Australia*: Papers of the Canberra CBC Seminars 1987–1993, B. Alderman and P. Clayton (eds). Thorpe, Melbourne, pp. 255–66.
White, K. (2001) 'A Look at Modern Classics', *Magpies* vol 16 no 1, March, pp. 4–7.
Williams, C.and Dillon, K. (1993) *Brought to Book : Censorship and School Libraries in Australia*. ALIA in association with Thorpe, Port Melbourne.

Chapter 18

Teacher-as-artist, researcher-as-artist: creating structures for success

Rosemary Ross Johnston

This chapter proposes the concepts of writer/illustrator-as-artist, teacher-as-artist and researcher-as-artist, as a way of crossing boundaries. It notes how the work of each of these comes together within the specific context of the classroom, and how they can collaborate to construct a powerful foundation for what Clay (1991) has referred to as 'the deep structures of success'.

It is appropriate that this should be the concluding chapter of a book that seeks to cross the boundaries between disciplines. If boundaries are going to be crossed, it is in the classroom that such crossings will truly take place. For the most part, it is here, in an educational context of influence, that children's literature becomes either inclusive entry point or exclusive barrier. For the most part, it is here that literature and arts become integral (as mind-openers, image-makers, spirit-feeders) to the sustainable futures of lifelong learners, or become unsustainable and unsustaining.

It is however important to consider the nature of the crossing that is being proposed, for while the above comments obviously refer to children, they are also applicable to the other players in the classroom cast, teachers. While researchers in arts disciplines are sometimes guilty of implying a type of intellectual superiority over educational researchers, teachers can express disgruntlement with researchers in both fields, perceiving their theoretical discussions as remote and irrelevant to what actually goes on in classrooms, where they and their students are coping with critical everyday issues: for example, achieving survival in a new language.

These perceptions constitute the real crossing: it is not so much a crossing of territory as a border dispute over intellectual capital. What is needed here is not a merger — the arts and education have their own rich and fertile spaces and their own prolific traditions of research and practice. What is needed, however, is freedom of access, a toing-and-froing that does not view either side distrustfully, nor require them to stand in the 'alien' queue, firstly to have credentials checked, and secondly to make sure that they are not carrying anything dangerous.

Research *does* inform practice; what is equally important to acknowledge is that *practice in turn informs research*. This simple fact engineers the bridge for the crossing, a wide thoroughfare that has traffic going both ways. One means of facilitating the construction of this bridge is to conceptualise a little differently the role of the key figures in the drama that is playing out around its environs: that is, in terms of children's literature, the roles of writer/illustrator, teacher and researcher. This conceptualisation does not so much change these distinctive roles as redescribe their distinctiveness in terms of a common denominator. This chapter will propose such a conceptualisation and suggest ways in which it may generate deeper understandings and commitment to each other's purposes; it will do so while locating the discussion in a school context. Specifically, it will focus on how literary theory and educational practice function conjunctively in the experience of literature in everyday classrooms, and how the explicit proclamation of this conjunction crosses disciplinary boundaries and is intellectually liberating for both teachers and researchers.

It is important to note at the outset that theory in a postmodern society is not separate from or above the concerns of the everyday: postmodernism has in fact invested everyday activities — that is, 'the routine, repetitive taken-for-granted experiences, beliefs and practices, untouched by great events' (Featherstone, 1992: 160) — with dignity and significance. As Featherstone further notes, in everyday activities 'there is an emphasis on the present which provides a non-reflexive sense of immersion in the immediacy of current experiences and activities' (1992: 160–1). This immersion in present is one of the distinctive features of classroom situations and one of the realities of a teacher's life (as may be 'the disorderly babble of many tongues' which Featherstone identifies as another element of the everyday!).

Classrooms are characterised by the doings of the everyday. They are reproductive immersions in *presentness* — continua of presents continuous rather than pasts and futures. Teachers know this in practice. Here then is a place for a crossing: cultural theory can be applied to describe teachers' everyday time-space (classrooms), using different language in relation to everyday experience, and so provoking new connections for both theorists and teacher practitioners. Revisiting practice equipped with a different language opens up new mental imageries and promotes deeper intellectual endeavours. Two examples come to mind. Firstly, conceiving of classrooms as 'time-spaces' describes the physical location of schools in literary–philosophical terms, and invokes at least some engagement with Foucault's metaphorical idea of space as 'a site or container of power which usually constrains but sometimes liberates processes of *Becoming*' (Harvey, 1990: 213). Secondly, although the Russian literary theorist Mikhail Mikhailovitch Bakhtin (1895–1975) may be a long way removed from Australian classrooms, and his writings are not about education but principally about the novel as genre, his research is similarly liberating in this context. Bakhtin spent much of his life as a teacher of teachers (at the remote Mordovia State Teachers' College, 1936–1961), and his theoretical writings about literature are deeply philosophical; they are writings about life, and contribute a stimulating conceptual framework for teachers and researchers in educational as well as literary fields. Bakhtin pre-empted postmodernism by, among other things, particularly highlighting the significance of everydayness — the material practices and processes of the everyday — and by recognising that the speeches of everyday life (that is, everyday utterances) are overlaid and underlaid with thousands of other, already spoken, utterances and words. Thus language is *dialogic* — every word takes its 'meaning' from other words around it and other utterances of it; 'meanings' then, in my words, are fluid, mobile, and osmotic. This relates to Bakhtin's idea of *heteroglossia* — all words are part of a matrix of forces that press down and up and around their usage in the everyday.

Heteroglossia is a concept that acknowledges, in linguistic terms, both centripetal and centrifugal forces. *Centripetal forces* are those that come from a metaphoric top — they are socially endorsed as 'good' and tend to homogenise and assimilate language; that is, they are the centralising forces of language that fit words into established social and cultural hierarchies. *Centrifugal forces* come from the metaphoric 'bottom' — the rough, crude heterogeneous languages that, in Bakhtin's novel world, belong to the clown, mimic and rogue, but that in this context readily incorporate into school and playground culture, and the books that represent it. Teachers are builders and deliverers of words and utterances, juggling both centripetal and centrifugal languages as part of their everyday.

Bakhtin relates the everyday to other ideas that are similarly interesting in this discussion and particularly relevant in the context of teachers and teaching. Two of these are *heterogeneity*, which relates to a sort of 'open messiness' — and *unfinalizability* (*nezavershennost*). He defines unfinalizability as the general chaos and mess and unfinishedness of the world, but notes that this is positive rather than negative: unfinalizability represents the potential and openness required for freedom and creativity. Heterogeneity is also an essential part of creativity — neatness of idea continually being challenged by a different idea, established hierarchies of thinking toppled by fresh, upstart concepts and ways of seeing the world. 'Open messiness' is not of course referring to physical mess (although arguably that may sometimes be part of it): rather it is the everyday juggling and flux of the thriving activity that characterises the type of dynamic classroom that I have referred to elsewhere as *a place for seeing* (Johnston 2001: 437).

We know this because good teachers have taught us that it is so — and those of us who are teachers may have found it out for ourselves. Here we are not applying research into practice; rather, practice is informing and corroborating research; this of course is part of the symbiotic relationship between research and practice anyway. It goes without saying that in this sense good teachers are also active on-the-spot, on-the-job researchers in their own specific fields. (Indeed, teachers constantly engage in what we could develop as a concept of *spot research*: working out through trial and error the best solution to remove a particular problem for a particular child in a particular situation.) This discussion, however, is concerned with relating literary research and educational practice; some may question the need or viability for doing this (that is, corroboration), arguing that such an application is an unnecessary backward step, contrived and wasteful. It is not.

Applying theoretical understandings in different disciplines to the everyday realities and practices of teaching is important; in terms of a literary paradigm, it is important because it endorses and *names* the process. Naming, as we know from folk and fairytales, is power; naming the process in a different, heterogeneous way is creative and sometimes subversive, releasing a whole lot of other, powerful, cross-disciplinary ideas that excite, but are messy and unsettled — that may lead nowhere but that may lead somewhere rather important. Thinking of classrooms in literary terms is itself heterogeneous; it helps us to take a little leap and recognise the creative skills of the teacher, whose classroom (and mindscape) is metaphorically open rather than closed, informally messy rather than uniformly tidy, not finalised and therefore always on the move.

Children's literature — which relates to literary theory, educational contexts, and the artistic continuum, as well as to writers, illustrators, editors, publishers, children, teachers, researchers, parents and community — is an apposite location for a cross-disciplinary discussion. Setting apart for the moment the many and diverse roles of the children (who are of course specific and individual rather than collective), and the infinitely various nature of their needs, there are three other main roles: the *writer/illustrator-as-artist,* the *researcher-as-artist*, and the *teacher-as-artist*. These roles are all linked by a common practice or set of practices; obviously, that of being an artist. There will be no dispute over the first category (writer/illustrator-as-artist) because writing stories and drawing pictures is society's traditional perception of what artists do. But it is interesting — and fruitful — to tease out this idea in relation to teachers and researchers, with a view to exploring ontological relativities.

An artist is someone who is skilled in the processes and products of human imagination and creativity, who develops a set of artistic practices and uses a range of media and materials that enable these creative products to be expressed in distinctive ways. For Adorno, art works (and he is using the term in the conventional sense) are instances 'of an infinity of the present' (1984: 282) — a phrase that could equally be applied for our purposes as a description of everydayness and the everyday. Menke comments that the distinctiveness, 'the uniqueness of art, is that it sets itself apart, that it separates itself off' (1999: 3). I will return to this apparently contradictory second idea a little later.

Let's consider the notion of teacher-as-artist. This gained some currency in the 1970s: Gueulette (1979) discusses an idea of the teacher-as-artist and alchemist, stressing the concept of illusion in visual art terms; Dinan (1979) defines the teacher-as-artist as one who 'deliberately creates disorder by unsettling the audience'; Lessinger (1976) discusses a notion of teacher-artist performance 'that harnesses the power of affect to the educational process'; Axelrod (1974) applies the idea in terms of aesthetics; Newland (1971) uses Dewey's theory of aesthetics to develop an analogy of the teacher-as-artist. More recently, Michael Park (1992) argues a model of teacher-as-artist. This current discussion is rather more heterogeneous, and considers jointly the endeavours of both teachers and researchers.

Teachers of course teach; that is, they are involved in the process of *educo*: they lead, invite, draw out, raise up, rear and train. From nine o'clock in the morning to three or three-thirty in the afternoon, five days a week for forty weeks of the year, for at least fifteen years of the growing child's life, teachers articulate beingness to children. How? They do so through language: 'the boundaries of language,' writes the Austrian philosopher Ludwig Wittgenstein, 'are the boundaries of life-world' (Winch et al., 2001). A teacher educates by using the art forms of words and pictures. A good teacher is a craftsperson of words, an artist who places words carefully, both public words (addressed to the class as a whole) and private words (addressed to individual children). Words may not be able to break bones but they can break spirits: Susan Price's *The Ghost Drum* (1987), a book now unfortunately out of print, is a brilliant explication of the magic of words: ' ... the sound of them, the use of them, the shock, the smart and soothing cool of them' (p. 37). Chingis, the protagonist, is taught that:

> Words can alter sight and hearing, taste, touch and smell. Used with a higher skill they can make our senses clear and protect us from the simpler magics.

> (Price, 1987: 37)

It is Mark Antony's word magic that changes how the mob feels about Caesar's death; Cassius warns Brutus:

Know you how much the people may be moved
By that which he will utter?

In just the same way, teachers use the art of words to move, to help students see things differently, to change. A good teacher is one who makes word pictures that impart knowledge, that entice and even cajole children into learning, that connote possibilities of achievement and reflect probabilities of positive outcomes. These word-pictures tell stories that create images, paint and sculpt physical and mental landscapes, and proliferate media of response. They are inclusive pictures in which children can see themselves, being and doing; most of all, they are pictures in which children see themselves as success stories. In the context of reading reluctance, Martin (1989) notes, 'Remedial reading should begin with every child playing himself as a successful reader of books'; these comments, reminiscent of Heathcote's notion of the 'mantle of the expert', are applicable to all teaching situations.

Teachers are not only writers and painters of words and images; they are also directors of the day-by-day performance of the everyday classroom. They assign roles — 'You're good at this, aren't you?' — 'Why are you always the last one to finish?' — 'And you, sit over there and try to do something right for a change!' These roles and their associated directions become cumulative and, just as they do in dramatic performance, they create characters, suggesting behaviours and actions. As in theatrical performance, these words echo in private worlds long after they are uttered in public worlds. The power of words (signifiers) can bring about the reality of the signified; as Bakhtin writes:

Not from the thing to the word, but from the word to the thing; the word gives birth to the thing.

(Bakhtin, 1981: 153)

Every utterance builds on other utterances, every word is filled with intentions, implicit or explicit. Words form, manipulate, change. To quote again from Susan Price's *The Ghost Drum*, consider this passage where Chingis is taught how words can be used by those in power:

Suppose that a Czar or Czaritsa ordered their people to fight a war, a stupid war, a war that should never have been fought. Thousands of people are killed for no good reason and their families left to mourn them. Much, much money is spent on cannons and swords, so there is no money to spend on other, better, things … The Czar is afraid that if the people find out how foolish and wasteful the war was, they will be furious and do him harm. So the Czar uses word magic. He says to the people: 'The war was not foolish — no! It proved that our people are the bravest and best in the world because they died for us, and killed so many of the enemy. I know you are starving, my children, but that shows how noble you are and how willing to make sacrifices for the Motherland. I, your Czar, am proud of you!' He says this and repeats it over and over again, and he makes his servants repeat it over and over to everyone they meet — and the magic works. The people forget to be angry. They grow *glad* that their sons and brothers were killed, and proud that they themselves are cold and hungry.

(Price, 1987: 36–7)

All of this constitutes an artistic meeting place, teacher-practitioners, writers and researchers meeting together, grafting and propagating as part of intellectual endeavour, nurturing buds of new growth. The same deep idea is being given different forms of artistic articulation. In Bakhtin's words:

> [L]anguage has been completely taken over, shot through with intentions and accents. For any individual consciousness living in it, language is not an abstract system of normative forms but rather a concrete heteroglot conception of the world. All words have a 'taste' of a profession, a genre, a tendency, a party, a particular work, a particular person, a generation, an age group, the day and hour. Each word tastes of the context and contexts in which it has lived its socially charged life; all words and forms are populated by intentions.

(Bakhtin, 1981: 293)

Bakhtin is an example of a researcher-as-artist. Sometimes, as above, theory endorses practice, rather than informs it. More accurately, it expresses it in such a way as not only to describe what actually happens, but to draw striking word-pictures for teachers of what teachers actually do, exciting a language of possibilities that injects new ideas and enthusiasms. This is one of the roles of the researcher-as-artist. Researchers-as-artists choose words carefully and aesthetically not only to describe but to inspire, and to construct new stages for debate and discussion: 'Suppose', writes Margaret Meek (a wonderful example of another researcher-as-artist), 'we now began to speak of reading in terms of *dialogue* and *desire;* would that not be a better beginning?' (1991). Edward Wilson refers to science as a 'culture of illuminations' (1998: 45); discussing contemporary society, Geoff Mulgan writes that democracy 'can become more of a permanent conversation' (1997: 16). Hagerstrand develops a metaphor of 'time geography' that conceives of individual biographies as 'life paths in space' and describes daily routines of movement — such as going to school — in terms of geographical 'stations' and 'domains' where, in Harvey's words, 'certain social interactions prevail' (Harvey, 1990: 211). Derrida is an artist researcher–philosopher. He pushes us to the limit but articulates what we can't say but intuitively, deeply, understand:

> There is in literature, in the *exemplary* secret of literature, a chance of saying everything without touching upon the secret. When all hypotheses are permitted, groundless and *ad infinitum,* about the meaning of a text, or the final intention of the author whose person is no more represented than non-represented by a character or by a narrator, by a poetic or fictional sentence, when these are detached from their presumed source and thus remain in secret (*au secret*), when there is no longer any sense in making decisions about some secret beneath the surface of a textual manifestation (and it is this situation that I would call text or trace), when it is the call (*appel*) of this secret, however, which points back to the other or to something else, when it is this itself which keeps our passion aroused, and holds on to the other, then the secret impassions us. Even if there is none, even if it does not exist, hidden behind anything whatever. Even if the secret *is no secret,*

even if there has *never been a secret, a single secret.* Not One.

(Derrida, 1997: 109)

In the following passage, Harland refers to the researcher as critic, but in arguing a conceptual linkage of critic and reader, he interrogates common perceptions and stimulates ideas:

> The empowerment of the reader is simultaneously the empowerment of the critic, who stands in as the reader's representative. The relation of critic to text is no longer that of knower to known. Producing meaning on the text's own level, the critic operates as a doer rather than a knower – and certainly not a detached or impartial knower.

(Harland, 1999: 242)

Researchers and teachers meet at pragmatic levels, but they connect with greatest significance at the level of knowing and doing, which I am arguing is an artistic nexus. Both are knowers and both are doers; they know and do different things — but not always, sometimes they know the same thing differently. This interaction demystifies, communicates and enriches. For example, children's literature researchers of the last decade focused to a great extent on ideology (Hollindale 1988, Stephens 1992). Those discussions have linked in educational fields to the debate about multiple literacies, in particular, *critical literacy*, which is defined as:

> … reading with a knowledge of the workings of a language, reading with an awareness of what and how the text is making you feel, and reading with the ability to discern the ideas and attitudes and assumptions behind the text.

(Johnston 2001: 320)

In other words, the concepts of *critical literacy* and *ideology* emerge in different fields, but emanate from the same intellectual impulse.

It is interesting to consider Julie Kristeva here. A very brief introduction to Kristeva's work would note its breadth and its depth. She resists easy classification; in the bounded, discipline-driven research agendas of the twentieth century Western world, her work is characterised by its interdisciplinarity and 'outsideness' — to use another Bakhtinian term. Although she was a part of very influential intellectual circles, a student of Barthes, and is commonly labelled as a feminist, she moved in her own space on the edges. Barthes wrote of her first published book:

> And now I have been made to feel again … the force of her work. *Force* here means *displacement.* Julie Kristeva changes the order of things: she always destroys the latest preconception, the one we thought we could be comforted by, the one of which we could be proud: what she displaces is the *already-said* …

(Moi, 1986: 1)

Kristeva (a Bulgarian who spoke fluent Russian and had a strong grounding in Marxism and Russian Formalism) was of course a foreigner in Paris, and as Moi notes was 'always foreign to the theoretical scene she was in' (1986: 3). This foreignness — outsideness, apartness — was her strength and her art as a researcher-as-artist.

The idea of teachers and researchers as artists — as communicators, philosophical inquirers, self-reflexive thinkers, creative and aesthetic organisers of material, performers, interpreters, dramatists, actors, music-makers, directors, producers — crosses boundaries and provides thoroughfares, but does not need to preclude distinctiveness: each has its own role and difference. The nature of the relationship, however, must be as open, not closed, systems. Kristeva's description of adolescence in her essay on the adolescent novel provides a fine analogy:

> I understand by the term 'adolescent' less as an age category than an open psychic structure. Like the 'open' systems of which biology speaks concerning living organisms that live only by maintaining a renewable identity through interaction with another, the adolescent structure opens itself to the repressed at the same time that it initiates a psychic reorganisation of the individual …
>
> (Kristeva, 1990: 8)

The relationships between literary theory and teaching offer sites of multiple 'renewable identities'. We have already mentioned the idea of outsideness; this refers not only to an awareness of others (the common usage), but, more importantly, to an awareness of self as other (the sense in which Bakhtin used the term). Such an awareness is of course a more sophisticated expression of one aspect of cultural literacy; that is:

> … the knowledge, understanding and appreciation of diverse ways of being. This knowledge, understanding and appreciation of diverse ways of being … means being open to and experimenting with different ways of doing things, different sorts of formats, different ideas about beginnings and endings, different ideas even about what language should be, and different ideas about literacy.
>
> (Johnston, 2001: 292–93)

More pragmatically, there is a 'concentration upon procedures from both traditions that can be cooperatively employed to serve a line of research' (Smith and Heshusius, 1986) — and we could add, a line of teaching.

I have already noted Menke's seemingly problematical comment (in the context of this discussion) that art separates. The teacher-as-artist does not actually separate, but she or he does know when to step back, when to operate at a remove, and allow space for the fledgling first steps of learners. Teachers know how to use physical space in the stage that is the classroom; they also know how to use mental space. The work of the teacher, like the work of an artist, is intuitive, aesthetic, expressive, creative. It is also deeply, intensely communicative. Most art is addressed to someone else — an audience, a reader, a viewer, a beholder, a performer, a listener. In fact, pushing the argument further, the aim of all artists is to get their message across, to transact, negotiate, arbitrate and evoke. The word 'arbitrate' is new to this discourse; it does not here pertain to teacher-as-judge or decision-maker. Rather, it infers a particular process that leads to the resolution of differences between what children know and don't know. The artistry of words and pictures helps to embed new knowledge in the already-known as part of an arbitration kit.

Here teachers can draw on the powerful resources of the creative arts, which allow children the option of moving outside their own private worlds to try on other selves and roam in other subjectivities. 'Creative arts' is not, as some curricula suggest, only a separate group of subjects that includes art, drama, music, dance (important as these are); rather, creative arts are a plurality of *interdisciplinary, core-disciplinary, artistic practices, processes* and *paradigms* that spill over, usually at the deepest point, into all disciplines. A scientist's discussion of string theory and superstrings describes the dimensions of the universe as being 'tightly curled up in the folded fabric of the cosmos'; the same scientist notes that the microscopic particles within protons and neutrons are called 'quarks' after a passage in Joyce's *Finnegan's Wake* (Greene, 1999: 6–7). Here scientific facts are expressed creatively, in poetic metaphor. These creative arts represent the human need to produce and to read narratives, to describe and create and imagine and dream — linguistically, visually, aurally — stories and images of human experience. 'Creative arts' must include literature; it must in particular, in school curricula at least, include children's literature — words and pictures, semantics and sounds, design and orthographies. The practices, processes and paradigms of the creative arts include literary and visual grammars (see, for example, Kress and van Leeuwen, 1996), metaphor, imagery and representation of subjectivities. These can be conceptualised as what we could develop into an idea of the metacognitive *arts of knowing*. Indeed, it is these metacognitive arts of knowing that allow us to 'know' at the deepest level (beyond the superficial) — to perceive, receive, become aware of, think about, learn about, interpret, remember, imagine and sense. And it is these metacognitive arts of knowing that give artists the languages — words, pictures, musical, dramatic — to describe their 'knowing' to others.

In a so-called knowledge society, where knowledge seems to be increasingly situated as an autonomous commodity, creative arts and creative artistries provide personal, relational, handholds. For children, they provide media for involvement and response in all sorts of non-traditional ways. Through the processes of the creative arts, children can step out of self and respond in the safety of role. They may do so just by wearing masks (thus to hide, appear as other, or assume another identity of choice). They may bypass words altogether and paint responses and other selves; or dance a different idea of being, or they may simply sit and think and imagine. They may disregard formal linguistic structures and create word pictures that bypass lack of grammatical knowledge and emerge as poetry. Poetry can be a response to a scientific process (consider the notion of chemical reactions). Dance can be a response to the multiplication table (imagine dancing the three-times table). Extreme? Perhaps, but worth trying. The teacher-as-artist, working in open collaboration with a researcher-as-artist such as Howard Gardner, makes opportunities for as many different ways of responding as possible, offering options of success other than in traditional written and spoken forms. Writing and speaking will follow, but they should not always be pushed for first. Gardner's idea of multiple intelligences describes the many different forms of learning: bodily/kinaesthetic as well as logical/mathematical, musical/rhythmic as well as verbal/linguistic, visual/spatial, and intrapersonal as well as interpersonal. Whereas interpersonal intelligence relates, in Gardner's words, to 'the ability to notice and make distinctions about other individuals' (1984: 240), intrapersonal intelligence has as its core capacity *'the ability to access one's own feeling life'* (1984: 240, my emphasis). Both these are related; Gardner discusses them together — and they both clearly represent what happens in the literature/creative arts/educational domain. But it is the latter that I think is of pivotal importance in classrooms that are moments of continuous, everyday, becoming. Children need a sense of their own 'feeling life', even — particularly when — they cannot articulate it for themselves, even — particularly when — they are most divorced from any sense of it.

Here of course is where children's literature comes into its own. Literature represents in user-friendly ways diverse representations of 'feeling life': of the emotions and quandaries of being human. Its words and pictures give 'seeability' (Cassirer, 1996) to the most abstract of ideas, and express those abstractions in ways that reach children and touch children's lives. The picture book by Margaret Wild and Ron Brooks, *Fox*, expresses a range of such abstractions. Its text is a child-like hand-written script that is often crooked, that can be read in various ways and held different ways up, and that includes mistakes and cross-outs in the publication details. The abstract ideas include particular slants on the nature of friendship (as in *Huckleberry Finn*), fear (as in *A Passage to India*), jealousy (as in *Cinderella*), love (as in *Romeo and Juliet*), temptation (as in the Biblical account of Peter's denial of Jesus: 'And when at dawn Fox whispers to her for the third time she whispers back, "I am ready" '), loyalty (as in *Middlemarch*), vengeance (as in *Hamlet*), treachery (as in *Julius Caesar*), trust (as in *An Imaginary Life*), the pain of loneliness (as in *King Lear*), and the absolute integral significance of life itself (as in *To Kill A Mockingbird*). These complexities are part of textual 'understory' (see Johnston, 2001: 325). The writer and illustrator illuminate this understory in the artistry of their story and illustration — dramatic pictures, and simple words with sound effects within them:

> Magpie feels the wind streaming through her feathers and she rejoices. 'FLY, DOG, FLY! I will be your missing eye, and you will be my wings.'

There are rich, intertextually dense, metaphors:

> After the rains
> when saplings are
> springing up everywhere,
> a fox comes into the bush.
> Fox with his haunted eyes
> and rich red coat.
> He flickers through the trees
> like a tongue of fire,
> and Magpie trembles.

The visual chronotope — that is, the visual representation of people and events to time and space (see Johnston, 2001: 348, 408) — is a time-space that is simultaneously freedom and imprisonment, an 'occasion' (Ozouf, 1988: 126–37) which, like the experience of Australia to the early settlers, is at once exile and utopia. It also represents a compressed time-space that is another, darker version of the wild, and 'where the wild things are'. *Fox* is a story of tangled emotions, and there is no easy resolution — we hope Magpie makes it home but the odds would seem to be against her.

Fox is a text that the researcher-as-artist can discuss at a number of levels, making connections to the artistic continuum of which it is a part (as above), describing it in terms of familiar narrative patterns such as the quest, the fable genre, the potential rupture of the open ending; and noting the changing endpapers, from the blaze of desert colours at the beginning to the same scene transfigured by deep colours of darkness at the end. It is also a text that, I would argue, indicates at least to some extent the influence of researchers on writers and illustrators: deliberately postmodern in presentation, poetic, open and intertextually dense. *Fox* is a fable of becoming.

The teacher-as-artist reads this story in classroom community, savouring its magic, but doesn't necessarily ask any questions at all about what it 'means'. Rather, children are offered the opportunity to create a response to the story, corporately or individually. The response can be in any medium: it may be a debate, a dance, a piece of music composed on recorder or keyboard, a radio play or report for a newspaper, a film script or play, a painting or sculpture or collage or installation of some sort. These responses will naturally promote talk and discussion, and writing of one sort or another. Children can choose the medium for response in which they feel comfortable. 'Teachers need to be imaginative and pluralistic if they hope to stimulate revealing performances of understanding,' writes Gardner (1999: 178).

Literature represents the processes of becoming in fictional lives and worlds; despite some critical rejection of the idea, it also plays a major role in the processes of becoming in real lives and real worlds. 'All literature,' writes Bakhtin, 'is … caught up in the process of "becoming" ' (1981: 5) — a comment which clearly relates, in different paradigms, to both Montaigne and Foucault. What does a notion of 'becoming' mean, however, in classrooms where there are children who are having difficulties? What are they 'becoming' — or likely to become? In terms of literacy, for example, there are students struggling in a second language, in a first language, as reluctant readers, as reluctant writers, students who for a host of reasons are disadvantaged. Stanovich (1986), after reviewing the research, concluded that the biblical maxim propounded in the Gospel of Matthew can be applied to reading as well: 'For to those who have, more will be given, and they will have an abundance; but from those who have nothing, even what they have will be taken away.' (Matthew, Ch 13: v 12). These children will continue to struggle unless researchers and teachers use their artistry to intervene — painting enticing backdrops, opening up scenes of success rather than failure, offering other ways of response. Literacy, says Lyotard, is not a technology of knowledge appropriation; it is what he calls 'a relentless re-reading of reading' (Godzich, 1992: 135), an anchor to surroundings. Of course, not all reluctant students are 'poor' readers or writers; some children are skilled but not motivated to achieve. Goldberger's definition of a reluctant reader as someone who is not motivated to read and who 'is likely to have a permanent non-reading habit' stresses that this may, or may not, be linked to low reading ability and poor grades (1978: 382). Nonetheless, the child who doesn't like being in school is usually a child whose reluctance is symptomatic of a lack of success, a perceived lack of success, or fear of a future lack of success.

What structures for success can the collaborative enterprise of writers/illustrators, teachers and researchers construct for children under threat? Stanovich's analogy is a brilliant example of the artistry of researchers in drawing attention to findings and proposals in mind-catching ways. Teachers know that the principle that success breeds success, and failure breeds failure, is true across the spectrum, and that the most important attribute for school success is a *sense of self-confidence*. Theory supports this: in a study of cognitive and motivational determinants of reading comprehension, Ehrlich, Kurtz-Costes and Loridant note the diversity of poor readers as a significant factor; but stress (and the research literature unanimously agrees) the importance of self-confidence:

> We suspect that for many of the poor readers, continued failures serve to exacerbate their lack of confidence, and beliefs that academic outcomes are not controllable.
>
> (Ehrlich, Kurtz-Costes and Loridant, 1993: 375)

What Lowe calls 'relationship with self' (1994: 3) commonly appears to be negative in the reluctant reader and it is obvious that a poor reading self-image escalates as time passes and with each unsatisfactory experience. In fact, the one factor reluctant readers appear to have in common is a lack of confidence. In terms of second language learners, Tarone and Yule note:

> Although it is not always included in discussions of the language learning process, self-confidence is normally assumed to have an influence on successful learning. When affective filters are explicitly discussed, there seems to be a consensus that the general notion of self-esteem may be a crucial factor in the learner's ability to overcome occasional set-backs and minor mistakes in the process of learning a second language.
>
> (Tarone and Yule, 1989: 139)

The Catholic Education Office also notes that the basis of all successful learning is 'the positive self-esteem and well-being of the learner' (*Diversity*, 1993: 29).

Without a positive self-image, children are for the most part going to be unhappy in the school situation and will be recalcitrant students. Here is where research and practice must collaborate to enlighten and inform how negative spirals can be interrupted and reversed. Part of the answer at least will be in allowing children a multiplicity of ways of expressing their 'feeling life'. Part of the answer will also be to affirm and value the knowledge and skills they already have — a gift for drawing comic characters, for playing drums, for tap-dancing, for singing, a keen interest in a particular sport, or in popular songs. Teachers-as-artists find ways to celebrate whatever prior knowledge children bring to the classroom.

A positive self-image relates to confidence; confidence encourages risk-taking. Negative spirals need to be broken — and quickly — just as the negative cycle in poor reading needs to be interrupted as soon as it is recognised (see, for example, Clay, 1991; Muehl and Forell, 1973). Pressley, Borowski and Shneider (1987) have developed a model of metacognition based on the argument that successful strategy use enhances self-concept and attributional beliefs and that these motivational states thus determine the acquisition of new strategies.

This is part of making children feel a *sense of belonging* in the teaching/learning situation. A lack of cultural knowledge can help to exclude children, particularly children from other language backgrounds. Using literature creatively can help to fill gaps in cultural knowledge; teachers can also choose texts that carry cross-cultural ideas: *Fox* (Wild, 2000), for example, is a story that could emerge out of a number of cultures. Reading is a psycholinguistic process, a process in which the schemata — the knowledge of the world — brought to the text by the reader will not only influence but may in fact determine the knowledge acquired from reading. The early research by Anderson et al., notes:

It may turn out that many problems in reading comprehension are traceable to deficits in knowledge rather than deficits in linguistic skill … that is, the young readers may not possess the schemata needed to comprehend passages. Or they may possess relevant schemata but not know how to bring them to bear. Or, they may not be facile at changing schemata when the first one tried proves inadequate; they may in other words, get stuck in assimilating text in inappropriate, incomplete, or inconsistent schemata.

(Anderson et al., 1977: 378)

Another strategy for success is to give children a *sense of purpose*. The creative arts reflect multiple purposes and give opportunities for finding and describing 'meaning' in different ways. Reading is more than decoding; if the reader decodes, but fails to attain *meaning*, the process fails to have purpose. 'Getting words right' is not the task, writes Meek; the task is 'to interpret the meaning beyond the signs' (1991: 200–201). Teachers encourage the perception of purpose by offering diverse choices for expression of response — expressions which children can 'own' in some way, and feel confident about. Children who do not choose to read, who find reading 'hard work' and 'boring' (Lowe, 1994: 39), and who stop reading will develop linguistic and cultural deficits; such children will soon lose control of the reading situation. In fact, the only control option for them is a negative one: they can overtly or covertly refuse to participate in the reading process at all, a point which Lowe notes (1994: 7).

Meaning and purpose is wrapped up in story, and story begins in the classroom with *teachers reading aloud to children* — even when the children are perfectly able and competent to read for themselves. When a child is being read to, or read with, the classroom becomes a community — listeners, participators, imaginers. This is when teachers introduce stories that children are unlikely to choose for themselves; as Holdaway points out, 'the orientation to book language develops in a rich exposure beyond immediate needs' (1979: 40). Reading aloud also gives opportunities for all sorts of paralinguistic cues to meaning (voice and facial expression for example), it gives the child the opportunity to listen, to soak in the language aurally, taking from the reading what they will. Reading aloud, just for fun, sets up a structure for success.

Another structure for success is the *affirmative classroom*, where creativity and artistic response is facilitated, and learning is celebrated not as a singularity that can be ticked off, but as an underlying principle of holistic growth. This classroom offers opportunity for diverse, non-finalised activities relating to mental creativity, objective abilities and the external world. The less successful student has learned not to be a risk-taker and needs to be encouraged into actions that are not marred by histories of failure and that clearly offer possibilities of success. Drama, readers' theatre, dance and music, mime and clowning, writing and drawing illustrations, making a comic strip, composing songs or music to tell story in different ways, designing costumes for characters, making a collage of 'understory', adapting events into own words as poetic response, or as radio play, or as film script, or as Internet role play; all of these are ways of retelling story in one's own language of choice. This constitutes a scaffolding and safety net for the risks involved in participating in new learning.

In this scenario of success, the writer/illustrator contributes texts that captivate, that set imaginations racing, that draw new personal imageries and expand mental multiverses. I have written elsewhere (1995) about the type of texts that can be chosen and used with great success in classrooms where there are particular needs. The research — and Harry Potter — indicate that children like the unfamiliar planted in the safety of the familiar. Folk and fairy tales lend themselves to endless replays and retellings and seem to have a common appeal, as Wallace points out:

> … the classic folk tales offer the most predictable genre for linguistic and cultural minority readers.
>
> (Wallace, 1988: 30)

These can be related to non-readers' worlds by setting up connection points to things they know and are comfortable with, including popular music and film. Folktales tap into indigenous stories and their archetypal similarities can provide cues and clues in the reading process which children can use to predict. In another way, this helps to serve as an example of Clay's notion of the 'predictable text'. Predictability in this sense has, as Clay herself notes, different meanings but it does not simply mean repetitive or dull; it can, again as Clay notes, be constructive (1991: 184). The predictable text contains familiar material; the pattern of story is known even if the actual linguistic representation of that story is not. In this way, children are playing the role of reader (another version of Dorothy Heathcote's 'mantle of the expert') and learning to use what they know to help with what they don't know. In other words, says Clay, support is coming from the child's own prior reading; familiarity is encouraging independence and 'the smooth orchestration of all those behaviours necessary for effective reading' (1991: 184).

Children respond to the *sounds* of language, to rhyme and to rhythm. Like pictures, rhyme and rhythm can provide helpful clues for the less successful reader: patterns of rhyme can help a child to guess how a word is going to sound, and patterns of rhythm aid pronunciation as well as memory. A 'big book' such as Margaret Mahy's *When the King Rides By* provides a non-threatening and energetic reading experience for children of all ages. This book lends itself to oral activities: to reading aloud, to reading in a group (providing a safe structure in which the child may dare to speak without fearing mistakes), and to all sorts of language play. For example, groups can create their own line of nonsense verse: 'the lions roar and the trains rush by', 'the kangaroo jumps and the eggs all fry'. Children become creators of texts. In having fun with the language in this way, children are unconsciously responding to its metres and cadences; they are also unconsciously becoming familiar with how language works. Grammatical constructions such as participant and process relationship and agreement are being accumulated, practised, and confirmed.

The teacher-as-artist knows and trusts literature, trusts the creative responses that it can evoke, trusts its private maps and mindscapes; knows that children's literature is part of a wonderfully diverse and vibrant artistic continuum, and will find creative ways of displaying parts of the whole continuum to the gaze of the class. This class will have words read to them, just for aural edification — there will not be endless written responses about character and plot. Literature is more than comprehension: it is sounds, rhythms, feelings, glimpses and dreams of 'otherworlds'. In the past 'literature' has been perceived as too hard and too complex and has been watered down and simplified sometimes to the point of banality for 'problem' children. It is my experience that children often enjoy what they may not completely understand. Contemporary conceptions of *meaning* as interaction between the world of the reader and the world of the text infer the significance of the cultural base of literature and implicitly acknowledge its constant permutations; literature, however, is a part of both worlds. It is as much a part of the world of the reader as it is a part of the world of the text. Here again Bakhtinian theory recognises the significance of the continued interaction of the worlds of readers with texts:

> The work and the world represented in it enter the real world and enrich it, and the real world enters the work and its world as part of the process of its creation, as well as part of its subsequent life, in a continual renewing of the work through the creative perception of listeners and readers.
>
> (Bakhtin, 1981: 254)

The success of the Harry Potter books proves that the new technologies have not made the reading of books redundant: the pleasures of the text have survived the advent of the World Wide Web and the Internet. The Potter books, with their mix of genres — Cinderella story, school story, fantasy — and their sophisticated language and overt existentialism, indicate that the pleasures of reading are many and various. They include: what Rushdie calls 'what happens nextism'; the fantastic promise of another self who has great powers and who is highly respected within a circle of those 'in the know'; an understory that reaches out and touches children's private worlds, including both their fears and their dreams; an accessible but not over-simplified text, thus providing a sense of reading challenge; peer approval; dark questions answered within the security of a community where ultimately good survives; and clever plays on words that peg the texts to everyday culture and the real world. It seems to me that these ideas offer teachers a structure for understanding effective classroom strategies: presenting teaching/learning experiences as exciting and as a promise of other worlds; creating a classroom atmosphere of security and confidence; retaining the challenge of new learning without over-simplification and 'dumbing-down'; embedding new learning in a rich classroom environment that presents more than one option of response (writing an answer). Story can captivate children as it captivates us: the teacher-as-artist uses everything in his other power — voice, dramatic techniques, props — to present new learning as a story with a happy ending (that is, a story in which the child, like Harry, will ultimately succeed, even when there are setbacks and difficulties).

Discussing aestheticism, Sussman concludes that the purpose of all of the many strategies he enumerates is to bring about in the reader what he calls 'an awakening' (1997). The postmodern classroom is a performance space for such awakenings. Barriers and boundaries are removed; in Bakhtinian terms, this classroom is a stage 'without footlights': everything is performance, and everyone is performer. This democratic classroom appears free but is securely grounded in 'deep structures' that proactively work for success, especially for the success of those for whom success is the most problematical. The art of the writer-illustrator (beyond the footlights) makes the invisible visible, giving seeability to abstract ideas and complex thoughts. In an era of multiple literacies, the artistry of researchers and teachers meets to provide numerous points of entry and invite connections with the many provinces of the multiple realities of the classroom players. In the art form of children's literature, all have a role to play, and a real contribution to make to the life-worlds of those who are at the centre of what we do, children.

Bibliography

Adorno, (1984) *Aesthetic Theory* (translated by C. Lenhardt). Routledge and Kegan Paul, Boston.

Anderson, R.C., Reynolds, R.E., Schallert, D.L. and Goetz E.T. (1977) 'Frameworks for comprehending discourse', *American Educational Research Journal* 14, 4, pp. 367–81.

Axelrod, J. (1974) *The University Teacher as Artist*. Jossey-Bass, San Francisco, California.

Bakhtin, M.M. (1981) *The Dialogic Imagination* (Michael Holquist, ed., translated by Caryl Emerson and Michael Holquist). University of Texas Press, Austin.

Cassirer, E. (1996) *The Philosophy of Symbolic Forms*. Yale University Press, New Haven and London.

Clay, M.M. (1991) *Becoming Literate. The Construction of Inner Control*. Heinemann Education, Auckland.

Currie, M. (1999) *Literary Theory from Plato to Barthes*. Richard Harland, London.

Derrida, J. (1997) in John D. Caputo, *The Prayers and Tears of Jacques Derrida*. Indiana University Press, Bloomington and Indianapolis.

Dinan, J. (1979) 'The Classroom as Playground', *Viewpoints*, Minnesota.

Diversity (1993) 'Children's Literature and Second Language Learning', *Diversity* vol 8 no 1, Catholic Education Office, Victoria.

Ehrlich, M-F., Kurtz-Costes, B. and Loridant, C (1993) 'Cognitive and motivational determinants of reading comprehension in good and poor readers', *Journal of Reading Behaviour, A Journal of Literacy*, 25, 4.

Featherstone, M. (ed) (1992) *Cultural Theory and Cultural Change*. Sage Publications, London.

Gardner, H. (1984) *Frames of Mind: The Theory of Multiple Intelligence*. Fontana Press, London.

—— 1999, *Intelligence Reframed*. Basic Books, New York.

Godzich, (1992) Afterword in J. Lyotard, *The Postmodern Explained*. University of Minnesota Press, Minneapolis.

Goldberger, J. (1978) 'The rule of the reluctant reader', *Booklist* 75, 4.

Greene, B. (1999) *The Elegant Universe*. Vintage, London.

Gueulette, (1979) 'Curriculum: Managed Visual Reality', paper presented at the Annual Convention of the Association for Educational Communications and Technology, New Orleons, Louisiana.

Harland, R. (1999) *Literary Theory from Plata to Barthes*. Macmillan, London.

Harvey, D. (1990) *The Condition of Postmodernity*. Balckwell, Massachusetts and Oxford.

Heathcote, D. and Bolton, D. (1995) *Dorothy Heathcote's Mantle of the Expert Approach to Education*. Heinemann, Portsmouth, UK.

Holdaway, D. (1979) *The Foundations of Literacy*. Ashton Scholastic, Gosford.

Hollindale, P. (1988) *Ideology and the Children's Book*. The Thimble Press, Stroud, Glos.

Johnston, R.R. (1995) 'Of Dialogue and Desire: Children's Literature and the Needs of the L2 Reader', *Australian Journal of Language and Literacy* 18, 4, pp. 293–303.

—— (2001) 'Children's Literature', in Winch, G., Johnston, R.R., Holliday, M., Ljungdahl, L. and March, P., *Literacy: Reading, Writing and Children's Literature*. Oxford University Press, Melbourne, pp. 287–437.

Kress, G. and van Leeuwen, T. (1996) *Reading Images: The Grammar of Visual Design*. Routledge, London and New York.

Kristeva, J. (1990) 'The Adolescent Novel', in *Abjection, Melancholia and Love: The Work of Julie Kristeva*, J. Fletcher and A. Benjamin (eds), Routledge, London.

Lessinger, L. (1976) 'Increasing Productivity in Education: A Few Seminal Ideas', Elemenatry Education Act Title V.

Lowe, K. (1994) *Growing into Readers*. Primary English Teaching Association, Newtown.

Mahy, M. (1986) *When the King Rides By*. Bookshelf, Ashton Scholastic, Gosford.

Martin, T. (1989) *The Strugglers: Working with Children who Fail to Learn to Read*. Open University Press, Milton-Keynes, England.

Meek, M. (1991) *On Being Literate*. The Bodley Head, London.

Menke, C. (1999) *The Sovereignty of Art* (translated by N. Solomon). MIT Press, Cambridge, Mass. and London.

Moi, T. (1986) *The Kristeva Reader*. Basil Blackwell, Oxford.

Muehl, S. and Forell, E.R. (1973) 'A follow-up study of disabled readers: variables related to high school reading performance', *Reading Research Quarterly* 9, pp. 110–23.

Mulgan, G. (1997) *Connexity: How to Live in a Connected World*. Chatto and Windus, London.

Newland, G. (1971) 'Teaching and the Aesthetics of Learning', *Journal of Thought* 6, 4, 254–9.

Ozouf, M. (1988) *Festivals and the French Revolution*. Blackwell, Cambridge, Mass.

Parks, M. (1992) 'The Arts of Pedagogy', *Art Education* 45, 5, pp. 51–7.

Price, S. (1987) *The Ghost Drum*. Faber and Faber, London.

Stanovich, K.E. (1986) 'Matthew effects in reading: Some consequences of individual differences in the acquisition of literacy', *Reading Research Quarterly* XXL, 4, pp. 360–406.

Stephens, J. (1992) *Language and Ideology in Children' s Fiction*. Longman, London and New York.

Sussman H. (1997) *The Aesthetic Contract: Statutes of Art and Intellectual Work in Modernity*. Stanford UP, Stanford.

Tarone, E. and Yule, G. (1989) *Focus on the Language Learner. Approaches to Identifying and Meeting the Needs of Second Language Learners*. Oxford University Press, Oxford.

Wallace, C., (1988) *Learning to Read in a Multicultural Society The Social Context of Second Language Literacy*. Prentice Hall International, London.

Wild, M. (2000) *Fox* (illustrated by R Brooks). Allen & Unwin, St Leonards, Sydney.

Wilson, E.O. (1998) *Consilience: the Unity of Knowledge*. Alfred A. Knopf, New York.

Winch, G., Johnston, R.R., Holliday, M., Ljungdahl, L. and March, P., (2001) *Literacy: Reading, Writing and Children's Literature*. Oxford University Press, Melbourne, pp. 287–437.

Note

Some of the ideas in this chapter appeared in an earlier paper, 'Of Dialogue and Desire: Children's Literature and the Needs of the Reluctant L2 Reader', *Australian Journal of Language and Literacy* 18, 4. Those interested in this specific area are referred to this paper, which has a much more particular ESL focus.

Index